William Wilberforce Nevin

Vignettes of Travel

Some comparative sketches in England and Italy

William Wilberforce Nevin

Vignettes of Travel
Some comparative sketches in England and Italy

ISBN/EAN: 9783337211981

Printed in Europe, USA, Canada, Australia, Japan

Cover: Foto ©Andreas Hilbeck / pixelio.de

More available books at **www.hansebooks.com**

INTRODUCTORY.

THESE papers are in part a recast of some letters contributed to the public press of the United States during a visit to Europe in 1879 and 1880, and in part fresh matter from original notes then taken. The wide republication here and abroad of many of the newspaper letters suggested the preparation of this volume.

The several sketches are mainly in the direction of comparative studies of social and political life in other countries. The volume is, however, less symmetrical in this respect than I could have wished now, for the reason that this line of treatment was not an original plan—the work only drifting that way in the gradual course of travel and writing.

Comparative study has been the rule of advancement in all knowledge this century, and advance in the sciences of politics and society will best be made by the same means. We cannot compare our own institutions and form of government with those of other nations until we understand them, and we can never thoroughly understand them until we see them brought out in relief against the background of other countries.

In other countries and in former times responsibility for the social and political progress of any nation has been confined to a small and highly-favored class. With us it rests upon the whole people. The education of foreign travel—once the privilege and pleasure of a few—has, therefore, become the duty of every American citizen. The citizen is the statesman now. If this is not the Providential intent of the flood of European travel which annually leaves our shores, it is certainly its fortunate opportunity.

Any contribution, however imperfect, to this comparative study of ourselves ought to be of some use to some portions of our people. In Chapter XVII. of this work I have attempted to show that aid in this work is the most useful function now left to our diplomatic service and the best reason for its present existence.

Along the pathway of travel and study I have endeavored

3

to give, wherever possible, some of that more intimate and personal information which every educated traveller so often feels the want of, and which for some reason will not get into the guide-books—the special uses of special places, the best economies of time and route and intellectual energies, the tried and tested equipment of books,—that kind of information gotten only by experience, always costly, and which to one *en route* for the first or only time generally comes too late for use.

And in this matter of information, a closing word of counsel. Much of the higher value of travel is often lost for want of some reasonable provision beforehand for taking all of the advantage of foreign life. Old lands, with their endless associations, have such charms for the New-World citizen that he is apt to think of nothing but the pleasure of wandering at will among their ruins, their grandeur, their unaccustomed and suggestive sights and sounds.

The highest expression of any living land, however, is its society, which is the fruit of all its years or centuries of struggle and longing. He only sees a land who knows its people. England, for instance, which, by reason of language and race is the most profitable ground for American travel, one can only begin to appreciate by meeting personally some members of some of its distinctive and defined classes, and seeing them in the setting of their own homes. A single day spent in a cathedral close ; in an old castle, with an historic family, still its living soul, yet in it ; in an English gentleman's country-house, that charming flower of a well-perfected order of life ; in the college-cloisters of one of the ancient universities ; in a substantial farm-house ; or, if one cannot do any better, in a humble, out-of-the-way inn, will give more insight into the social structure and historical civilization of England than a whole cycle of existence in hotels or helpless rambling with red books among show ruins and over beaten highways. These are the pictures which are the real historical paintings of the country. To get a stereoscopic view of England one should enter all these doors and many others. That good fortune, of course, can only come to very few, but all may enjoy some one " interior," and from it, like a skilled anatomist, construct to his own conception the whole fabric of the body politic and social.

PHILADELPHIA, November 15, 1880.

CONTENTS.

ENGLISH TOWNS.

CHAPTER   PAGE

    I.—CHESTER 9

   II.—YORK 19

  III.—SHOTTERY 25

  IV.—READING IN BERKSHIRE 30

   V.—LANCASTER 36

  VI.—UNIVERSITY TOWNS: OXFORD 44

 VII.—UNIVERSITY TOWNS: CAMBRIDGE . . . 61

ENGLISH POLITICS.

  VIII.—ENGLISH POLITICAL LIFE 79

   IX.—GLADSTONE 84

    X.—AN ENGLISH ELECTION 92

   XI.—THE INTERROGATION POINT IN POLITICS . . 99

  XII.—COMPARATIVE COST OF GOVERNMENT . . 103

 XIII.—PARLIAMENT,—THE HOUSE OF COMMONS . 109

 XIV.—PARLIAMENT,—THE HOUSE OF COMMONS . 118

  XV.—PARLIAMENT,—THE HOUSE OF COMMONS . 126

 XVI.—PARLIAMENT,—THE HOUSE OF LORDS . . 142

XVII.—FOREIGN SERVICE 145

XVIII.—COMPARATIVE POLITICS 151

LONDON.

  XIX.—WESTMINSTER ABBEY 165

  XX.—THE LONDON PULPIT 175

 XXI.—THE PLAY AND THE THEATRE 189

XXII.—THE LONDON TIMES 196

XXIII.—HISTORIC TAVERNS 207

SCOTLAND.

CHAPTER   PAGE

XXIV.—Entering Scotland 223
XXV.—Scottish Notes 230
XXVI.—Towards the Hebrides 238
XXVII.—Iona 247

NORTHERN ITALY.

XXVIII.—Venice 265
XXIX.—Genoa 276
XXX.—Pisa 286
XXXI.—Siena 293
XXXII.—Orvieto 305
XXXIII.—Pistoja 314
XXXIV.—Ravenna 322

ROME.

XXXV.—Rome the Centre 331
XXXVI.—St. Peter's, and Italian Preaching . 336
XXXVII.—The Pantheon 346
XXXVIII.—Prison of St. Paul and St. Peter. . 353
XXXIX.—The Palace of the Inquisition . . 362
XL.—Constantine's Battle-Field . . . 367
XLI.—Ostia—The Pompeii of Roman Civili-
zation 374

MODERN ITALY.

XLII.—New Rome 385
XLIII.—United Italy 393
XLIV.—Garibaldi 402
XLV.—Modern Italy 409
XLVI.—The Italian Life 422

APPENDIX.

Hints of Travel 435

ENGLISH TOWNS.

.

CHAPTER I.

CHESTER.

The Entrance-Porch to England—An Initial Walk—
The Old Home—Vitiation of the Language—The
Soldier and the Beggar—Coming Differentiation of
the English and American Language—The Vignette
Cathedral Scene of England.

CHESTER is the vignette scene of England, and a
very charming one. Within fifteen miles of Liverpool, and trains running out almost hourly, the experienced traveller can, and the judicious one will, avoid
that monotonous town consecrated to trade and lucre,
and spend his first night in England in a little country
village representative and typical of the most English
of English scenery. Indeed, if circumstances permit,
I would advise that the visitor walk from Liverpool
to Chester. It is a short distance, over excellent roads,
and the walk will give one at once an idea of English
landscape which it would take weeks of railway travel
to acquire.

The walk will be made along green lanes and by
hedges and under avenues of great trees which form a
picture not to be forgotten, and answering completely
to what is, perhaps, the conventional conception of any
well-read person of rural England. To an educated
American, indeed, all England is so familiar by pictures, literature, and legend that, entering it for the
first time, he feels as if he were coming home again
instead of visiting a strange land,—as if he had been
there before in a half-remembered childhood or in a
dream, and were part of it. This indefinable sense of
a previous knowledge is not, I think, a mere intellec-

9

tual photograph or illusion, the impression of years of
early or long reading. It is the assertion of a race instinct. Froissart—that most picturesque of old chroniclers—does not prepare one so for Normandy, nor does
Boccaccio for Italy. Any one who goes to Rome for the
first time recognizes at once the Pantheon or the Colosseum, and the stranger at Paris enters the Madeleine
confidently without question of guide or guide-book,
but he knows them, however, as he knows the pyra-
mids and obelisks, and he has not that feeling of kin-
dredship, that sense of his own merger in them, which
is one of the great charms of English travel.

Although to American eyes simply a charming
country village of a few thousand inhabitants, Chester
is by English law a city, being a cathedral site, and
fairly bubbles over with tradition, legend, and history,
so that one feels like looking on its very humblest
people with respect as the richly-dowered "heirs of all
the ages." These heirs, however, save the cultured
aristocracy, who are few in numbers and mostly of ecclesiastical savor or relation of some kind to the cathedral, with its ancient establishment, seem poor and
struggling, and I fancy would gladly give up all their
historic privileges for a quarter-section of American
prairie.

Our Pennsylvania town preserves the full name and
tradition of this site better than its English ancestor.
For long periods of history this old Chester was known
as West Chester,—just what it was under the Romans,
the "west camp" of the province, "Chester" being the
very natural corruption of our rude forefathers for the
Latin *castra*. Chester's first interest, indeed, comes to
us from its associations as an ancient Roman fortress or
stronghold. Here, about the time of Christ, was sta-
tioned the Twentieth Legion (about a brigade of our
army), keeping down our barbarian ancestors. Stone
coffins and other Roman antiquities are still dug up
from time to time, and one or two handsome Roman

crypts, discovered after centuries of disuse, have been put to modern use as wine-cellars. It is a natural military position, having been seized on by those excellent soldiers, the Romans, and well fortified, and has been a centre of tough fighting ever since. Its distinction in this respect is grounded on sound military and geographical reasons, and will endure. When the Romans had gone, the Danes held its abandoned walls to the bitter end against King Alfred. It was the last point taken by William the Conqueror, the last fortress to lower the Saxon standard before the Norman banners. From a tower on its walls, which is now a relic, they show you the spot where King Charles I. stood and saw his army and his kingdom melt away before his eyes down on the moors below. There will be a battle here again when the Germans invade England, if Englishmen still keep up their fathers' fashion of fighting for their soil inch by inch. From a military point of view, Chester is topographically "the last ditch" of a lost cause in England.

All the town is surrounded by a huge wall with balustrades of brick, and at the angles fortified with towers, which in their day swept the faces of their sections of the wall and commanded its approaches. Along the top of this wall you walk now, and see on one side the moors—which, I suppose, in the old times, when defence was the first consideration, could be flooded by the Dee, a tranquil little stream answering in size and appearance to the American creek—and the other the near hills of Wales. Our guide, an enthusiastic and slightly bibulous "freeman" of Chester, looked on these hills yet with only half-repressed indignation as the abode of marauders and thieves, whom we might momentarily expect to swoop down. Indeed, in the excitement of historic declamation, relating the past military and ecclesiastical glories of his native city, I think sometimes he got the centuries mixed up, and mingled his own troubles with the statelier tragedies which marked the fall of thrones and turned the course of history.

Inside the walls, in the "old city," every building and street is quaint and picturesque, and the narrow ways are fairly crowded with houses that are historic and pregnant with suggestion. There is the summer residence of King Henry VIII., a low, mud-walled building, not twelve feet high, but which so short a time ago was a fit dwelling for a monarch. It sounds rather comical now, but there is in Chester a charitable foundation of this many-wived King Henry for the perpetual support of "six widows." The widows are to-day enjoying this benefit.

Through a brick alley-passage not five feet wide you come on the ancient palace of the great Earl of Derby, a soldier and statesman, who in old times headed armies, levied war against his king, and for that act parted with his head on the scaffold. This place is a rackety structure of two low stories, hardly high enough to stand up in, and is now occupied by a family of the poorest sort in a city where poverty is squalid and wretched to an extent that we happily know nothing of. A dirty, red-haired girl with torn petticoats and a hungry-looking face received us on the threshold and offered the modern hospitalities of the palace.

Another building strikingly quaint and suggestive of ancient manners is a long, low structure, gabled and antique, which, some six or seven hundred years ago, was the residence of a great bishop who ruled in Chester. It is more spacious and imposing than either of the others just mentioned. Along the entire front, of some eighty feet, runs a gallery something like the inclosed porch of a Lancaster County hotel. The whole front of this house, from the roof to the ground, is covered with carved and graven images in wood of curious and often grotesque design. Two entirely nude figures, man and woman, are shown you by the guide, and one façade has been cancelled and shaven plain, the imagery being too gross for modern eyes.

These odd old buildings, their whole fronts covered with curious wooden carvings, and many of them devoted now to the commonest and humblest uses, give a general effect to Chester which is stronger and more impressive than any of the detached " shows" which here, as in any locality, are always forced on the stranger. This fantastic tracery of steep gables and overhanging eaves and brown skeleton rafters, the lean ribs of centuries, and quaint relievos, half-religious, half-pagan,— this and the beautiful view stretching out over peaceful water and meadow to the delicate filmy contour of the Welsh mountains are the pictures of the place.

The great sight of Chester, of course, is her cathedral, the central point which gathers up her history from the time of King Alfred. It is not large compared with others in the island, but, half in ruins, is beautiful and picturesque beyond description. This cathedral, like all the great churches of England, is a pantheon. In St. Paul's and Westminster lie the dead of the nation. In Chester and other country churches or cathedrals sleep the local great. These grand graves, where those men who have deserved well of their country and their fellows are gathered in noble companionship and honored for ages, are a powerful stimulus to great thought and heroic action, and must tend strongly to elevate those who live near them and worship in them, drawing them daily away from the ignoble struggle for mere gain of money, and lifting them up to better things. For in all this country, for which wealth has done so much, I have not found one name enshrined there in honor merely for its riches, and any man or boy may be buried in the greatest church of his county or the kingdom if he does some service to his fellows worthy of recognition and remembrance. In this beautiful cathedral of Chester, consecrated by art, legend, and religion, among the bishops and statesmen and generals

2

of centuries, I have found the names of young soldiers, without rank, fortune, or family, who died only a few years ago in the Crimea.

In St. Paul's grand pile, where lie Wellington, and Nelson, and Sir John Moore, and Dr. Samuel Johnson, and John Howard, and Bishop Heber, and Sir Joshua Reynolds, there are inscribed, with equal honor, the names of some poor unknown ship-boys who in a great naval action went down nobly, standing to their duty as grandly and as faithfully as admiral or general. As I looked at this tablet some young sergeants, proud of their early chevrons, and of a regiment on its way to the African war, were poring earnestly over the names, and I knew that the real service of this cathedral would be offered some day in silence on the battlefields of Zululand.

It is impossible, of course, to describe in words such a cathedral as this,—a building which is the result of the consecrated labor, art, and devotion of centuries. And it is but one of many. They must be seen to be conceived, and when seen can only be known through the eye of culture and history.

Chester cathedral is not by any means the one to select as the prelude to a course of systematic study, but it does well enough to break in with. One must do his æsthetic teething somewhere, and Chester answers very well for that purpose.

Right here at Chester, on the threshold of England, one strikes an English habit which is offensive to American taste, and which will jar on the ear during one's entire stay in the country,—viz., the corruption, by illiterate contraction, of the language. This process of deterioration is going steadily on in all classes. Cheshire, the county name, is slovenly and ignorant English for Chestershire, but it has been adopted by all England, although its origin must have been from the thick-lipped hinds. Cheshire is clownish, and means nothing; Chestershire is sonorous, stately, and records two volumes of English national history,—the Latin rule of the camp and the Saxon rule of the shire.

The lower-class Englishman is thoroughly illiterate, and often succeeds in stamping his illiteracy on the nation. There cannot be a neglected class in any community without the whole community suffering for it. Just as the Southern people in our country acquired a negro twang and dialect, the black nurses teaching it to the white children, so to-day the English language in England suffers at the hands of its large uneducated and neglected class, and it has come to pass that English gentlemen cannot keep even their aristocratic names intact, but accept them back from their servants mutilated and vulgarized in sound. Thus Beauchamp has deteriorated to Beacham, Beauvoir to Beaver, Stanhope to Stannup, Cholmondeley to Chumly, St. John to Sinjin, Marjoribanks to Marshbanks, Worcester to Wooster, Leicester to Lester, Greenwich to Greenitch, Chaworth to Chorth, Woolwich to Woolich, Haworth to Horth, Hawarden to Harden, Warwick to Warick, Taliaferro to Toliver, St. Botolph's-town to Boston, Sandys to Sands, Wemyss to Weems, Dillwyn to Dillan, Strachan to Strawn, Mainwearing to Mannering, and so on from one end of the island to the other.

This vulgar and servile pronunciation, especially of the lordly old Norman names, is very marked and very unpleasant to a stranger. But it is retribution. England has not been true to her trust in the matter of common education. With universities and schools far beyond anything we can pretend to, with a clergy educated greatly beyond our grade and enjoying in the days of priories and abbeys the monopoly of education, she has kept her talent of learning selfishly folded in a napkin for the exclusive uses of one class. Now the wronged classes avenge themselves.

Indeed, the wrong against the noble language of Milton and Shakespeare is very prevalent throughout all

England, high and low. If the lower-class Englishman drops his "h's," the upper-class Englishman drops his "w's;" and I do not know that the offence is in any way mitigated because fashion approves the one elision and disapproves the other. "Extraordinary" is a good shibboleth with which to test the Englishman. Very rarely does he successfully master the "d."

It sometimes seems as if the special function of the United States with regard to our common English language were to be its preservation by the general education of the whole people. England has shown that no special centres of education, however excellent, respected, or sacred, will protect the purity of the tongue against masses of ignorance and servility.

This lazy vitiation of the English by the dropping of letters, and sometimes of whole syllables, is in constant progress in England on a grand scale, enervating the language in form and sound, and were there no communication between the two countries would soon, with other influences, result in two tongues related to each other like French and Spanish or Spanish and Italian. As it is, the process of differentiation has already set in, but it is hourly counteracted by the incessant intercommunication of the two peoples.

As this different use of words will confront the stranger all the time in England, I give here some illustrations to show on how large a scale the variation has already begun :

English.	*American.*
Shop.	Store.
Shopkeeper.	Storekeeper, merchant.
Shares, shareholder.	Stock, stockholder.
Chairman (of a company).	President.
Railway.	Railroad.
High level (railway).	Elevated.
Station.	Depot.
Shunt.	Switch.
Stoker.	Fireman.
Guard.	Conductor.
Driver.	Engineer.

English.	*American.*
Booking-office.	Ticket-office.
Goods.	Freight.
Carriage.	Car.
"The cars."	"The train."
Line.	Track.
Chemist.	Druggist.
Lift.	Elevator.
Tram, tramways.	Street-cars.
Outing.	Excursion.
Post.	Mail.
To book.	To charge.
To post (a letter).	To mail.
To book (a seat).	To buy a ticket.
To "take in" (a newspaper)	To subscribe for.
Quite, in the sense of	Entirely.
Public-house.	Tavern.
Spirits.	Liquor.
Meat-shop.	Butcher-shop.
Tub.	Bath.
Cab, cabman.	Hack, hack-driver.
Inn.	Hotel.
Luggage, luggage-van.	Baggage, baggage-wagon, -car.
To register (luggage).	To check (baggage).
Stick.	Cane.
The hustings.	The stump.
The Ministry.	The Cabinet.
Member.	Representative.
"Contesting a seat" for Parliament.	"Running" for Congress.

Who can translate into exact American "young person" as uttered by a British dame? How shall one express, under our different social conditions, the contempt and disgust of "cad"? What equivalent have we on this side of the Atlantic for those great structural vertebræ of an Englishman's speech, "really," "ah," "haw," "now"?

Were it not for the large and continuous intercommunication of books and magazines and newspapers, of letters and telegrams and travel, the languages would even now be standing widely apart.

The "Rows," the guide-book feature of Chester, were a disappointment. They are a curiosity, of course, but

greatly overrated. The best description, perhaps, is in
one of Dickens's later novels, but the great novelist
wrote of them like a reporter paid by the column, and
from his trained imagination built up a curiously involved and very interesting structure on a rather commonplace foundation of fact. The Rows run only for
a few short blocks, and are simply a deep porch set far
in each house and open from house to house. One
can walk continuously for the distance of a block along
the porches just as on the street below. At the end of
each block, however, he must descend to the street,
ascending again at the next block. In time, small shops
have been opened in the second story, and you have
thus a double shopping-front for a small distance. It
is only this, and nothing more.

Chester's greatness and interest lie in her historic
riches,—her wealth of culture, legend, religious tradition, and power,—and it seems a pity that she should be
labelled and ear-marked for travellers by what is at best
but a curiosity and but an item in her vast repertoire
of things curious and quaint.

Entering this pleasing vestibule of England, you
meet at once two figures unpleasant to the American
eye,—the soldier and the beggar. Here they are in
these quiet sylvan shades and echoless cloisters, and
they never leave you wherever you go in Europe. The
poverty and beggary of Chester are very repulsive to
one unacquainted with the squalor and wretchedness of
this continent, and it is something very sad to see them
in a village town whose chief monument and distinction
is a venerable cathedral, and which itself is almost a
cathedral close. The British scarlet and gold, too,
flashes along these leafy streets and under ruined walls
and still moss-grown arches,—wherever, in fact, a British nursemaid strays. The English drum-beat echoes
every day around the entire globe, which is grand, but
it is also heard every night in every peaceful county
of England, which is not so grand.

CHAPTER II.

YORK.

An Old Cathedral City—The Gateway to Historic England—A Traveller's Plight—The English Cathedrals
—Story of their Building and what they Cost—The
new Uses of the Old Temples Stripped of their Pictures and Idols—An English Rest.

York is the historic gateway by which to enter England. The stress of modern travel carries one to
Liverpool, and, while its suburban confine of Chester is
a very picturesque and pleasing vignette portal, it has
no historical significance. The traveller who comes to
study England will do well to leave there after a day
and strike directly for York. This is in conflict with
all the modern routes of travel; but, as these routes
have been determined for the use and advantage of
railway companies rather than the pleasure or profit of
travellers, they are no guide to an intelligent seeing of
the country, and are often a harm.

York was a stronghold of our ancient Briton fathers
and a capital seat of rude power away back in the mists
before the time of Christ. It was the capital of the
Roman empire in Britain, and the old Roman military
walls around the city are still standing in a wonderful
state of preservation. You could fight a battle from
them to-day did the conditions of modern warfare allow
it. In the streets and buildings and remains you see
the record successively of the Roman period of English
history, the Saxon, the Norman, and modern England
from the Plantagenets through the Commonwealth down
to Victoria. In the walls and arches of the great
minster you read the whole history of English archi-

tecture,—Saxon, Norman, Late Norman, Early English, Decorated, Early Perpendicular, Perpendicular, Late Perpendicular. York is a kindergarten of English history for grown folks.

In its name York is another illustration of the inherited and hopeless tendency of the Englishman to a corruption, by contraction, of the language. "York" is the stately and civilized "Eboracum" of the Latins as it has come down to us through the thick-lipped Saxons and half-articulating Britons, only the rude guttural remains of a once polished word.

Coming to York on the last day of a racing week, I had an experience very odd to an American. This town, with a modern population of fifty thousand and some twenty centuries of dignity, has hardly the hotel accommodation of one of our Western towns of ten thousand people. Every inn was full, and the landlords did not seem to feel under the least obligation to provide for any one. When all their rooms were full they seemed to think their duty ended, although this thing must occur again and again. In nearly all the old towns of England the hotel provision is simply ridiculous, judged by our necessities. After driving to the half-dozen or so modest-sized inns of the place without getting a lodgment, I was about taking the train again to find a roof for the night, when some citizen who had watched the quest directed me to a private house where lodging, he thought, might be had. I found there very good apartments and fair service and meals, but at a cost greater than the Windsor in New York or the St. George in Philadelphia.

Much of the interest of the town attaches to its Norman period, as you read it in castle and bar and ruined abbey, although in this epoch of its splendor and power York was but a town of ten thousand inhabitants. The Normans, however, cared very little for monotonous figures. Although great sailors, they had only moderate capacity as traders; but as soldiers, priests, artists, poets and builders, the force of their time, they left their stamp indelibly. They made history rather than textile fabrics or patent machinery.

The glory of York, however,—as it is one of the glories of England,—is its great cathedral or minster; and it is the object chiefest worthy of study in the place. It is indeed a very good specimen with which to begin the study of the English cathedrals. These noble cathedrals of England, spread over all the land, are one of the first and strongest impressions of the kingdom on the stranger. They are so grand, so beautiful, so living, like breathing hearts of stone, that seeing them one feels at once as if he had never seen a church before. They seem not of this world, but of some other world; higher and better houses not made with hands, but born of an art and a conception beyond our modern powers.

But when one reflects what they are and what they mean, they start a singularly involved social problem, and the cold judgment inclines against them. They are the product and represent that dreary and profitless stretch of English history from the Norman conquest to the Reformation,—five wretched centuries of want and ignorance and human suffering and stagnation. They are the outcome, and with a few castles and splendid abbeys the whole outcome, of the five hundred years in which England was a province of the modern Roman empire, the people and the kings of England ruled over by cardinal-princes,—the ecclesiastical proconsuls of Rome. During this period all the other countries of Europe were similar provinces, and these wonderful cathedrals went up in them all. You recognize at once the essential idea of them, the grand conception, the spirit of the work, as you meet them again in France and Germany and North Italy. The cathedral stands out everywhere as the dominant idea of that period and the symbol of its power. This idea in the different development of our day is lost, and you

cannot reproduce these old cathedrals now. It has
been tried, but with inevitable failure. No study or
imitation of the old proportions will fashion a building
like unto those which yet speak for their dead age.
You may get something which is like the form, but it
is not the living form : it is a corpse. The soul has
forever fled.

Now, what is painful to think of in relation to these
lovely cathedrals is this : These magnificent buildings,
that seem almost to glow with faith and beauty, drank
the life-blood of England. During the period of their
building England was almost stationary. There was
no social advance and no social hope. There were no
homes in England as we know them now. There was
no freedom as we know it now, little of comfort, and
nothing of progress. From A.D. 1100 to A.D. 1400 the
population of England advanced but ten per cent. a
century, less than one-tenth of one per cent. a year.
For the people there was no wealth, no education, no
trade or commerce. There was deficient food, shelter,
and clothing, and, in consequence, continuous disease
and epidemic. There was chronic war. It was a time
of plague, pestilence, and famine, of battle and murder,
and of sudden death. There was no science, there was
no art save in the direction of ecclesiastical architecture
and adornment.

Yet it was the same England, with the same people,
soil, climate, and resources, as to-day. But one-fourth
of the adult population of that time are computed to
have been priests, monks, nuns, and their hangers-on
and attendants, non-productive persons and an eco-
nomic burden on the other three-fourths, whose productive powers were still further lessened by a long list of
saints' days, and a heavy drain for military purposes.
This is the England of these beautiful abbeys and venerable priories and stately cathedrals. All over Europe
these buildings are a magnificent demonstration of organized ecclesiastical power and a wonderful flowering

of æsthetic force, but it has been all at the cost and sacrifice of the common people, whose " bodies are the temples of the living God." For them these silent gray cathedrals meant intellectual and civil starvation, social degradation, physical ill health, and the shortening of life.

For one who wants to drink in the beauty of the cathedrals of Europe it is better to begin with those of England,—Lincoln, and Ely, and Peterborough, and Durham, and Lichfield, and Canterbury, and Salisbury, and Exeter, and Winchester, and Wells, all of which are worth a visit, and many others. It is better to begin with these English cathedrals and enjoy them while one may; for, with all their impressive splendor to our unaccustomed Puritan eyes, they come to look empty and bare and cold after one has once felt the sensuous glories of the churches of Southern Europe. The beauty of these Northern churches is too severely intellectual in contrast with the warmth and rich color of the South. Coming back from there, one feels the nakedness of the stern gray cathedrals of England and longs for the Madonnas and bright coloring of Italy, the ascending incense, the burning lamps and warm pictures, the family altars, the noble armies of saints, the marble flight of pure white angels,—thousands and thousands of them,—and the splendor of the trembling altar with its sacred lights flaming over silver and precious stones.

To tell the truth, although our Church-of-England friends never quite like to hear it, these great cathedrals of theirs were built by the Roman Catholic Church. They belong, with all their splendors, to it, with all its defects. Their present use is unsympathetic and an anachronism. Robbed of their saints and swinging censers, their beautiful idols and graven images and polytheistic chapels, they are a cold void. For the present Church-of-England service they have little more special appropriateness than has a Greek temple. And so it has come to pass that in some of them the choir is inclosed from floor to roof on all sides, and fashioned into a new Protestant church within the old cathedral, conformed to the exigencies of the modern worship.

For the American stranger, to whom the outside of the Old World is all a poem, York is a delightful old town just to wander through alone and at will. It is full of quaint and ancient little streets, overhanging houses, antiquated stone seats and remains, odd nooks and corners that have come down from the Middle Ages. In all its streets you read the legend of Roman and Saxon and Dane and Norman and Puritan. On its walls you see the Plantagenet and Tudor emblems. At one sweep in a few hours in York you may find Roman altars and coffins and forgotten household gods, Saxon monuments, Norman fortifications, the poor dwellings of the people in mediæval times, Elizabethan manors, and the unimpressive because familiar building of our own day.

York was once the northern metropolis of England, a centre of fashion and political life, and dividing ecclesiastical power with Canterbury and London at a time when ecclesiasticism was the force of the realm. Now the railways have drawn all that to London, and York is a quiet, easy-going old cathedral city, eminently respectable, aristocratic, and rather sleepy. As a social study I have no doubt it is interesting and worth investigation, but it was not my fortune to know it save from the outside. A cathedral city is itself an order of life and society unknown to us, and which it would take a novel to reveal.

There are three clubs in York, and they show how the lines are drawn. One, and the leading, the Yorkshire, is for "county gentlemen"; the York is for "city professional gentlemen"; while the third and last, the City, is for "tradesmen."

York, with a population of fifty thousand, and the

capital of the largest county in England,—Yorkshire,—
covering a population of about two and a half millions
of souls, has just three *weekly* newspapers.

It is an English town from top to bottom, old-
fashioned, comfortable, dignified, and satisfied with itself. There is nothing in our land with which to contrast it or run a parallel. There is probably no way in
which a stranger would get a better inside conception
of English provincial life of a high order than by living
for a few weeks in York; and if one were fatigued or
exhausted by the wear and tear of the ocean, it would
be an excellent and profitable resting-place.

YORK, ENGLAND

CHAPTER III.

SHOTTERY.

ANNE HATHEWAY'S COTTAGE AS IT STANDS TO-DAY—A FARM
VILLAGE—SHAKESPEARE'S LOVE IN THE THATCHED COT-
TAGE—THE LOCAL AFFECTION FOR THE STORY.

I HAVE walked to-day from here to the neighboring
village of Shottery to see the cottage where Anne Hatheway lived and where Shakespeare won her. It was a
charming bit of representative English scenery, that
landscape and view so unlike our own, and yet so
familiar through literature and tradition that it always
seems to me as if I had seen it before in dreams or some
previous condition of existence. I followed a footpath
across the fields, with old-fashioned stiles at every fence
and hawthorn hedges along the lanes,—the very path
trod by Shakespeare in his quest of Anne. Tradition
does not say how often he had to walk it.

The cottage, a quaint, straw-thatched building covered with ivy and rose-bushes, is in a good state of preservation. The old house, which was, for its time, commodious and of some pretensions, is now occupied by three families,—farm laborers. The central division, which is formed of the hall and main fireplace, and the sitting-room of the old building as it stood in Shakespeare's time, is now known as the Hatheway cottage, and is kept much as it stood then, with some of the old furniture and heirlooms of the family. An elderly woman, with the pleasant manners of the humble classes here, received me, and showed a real and intelligent interest in explaining the legend and relics of the place. In answer to a question, she told me she was herself a Hatheway, and that her family had lived on the spot ever since the time of Shakespeare, as well as for generations before.

Although the exterior of the house is of humble appearance, the Hatheway family must have been of the better sort in their days. The room where Shakespeare made love—or where Anne made love to him, as a somewhat cynical and mature damsel of the place, who seemed to look on my walk to Shottery parish as a kind of mild lunacy, informed me—is a large room, some fifteen feet square, handsomely panelled in oak. It is flagged with broad stones, worn smooth by the steps of generations, looking rude to us, but which was the comfortable custom of the time. The great feature of the room is the wide, old-fashioned chimney-place, in which you can sit, and sitting look up through to the sky. In the left wing of this capacious fireplace, as you face it, there is cut or built in the wall the bacon-closet, still serving that homely use for the Hatheways of 1880. On the right side stands the "courtin'-settle," as my old friend phrased it, a very rude wooden bench, some five feet long, with back and low arms. This seat my guide was sure was the real and veritable place which did the work, and carried the Hatheway family into legend and history. On it sat at the time of my visit a young girl of sixteen, sewing some homely work,—a Hatheway without a Shakespeare.

Up a narrow and humble wooden stairway you reach the half-story rooms, which are now and were in the sixteenth century the sleeping-apartments of the family. The bedstead, the central feature, is further evidence of the substantial standing of the family. It is handsomely carved with scroll-work and human figures, some of them resembling the grotesque carving seen in ancient cathedrals. This work appears, by its style and class, to date about four hundred years ago. The bed has been in the Hatheway family ever since their name became a matter of interest, and is believed by them to have been used for generations before. It is not in use now, and is furnished with very heavy and soft linen, woven in the family, and hemmed with wonderful elaboration. This, too, an heirloom from more prosperous times. In this bedroom is a spinning-wheel seat, alleged to have been immortalized by Shakespeare, but the good dame would not give the passage by which his kindly remembrance had carried the homely object into literature.

This room, the old state bedroom of the family, like its adjoining mate, the present sleeping-apartment of the house, is so low that you touch the ceiling everywhere except in the centre, and the joists and rafters are joined together not by nails but by wooden pegs.

The Hatheways of Shakespeare's time were "yeomen," a class of British society that has pretty much disappeared. The people who live in their cottage to-day are farm-laborers, a class so poor and ignorant and hopeless of any future that we happily have no equivalent to it in the United States. This fact accounts for much of the contrast between the substance and comfort indicated by these relics and traditions of the past and the meagreness and poverty of the family to-day. It makes this humble cottage, also, an instructive illustration of a very unsatisfactory change that has been going on in the lower order of English society.

Visitors, the Hatheway dowager informed me, came often, but not so many in these hard times as in years before. The Americans, she said, were " the best;" and to my inquiry as to what was best, she said they took most interest and seemed most pleased. I was pretty sure my hostess took me for an American prince, and so, *noblesse obligé*, gave her a shilling, where I think a sixpence was the usual gratuity. This modest British coin brought me a shower of blessings and kind wishes, and, what was more practical, some snowdrops and " rosemary for remembrance" from the garden. Indeed, the real gratitude which a shilling given to a decent man or woman in this land always evokes is sad evidence of the narrow margin of existence here. Life is a struggle, and the poor go into it burdened and handicapped almost beyond hope.

In the modest garden of the cottage, planted with box, lavender, marigold, rosemary, pansy, thyme, and other familiar English flowers and shrubs, stands the well of pure cold water, in the same place and serving the same homely uses as of old. It is doubtful, however, if Shakespeare ever drank of it. The Englishman of the sixteenth century, like the Englishman of the nineteenth, I suppose, confined himself to ale.

In my walk across-fields from Stratford-on-Avon to Shottery, the footpath of course often diverged, and I was forced to inquire of those I met the way. I was much struck with the familiar knowledge of all with the story of Shakespeare's love, and their simple pride in it. In other localities where there were famous churches, in which good knights and old earls famous in history lay buried, I have often inquired of respectable-looking people and found them ignorant of or only half acquainted with the great historic features of these places. In Warwick, for instance, I found several worthy people who seemed to know nothing of the great Earl of Leicester, and not to care much whether his body was in their church or not. All around Shottery, however, the name of Anne Hatheway was a household word and the humble thatched cottage a shrine. Some rude farm-laborers, who spoke so thickly I could hardly understand them, and used language so provincial as not to seem English to American ears, and some bright little boys hardly twelve years old, alike gave intelligent answers, showed a friendly sympathy in my quest, and seemed to think my pilgrimage the right and proper and natural thing to do.

This is "Shakespeare land." The town lives and moves and has its being in his memory and tradition. His body lies buried here in a beautiful and stately edifice,—a noble shrine to which the culture and genius of the world come to worship; the house in which he was born has been carefully and faithfully restored, and is held in honorable trust for the use and devotion of posterity; the dwelling in which he died is set apart from common uses, and is to be the site of a grand memorial monument; but the hearts of this people go out in simple love and affection to the little cottage where he loved, even though historic gossip suggests and calm reflection convinces one that the passionate fascination of a boy of eighteen for an innocent creature of twenty-six was not a purely idyllic romance.

I am staying here at the Red Horse Inn, a house which has the enviable distinction of having its advertisement drawn by Washington Irving. He introduced it into American literature in his first letters from England, and it has ever since enjoyed a rich custom of American travel, and is worthy of it. Irving, long years ago, wrote with grateful feeling of its good cheer, its solid comforts, its homelike domesticity, its honest wines, and its pretty waiting-maids, and the house keeps up well its reputation in all these essential points. Of the inns of England suffice it to say that, while somewhat expensive as compared with our hotels, they are a delightful experience in life which I fear we shall never have in our country. Neither our landlords are solid and unassuming enough to give them nor our people sensible enough to demand and have them. I have tried three now,—the Craven Arms, at Coventry, the Warwick Arms, at Warwick, and the classic Red Horse here,—and understand the reason of their affectionate remembrance in English literature.

STRATFORD-ON-AVON.

CHAPTER IV.

READING IN BERKSHIRE.

READING OF ENGLAND AND READING OF PENNSYLVANIA— COMPARATIVE PICTURE OF TWO COUNTY TOWNS—BLOOD IS STRONGER THAN WATER.

READING of England, like the familiar Reading of our Pennsylvania, is the capital town of the county of Berks, here often called Berkshire,—the shire or shrievalty of Berks. The two towns are almost about the same size,—42,000 to 45,000 inhabitants. Reading of England figures in the directories at 27,000, but the town of Early, which is built into it so that the stranger cannot tell in which municipal corporation he may be, is substantially and popularly a part of Reading, and brings its population up to the figures of its New-World namesake.

England's Berks County has a population of 196,475, and an acreage of 450,132 acres. The Pennsylvania Berks has a population of something over 100,000, and an acreage something over 600,000 acres. They are near enough to make a parallel have some interest.

Politically, all comparison ceases. Berks of Pennsylvania, with its Reading in it, sends one member to the House of Representatives of the United States, and sends him by male or manhood suffrage, every male citizen of age and not convicted of an infamous offence having an equal voice in the selection of the representative. The Berkshire of England, with only 7741 legal votes, sends to the House of the Commons of the United Kingdom three members, two of whom are Conservatives and one Liberal; while Readingtown in its own right, on a registry of 4721 votes, sends two more members, both of whom are in this Parliament Liberals. Then Abingdon, with 890 votes, Wallingford, with 1204 votes, and Windsor, with 2054 votes, all boroughs in the same county, send one member each, two of whom are Conservatives and one Liberal. Eight members, therefore, are sent from the county of Berks, and, as it may often happen under the peculiar British system of voting and representation, they are exactly divided as to party. Berks County, therefore, pairs itself in the House of Commons. I write of the House which expired in 1880.

The county is represented in the upper house by all its peers, be they one or twenty. It is to be said, however, for the honor of the peers, that its members when sitting as legislators rise above sectional or local feelings and sit for the whole country,—*i.e.*, when that does not conflict with their sitting for their own class. I am glad of the opportunity to make this political contrast, for it is only by such pictures that one can set forth the wide differences of detail in the practical politics of the two countries.

The Reading I write from is a very ancient site. It emerges in a shadowy way out of the night of history, and first appears in recorded tradition as Redinges, which has very naturally softened into Reading. The Danes and Saxons fought around here one thousand years ago. King Alfred the Great once or more visited the spot. Parliaments of England sat here when the Parliament was a peripatetic and experimental institution, wandering around as our own Continental Congress

once did through York and Lancaster and Philadelphia.
Archbishop Laud and John Bunyan were familiar with
its streets. An old King Henry, about 1100, founded
for it a magnificent abbey to house and accommodate
two hundred Benedictine monks,—the same fortunate
fellows who once enjoyed the historic cloisters of Westminster Abbey and were a great order in England.
The stately ruins of this grand old abbey, artistically
clad in fresh and neatly-kept ivy, jealously guarded
from decay on the one hand or too perfect restoration
on the other, are now the pride and glory of the Reading
of to-day. It is, in truth, a very striking and venerable pile. The great old walls, with gates and archways and massive works still standing in the rough
outline of hall and chapel and cloister, are quite remarkable in their composition, the masonry resembling
that natural conglomerate formation of rock popularly
known as pudding-stone. The huge walls in front have
been built entirely of pebbles or bowlders of a hard,
smoky crystal or quartz, imbedded in some kind of
mortar, which formed the whole into one solid mass.

These are the things which old Reading has in advantage over our new Reading. And these legacies of the
past are not only a wealth of tradition and legend and
inspiring associations, but a substantial material bequest
of brick and mortar. Her churches, her public buildings, her roads,—in part at least,—come down to her as
the gift of previous generations. This is the advantage
which every English town has over us, and it is a great
one.

These things apart, there is a strong similarity between the two towns,—the Readings of England and
Pennsylvania. In both the houses are solid, comfortable, respectable,—the dwellings of a substantial middle class of people. In both the streets are spacious
and fairly well kept. In both brick is the predomi-
nating material of structure, and in both there is a distinctly visible new and old order of building. The

pavements of the Pennsylvania Reading are roomier than those here, and the accommodations for travellers on a larger scale. Although three railways run into or through the place, there does not seem to be much travel, and consequently little provision for it. The business of Reading is largely as a distributing centre for Berks County, which comes in and goes out the same day, while the nobility and upper classes rarely have occasion to use a country hotel, visiting at one another's houses. These facts, of course, limit the necessity of providing for travel. I am staying at the traditional county-house, a good old English inn, which, although comfortable and excellent in its way, is quite primitive and thoroughly provincial. Our Reading is quite " smarter."

It is to be said further for this Reading that its best does not show on the outside. The nobility and landed gentry, of course, eschew a town and spend their large means in building country establishments, which, being seated in the heart of vast estates, are out of sight even from the high-roads. The presence of this class in the town is seen only in an occasional drag on the streets, or the "boxes" and ponies and coroneted equipages and heavily-built hunters which indicate the neighborhood of gentlemen's stables. Were all the houses of the wealthier people of our Reading to be withdrawn from its town limits, it would lower the level of the appearance of the place very greatly.

The environs of the town here are for this season very beautiful and attractive. As you pass along the road you catch continuous glimpses of homes of ease and elegance and refinement hidden in the trees or nestling quietly and warmly in the midst of broad and abounding acres, golden now with wheat, and bordered by thorn-hedges red and fragrant with roses.

This Reading of England, like ours, is also somewhat famous for its breweries,—its fountains of beer. It has, too, noted iron-works, a fairly gigantic biscuit-

c

factory known all over the kingdom, and other manufactories, and has become quite a centre of the seed
trade in England. In fact, this trade is the most conspicuous in this place, the seed depôt of the main house in
the business being an enormous affair entirely dispro-
portionate in size to anything else in the town. Being
on the junction of the Thames with another small
stream, this Reading has also some shipping and fishing
interests, which our town has not, and the Oxford students come down to it often in racing- and boating-par-
ties. The boating is, indeed, quite a feature of the
place, giving a distinct local color to the town.

Anglican Reading, finally, has a park with which, I
suppose, our younger town cannot compete. It is not
large, but speaks well for the cultivation and æsthetic
advancement of the people. Its laying out evinces a
thorough acquaintance with the best principles of land-
scape-gardening, and fully doubles its apparent size
and all its uses. Its treasures of ornament are quite
effective,—wonderful old trees always the centres of
little systems of walks, a grim, black cannon, "cap-
tured at Sevastapol," fountains and basin grass-plots
relieved with rare flowers and exotic foliage, and, last
and best, the crowning feature to which all avenues
finally lead you, that stately old abbey, with its royal
ivy and arched vistas, and scattered fragments and
capitals, and the stone sarcophagus, and all the "properties," in fine, which any well-regulated, picturesque
old English abbey should have.

Like our own Reading, this one, too, rests in a magnificent background of generous farms and agricultural
wealth. The good cheer of the country is everywhere
visible,—in the fruiting-fields, in the warm, rubicund
faces of the burghers, in the heavy, well-fed horses,
and in the general well-to-do and contented look of
everything and everybody. The farms of Berkshire
are reputed through England, and the famous Berkshire pigs are known to breeders the world over. In

the old country, as in the new, the county of Berks is the solid foundation of Reading city.

This Reading has just three weekly newspapers and none daily. Compare this with the vigor and energy and journalistic excellence of the large press of American Reading, daily, weekly, and monthly, and you know which country you are in.

To trace this parallel between these two towns of our two countries, although starting in the accidental point of similarity of name, has been very interesting to me, and I trust will be equally so to some of my readers. The two people are very much alike; their dwellings are similar; their ways and habits of living about the same, even, notwithstanding the strong infusion of Germanic blood into the human stream of our Reading. But what is that again but the repetition in modern times, and on a small scale, of the ancient race history of England? The two towns represent also the substantial middle-class population of both counties, and it is interesting and instructive to observe that like conditions of life, or nearly like, produce on both sides of the water about the same results, notwithstanding the great differences of politics, government, and social structure which exist between us. It is evidence of our common blood and race,—a blood that goes back of modern history and takes in German as well as English stock.

READING, ENGLAND.

CHAPTER V.

LANCASTER.

Two Towns in the Old World and the New—Tracing the Lineaments of the Pennsylvania Town in the Blood and Soil of England—English Electoral System —Voters with Three or more Votes—The Celtic Tinge —A Missing Link—The Old Time Colonial Lancaster of Pennsylvania fresh in England Yet.

PENNSYLVANIA, in her State nomenclature, bears perpetual testimony to the affectionate remembrance in which the early English settlers ever held their old country, keeping green in the names of the new land the memory of the old homes they should see no more in this world. The extent and detail in which this has been done is quite remarkable, although it often escapes notice until it is forced on one's attention by finding in a strange land place after place with the old familiar names. This systematic reproduction sometimes almost makes the new land seem like a shadow of the old.

There are here a Carlisle town, " on which the sun shines fair," which is the county-seat of Cumberland; a Reading, the county-seat of Berkshire; a Lancaster, the county-town of Lancashire; a York, the county-town of Yorkshire; a Chester, the cathedral city of Cheshire; a Huntingdon, in Huntingdon County; and a Bedford, in Bedford County. There are a Bucks County, a Montgomery County, a Westmoreland County, a Northampton County, a Somerset County, a Northumberland County; and in detached towns and villages, streams, townships, and so on, one might run the list out indefinitely.

In this Lancaster from which I write one can trace the family relationship even to minuter detail.

There are here from old a King Street and a Queen Street and a Little Duke Street, and St. Mary's, James', High, Market, Water, Ann, Church, and Middle Streets. Our Prince Street is here Prince Regent Street. There are a St. Peter's Roman Catholic Church and a Phœnix Foundry, which may, for aught I know, be the parent of our Phœnixville Iron-Works.

England's Lancaster, like Pennsylvania's, is a town of something over twenty thousand people and the centre of a Lancaster County, but between the two counties there is no parallel. England's Lancashire has nearly three millions of population. It is relatively one of the largest counties of England, having an acreage of one million two hundred and eight thousand acres. During this century it has become the centre of the cotton trade, and cities like Manchester and Liverpool, with their hundreds of thousands of inhabitants, have sprung up within its borders, but little Lancaster town, with its old church and castle and the prestige of its Roman camp, is still the historic county-town, the seat of its dignity and honor. England rather looks down on new-made wealth unconsecrated by religion, learning, blood, or traditions of arms.

Although a place of perhaps several thousand inhabitants less than our Pennsylvania town, this Lancaster presents a much more imposing appearance. It is built entirely of stone, giving it a very solid and substantial air, while the tints of the stone, grays of every hue, produce a much handsomer effect than anything that could be gotten from bricks. The central view from the old Main Street, looking up the rising slope of the hill, covered with quaint gables and buttressed walls, and finally culminating in the castellated masses of John of Gaunt's great tower, is one of the finer pictures of interior England, and architecturally quite striking. It is an irregular town of narrow streets, rambling up and down hills of even steeper grade than those of our own Lancaster, and plunging every now

and then into dark and dingy hollows that are more
picturesque than reputable. It is, however, very
reasonably free, for England, from beggary and want,
and its approaches to the country are generally through
pleasant lanes lined with comfortable cottages or small
houses festooned with flowers, and each with its little
garden of green grass or foliage presenting a pleasing
picture of comfort and modest refinement.

It was on a market morning I came to Lancaster,
and the look of things was very familiar. King Street
was lined with unhorsed wagons and carts and vehicles
of all kinds from the country. In the large, spacious
courts or interior yards of the inns were throngs of
people surging out into the streets and back again. In
the stalls and tap-rooms the men were gathered, talking
and selling and buying; in the stores and shops, the
women. Farther down into the town the scene became more distinctly English and provincial, the market
shifting into a kind of fair,—noisy, cheap, and rough.
Here all kinds of things were being sold at vendue,
half a dozen rude auctioneers standing almost with
their backs to each other, each with a barrel covered
with a sheet-iron plate as his stand or counter. All of
them cried their wares at the top of their voices, and
pounded with a hammer on the iron plates in order to
emphasize their yelling. The music was *Wagneresque*.
It was a simple realistic opera that told very well the
story of rustic England. Nevertheless, through all
this din and disorderly noise the transfer of property,
after a fashion, went pretty rapidly on. The things
sold were small wares of a cheap kind,—rough china,
tin, ready-made clothing. Everything was rude, petty,
and humble.

One touch of local color which I certainly thought
to have come on here is conspicuously wanting. I had
surely expected to see again in this ancient Lancaster
the " Red Lion," and the " Leopard," and the " Black
Bear," and the " White Swan," and the " Cross-Keys,"

and "The Grapes," all in goodly state with substantial coaches in front of them, and sanded floors, and burnished pewter, and warm welcome, and good cheer inside, but they are not here. Nor did I find any inn signs or names at all in the old place which have survived in the new,—a missing link in the chain of succession which seems rather singular.

The most marked contrast between the two Lancasters is the entire absence here of any Teutonic element. The place is very English, with even less trace of the Saxon than in most parts of England. Lancaster has very sensibly felt the influence of the Celtic settlement to the north, south, and west of it,—Scotland, Wales, and Ireland,—and you see this blood-stamp clearly in the forms and structure of the people, especially in the women, who have more of the French and Irish race characteristics of feature and movement than any I have met in any part of England. This was easily distinguishable both in the farmers' daughters in the markets and in the faces and carriage of the townswomen whom I saw in church. There was a distinctly warmer coloring of hair, a greater elasticity of step and fluency of motion, than belongs to the average English woman of other sections of the land. Being the last stronghold against the Danes and Saxons and invading Northmen of all kinds coming in from the east, it is but natural that this northwest quarter of England should retain most strongly the blood and features of the earliest races.

From the time of the Wars of the Roses, Lancashire has always been a place noted for its political activity, and just now it is in active motion, organizing already for the next Parliamentary election. At present it sends a strongly Conservative delegation to Parliament, notwithstanding the radical leaning of such places as Manchester and Liverpool and Preston, a manufacturing town of one hundred thousand. The county, apart from these towns, sends eight members, all Conservative, two of whom are in the Cabinet. Preston sends two Conservatives, Liverpool two Conservatives and one Liberal, and Manchester two Liberals and one Conservative, these latter two great towns just pairing off each other's influence. The voting list of Lancashire, when all the districts are footed up, seems pretty high, but it must be remembered that under the English system one man may easily cast three votes, or even more.

For instance, in Lancashire, a man living in Preston or Liverpool might easily have *three* votes, thus :

1. If in his town he is a registered property-owner or rent-payer, he has a vote there. This is the first, and, according to English feeling, the lower grade of franchise. The man votes as one average, industrious, respectable subject of the kingdom.

2. If this same man is of a county family, owning estates in the county, he may also vote on the county list. Here he votes his family birth and historic connection with the kingdom.

3. If this same voter, who has already cast two legitimate votes, is an educated man, he may vote again on the registry list of his university, which sends its members to Parliament. Here he votes his education.

Lastly, as far as he may be able to influence or assist in the appointment of a bishop, he also votes again, the bishops being lords, who sit in the upper House.

It is this delicately-adopted system of the representation of interests, of birth, of education, of religion, of classes, of labor, of money, etc., which makes all mere figures so deceptive and illusory in treating of English politics. The English statesman resents the mathematical basis of representation as being merely an averaging and levelling process.

English Lancaster has just three weekly newspapers. Here, as in the case of Reading, our Pennsylvania towns so far outstrip their old-country parents that any comparison is out of the question. It is the same way in old Carlisle, which, with a population of thirty-five thousand, publishes only weekly journals, and but three of them.

Our young Lancaster of the New World—if you will subtract from it all the presence and influence of the great German blood, which it could so ill do without—is a pretty fair reproduction of this old town. That is the only marked difference. You do not hear a grateful German word here, or see the trace of a single Germanic custom, usage, or tradition.

There are no great barns here; no red-faced farmer boys with their shining buggies and well-fed horses in the streets; no staid and decorous Mennonite elders with solid and prosperous air; no German books or papers or almanacs in the shop-windows; none and nothing of that honest, strong, and historic race which has contributed so much to the wealth and glory of our Lancaster County, and which is now perhaps its better half,—only their English cousins of like manner and degree. You find here fresh and in clear outline the Lancaster of our young past; the Lancaster that clustered around the old-fashioned court-house; the Lancaster of old King and Queen and Duke Streets; the Lancaster of the Old Bar and of the country "manors" of gone times; the Lancaster that used to come in from Carnarvon and Coleraine and Little Britain and the "lower end;" the Lancaster of the Yates and Cunninghams and Lardners and Montgomerys and Franklyns and Jenkins and Bartons laid away in their family graves forever. Here it is, drinking port and sitting in stately old Windsor chairs and burning wax tapers and swearing at dignified butlers and powdered footmen yet.

In their respective relation to the adjacent country there is a strong resemblance between the two Lancasters. Lancaster of England is situated on the pleasing river Lune, which, when the tide is out, is nearly as respectable a stream as our Conestoga Creek; when the tide is in it is something larger. While the county of

Lancashire is distinctively known as a cotton-spinning
district, that portion of it which lies immediately
around Lancaster town and forms its beautiful setting
is a fine, rich agricultural sweep of land rolling pretty
much as do the farm-fields from Lancaster to Millers-
ville, in Pennsylvania. It looks rather richer and
more bountiful than our land, because the generous
green of the meadows and fields is not broken by the
arid lines of dusty roads and dry fences. The sweep
around this Lancaster is one broad field of living green,
the various divisions of property marked only by the
darker olive shades of the hedges. The roads are narrow and deep, and so hedged by hawthorns and box
and bushes as to be hardly seen, and not at all to break
the picture of the landscape.

Altogether, there is quite a family resemblance between the two towns,—their people and life. There is
the same size, the same equable comfort and rest and
substance,—the golden mean of blessing. The general
features of every-day life—on the outside and out of
doors at least—are much the same. There is a reasonable distribution of wealth among the people of both
towns, and a comparative freedom from want.

Lancaster of England—with its solid structures of
stone; its fine gray tints unbroken by the glare of red
brick or white paint; its old-fashioned domestic houses,
with quaint armorial bearings or scriptural legends
carved above the doorways; with its venerable walls
and gateways clad with ivy and lichens; with its famous
round castle, which has

> " Oft rolled back the tide of war,"

and from whose parapets surly cannon are even now
trained on the peaceful fields; with its mediæval legacies
of dungeon and keep; with its authentic traditions of
Roman empire; with its towers and turrets and spires
of modern time and use; with the British soldiery of

to-day, brilliant in scarlet and gold, filing through its streets to the calls of drum and bugle; with its local peasant dialect, unintelligible to American ears, and the clang of the wooden shoe—is by far the more picturesque and impressive of the two places.

Lancaster of Pennsylvania, however, has solid advantages over the older city. She has already public buildings far beyond those of this town at the same age. Give the Lancaster of the New World one thousand years more and I doubt not she will be a greater city than even this one, and in tradition, already in her infancy, has she not the names of Muhlenberg and Mifflin and Fulton and Buchanan and Thaddeus Stevens,—men as great and historical as any of the heroes of the Wars of the Roses? She was for a brief space, in times of turmoil, also the capital of the nation, a seat of government just as respectable as the court of Henry IV., which for a short time was held here.

And to-day, in many of those things which mark the strength of this century,—in newspapers, in schools, in broad streets, in commodious pavements, in spacious hotels, in fine stores and the goods in them,—our Pennsylvania town is far ahead of its respectable old English parent. The glory of this Lancaster lies in its past: ours is yet to come.

There is one fact forces itself on one in drawing this parallel between the two towns from the old home site which is rather strange and somewhat sad. The name of our new Lancaster, the establishing it as the seat of a county of Lancaster, the naming of the streets after the old ones even to the detail of rank, King and Queen and Prince being the great streets here and the others mentioned minor ones,—all force the conclusion that our American Lancaster was laid out by Englishmen of Lancashire, who lovingly traced in the soil of the New World the very lines and features of their old home. Yet in the county paper of to-day, on the signs of the shops in the streets, on the mouldering and sunken tombs and gravestones in the old churchyards, I have not found a single one of the old colonial family names of the Lancaster of Penn. Literally, " the places that once knew them know them no more."

LANCASTER, ENGLAND.

CHAPTER VI.

OXFORD.

An Idyllic Seat of Learning and Conservatism—Curious Superstitious Survivals—Historical Development of the Modern College—The American and the English College—Ecclesiastical Oxford—The Martyrs—An Old-Fashioned English Country Inn and Four-in-Hand Travel — Gentleman-Coaching in England — A County Institution.

> " A citie seated riche in everye thinge,
> Girt with woode and water."

OXFORD—the ford where, in old Saxon times, the oxen crossed the river, and now the ford where, for five hundred years, England's youth have crossed a greater stream—is a charming picture of rest and sylvan beauty, —an academic idyl. It is a picturesque old place of that mediævo-ecclesiastical architecture, half religious, half military, which tells so impressively the story of its day; a town of towers and turrets and spires; of ancient walls and buttresses and quaint gargoyles; of glorious stained-glass windows, oriel and rose and arched and catharine; of lovely academic garden-parks; of quadrangles and chapels and cloisters for the monks of letters; of forgotten bastions and redoubts, and long, stern walls with battlemented walks, now peacefully crumbling under ivy and roses; of stately oaks and beeches, and grand old trees venerable with moss and lichen and tenderly watched and cared

for in their green old age; of Gothic arches and gateways and falling ruins; of wooded walks and gentle
waters; of smooth, soft meadows, all shaven and shorn,
"and fields of living green;" of noble bits of forest,
carefully tended and stocked with antlered tenants;
of prisons of the martyrs and precious altars where, in
flame and fire, they won their crowns; of crosses and
statues of great men and good women and strange
beasts, grotesque symbolic images in stone; of quiet
churchyards and chiming bells and peaceful graves;
of gray stone and clinging green and ancient gables;
of scented gardens filled with old-fashioned English
flowers with homely Saxon names; of rustic inns; of
classic streams and time-stained halls consecrated by the
traditions of faith and learning, and hallowed with the
names and memories of the great and good of England.

> "Were ever river-banks so fair,
> Gardens so fit for nightingales, as these?
> Was ever town so rich in court and tower?"

When the American college graduate sees all this
wealth of culture and of the tradition and legend of
learning which is lavished so generously on the foundations of scholarship here, he feels sharply the bareness
and poverty of the surroundings of our best academic
life. The English student, even if he never studies much,
may get unconsciously, almost by absorption, a generous
education. His training, apart from the tuition of the
schools, is liberalizing and humane, for he enters at once
in his daily life and being into the fellowship of centuries of learning and intellectual dower. It is his inheritance.

I think no American alumnus will ever visit an
English university without a feeling of poignant regret
for the opportunities which have not been his and a
vain instinctive wish that he might be born again.
But it is not fair to compare our young American colleges with the English school, the heir of all the ages

of Anglo-Saxon culture, piety, and intellectual growth. Not only are they separated by centuries of care and sacrifice and endowment, but to-day they represent different conditions of society, and different stages in the development of history and education.

Nor would it be wise for an American student to take his full academic course in an English university, however superior the advantage and pleasure as far as scholarship and cultivation are concerned. The friendships one makes at college will largely influence and control his future life, and for Americans this association should be American. An American boy who studies at a foreign school simply expatriates himself for life. He comes home a stranger in his own land.

I would, however, strongly advise every college-bred man of our country who is yet within, say, five or six years of his graduation to complete and finish his course by a year at Cambridge or Oxford. Such one year of post-graduate study will sum up and round off all that has gone before, and in the way of broadening thought and widening the range of his intellectual activities double the value of all the years of his American *cursus*. Even one day in Oxford or Cambridge will yield a rich return to a trained mind from our schools. The acquaintance made, too, of English and continental young men—men who will rise to power and influence in foreign nations—will always extend one's power and influence at home if he can make them available from a wide basis of home acquaintance.

If, however, one must be restricted to a single course of a few brief years, for an American the American college, with all its barrenness, its lack of refinement, its poverty of intellectual wealth, is the proper place. The two schools represent different stages of society, and the progress of learning and the education of the American college will, on the whole, best answer the present demands of American life, social and political.

Education, in our Anglo-Saxon times, has so far developed three grand stages or epochs:

I. The monk and the convent represent the first stage of learning in our modern civilization, or renewal of lost civilizations. During this period education was a monopoly, held strictly and exclusively within the control of the Church. This was the mediæval period. Education was shut up in the cloister. The very word *claustrum* describes it.

II. Next comes the fellow and the college. The modern college, with its foundation, its endowed and permanent masterships and fellowships, all the fortunate holders of these franchises housed and living together with their precious stores of tradition, association, honors, books, manuscripts, and appliances of learning, is the legitimate child of the convent, and has been often actually and literally its heir. Here, too, education was at first held to the Church, but within recent centuries it has been emancipated to the learned professions,—comparatively limited bounds. Knowledge, however, was still *in collegio*, and not free. This is the period of modern Europe and the second stage.

III. Third comes a stage which has not yet taken definite shape or outline,—the stage to which we are tending, and for which the American college in its present condition is the preparation and vestibule. The work of this stage I take to be the emancipation of learning and education from any class bounds, and its free distribution among all the people,—perhaps even at their homes,—the fixed centre being a limitation and a thing of the past. The system of university examinations which now covers all England like a network, and which Harvard has introduced in the United States, is a pronounced movement in this direction. This is the period of the near-impending future.

We are now in transition from the second to the third stage, and must endure all the unpleasant features of transitional existence.

But while we may not reproduce the English college on our soil, we cannot, therefore, affect to ignore or despise it. We are its heir, entitled to all its wealth of life, just as the college inherited the treasure and historic existence of the convent. And it should be our study to get this in all its fulness, and as soon as possible. There are many features of English university life which might at once be advantageously adopted or adapted here, and I think a most useful training for an American college president or professor would be a personal study of English university life,—its organization, academic discipline, relations to society, and daily school and individual life. There could be no better qualification for an academic leader.

Oxford, as a village, is a far lovelier and more picturesque place than Cambridge. Indeed, as a picture to a stranger it is one of the loveliest spots in all England, and I much wonder that it is not more of a place of summer resort for travellers, especially as during the long vacation chambers are to be had cheap. Living, indeed, is always cheap as compared with the cost of our life. I noticed in Oxford a placard offering fourteen small houses for rent at a gross rental of one hundred and fourteen pounds. They were houses for working-people, four rooms and back-closet and shed, built of solid stone, well finished, in a healthful and clean locality. This is about forty dollars a year of our money.

Apart from its academic life and glory, Oxford presents many features of attraction to the visitor. Its authentic record dates from A.D. 900, and one reads the history of England down from that time in its venerable walls and crumbling ruins.

It has religious associations and memories of surpassing interest to Protestant faith. In its streets once flamed the most famous fires of martyrdom in England; in its halls and chambers preached, in its towers

were imprisoned, and from them led to death, the deathless martyrs. An imposing memorial cross, after the
general fashion of the handsome Queen Eleanor design,
erected in the middle of a handsome street, marks the
neighborhood of the spot where Archbishop Cranmer
and Bishops Ridley and Latimer were burned to death.*

> "Then God was with them, and the glare
> Of their death-fires still lights the land to truth."

This splendid monument was erected in 1841, and I
take it was intended as a mute and imperishable memorial against the Tractarian movement, then in alarming
progress. From a stern and gray church-tower still standing near this spot you see the window from which that excellent authority, Burnet, says Cranmer in prison looked
out and saw his comrades, Ridley and Latimer, burned
at the stake. He was near enough to see their faces.

There are several of these martyrs' towers in Oxford
in which distinguished scholars and prelates and statesmen were confined for conscience' sake, and it is depressing to think that most of them were church-towers,—
parts of houses dedicated to worship and to the preaching of a gospel of love, and that men did and could
worship in them at the very time they were desecrated
to such unholy and unchristian uses. In those dark
days of Oxford church towers seem to have been built
with perhaps an ulterior "eye to the glory of God,"
but practically and immediately for the purpose of con-
fining in them such persons as differed in views and
opinions from the builders or custodians.

Among the records of Oxford are two sickening bills
of the executioner in these martyrdoms, charging by
items for the services of his assistants and for materials,
fagots, etc.,—significant now as monuments of the con-

---

* The original picture, by the way, of the "Burning of Ridley
and Latimer at Oxford," by Sir George Haytes, left England
some time ago for Philadelphia, having been purchased by Mr.
Latimer, a direct descendant.

dition of civilization and religion in the sixteenth century. The entire cost of the burning of the two bishops was £1 5s. 2d.; of Cranmer, 12s.

Oxford has always been noted as against Cambridge for its religious activity and coloring of thought. It has been in all its history the home of polemics and controversy and doctrine. From the pulpit and the stake, and in later and more gentle years the "commons room" of its precincts, nearly all the great religious movements of modern English times have taken their start. To-day I believe it furnishes a much larger proportion of its graduates to the orders of the Church than does its sister Cambridge.

In the list of its graduates you can almost read the religious and ecclesiastical history of England.

Among them are John Wiclif the Reformer, Tyndal, (translator of the Bible and martyr), Archbishop Laud, John Foxe ("Book of Martyrs"), Cardinal Pole and Cardinal Wolsey, Archdeacon Philpot, martyr, Bishop Hooper, martyr, Cardinal Moreton, Bishop Jewell, Bishop Bonner, "the bloody," Sir Matthew Hale, Campian, the noted Jesuit, Jeremy Taylor, Richard Cecil, Bishop Heber, Dean Milman, both the Wesleys, John and Charles, Hooker, the writer, Bishop Butler ("Analogy"), Sir Thomas More and Sir Thomas Browne ("Religio Medici"), Bishop Lowth, Dr. South, John Keble, Rev. F. W. Robertson, Dr. Edward Young, Archbishop Whately, Cardinals Manning and John Henry Newman, and Dr. Pusey. Cranmer, Ridley, and Latimer were Cambridge men, but they were all burnt here.

I might lengthen out this list almost indefinitely by going into the names of distinguished living clergy and dignitaries in the English Church, would it not seem invidious to make selection. I have mentioned none of the men now alive save only the two able princes of the Roman empire who claim to rule in England. But a glance at this list shows that the great Methodist and

Tractarian movements, so unlike in character and tendency, were cradled here; that the rehabilitation of the Roman Church on English soil in the nineteenth century found its leaders here; that many of the minor currents of modern theological and religious thought started here; and that here surged·in merciless force the fluctuating waves of the English Reformation, out of whose conflict, through fire and sword, arose the present Churches of England.

Sydney Smith and Dean Swift, who illustrate how oddly the English semi-social, semi-political system of filling pulpits sometimes works, were also Oxford men.

Oxford has been in all its history distinctively the Church school, and to-day stands nearer the cloister than Cambridge, which, in many features, is tentatively stretching forward to the new era.

Oxford, like Cambridge, has a university press, known the world over for the finish and scholarly thoroughness of its work. The distinctive feature of the Oxford press has come to be the printing of the English Bible. Here you get the authorized King James version in absolute purity of text, every letter and point established with critical accuracy and judgment, and the whole book produced in the highest finish of paper, composition, press-work, and binding. It is the best memento to bring home from Oxford, and you can get it in editions of every kind and style and price. It claims to be the best-printed Bible in the world, and, I suppose, is, and certainly it is invested with more interesting traditions and associations than any edition that issues from any other press, for it comes from the school-house of Wiclif and Tyndal, and the martyr-fires of Cranmer and Ridley in Oxford's streets made the circulation of our English version possible.

It is a curious fact that the traces of an extinct re-

ligion survive longest in the forms of the new religion
which takes the place of the dead one. Long after the
life of the old faith has fled it still is preserved in the
ceremonies of the new. In Italy to-day nearly every
striking fête and feature of the Roman Catholic
Church is traceable· to customs and rites of the old
classic faiths which held sway there before the Christian
era. So in Oxford, a historic religious centre of England, and, as the centres of learning always are, a most
conservative spot, the vestiges of the forgotten beliefs
and usages of early paganism in Britain are clearly
visible in a number of traditional ceremonies which
have been handed down from the centuries, and whose
observance is yet jealously maintained, although their
meaning and original life are long lost.

The beautiful Magdalen Tower is the pride of Oxford, and well it may be, for in grace and symmetry
of architectural design, and the lovely picture of cultivated glebe and wood and water which surrounds it, it
is one of the finest sights of England.

On the castellated summit of this tower, every first
day of May, "at five o'clock in the morning," the choir
of St. Mary Magdalen College, in vestments, assemble
and chant a Latin anthem, and in reverential orison
hail the rising of the sun. Hundreds of people gather
on the streets and in the parks at the foot of the tower
to witness this ceremony. This matin rite means nothing any more now, but is admitted to be the survival
of some pagan solemnity,—as most May-day customs
are,—probably of sun worship.

In Queen's College, to this hour, the " ryghte merrie
jouste of ye boare's heade" is yet observed with cere-
monial state on every Christmas day. At dinner in
the great arched college hall on that day a fine old
boar's head, bedecked with bays, is solemnly borne
around the oaken floor, while the college chant the
sonorous old carol whose words and music are so
familiar to academic memory :

> " Caput Apri differo
> Reddens laudes Domino.
> The boar's head in hand bring I,
> With garlands gay and rosemary ;
> I pray you all sing merrily :
> Qui estis in convivio."

This observance is most probably a transmitted vestige of the Feast of Freyr, the Scandinavian god of peace and plenty, held at Yule-tide, when a boar was always sacrificed in his honor and as an offering of thanks and gratitude. The words of this semi-pagan canticle date from the sixteenth century, and, although the whole thing is a Norse relic, it was certainly a more Christian diversion than burning bishops.

Non-academic Oxford is a typical English village of the prettiest kind,—a village of green hedges framing picturesque bits of wood and valley and charming homes ; of slumbering churchyards toned with gray tombstones and dark yews ; of quaint gables and rambling streets stocked with old-fashioned country inns, each one the fitting background of an ever-changing picture of rural sights. All the traditional inn names of England seem to be gathered here, and they make one of the features of the town. There are the King's Head, and the Red Lion, and the Saracen, the Three Jolly Farmers and the Three Cups, the Maidenhead, and the Crown, and the Roebuck, and others I cannot recall.

I put up at the Mitre,—the traditional old county and university inn,—an interesting historical picture in itself of past social life and customs in England. The Mitre is to-day but a survival of a past generation, of a glory of Oxford that is gone ; but it is still an instructive and pleasing remain to an American stranger. It is an old-fashioned county inn of the once aristocratic kind, of a High-Church and horse-racing flavor, redolent of old port and strong red ale, patronized by young country squires, who lunch on cold

ham and champagne, and by broad-shouldered, florid-
faced, cheery Englishmen born of the soil, and " who
they themselves have said it." Its very name is a defiant shout for prelacy and Establishment, an echo of a
war-cry which carries you back to the old days of
trouble and party-passion,—the days of Church and
Crown.

You enter through an unpretending wooden door,
heavily barred and crossfastened, into a low broad hall,
and the first sight which greets your eyes are stout
rounds of beef and generous flitches of bacon and game
of various kinds hung by hooks to the unplaned rafters
overhead ; you step hastily from under to avoid the
drops of fat which threaten the unwary lounger (the
experienced habitués, I soon found out, knew just
where to stand), and in doing so confront the useful
young woman who answers as bar-maid, room-clerk, and
cashier in a British inn, who welcomes you personally
and pleasantly to the house. Some four-in-hand coach-
ing-whips of approved pattern and trial ornament the
hall-way, professionally and gracefully coiled on the
walls. The guards' loud livery hangs on the pegs with
some gentlemen's overcoats. Several handsome and
affectionate hounds mingle intelligently with the other
functionaries, guests, and dignitaries, and you know you
are at a respectable centre of coaching, hunting, racing,
and English country sports generally.

But the bishop's mitre is the trade-mark of the
house and the historic crest of the place. This prelatical
symbol confronts you everywhere and all the time. It
is panelled in the halls, painted on the walls, carved on
the doors, burnt in the china, engraved on the glass, the
silver, and the pewter, and woven in the linen. It
blushes through your wine, lies placidly under the water
in your wash-basin, consecrates the stables and dog-ken-
nels, and seems to rest in contented benediction on your
ale-tankard. Even the napkins are loyally folded in
this respectable episcopal device.

But it is the benediction of the past which comes down on the American traveller when he enters these old-fashioned doors. The Mitre claims to have stood here from A.D. 1400, dispensing food and shelter for man and beast. Fifteen generations of fathers and sons have purchased its hospitalities. In its low-ceilinged coffee-rooms men sat, near five hundred years ago, much as we sit now, and when they talked politics or told the news they spoke of Agincourt and glorious King Harry, of the execution for treason of the Lollards, of John Huss burnt, of the strange maid Joan, the sorceress of Arc, luring English soldiers to defeat and shameful death on the fields of France, or of how the rude but resolute Parliaments of England were wrestling with the crafty and learned legates of the pope. This is the Mitre tavern which the American crosses the seas to see, and which, I think, his English cousin on the spot never sees.

The Mitre tavern of Oxford, however, as it exists in the flesh to-day, is a thing of the past, and I cannot conscientiously recommend it to the modern traveller. The times have changed and it has not changed with them, except, perhaps, to keep abreast with the modern extravagant prices. Flavor and picturesque traditions are very good in their way, but they will neither feed, lodge, nor care for one's comfort and cleanliness. There are other and better hostelries now in Oxford,—those of our own century.

The link which connects the Mitre with the present time, and drags it, half-alive, into this nineteenth century, is stage-coaching. I entered Oxford on the top of a stage-coach and left it in the same glory, and warmly advise every traveller for pleasure or study to do the same. One sees the country, the estates, and the common people for miles as he can by no other way, and, by a half-mental, half-physical process, arrives at the consciousness of the Englishman's conception

of the height of human happiness. The Mitre, by
virtue of its lineage and traditions, is the hostel where
"the coach" puts up, and hence its *raison d'être* and
existence now.

Four-in-hand stage-coaching in England is something
more than a rich man's amusement. It is an institution.
It is the assertion of a national and class tradition, and
when an English gentleman assumes charge for a season of a coach line it is looked on as a patriotic act,
and the man himself in doing so is deemed to have deserved well of his country.

The stage line from Oxford *via* London to Cambridge
is owned and driven by a gentleman of the county,
Captain B.,—his commission in the local militia, I believe,—who pleasantly gave the full details of his work
as we drove along. His line of road is one hundred
and twenty miles, and his coach stable is stocked with
just one hundred and twenty horses,—a horse to the
mile. He drives this entire route in one day, returning the next, and resting only on Sunday. The schedule
time either way is twelve hours, starting from the
Mitre, Oxford, on Monday at nine o'clock A.M., and
pulling up at The Bull, Cambridge, at nine o'clock P.M.,
reversing the trip on Tuesday, and so on through the
week. This schedule allows thirty minutes in London
for luncheon.

Captain B., a gentleman of about thirty-six, of
wealth and position, does this work regularly every day
for a season of some five months each year. I spent a
week at Oxford, and also at Cambridge, and was personally witness to the unfailing punctuality of departure and
arrival at both places. There is no railway in our country
or in England which does better,—perhaps none which
does so well. He and his coach were immensely popular
all along the line. The little villages were always in a
tumult as we rolled through them. All day every wagon
or carriage of high or low degree drew off and gave the
road to "the coach;" the ladies were gathered at many

a tempting-looking hall or park gate to see the spirited
horses, well in hand, dash by foaming and glossy. The
landed gentry of the neighborhood frequently timed their
walks so as to come in with us at the changing-places and
exchange a word of greeting or welcome. Every one,
high and low, gentle and simple, the entire route
through, knew all the teams and their respective
merits, and every inn and station was full of tales and
legends of them and their driver. From one end of
the drive to the other the coach was a county institution
and the captain was a county hero, and to understand
the meaning of this you must remember that "the
county" is the corner-stone and foundation of English
life.

Captain B. had perfected with a master-hand every
arrangement of detail in his enterprise, and both the
safety and pleasure of the passengers were looked after
with scrupulous regard. He carried with him three
servants, a guard, a valet, and a relay driver in case of
emergency. While everything was thus provided to
support and sustain him and keep him in good condition, he personally did the work of driving, and it was
one whose magnitude and steadiness would, I think,
appal most American gentlemen. It was not a party
or an excursion, recollect, or a spurt, but regular daily
work, in wet weather or fine,—this year nearly every
day wet,—and carried on often without even the relief
of a congenial companion.

At the end of the season, the captain told me, he sells
all his horses by auction at Tattersall's, and sometimes
makes on them. Having been driven for a season in
the coach is a good character for a horse and commends
him in the market. It is a guarantee of careful and
experienced training. Part of the work and pleasure
of coaching during the season is the breaking in of the
new horses.

There is no one day of English travel which is better
worth taking than this enjoyable four-in-hand drive

from Oxford to Cambridge, or *vice versâ* if you are at
Cambridge first. You see five counties of England,
much of its best farm land and southern scenery. You
enter London and leave it on a seat from which you
have a view such as you can get in no other mode of
conveyance. You see the city shading into the country
for miles and miles on either side, and gain an idea of
its vast size and of the dense population of rural England such as no reading, statistics, or thinking will give
you. In London you rest half an hour and lunch at
the White Horse Cellar, just as English gentry were
supposed to have done a hundred years ago. It is a
veritable cellar, down steps, and with a humble and
unmarked front, but right in the centre of fashionable
Piccadilly, and preserved in all its original features with
pious care.

And best of all you see the English stage-coach in its
glory,—the struggling survival of the eighteenth century. This is a historic study, and alone is a picture
worth coming to England for. It is a sight to see the
coach roll off: it is a greater sight to see it come in at
the end of the day amid the popular acclaim and enthusiasm that might attend a victorious general returning from conquest and battles.

Fully an hour before the time of starting the boys
and idle men of the town begin to gather around the
main court-yard and gaze in silent and satisfied contem-
plation on the great lumbering red-and-yellow vehicle
which stands empty and unhorsed before the door.
Then, in due time, the stately guard makes his appearance with a burden of responsibility upon his serious
features. One or more young porters attend his decorous
footsteps. A hush falls upon the vulgar crowd, and
then, in measured and authoritative tone, begins the
issuance of official orders. Ah! it is a sight to see the
grandeur of this functionary, conscious that the eyes of
all the county are upon him, in gorgeous livery and
high beaver hat and huge bouquet in button-hole,

pinned there by the buxom barmaid; the ministerial air with which he determines the proper location of the luggage; the judicial gravity with which he decrees for or against a trunk; the grave halt over the proper strapping of a box; the utter repression of any levity on the part of his youthful subordinates; the more than Olympian front with which he accepts the grateful incense of the common herd; and the swelling sense of importance of every favored servant who is intrusted with a duty about the wheeled throne, their official communications with each other; the distended dignity of every groom and footman; the nervous, expectant look of some town youth halfway up in society, who lingers by the team and boldly essays to stroke the near wheeler, anxious to receive a nod, perhaps, happy moment! a condescending word of recognition,—to be seen talking with the swell demigod of a driver when he in due time appears.

Punctually at 8.59 the lord of the coach, with his buttonhole flower, too, and irreproachably dressed, walks out of the open door through an aisle of living flesh, which opens deferentially before him, ascends the box, accepts the reins, and sits for a moment like a statue. The guard and the proprietary driver compare gold watches,—an awful instant of suspense,—a last moment of rapid comprehensive inspection; the guard reports all ready, the horn rings out, and the state carriage of the county rolls off as smoothly and noiselessly as a perfect locomotive, in the hands of a perfect engineer, draws its train out of a well-appointed depôt.

As a matter of pride and point of finished etiquette, the guard, who has been clambering all over the stage, on and off a dozen times, makes his final report from the ground, and then leaps lightly on the wagon after the wheels are in motion. His easy professional ascent of the coach diagonally is the last touch to the picture.

The arrival of the coach is a still more inspiriting scene. In an English village all work has stopped at four o'clock in the afternoon, perhaps three, and by nine P.M. the whole town, men, women, and children, are thrown painfully on their own resources for amusement or occupation. They are, therefore, more than ready for the discharge of any public duty. I have repeatedly seen the streets, both at Oxford and Cambridge, densely packed for squares awaiting the coming of the coach, whose horn was to be heard out of the darkness at 8.57, growing clearer and livelier as it grew nearer. And this not on any extraordinary occasions, not to meet any prominent guest, but only to welcome "the stage-coach." We simply cannot understand the feeling with which the Briton clings to an old institution, and honors and worships the man who sustains and asserts it.

A shout goes up as the heads of the impatient leaders, who snuff excitement in the air, touch the crowd. The human walls form themselves again, the coach rolls into the stand, and, with the solemn air of a great duty done, the driver drops the reins into the hands of the local grooms, who contest for the honor of receiving them. Then the cheery welcomes, the questions as to the events of the past two days in which the worlds of the village and of the coach have been sundered, the orders for dinner, and the form and ceremony of the landing. The formal service of the morning is all repeated in inverse order, and, last of all, the tired and triumphant horses disappear into the night, led away like heroes, amid thronging masses of attendant Britons.

I have seen a cabal of veteran politicians decide on the policy of a momentous national campaign. I have seen battles forced in a flash, and anxious generals strike out a plan of action in the saddle and almost in the moment of execution. I have seen a council of officers, with defeat around them and their dead among them, answer with solemn defiance a summons to surrender. I have seen half a dozen army corps deploy their massed battalions in silence on to a field of history and death,—but I have never seen anything half so impressive, so utterly and overwhelmingly imposing, as the arrival or departure of a swell English coach-and-four in front of an old-fashioned English country inn.

OXFORD, ENGLAND.

CHAPTER VII.

CAMBRIDGE.

IN COLLEGE CHAMBERS IN THE UNIVERSITY—THE PURITAN COLLEGE THAT GAVE BIRTH TO HARVARD—THE COLLEGE-DAY AT CAMBRIDGE—THE SUPPRESSED UNDERGRADUATE—DINNER IN THE COLLEGE HALL—A SURVIVAL OF BARONIAL TIMES—ENGLISH COLLEGE EXPENSES—A COMMONWEALTH OF LETTERS.

SOME months since, in Rome, I spent an afternoon in the convent grounds of San Gregoriano, from whose pleasant shades St. Augustine carried, hundreds of years ago, the seeds of learning and Christianity to savage England, leaving the refinement, the culture, the religious fellowship of civilization to bear the faith to our rude Saxon forefathers.

To-day I write from the Puritan cloisters of Emmanuel College, Cambridge, the historic walls from whence the germs of civil freedom, and that education which alone can protect and perpetuate it, were borne to our *New* England. It was from this Emmanuel College—that Puritan foundation established in faith away back in the stormy days of the Commonwealth—that went forth the early divines and educated laymen who, in our colonial times, laid the firm foundations of the civil and religious liberty we enjoy in this land, in this generation. And to-day it is grateful and

6

pleasing to know that, foremost among the traditions of Emmanuel, and cherished among her wealth of pious, civic, and scholarly associations, are the memories of these graduates, the Harvards and Hookers and Wards and Bradshaws of 1600–1650, and the great work they did, in which the mother-college claims her deserved share. "Among those chiefest worthy of honor," says Bacon, "are the founders of states;" and Emmanuel hopes to have securely founded in the New World the Commonwealth which went to pieces so disastrously in the Old. It is her crown. That staunch and learned old Puritan statesman, Sir Walter Mildmay, whose liberality and faith laid the foundations of Emmanuel in the darkness of uncertainty and political trouble, builded better than he knew.

The language of the charter or deed of foundation of the college given by this scholar, soldier, and statesman, which I regret I have not at hand to quote at this moment of writing, is often touching, and read now, in the light of history, is in places dramatically prophetic. He held high office under the government of Queen Elizabeth, and the fact of his freedom to found, in express words, an establishment for the teaching and culture of Puritan principles is strong evidence of the civil liberties of England in that brilliant epoch of her history, and of the intellectual breadth and liberality of her political leaders. As the direct ancestor of Harvard University, Cambridge, Massachusetts, Emmanuel College has always had a special interest and attraction for the American scholar, and some of our best New England and New York families have sent their sons to it for their collegiate education.

From Cambridge of England, however, the interest of Emmanuel College takes a wider sweep and range. As the academic fountain of Puritanism she looks on our whole land, people, and history—in one sense, the religious and political development of Puritanism—as her child and descendant.

A good friend in London, who recognized the Puritan in me, and who was himself a fellow of Emmanuel in residence, was kind enough to invite me to spend a week in Cambridge in college quarters, placing at my disposal a suite of undergraduate chambers then vacant, it being the long vacation.

The college life of Oxford and Cambridge, the munificent development of ages of faith and learning, is something so infinitely deeper, broader, richer, and better than anything we have in our land, and withal so different, that it is difficult to know how to describe it or where to begin the attempt. I do not know, however, that I can commence in any better way than by attempting a picture of my quarters and working out from thence.

Cambridge University, as I suppose every one knows, is a collection of independent colleges, each with its own separate government, buildings, grounds, history, and associations. These colleges to-day are seventeen in number, and they make up both the university and the town. If you will take seventeen silver dollars and half-dollars, and throw them down on a piece of white paper irregularly but rather close together, draw circles with a pencil around each of the coins, and then connect these circular inclosures by convenient lines indicating streets and walks, you will have a pretty good idea of the plan of Cambridge town. It is simply a village which has grown up and around the grounds—or what, in Pennsylvania, is called the "campus"—of the several colleges.

What first strikes an American stranger with some surprise is the comparatively limited extent of these grounds,—the territorial plant of the college. In our imaginations these colleges—venerable in age and tradition, and dowered with the associations of centuries—rise in magnificent proportions, and seem to stand in princely domains in glebe and forest. As a matter of fact, the average college at Cambridge or Oxford has not a greater acreage in its grounds than the average American college; in fact, has not so great. Harvard, I am sure, has larger grounds than most of the English colleges. So have Princeton and Union, and, I believe, Yale. Pennsylvania is already very generously endowed in this respect. Few of the English colleges have grounds equal in extent or in artistic possibilities to those of Jefferson and Washington at Canonsburg, or Franklin and Marshall at Lancaster, or the Lehigh at Bethlehem, or Dickinson at Carlisle, or Lafayette at Easton, or the institution at Mercersburg, or even of our University of Pennsylvania, planted on costly acres in the built-up streets of a great city. All these have greater advantages in the way of scenery and room and possible embellishment and artistic enrichment of their grounds than the average English college of the two great universities. Some of the college-buildings here consist of but a single structure, with such grounds only as are inclosed in the interior court.

On these limited academic fields, however, the consecrated wealth of long centuries has been lavished, under the guidance and direction of the highest art and cultivation of the time. The grounds of some of the larger colleges of Oxford and Cambridge are often laid out with park and landscape effects such as have hardly been reached anywhere in our country. Even the smaller ones are carefully dressed and worked, so that an acre or two will often set forth a wonderful study of foliage or hue. And all are crowded with grand old tombs, mouldy, half-decipherable legends, armorial bearings, monuments of history, the graves of martyrs, statues, arches, solemn ruins, memorial gateways, monumental crosses, picturesque cloisters, and a thousand works of art and ennobling associations. In the successive architecture of many of these noble edifices and in the chain of names and graves and monuments you can read the history of England from the twelfth century down.

It is this splendid endowment of tradition, this continuous legended memorial of the scholarship and piety of ages, which is the wealth of the English college. It is the contrast with this which makes our own college life, so far, seem so poor and thin and meagre.

Another disillusion is the fact that the number of undergraduates in these English colleges does not differ materially from the number in ours. This runs from sixty or·seventy up through the hundreds, in some one or two cases touching a thousand, just as in our detached American colleges. It is the massing of these English colleges in one column and bringing them all under the influences of one another which gives them their intellectual force in the world of thought. The seventeen colleges of Cambridge are not educating any more young men than seventeen isolated American colleges, but they are as an organized regular army is to a body of loose militia regiments.

Emmanuel College holds about a medium rank as to the extent and decoration of its grounds. The extensive front of the great college-building is Greek, with some adaptation of English style,—this in the way of protest against the ecclesiastical architecture of most of the other colleges. The central feature of the main edifice to an American eye is the high quadrangle or interior court, faced on two sides with arcades, and bright with its shaven lawn of grass ever green and smooth and fresh. The entrances to the chambers of the fellows and undergraduates open on to this court, always known over Cambridge in college vernacular as the "quad." Although. this residence portion of the college is but one building, it is divided into sections or grand compartments, very much like the separate houses of a city row, having no communication with one another, and each section entered only from its own front door. These sections, or houses, consist of about six or eight sets of chambers, two or three of which are occupied by fellows, the remainder by undergraduates. In older times this was the family, the fellows being charged with some care of the students. This is not the case now, although the fellows always take a kindly interest in their undergraduate neighbors, feel, perhaps, some little historic responsibility, invite the boys, at all events once or twice, to breakfast with them, and if there is any community of tastes or feelings it results in a valuable association and acquaintance ·for the undergraduate. He is in the care of an older man, who feels for him as a brother.

Now for the life of the undergraduate, the only college-life known in our country. My quarters, as I have said, were the ordinary suite of chambers of an undergraduate student, absent at the time, and their description will appear rather sumptuous to the American graduate who recalls the two-in-a-small-room accommodation of many a good Pennsylvania college. This suite consisted of three good-sized chambers, with a small pantry or closet-room. The main chamber, by which you enter your suite, is a fine large room about twenty feet square, looking out with three windows on the quadrangle.

In this sitting- and reception-room are served your breakfast and luncheon by your own servant, and attached to it is the pantry, a capacious closet for the storage of your table-linen and service, and large enough for your attendant to make a little coffee or tea, wash the dishes, or cook a slight breakfast. Out of this large room open two smaller ones, ten by fourteen feet, a bed-chamber, and a study or private retiring-room.

Each section, or house of six or eight suites, has its own separate servants, with their own quarters, to whose services each fellow or student has equal rights. This staff consists generally of a man and wife or small family, who can, between them, readily cook the breakfasts, prepare the morning baths, brush the clothes, black boots, and run the errands of the six or eight single gentlemen who form the family. Some of these servants, as is always the case around a college, become quite scholastic in appearance and demeanor. In Cambridge this male attendant is known as the "gyp;" in Oxford as the "scout."

The development of the undergraduates' quarters to the present generous provision illustrates somewhat the progress of social life and habits during the past century or two, and affords evidence of some curious changes. In early times undoubtedly two or more students were quartered together. "Chum" is a contraction of chambermen. It is likely, in remote times, that six students occupied a common sleeping-room with three or more beds in it; but even then each one of them, as the ancient buildings show, had his separate little cell, generally opening out of the common bed-chamber, to which he retired to read, study, or "muse." From this habit this little cell became known as the student's "museum." Here we have the history of another word now diverted to quite a different special use. The change in personal habit and feeling made by a few hundred years is quite curious. The student of Cambridge to-day would willingly read, write, or study in a common chamber with another man, but he would, under no circumstances, share his bed-room with him.

My rooms look out on either side on prospects pleasing to the eye, cultivating to the taste, and elevating in association and suggestion. On one side they command the classic green quadrangle, all shaven and shorn, with its cloistered arcades, venerable gray tombs, monumental legends, and the admonitory walls and columns of gone ages. On the other side the study and bed-chamber sweep a small stretch of college park, looking out on gardens with ivy and roses, and a clear little stream in which, from your windows, you can see the fishes swimming under the crystal waters, and on whose quiet bosom placid ducks and philosophic swans live in amity with their finny friends. Wide, roomy seats are built into these windows, in the pleasant old English fashion, and very delightful and restful they are when you look out from them on noble trees, charming gardens, and vistas of leafy boughs and lake and meadow. Compare this with the red brick walls and the bare wastes of clay, and, perhaps, the barren, neglected campus, which form the *entourage* of a new American school and leave their painful photograph forever on the minds of its children.

On the walls of these rooms hang some good engravings and a small painting, a mounted fox head and brush, a worn horseshoe, probably from the heels of some triumphant racer, whips, spurs, crossed oars, some hunting pictures. It is proper to add that there are also some books. The suites of the fellows are generally somewhat superior in accommodation to those of the undergraduates.

Life in one of the colleges of an English university is something very different from that of an American college. Intellectually it is something far higher and stronger. The undergraduate is not the central feature, as with us, but only an incident. The living college is the master and the fellows. The undergraduates are but the younger members of the academic family and on the threshold of the house,—the little children who are seen and not heard.

Again, not the least part of the liberal endowment of an English college is the tradition of social usage and habit which it carries down, by force of which any student coming to live within its walls and sharing its life receives the training of a gentleman, acquiring the personal habits and manners which fit him for association with the better classes of society. In the average American college the student leaves either a boor or a gentleman, just as he entered. In the English college, however, the home for hundreds of years of the sons of gentlemen, the habit of life has become fixed and traditional, and any boy going through it comes out with that as a part of his education.

The daily life of the English college-resident is simple, and differs from ours distinctively in the care with which it is arranged to distribute the time for work and exercise or rest, and the ease with which it consequently bears on the individual. The English student attains a far higher grade of scholarship than ours, but we never hear of his breaking down, of shattered nerves and prostrated brain. He takes more time, it is true, but saves his body and his head.

The order of the college day is roughly this: Bathe in your room at six or seven o'clock; breakfast served in your front chamber at seven or eight o'clock; reading until one o'clock P.M., when there comes a light lunch in your room, generally only bread and cheese and strong college ale.

Lunch-hour ends absolutely the day of study or work. At this point the whole college —master, fellows, and students—betakes itself to the open air, and spends the whole afternoon, until six or seven o'clock, out of doors, walking, riding, boating, fishing, or at athletic games. It is here the college boy builds himself up for life. At seven o'clock dinner, and from dinner to bedtime rest. This is the common schedule of an ordinary university day. I have heard that there are "reading men" who burn the midnight oil far into the night, but I write only of what I have seen.

The college dinner is an imposing and perhaps the central feature of the daily life of the university. Here, in the great hall, the whole college meets together in pleasant union, and it is, I believe, now the only general meeting of the day, compulsory prayers being abolished except on extraordinary occasions. The hall itself—a survival of the old baronial times of the days of the "boar's head and rosemary"—is always one of the most striking architectural features of the college building. It is a fine and lofty room, with arched or fretted or handsomely-designed roof, the walls adorned with rich panelling and carvings, statues, heraldic devices, armorial shields, and old inscriptions, and hung with the portraits of founders and benefactors, kings, queens, statesmen, and soldiers. It is generally oaken, with stone or wooden floors.

At one end of the great hall, the farthest from the entrance, on a raised surface, is placed the table of the master and fellows, extending across the room ; on the lower level of the floor are tables for the undergraduates, running the length of the room, and placed at right angles with the master's table. All are served at the same time and alike. When the hour for dinner comes, the master and fellows, with their guests if there are any, assemble in the combination-room, another fine chamber, of which anon, and move from there into the dining-room, the master leading. The same order of procession and seating of guests holds as at any gentleman's table. As the procession from the combination room enters the main hall, the undergraduates, who are already seated, rise from their benches and stand as the college passes. When the procession reaches the head of the table, one of the students reads or intones a brief Latin prayer, and all seat themselves. At the close of the meal the same ceremony is repeated, the undergraduates rising and standing at attention as the master and fellows pass out. In Queen's College, Oxford, I believe the summons to dinner is yet blown from a trumpet by a tabarder, but this is exceptional.

This college dinner, taken thus every day in the academic ancestral hall, in the presence of the effigies of great men and good women, the founders and ancestors of the house, in the midst of historic associations and venerable traditions, is the dress-parade of university life.

The dinner, I should have said before, is the ordinary

solid English evening meal of four or five courses,—
a soup, a fish, roast meat and vegetables, a salad and
dessert. Ale is served the undergraduates on allowance,
I believe. On the master's tables there are generally
wines, in some colleges on allowance, at others ordered
at cost prices. The Englishman, however, generally
always drinks a huge flagon or tankard of ale with his
wines, sometimes before and sometimes after. It seems
always to be in place to the British stomach. The college cellars, I need hardly add, are most excellent : tradition does its work kindly and gently even here, and
one generation takes care of the next.

Dinner over, the undergraduates are dismissed to their
rooms, while the master and fellows retire to "the combination-room," where over their coffee and after-dinner
wines the evening is spent in conversation and discourse.
The combination-room is a spacious chamber, large
enough usually to accommodate forty to sixty men, in
solid old-fashioned arm-chairs, with tables, rests, screens,
and stools. It is also hung with memorial paintings
of benefactors, masters, distinguished "fellows" who
have passed out into the world and become statesmen,
cardinals, generals, writers, martyrs, or won fame in any
way. Every old college has its gallery of these its
honored children, and they are among its chiefest treasures. The room itself quickly becomes a centre of interesting association and academic tradition. In our
combination-room at Emmanuel, for instance, more than
one hundred years ago, Dr. Samuel Johnson was a frequent visitor, and the spot where he always sat, just to
the left of the warm chimney-place as you face it, is
pointed out as a tradition to-day, and the broad chairs
we sat in this year were the same used then. It was in
the combination-room of Oriel College, when Keble,
and Whateley, and Newman, and Arnold, and Pusey
were fellows, that the celebrated "Tractarian" movement took its start.

The fellows of a college in residence at times may be

only eight or ten, when, of course, this room is too
large, but the little groups gather in the gloaming of
the fireplace, and the effect of the shadows around them
advancing or retreating into the dark recesses of the
spacious walls is very picturesque. Wax candles, I
may say here, with their antique religious light, are *en
régle* in a well-regulated old combination-room, gas
being too modern and shoddy. A solemnly stately butler, with white hair and portly, judicial air, is also an
indispensable property.

Smoking, I believe, is not customary in the combination-room, the fellows, who retire at their convenience
during the evening, going to their own chambers singly
or in squads for a pipe or cigar. At eleven or twelve
the English university man brews a pot of hot tea,
drinks it, and on this extraordinary sleeping-potion goes
to bed. Here ends the college day.

Emmanuel College was founded to nourish and assert the Puritan principles inside the Church of England, and for a long time it distinctively represented the
Puritan idea in English thought and history. Its very
name was a battle-cry. Emmanuel—"God with us"
—was the watchword and popular device of the early
Puritans. They wrote it at the head of their letters,
used it as a common form of salutation in their homes
and on the streets, and later on under Cromwell shouted
it at the head of regiments in the crucial hour of battle.
The chapel of this Puritan college, as a protest against ecclesiastical tendencies and superstitious usages, was built
plain as a Methodist meeting-house, pointed north and
south instead of east and west, and was never consecrated.

Those stirring old times are gone, and nothing is left
of them at Cambridge, not even the cold ashes of the
dead controversies. The ancient theological camp is
now the pleasant home of humaner letters and a passionless science which studies their remains as it would
the nerves of a frog or the traces of a prehistoric hab-

itation of the globe. Toleration, a spirit of judicial study, is the claim and intellectual boast of the Cambridge of to-day. It is its pride now that it never burnt a bishop on either side when the fires of hate and narrowness were flaming over all England.

Speaking one evening at King's College table of Whistler,—

"It may be heresy here," I said, "to admit to an enjoyment of his paintings."

"There are no heresies in Cambridge," promptly spoke up the senior fellow at the table.

In looking over the worn and somewhat defective records of the early years of Emmanuel College one sees very clearly the direct stream of its influence on the thought and history of our land. From its walls came Thomas Hooker, John Cotton, Nathaniel Ward, John Ward, and many of the lesser divines of colonial New England, John Bradshaw, president of the court which tried Charles I., and others of the famous regicides, some of whom sleep to-day on our shores, and also a large number of the historic "Assembly of Divines," who, in the palmy Parliamentary days of Puritanism, drafted the "Shorter Catechism" in Westminster Abbey.

After much search we found, on the original rolls, the date of the taking of his degree of M.A. by John Harvard, the early scholar who has given his name to the new Cambridge University of our country. It was in 1628. This date, I think, has never before been published, not being found in the large two-volumed history of Harvard. The record of graduation seems to have been lost, but the degree is taken in course.

Among the incidental library treasures of Emmanuel shown me was an autograph letter from Edward Everett, who visited the college some thirty years ago, examined with interest its records, and on returning home sent it some volumes of New England academic history.

It seemed at times rather odd to me to recall the

memories of the rigid old Puritanism of self-sacrifice and severe manners and personal austerity—the old Puritanism we know so well in our land—here in its modern home. The old Greek walls, with their once hard Pro*test*ant lines, are toned and softened and mellowed by time. The rigid distinctive intellectual principles of ancient struggles are lost in the broader culture and wider range of modern thought. The Puritan college of Cambridge to-day does not differ materially from the High Church college or the Broad Church college of the same university. The old names are there held in affectionate memory, like family portraits, but that is all. I hardly think the gaunt old Puritan of the seventeenth century would recognize his Emmanuel boy at Cambridge to-day. I much fear the undergraduate has a carnal knowledge of playing cards and running horses and boat-racing and strange wines and ungodly games, and I do not think the corporate fellows would object to having their college and now-consecrated chapel all covered over with Madonnas and saints and crucifixes, if only it were done in good taste and in the highest glory of marble and stained glass, and mosaic and oaken carving.

But these Puritan descendants have not forgotten their fathers. They may not lead their austere lives to-day any more than they should wear their quaint clothes, nor would it do any more good. But they give to all the freedom for which the Puritan fought, and thus afford the sweetest incense to his memory, and in the daily college life keep green the names of the founders and leaders. They venerate the ancestral manes; they honor their parents in the goodly land which the Lord has given them; and every evening the gathering in the combination-room is a reverent function *in piam memoriam.* The libation is generally claret, sometimes port.

I was interested in finding how moderate are the

expenses of the undergraduates at Cambridge in comparison with the generous provision for his living and tuition. An allowance of seven hundred and fifty to one thousand dollars a year will sustain a boy creditably. This sum will not only cover necessary expenditures, but enable him to bear his fair share in the college amusements, boating, cricket, etc., and mix on equal terms with his associates. My friends thought one thousand dollars a rather generous estimate, which should also cover the travelling expenses of the year to and from Cambridge from a home in England. For this sum the student not only gets the thorough training of a strong college, but lives in the strengthening atmosphere of seventeen colleges, with all their splendid inheritance of centuries of tradition and association.

In outward organization the university is a union of independent colleges forming a literary commonwealth. These colleges hold to the central government much the relation of our States to the national government at Washington. Indeed, following out the line of this comparison, the university might aptly be called the United Colleges of Cambridge. This phrase will, perhaps, best convey to the American mind the outline of its constitution. Each college manages its own internal affairs, regulates its own admissions, establishes its own *cursus,* governs its own students, administers its own endowment, and elects its own master. The university organization masses the forces of the whole of them as against the outside world. It confers degrees, elects members to Parliament, and generally deals with the outward or "foreign affairs" of the academic commonwealth.

Under recent acts of Parliament very considerable changes are being made in the constitution of the universities and the administration of the colleges, but they are too wide and complex to take up in the limits of this paper. The general movement I may say, however, is towards centralization,—the strengthening the University at the expense of the several individual colleges.

In fact, I must stop here, noting only in closing one mediæval touch of local color. Every night here, precisely at nine o'clock, the curfew-bell sounds. It tolls just the same strokes as in the troubled times of the Norman conquest, carrying us back hundreds of years, but it cannot carry us off to bed any more.

CAMBRIDGE, ENGLAND.

ENGLISH POLITICS.

CHAPTER VIII.

ENGLISH POLITICAL LIFE.

A Transition of Sovereign Power in Progress—The Eng-
lishman's Development from the "Subject" into the
"Citizen"—Government of the Great Families—The
Aristocratic Order—Land its Basis—The Blow to
English Society that Comes from our Prairies—The
English Castle and the Kansas Wheat-Field—A
Bloodless and Silent Revolution—The Runnymede
of 1880.

ENGLISH politics are an extremely interesting study
at this moment, because they are in a transition state,
and the old forces and the new define themselves more
clearly than when the country is in repose and standing
still. The government is passing from the hands of
an aristocracy into the hands of the people, and this
by reason of a change in the social structure of England itself. The old England whose corner-stone is
class and privilege is dissolving in the new political
acids of the nineteenth century. The stratification of
society—many classes and orders of the people, and
these classes resting one upon another—is giving way
to a new order of things, where, as nearly as possible,
society becomes homogeneous, rank is done away with,
and all classes are fused into one mass.

For many centuries England has been governed by
its great families. The castle was the germ of political
power, as the township is with us. The people were
not sharers in the management of the nation, but
"subjects," nominally of the crown, really of that
order—or, in American parlance, "ring"—of great
families who made and unmade kings and queens.

79

Now the Englishman is developing from the "subject" into the "citizen." This is the silent revolution, social and political, which is in progress to-day in England. It is noiseless, bloodless, after the fortunate fashion of the land, and moves ever without violence, but it is none the less radical and thorough.

No one can look on the landed aristocracy of Great Britain without a sense of profound admiration for the power and self-control which have constructed and sustained the order. For many centuries it has governed England absolutely, controlling to its own use and behoof the power of the crown, the Church, the army, the schools, and subordinating to itself and its own uses trade and commerce and wealth. There has been a breadth and intelligence and self-restraint necessary to achieve and keep all this which challenges respect and admiration. These great families acquired and held all the land of the country, and so held a nation as tenants. When votes became the coin of government, they kept all the votes to themselves. Withal there was a certain conscientiousness in all this princely plunder. They did not defend it as a lordly robbery. They wished to show a better title than the sword for this high estate, and so they held it all in trust for the nation. The ballot was a trust in the hands of the few to be exercised for the benefit and good of the many. This was Burke's famous theory, brilliantly elaborated in his brilliant style, and doubtless he believed it. And if you ask an English lord of to-day, he will tell you that he holds his magnificent estates,—hundreds of broad farms, villages, towns, counties,—not as a selfish personal possession, but in trust for all the people. Nevertheless, in both of these instances it is clearly a case where the trusteeship is more desirable than the usufruct.

The people have gotten the votes to themselves, and now they are getting the land. This is the revolution.

Without question, the large English holder by descent

does feel a responsibility over, which the American landowner by purchase never experiences. His fathers did acquire their land as a trust, to defend the kingdom. The trust has passed now into a different shape, and those who are conscientious recognize it. The defect of the theory is that those who are not conscientious or intelligent do not recognize it, and there is no way of making them. The suffering usufructuaries have no remedy. The submergence of the English aristocracy in the waves of the people is a sight which even the American republican views not without a certain sadness. The ultimate gain to the whole people is large. The immediate loss to the world is definite and sharp. As a class the aristocracy of England is probably the best and highest that has ever been. It has been more conscientious, more dignified, of a higher moral and intellectual grade, than the nobility of any other country. To its blood and birth it has added education and wealth, consecrating them to its high social and political uses. Thus it has become educated without pedantry, and wealthy without vulgarity. It is this trinity of hereditary power and education and wealth which has made it strong and permanent.

As a consequence of all this it has evolved a very high type of man and woman,—a flower for the enjoyment of all the world. In physical health, in personal cultivation, in gentle manners, in a delicate sense of honor, in the perfection of his mode and order of life at home, the English gentleman of our day stands without a rival. Other classes of other countries may approach or equal him in some one of these points, but in the combination of them all there is none that comes near him.

Now, the lower-class Englishman, in whom, by the force of numbers, he will be lost, is not a pleasing or desirable order of man. When the English aristocracy goes down it is not merely the dissolving of a venerable historical picture, like a ruined abbey or a fallen castle. It is a positive loss. Thoughtful Eng-

f

lishmen to-day will tell you that the imminent danger
to English society is the coming up of large masses of
uneducated wealth, which, presumptuous and vulgar just
in proportion to its ignorance, deteriorates and lowers
the tone of opinion and thus degenerates the fibre of the
whole social structure. This is so in every country, but
is especially so in England, for the lower-class Englishman is a peculiarly ungracious and disagreeable kind of
being. The safety of England and the hope of good
for all her classes lie in the fact that this change has
been going on very slowly.

Just at present, however, there are many indications
that a crisis is threatening that may hasten the course
of English history beyond its average slow movement.
Curiously enough, the impulse comes directly from our
side of the ocean.

Land is the basis of the English aristocracy. Its
rentals have been their revenue, and all of it, for a peer
could not go into trade. The rental of land depends
ultimately on its bread-yielding power,—the value of
the wheat it will raise. But land, having become the
corner-stone of social position and power of all kinds,
has come to have a fictitious value in England far beyond its wheat-raising value. The new-made millionaire
in England is nothing until he owns a large country
estate. This, and this alone, will give him any position
in the county and open, grudgingly and sparingly
enough it is true, the doors of society. Consequently,
the new manufacturer and tradesman buy it at any price.
Thus it has come to pass that in recent years, while the
rents or income of land have been coming down, the
price of land has been going up. The new men want
it without reference to its legitimate value.

With the rise of commercial fortunes values have been
going up all over England, as over the world. It costs
more to live, and the landed classes, even if getting the
rents of a hundred years ago, are relatively poorer. But

they do not get the old rents, for the value of wheat is going down all the time; and the value of wheat is the measure of the rent which the tenant-farmer can pay. It is the farmer whose profits support the landed aristocracy. The castle rests on the farm. Now, it is the tremendous importation, at ever cheaper rates, of our American wheat into England which is steadily lowering the market price of English wheat and the rental of English farms. Thus comes a dramatic situation. The Kansas farmer, the men of Minnesota, Nebraska, and Dakota, all-innocent of their work, are sapping away the foundations of the aristocracy of England. Every swath in a Western wheat-field topples a stone from an English castle.

The social and political fate of the strongest and ablest aristocracy of Europe is being worked out to-day on a foreign continent and by emigrants from Europe, —the stones which the builders rejected there. It is Nemesis.

This is the situation, and every year it is getting worse and worse, for every year the price of land will represent less and less its bread-yielding power and more and more its social power, and with the perfection of transportation and the opening of wider areas to cultivation American wheat will be laid cheaper and cheaper at English doors. Then, again, another pressure hastens the crash. Growing slowly poorer, the landed nobility have been for a generation or two doing what most other people do in like situation,—borrowing and mortgaging their land. To-day the landed estates of England, as a whole, are heavily encumbered, many of them up to their full value. As the power to pay off debt is steadily decreasing, this effort for relief only speeds the final disaster. One of the imminent questions which confronts most gravely the new Parliament is some plan for the relief by law of the landed estates of Great Britain burdened by the debts and charges of generations.

However radical the social and political changes in progress in England, there will not likely be any change in the form of government in our time : England loves a form too well. The great families administered their aristocratic government under the form of a monarchy. The people likely will administer a republican government under the same monarchical form. England to-day is as republican as we are in many things, but the old forms remain unchanged,—venerable and picturesque, but lifeless.

This is the revolution which is going on to-day in the England of our sight, and it is as great and important as any in her history, as sharp in its lines, as far-reaching in its consequences. Conventional travellers seek out the plains of Runnymede to sentimentalize or indulge in patriotic platitudes, but there is a current flowing through Westminster to-day, and at every election-poll in England, with a stream clearer and swifter and more fateful than ever ran the historic water-brooks of Surrey.

CHAPTER IX.

GLADSTONE.

The English Statesman in his London Home—A Pen-Portrait of the Man—The Scholar in European Politics—Mr. Gladstone on American Government Administration—The Payment of our National Debt—His Fundamental Republicanism—Free Trade.

I found Mr. Gladstone, the scholar-statesman of England, among books, letters and MSS., and volumes laid in successive strata on his table. The last number of the *Nineteenth Century* served as a paper-weight, holding down a mass of official parchments. A file of Greek newspapers peeped out from the covert of a pigeon-hole,—Cyprus was then the *bête noir* of English politics,—looking like erudite mummies among the strapped and indorsed bundles of parliamentary briefs and "orders for the day." The "Homeric studies" of the Oxford "double-first" scholar were coming into the most practical kind of play as a political force. Disraeli himself could not have asked a more dramatic situation.

Mr. Gladstone's London dwelling is a plain, spacious house, one of a substantial "row," with the ordinary architectureless front of a close-built city street. It stands on Harley Street, in one of the most solid and respectable quarters of London. Inside there is only the usual provision of the average well-off citizen,—a great deal of comfort, but no display. He avoids the palace-atmosphere in his own home, just as he eschews the glamour of imperial ideas in politics. Simplicity is, indeed, one of Mr. Gladstone's ruling characteristics. The visiting-card of the ex-premier of England reads simply "Mr. W. E. Gladstone."

This is, indeed, all the rank he is entitled to under the social laws of England, which are held more binding and sacred throughout the land than the acts of Parliament. It is one of the triumphs of the English social organization, which it has taken centuries to perfect, that at a London dinner-party Mr. Gladstone (out of office) would have to yield precedence to any hobbledehoy of a school-boy whose father chanced to be an earl.

In this modest house the work-room of the veteran statesman is a moderate-sized chamber on the second story, lined with books and very solidly furnished with heavy table, large, comfortable leathern chairs, and a few fine engravings, some of political, some of art interest, the day's papers on the floor. A vase of fresh flowers, full of color and bloom, smiled through the sombre smoke and muddy fog of London.

8

In personal appearance Mr. Gladstone is an active, lithe, muscular man, rather tall, and of well-proportioned frame. His face and figure have that clear-cut contour which generally indicates several generations of intellectual activity and personal leadership. Mr. Gladstone is the descendant of a long line of Scottish lairdmen of small wealth and limited possessions, but accustomed to stand first in their community, to think, and to lead. The face is scholarly, cultivated, its outlines boldly defined by that meagreness of muscle which distinguishes the intellectual athlete. There is not an ounce of superfluous flesh on it. The thin lips and well-cut mouth and chin betoken firmness, determination, and endurance. Seventy summers have sat lightly on Mr. Gladstone, but the years have brought their blessing of rest, and his face in general wears the repose of strength and experience, strongly lined with the record of struggle and thought. A new fact, however, or an aggressive opinion wakes the whole man with the fire of youth, and the eye flashes with eager light, and the body bends quickly forward, as if to grasp a fresh acquisition.

Like all strong Englishmen, Mr. Gladstone is a man of large physical power and endurance, fond of out-door air and work, and the ring of his axe at Hawarden, so familiar to England, has echoed even across the Atlantic.

An Eton boy and a Christ Church graduate, I found at Oxford that the great university had already in living memory enrolled Mr. Gladstone among her jewels of state, with Wolsey and Pole and Laud and Hampden and Vane and Clarendon and Sir Thomas More and Marlborough and Pitt, and the long list of her sons who have led in field and council, consecrating their trained powers to the service of their country. If Mr. Gladstone owes to his university the intellectual training and discipline which have enabled him to stand foremost among the political leaders of his time, he has amply repaid the debt in the conscientious devotion with which he has served at the altars of learning during a busy and eventful life, and a long one, for the premier's political career began within one year from his college graduation, when he was elected to the House of Commons as a Conservative. Within two years from that time he was in the ministry as an under-secretary.

Notwithstanding the strain of a continuous political career in a country whose political service is, perhaps, the most exacting in the world at this time,—its interests encircling the globe,—Mr. Gladstone has been a most prolific writer, his range of study and discussion running pretty much over all the fields of modern thought. His greater works, "Homer and the Homeric Age," "Juventus Mundi," "Ecce Homo," "Vatican Decrees," are, perhaps, as well known to the educated classes of our own country as to those of England. They do not begin, however, to represent the immense bulk and varied range of Mr. Gladstone's literary labors. These are best seen in the wonderful wealth of his magazine articles, which have flowed in a steady stream for a generation now through the periodical press of England. An edited collection just made by one of the London publishers forms quite a respectable library in itself. In fact, Mr. Gladstone's contributions to the magazine literature of the day have been more voluminous than those of many a professional writer.

In outlining Mr. Gladstone's literary rank and work one cannot help noting the absence of any high scholarship in American politics as contrasted with its marked presence in European statesmanship. Education, of course, is a prerequisite for the European politician, but, further, a respectable degree of scholarship may even be said to be demanded. Personal cultivation, I may add, is a further incidental qualification growing out of the social structure of the Old World.

A glance at the English political leaders of the day shows how thoroughly scholarship has entered into their lives. Disraeli, ex-premier, is a distinguished novelist. Of Gladstone, premier of to-day, author, essayist, magazinist, I have just spoken, and I might have noted his breathing Latin renderings of standard hymns which have gone into classic literature. The late Earl of Derby, another premier, is known the learned world over for his translation of the Iliad. Lord Brougham was almost the first scholar of his day. The Earl of Caernarvon, a distinguished reviewer, has just published a translation of the Agamemnon of Æschylus. The Duke of Argyll has published elaborate works on politico-theological themes.

Coming down a little farther, Lord Houghton finds leisure from his duties in the House of Peers to contribute a volume of poems, while such active political workers as Sir Charles Dilke, Mr. Edward Jenkins, Sir George Campbell, Henry Vivian, M.P., Lord Lytton, Sir Bartle Frere, Lord Dufferin, Sir Henry Rawlinson, and others, have all published popular books of more or less literary ability. Sir Garnet Wolseley is an accomplished military writer, author of an admirable "Soldiers' and Officers' Hand-Book." Henry Fawcett, M.P., is professor of political economy at Cambridge as well as a distinguished writer.

Coming to France, it is no less striking. Thiers has given to the world a *pièce de résistance* in twenty volumes. Victor Hugo, Girardin, Lamartine, Laboulaye, Montalembert, Jules Simon, Guizot, are names familiar and distinguished equally in politics and in literature. The Comte de Paris has produced the most elaborate and the best history of our civil war yet written, and perhaps the best of all the books called out by our great struggle. Olivier has a new work just announced, and Jules Favre one just out. Even Louis Napoleon felt it desirable to assume a virtue if he had it not, and issued an imperial "Life of Cæsar."

In Italy, Menghetti, prime minister of the outgoing Cabinet, is known for his large work on "Church and

State," and Pantaleone, senator and soldier, has brought out an elaborate volume "Against Infallibility."

In Germany—the greatest national force of the day —every Cabinet has some of its chairs filled by doctors of philosophy, and even the generals are trained scholars. In fact, in this country, where the entire mass of the nation has almost a finished education, the political leaders must be men of trained intellectual power.

Compare all this with our own poverty. General John A. Dix won some possibly permanent literary distinction by a scholarly translation of the "Dies Iræ." Charles Sumner was a vigorous and polished writer. The present Secretary of the Navy has entered the field of polemics. There are some New England names in politics entitled to be mentioned respectfully in the world of letters; but how brief the list, and how meagre for the whole country! The American legislator's education is pretty much confined to votes and voting, just that particular field of knowledge which English public opinion prohibits its legislator from entering, forcing him to relegate all this kind of work to "the agent,"—a special political institution over here,—as incompatible with the standing and character of a lawgiver. Like the "whip," the "agent" is a distinctive feature in English practical politics to which we have no direct equivalent. I shall describe them both farther on.

In the course of conversation Mr. Gladstone grew quite eloquent in praise of the work of the successive administrations of our government since the war, warming almost into enthusiasm as he recounted their achievements in reducing the public debt, and asking practical questions as to the internal direction of this uniform policy through so many administrations, and as to its popular political effects on the country at large. The well-considered, almost scientific character of these inquiries showed how thoroughly Mr. Gladstone has studied and how closely he has followed our course in this matter. Indeed, he has made great practical political use of it, from session to session, for some years, in fighting the Conservative party.

It was the ambition of Mr. Gladstone as leader of the Ministry of 1868-74 to follow in a modest way our lead in this direction, and he did grapple directly with the national debt of England,—monster as it is,—and initiated a very promising movement towards its diminution. Since his outgoing the movement has not been carried on, but I have no doubt the attempt will be renewed under his present administration.

In truth, in a general way Mr. Gladstone is rather extravagantly laudatory of our country, standing up stoutly to all the assertions in his recent famous " Next of Kin" article, so complacently received on our side of the water, so severely criticised on this. I told him frankly I thought he had done us some substantial harm by this brilliant paper, as our national sense of self-sufficiency is not, as a rule, in need of stimulant, but he avers that we were entitled to all he said.

Mr. Gladstone has unquestionably made a close study of our public men and measures of late years, and takes heart for England from our achievements, believing that the two great popular governments of the English-speaking peoples of the world must move in the same direction, and that what one can achieve the other can do. He has a familiar knowledge of the interior working of our political system, and of the work and character of our really prominent men,—the men whose speeches have shown thought enough to catch the ear of foreign statesmen.

Mr. Gladstone avers that our national integrity in the payment of our public debt—the efforts both of the people and of administrations made to this end—is something unprecedented in political history. To this point he returned again and again with unflagging interest, inquiring whether the nation never grew restive under the continued pressure of taxation,—whether it was made a leading issue in the campaign before the people,—and expressing his renewed admiration for the courage and integrity of the leaders who carried it through, and of the people who are capable of such things.

Mr. Gladstone, whom I met in the fall of 1879, when he was out of office, was kind enough to go at some length into the party situation of the hour, revealing his mental and political cast in this unstudied conversation, following its own drift, far better than in an elaborate speech or article. He has all the essential fibre of republicanism. He has that faith in the people which it is so hard to find in a country where society rests on a foundation of sharply-distinct and separated classes. He is, as a consequence, the instinctive enemy of imperialism and all it tends to and longs for, hating its dreams and ventures with a hearty hatred. He believes thoroughly in movement forward, which, for an old man in an old country, is a sign of a very young heart. The very atmosphere of Europe is depressing and calculated to make one lose faith in human progress. Indeed, I have noticed that even the American domiciled long in the Old World loses insensibly that sense of the recognition of a common manhood in all men which is a part of our inheritance.

Mr. Gladstone out of office was as much a power as in. The Marquis of Hartington was the technical leader of the Opposition, and did really "drive the political machine" on the floor of the House of Commons, but Mr. Gladstone was the heart of the party, the power around which the intelligence and personal confidence of liberal England gathered, as the parliamentary campaign of 1880 abundantly demonstrated. To-day he is again at the head of the England that is making history.

"Free trade" is a popular political enthusiasm or sentiment with the Englishman, something like the instinctive assertion of the Monroe doctrine with us, and in this matter Mr. Gladstone is the prophet of his people. For it he has labored all his life, and has a word, in season or out, to be cast on good soil or barren.

During this visit the subject had not come up, but at the door of the room, after having shaken hands, it seemed to strike Mr. Gladstone suddenly, and, coming out into the hall, he resumed conversation earnestly on this new tack, firing out some facts and arguments from a thoroughly unstudied and unconventional position over the banisters.

"Oh! I want to say a word, frankly and heartily, as we English always do: Why *do* you persist in your illogical policy of protection?" etc., etc. "You Americans are having everything your own way; you are competing against us all the time in manufactures; you will beat us finally in the long run. Why *will* you retard your own progress?"

"Well, Mr. Gladstone, I come from a city of manufacturers, and we are perfectly satisfied with our rate of progress; in fact, our great national danger is always of going ahead too fast, and the very best policy for us is one that does retard us a little."

And the momentary colloquy closed as discussions on this subject always do.

LONDON.

CHAPTER X.

AN ENGLISH ELECTION.

FIXING THE TIME OF BATTLE—THE BRIEF CAMPAIGN—RE-TURNING A MEMBER—MEETING OF THE ELECTORS—CON-TESTING A SEAT—NATURE AND COST OF THE EXPENSES OF AN ENGLISH PARLIAMENTARY ELECTION—THE ENGLISH-WOMAN AT THE POLLS—WOMAN AND SOCIETY IN POLITICS.

AN English parliamentary election is so different from ours, and the differences show so sharply some of the divergences in practice of our two political systems, which are so similar on paper, so dissimilar in fact, that they can best be developed and contrasted in describing the practical process of returning a member.

In the first place, the time of holding elections is not fixed by law, but depends on the will of either one or the other party,—an immense tactical advantage for whichever party is able to secure it. When Parliament dissolves, an *immediate* election is held for the next one. The party in power can dissolve whenever they wish, if there is any reason so to do. Disraeli was watching, for instance, the whole of the year 1879 for a desirable opportunity to dissolve the Parliament whose limitation of seven years was expiring, ready to do so at whatever moment he deemed the public mind was in a favorable condition to return a Conservative majority in the next. But while the party in power have the first shot for this great chance of fixing the time of battle, the Opposition, if it should find itself strong enough to defeat the Ministry, can bide its time for that, and force a dissolution, and the consequent election of a new Parliament at the moment of its choice. In either case the election takes place at the will of the management of either one or the other party, and is not at stated periods fixed beforehand by law.

In the second place, when an election comes the struggle is immediate, short, and sharp. Ten to twenty days is full time for a national political campaign in England. In that brief time all the work is done, and the struggle is over,—this, too, in a country where the public pulse does not beat nearly so fast as with us, and where ideas travel very slowly. From London to Edinburgh is in railway time about the distance from New York to Pittsburgh, but an idea will travel from Maine to California ten times faster than from Surrey to Scotland. Nevertheless, the Englishman puts through his political campaigns ten times more rapidly than we do.

The process of an election, or as they call it here "returning a member," is in this wise: When the time comes, either by a general dissolution or by cause of a special vacancy, a writ goes out from Westminster to each constituency (American, election district) to send forthwith, or within a certain brief time mentioned, the member or members which constitute its representation as fixed by law. This election district is not as with us a given number of population temporarily defined for that purpose. It is a borough, a county, a city, a university that has at one time or another acquired the right to a certain representation. This writ goes out to the returning officer, who is generally the head of the election district whatever it be, the mayor of a city, the high sheriff of a county.

This returning officer immediately calls a public meeting of the legal electors *to send a member.* This meeting takes place, I believe, generally about two days after the reception of the writ. The returning officer who called it presides. Any elector may there nominate a member. The nomination is generally made by the most prominent and influential gentleman in the county or borough. If it is seconded by four other gentlemen, so that five electors join in proposing, the nomination is duly and fully made. The presiding officer waits a due interval to hear if any other nominations are proposed, and, if none are, he then and there declares that the nominee proposed is duly returned, and issues to him at once his certificate, and the whole thing is over.

Should there, however, be any other candidates, their friends immediately put them in nomination, the names of five electors in each case being needed to bring a name before the meeting. When two or more have been so nominated the presiding officer announces that the electors have failed to make any return and that their choice must be decided by a ballot, and he fixes a day for taking this ballot, generally from two to ten days from the meeting. The ballot is therefore only a contingency in an English election, and not the soul of it, as with us. In ancient times it hardly came into play at all, and even in the general election of 1880 very many members were returned without its use.

This appeal to the ballot is what in England is called contesting a county or borough. "A contest" in England is not a scrutiny of the vote as with us, but exactly what we call "running" for any office.

Before any candidate, however, is declared duly in nomination, he must, if there is this contest, give bond to the returning officer, with two good securities, for his share of the costs of the election. The terms and amount of this bond are in the judgment of the returning officer. If the candidate cannot give it, his nomination drops. Up to this time the proceedings have cost nothing. If there has been no contest, the gentleman nominated has a seat in Parliament without the expenditure of a cent.

With the "contest" or running, however, the work gets serious. This bond is the check-rein to individual political ambition in England. A member of Parliament receives no salary; the costs of obtaining a seat by an election average at the least five thousand dollars; should Parliament dissolve in thirty days after it convenes, as is perfectly possible, the seat is gone and all is lost.

It is always a mystery to an American politician why the expenses of an English election are so heavy, and what they can be. I think the general belief among us is that this five thousand dollars—and it sometimes goes up to twenty-five thousand dollars or over— is simply a bribery and corruption fund, but it is not so necessarily, and hardly ever directly. In England an election is an affair of the candidates entirely, and not of the people, as with us. They hold it and conduct it, and not the state. Out of their own pockets, therefore, they must provide for all the expenses. They pay for the printing of the tickets and all blanks and forms, for the hiring of watchers, inspectors, and clerks, and for the rent of all the polling-places, which in a large district, as in some parts of London, may be enormous. These expenses they share among themselves, and it is to mutually secure these that the bond is given.

There are also other individual expenses which are legitimate, and which are special to England. The lower-class Englishman has not that taste for politics which is inbred with us, and great exertion is needed to "get out the vote," which is always light contrasted with our polling. Now, the most delicate attention you can pay the English voter is to haul him to the polls in an open two-horse barouche. The lower-grade vote generally insists on this, and as a consequence the outlay for carriages is always a tremendous item in a candidate's bill. A carriage for an election day also is apt to cost more than for any other day in the year.

Again, the canvass in England is conducted through "agents," whose functions will be explained farther on. These agents are generally local attorneys. As many are used as may be needed, and gradually the custom is spreading of having more and more, until now I am assured that in a rural election the entire local bar is often divided between the opposing candidates. These attorneys' fees, too, are sometimes regulated on the same principle as are the bills of the livery-stable keepers. There is no trouble at all spending the five thousand dollars—when one understands the customs of the country.

Finally, the count of the vote is made by the candidates themselves, and not by the state. On their mutual report of the result the returning officer makes out his certificate.

The most novel feature, however, by all odds, of an English election to American eyes is the presence of women in it, and the active part they take in the canvass. There is no Duchess of Devonshire to kiss the butchers nowadays, but the ladies of England freely lend their charms to the adornment of the hustings all the kingdom over, and take a personal share and intelligent sympathy in the work. The wife, mother, and sisters of the candidate, and sometimes his cousins and his aunts and his friends, appear on the platform with him, or ride in open carriages with him and his party from point to point during the canvass of a city, or on the critical day of the polling, and their names, movements, and appearance are duly chronicled in the daily prints. Gladstone's wife and daughters it will be remembered were with him through all his wonderful invasion of Scotland, and they also "assisted" his son in his contest for an English seat. A youthful Lord Ramsey ran on the Liberal ticket for Liverpool during my stay in the country. His young wife accompanied him everywhere, and her presence really seemed to be popularly his strong point. The Liberal papers referred editorially again and again to "this interesting couple," and kept the picture steadily before the people. It evidently was a political force. The canvass of a county whose political control is in the hands of a great family, may be almost a kind of picnic. The candidate drives out every day from the castle with a brilliant party of lords and ladies, and if he is fortunate speaks on the platform from the centre of a bouquet of countesses and Honorable Marys,—a lovely kind of election committee forever out of the reach of an American politician. On occasions the candidate and his friends who speak with him appear in evening dress and with bouquets at the button-holes,—a proceeding that would be rather desperate here. In England society is a power in politics ; here it is something which the average voter resents.

The women of course enter into politics with that charming disregard for principles and regard for men which is so pleasing a characteristic of the sex everywhere, and their participation lends a piquant flavor to a political campaign entirely lost to us. The politics, like the Church, of an old family, however, is generally a matter of descent.

It is not likely that this phase of political life will ever obtain here. In England politics enters into the very fibre of society, and is part of the social structure. The family is the unit of society there, and not the individual, as with us. The government of the kingdom up to this time has been entirely a matter of certain great families,—part of their property and occupation,—and naturally all the family take an interest in it. Gentlemen—the young sons of peers or influential county families—as little able to do any political work as school-girls themselves, also often go around with the party, lending the influence of the family and name by their presence. It is something like sending the empty family-carriage to a funeral, but it does the work with the English voter.

Englishwomen, it should be added, by the force of this kind of education learn, after a fashion, a good deal of politics, and have a knowledge of public affairs and take an interest in their country which the American woman does not. When a girl can help her lover into Parliament, which, in England, means something much more than going to Congress here, or a married woman can distribute secretaryships or curacies for social vassalage faithfully performed, politics becomes fully as interesting as dancing or millinery.

London.

CHAPTER XI.

THE INTERROGATION POINT IN POLITICS.

AN ENGLISH USAGE—THE GOVERNMENT AT THE BAR OF THE
HOUSE OF COMMONS—THE MEMBER AT THE BAR OF THE
PEOPLE.

THERE is one practical point in British politics so unlike anything in our own, and so marked in their system, permeating it from top to bottom, that it is worthy of special presentment. It is the usage of interrogation.

From first to last, the Government to the House of Commons, the members of the House to their respective constituencies, are always on the stand, bound to answer clearly and explicitly any question asked in good faith and in the language of gentlemen. Information from the Government to the people is not, as with us, given in lengthy argumentative messages or elaborate speeches, but daily, and in brief, direct replies to specific inquiries. It is simple question and answer, as plain and unequivocal as the talk between two men on a matter of business.

This usage probably grows out of the admitted candor and straightforwardness of the British character, which loves simplicity and directness and honors them, and which hates indirectness and concealment.

I can best illustrate this point of practical politics by describing briefly its mode of use in the two instances in which it is brought into most marked prominence, —viz., the interrogation of the Government in the House of Commons, and of the representative, or "member," as he is here called, when he appears before his constituency from year to year, either to stand for election or report to his county the action of the House during its expired session.

In Parliament there is one distinctive feature to which there is nothing of parallel or analogy in our Congress. When you enter the House of Commons the object which perhaps strikes you first is "the treasury bench," a large, solid table-desk, covered with papers, and standing directly in front of the Speaker's desk. If you are acquainted with the *personnel* of the politics of the day, you see around this table the familiar features of the leading ministers,—the Ministry of England, the Cabinet of our Government. They are there with their briefs and data, and sometimes with clerks to answer squarely and directly and immediately such questions as may be put to them by the representatives of the people. This is done daily, I might almost say hourly. Sometimes, indeed, a whole session may be simply a fire of question and answer,—the questions a brief sentence or two, carefully framed, the answers equally short and well weighed, for on these answers the Government must stand. It cannot shelter itself behind a mountain of words.

On this right to demand of the Government full and explicit information on any subject at any time there are no limitations by law. There are limitations, however, necessarily, by usage. The same love of fair play which has evolved this system of interrogation demands that, in matters so weighty as affairs of state, fair and due notice shall be given of the question to be asked. An immature or hasty answer might be injurious to the best interests of the country, and, besides, would not be entitled to the weight and consideration of one duly matured and carefully framed.

Accordingly, it has grown into a usage that the questions to the Ministry shall be submitted to them in writing at least one day before the answer is demanded. The questions are, therefore, generally handed into the treasury bench on the floor of Parliament the

day before an answer is publicly asked on the floor.
Sometimes they are read aloud, and sometimes only
quietly handed to one of the ministers in the most
informal way, pencilled on a bit of paper, the back of
an envelope, or anything that comes to hand.

There being no limitation by law, any member of
course, if he chooses, may spring any question without
a moment's notice, and demand a snap answer. This
however, is considered "bad form," only injures the
individual who attempts it, and the public sense of
fairness justifies the minister in declining to reply until
he has had proper time. I have seen this done, and
am satisfied that the "smart" member who attempted
it only hurt himself; and, in truth, the minister's dignified refusal to return any answer until he could give
one worthy of a responsible Government was applauded
by the Opposition as well as by the Right.

The Ministry, again, may decline to answer any
question when, in their judgment, the answer would
be detrimental to the interests of the nation at that
time. This is, the same as with us, a right which
must be exercised judiciously as well as honestly.

Lastly, the questions must, of course, be put in good
faith and couched in respectful language. The buf-
foonery which so often obtains at Harrisburg or the
rough vulgarity of Albany would simply put its users
out of the doors at Westminster.

It is on the hustings, however, that this custom of
interrogation takes its most striking and popular form.
There the member answers to his constituency face to
face in their home, just as the Government answers to
the members in the House. The same general rules as
to notice, good faith, respectful language, etc., prevail
as on the floor of Parliament, relaxed a little, perhaps,
by the popular character of the assembly and place.
It is deemed better, on the whole, not to notice a vulgarity on the stump,—or perhaps to cautiously call
attention to it,—but to go on and answer the question

anyhow. These questions take the widest possible range, and are always intensely practical. What are the member's views on the Eastern question, and on "farmers' rights" and "game-laws" at home? How did he vote on the Indian appropriation, and how were his tenant-leases drawn this spring? What are his views on shooting rabbits or burying dissenters? The candidate, or member, is sometimes owner of half the county, and half the voters are his tenants. There is great latitude in these interrogations, and some of them are very curious and personal. They illustrate thoroughly, however, the campaign, and enable a stranger to understand the situation rapidly, and better than he would from listening to a dozen of one- or two-hour speeches.

There are advantages and disadvantages to this system on which I have not room at this time to dwell, but which every expert in practical politics will readily see for himself. In England the dangers of the practice are largely lessened by that spirit of fair play and directness which animates the nation and governs all its popular assemblies. There would be danger in many parts of our country that freedom of interrogation would degenerate into license and insolence, which would be thoughtlessly applauded.

The advantages are very great. It tends to check sophomoric speech-making; it brings the representative and his constituent in direct and very satisfactory relation; it clears up popular doubt or uncertainties, because the issues are framed in popular form by the voter, not for him, and answered direct Yes or No; it lets the member know clearly what his constituents want, and on what issues they are interested; and, lastly, it is essentially democratic. The Government is always at the bar of the House, and the House is always at the bar of the people.

LONDON.

CHAPTER XII.

COMPARATIVE COST OF GOVERNMENT.

GOVERNMENT SALARIES IN ENGLAND AND THE UNITED STATES
—EXPENDITURES, TAXES, AND DEBTS—THE MONEY ECONOMY
OF REPUBLICS.

THERE is a certain element of ignorance and discontent in our country which is always complaining of the extravagance and cost of our republican Government, national, State, and municipal, and flippantly referring to European Governments, most generally that of England, as being something better, more satisfactory and economical. I propose to show the folly of this kind of talk, not by any argument, but simply by citing some facts which will illustrate the cost of government abroad.

I quote England, because, first, that kingdom is most frequently held up to us as an example; and, secondly, because it is a constitutional Government of large freedom, and the circumstances of comparison with ourselves are, therefore, fairer.

The Lord Mayor of London receives a salary of $50,000 a year and a fine residence,—the historic "Mansion House" of the city,—just what we give the President of the United States.

The young Marquis of Lorne, as governor-general of Canada, receives a salary of $50,000 a year and a residence; again just what we pay our highest officer.

The English ambassador at Paris receives a salary the same as that of our President, $50,000 a year, as also does the lord high chancellor.

The money cost of our chief executive is, therefore, only that of a whole class of officials, say, of third-rate rank and importance in this monarchy and empire. We begin our scale of salaries at their third degree.

The Lord-Lieutenant of Ireland receives a salary of £20,000, or $100,000 a year, for governing a small state with less than six million inhabitants. He gets, also, in addition, $35,000 more in salaries for his household,— not an official household, but a personal one,—chamberlain, ushers, " gentlemen-at-large," master of the horse, gentlemen of the bedchamber, etc. This official starts with just twice the salary of our President and ten times that of the governor of Pennsylvania.

The Prince of Wales for serving the state in " that station to which it has pleased God to call" him, gets $200,000,—four times what is paid by us for the services of a chief ruler.

The Queen of England for the royal family—herself, her children, and her relatives—receives from the state annuities amounting to the total sum of £547,000 —say $2,735,000. We have no charge, burden, or outlay of any kind with which to compare this.

The "Church Establishment" is another political tax with which we have nothing to place in comparison, and is a very substantial item to the taxpayer. The Archbishop of Canterbury, for instance, is paid $75,-000 per year; the Archbishop of York, $50,000 per year; the Bishop of London, also, $50,000 a year,—up to and over our Presidential grade. The bulk of the bishops, however,—there are twenty-eight,—receive but from $20,000 to $25,000 per year.

As an incidental evidence of the comparative scale of cost of British Government, I may mention that the English minister to Switzerland receives from his country a salary more than twice as large as that received by the president of the Swiss republic himself. The British minister at Washington also receives $30,000 a year, three-fifths of our President's salary, and more than the salary President Lincoln was paid.

Castles and palaces, sometimes furnished, and with

even the silver provided, are "thrown in" with these generous allowances.

The British Cabinet officers receive generally $25,000 against our $8000 for the same duty.

Now for the "territories," or provincial possessions, of England. The governor of Ceylon receives $35,000 per year; the governor of New South Wales, the same; the governor of Victoria, an Australian province, $50,-000; the governor of New Zealand, $37,500; the governor of Jamaica, $35,000, and Sir Bartle Frere, in Africa, has been getting $30,000; and so the list might be extended in all quarters of the globe. Compare this with our modest territorial budget.

But let us come to some departments of expenditures not personal and contrast our burdens.

Take a single item. The estimate of appropriations asked for the army for this year by the Conservative administration was over $75,000,000. This sum has already been exceeded, it is believed, by about 33 per cent., making the cost of the army this year $100,000,-000 or over. And this is cheap for Europe, for the English army is a small one when compared with the continental masses of legions. In France the military burden is worse, and in Germany it is appalling.

The amount asked for the English navy for the current year is £10,860,901,—nearly $55,000,000. This one sum of naval cost is more than our entire "civil service and miscellaneous" expenditure for 1878. Or put it this way: The cost of the army and navy to England for one year is about equal to all our current expenses of all kinds, saving the item of interest on the public debt.

There is always some difficulty in getting the exact expenditures of the English Government, but the revenues raised in 1879 from the kingdom alone—the small territories of England, Wales, Scotland, and Ireland, and not the empire of foreign possessions—amounted to £83,-000,000, or about $415,000,000. As England is constantly going deeper into debt, this sum represents some millions less than her expenditures. Our national expenditure, including interest on the public debt, was, for the year ending June 30, 1879, $261,000,000. In other words, our cost of government is but three-fifths of that of the English, while our population is one-third more, and our area of territory is twenty-five times as great.

The final proof, however, in the comparative burden of government will be found in the public debts of the two countries. It is they which represent the sum of costs and the *weight.* Here the contrast is sharp: our national debt is something under two billions of dollars, and is *diminishing,* and England's national debt is £777,781,590, the enormous sum of almost four billions of dollars, and *increasing.* As a matter of fact, they count it now only by the interest, which, in 1878, at their low rates, amounted to £28,412,750. The country has lost all hope of paying off the principal; but that is not the worst,—it is not keeping it down; and in that is seen the weight of the burden of the cost of government, which is greater than the people can or will bear. Since 1862, when the interest on the debt was £26,000,000, there has been a steady and gradual rise, sometimes halting for a year or experiencing an inappreciable diminution, it is true, but never holding the gain, until it now stands at over £28,000,000.

And now, how is all this to be met? This is the individual question for our grumblers to confront. The Englishman staggers under taxes of which we happily know nothing at all, or very little,—a searching income-tax, to begin with, stamp acts and excise, probate and customs levies. Many of these are of heavy weight when contrasted with ours, even under the pressure of war. The probate of a poor man's will costs two per cent. on the sum proved. A tax answering to our "collateral inheritance" statute lays a levy of one per cent. on direct or lineal succession,—*i.e.,* the passage of property from father to son. When the legatee is farther out than a grand-uncle or aunt, this tax rises to ten per cent. Patents for inventions cost $25 at every step, the final issuing of the patent costing from $250 to $500 in addition. There are *pro-rata* taxes on insurance policies, on every lease, on mortgages, on conveyances, on settlements, on bonds, on covenants and bills of exchange and bank-notes. Then there are stamp-taxes,—a tax on every receipt given for a sum over $10, on licenses, on houses, on liquors. An attorney must pay down $250 to the state on his admission as barrister; a notary public, $150 on receiving his commission. You pay $2.50 for the privilege of carrying a gun, and $3.75 for the right to call yourself a servant and hire out as one; a marriage-license costs $10.50, and, if you want to marry without previous residence in the parish or district, the special license costs $150.

This list might be extended almost indefinitely. I only cite a few instances at hand to illustrate the weight of taxation in a well-governed European state, and how it presses in on the individual, annoying, hampering, and embarrassing him at every point and turn.

In fact, we have no idea at all in our fortunate country of what taxation in Europe is. In Italy, for instance, a country where the vast mass of the people are wretchedly poor,—so poor that one who has not seen them can have no conception of their poverty,— the annual expenditure of the national Government is greater than ours, and there are but 27,000,000 people to raise it from, instead of 45,000,000, as in our case. The taxation to meet it requires a levy of over $10 per head. As a sample of their power to bear taxation, I may mention that there is an *income-tax of thirteen per cent.*, which is deducted from even a foreigner's interest on an Italian Government security.

It is to be said in favor of England, at least, that, while the people pay high for public service, they get good work,—a better return than we do. Their public work is very thorough, and the grade of the public servant higher than with us. All this insures a certain economy in the long run, and inures to the stability of government and the good of the community.

I am not writing to this question, however. Ours is better for the cost than theirs is for their cost. It is likely that we both err,—they in having too costly a public service, we in demanding too cheap a one. The point I want to make is the immense cheapness of government under our system as compared with that of any other. It would be better if we would pay a better price for all public service and demand a better service, more solid work, and a higher class of men to do it,—men of education, character, and responsibility.

These things, however, are other questions, and open up endless argument in a hundred directions. The one point we are considering now is the immediate cheapness of republican government. It is rather fashionable among a certain class of people to be forever declaiming about the wastefulness, cost, and extravagance of a government carried on by the people, and not by a special class trained or born to the work. I maintain that a people's government is the cheapest on earth, and the republics of the United States and Switzerland and France are the proofs. An analysis of the national administration of France will show that all those departments of the Government which are new and distinctly republican are managed cheaply or at a moderate cost to the nation. Those departments which are yet run in the old monarchic grooves, as the diplomatic corps, for instance, are costly. Switzerland, a republic with a population of 3,000,000, has a yearly governmental expenditure of $8,500,000; the 4,000,000 of economical Hollanders, who indulge, however, in the luxury of a monarch, spend $50,000,000.

In fact, economy is an incident of republican government.

LONDON.

CHAPTER XIII.

PARLIAMENT.

Political Topography of the House of Commons—Sitting in Line of Battle—Plan of the House—Taking the Ayes and Noes by a Human Count—Sanctity of the Floor—The "Whip."

THROUGH the attention of one of the leaders of the Conservatives, the party in power in England at the time of my seeing it, I enjoyed the courtesy of seeing the House of Commons from its own floor. This is rather an exceptional privilege and a very desirable one ; the strangers' gallery, which is cramped and closely enough guarded too, giving one a view of only half the house, and a very unsatisfactory one at that.

Everything in England preaches history if you have ears to hear and a mind to understand, and this jealous guarding of the privacy of Parliament comes down as a usage from troublous times when, if the chamber of the House of Commons had been open to visitors, improper influences might have controlled the action of its members. Even now the chance presence of the Prince of Wales in the galleries is absurdly remarked on, and so great is the sanctity of the floor of the House of Commons that the messengers and servants of the House itself dare not tread on it when the House is in session. If a message is brought to it from the House of Peers, the messenger advances to the bar of the House,—an imaginary barrier supposed to be swung across the floor from the ends of the lower benches on each side of the room,—and it is there taken from him by the clerk or a member and conveyed to the Speaker's desk. In the same way, if you send in your card to a member, no page or servant delivers it at his seat. This messenger again halts at the bar. The nearest member, seeing it is a private message, takes it and passes it on until it reaches your friend or acquaintance. This service of courtesy the members hourly do for each other rather than suffer a sacred old form to be infringed on or weakened.

The reserved place on the floor which the modern centuries have wrested from the old fear and conservative tradition is a small compartment capable of seating seven persons, or eight if they squeeze. It is on the floor of the House, but carefully railed off from the members' seats. You can communicate with the members, however, who are in the habit of coming up to the "reservation" and speaking with their friends across the railing. Admission to this bench is given only on the special order of the Speaker in each case. When once you are in this intimate inclosure, which in appearance much resembles the prisoners' dock in our county court-rooms, you have an excellent view of the whole house and everything that is going on. You can see everything and hear everything. In the galleries, a large portion of the time, you can do neither.

On taking my seat inside of this modern and very moderate indentation into the British constitution I was amused to see how very thoroughly the American was there. The theory of this "private bench" is that it is a place where members may have an opportunity to speak to and see influential personages of the kingdom whom they ought to be able to consult or communicate with without leaving the chamber. Of the persons who occupied the bench this evening of which I write, one was an ex-senator of the United States, a second an American doctor of divinity, a third an ex-Cabinet minister of the United States, and another of the two remaining was certainly a fellow-citizen, but I did not know him. Five of the seven seats were thus held by the Yankee,—a small army of occupation.

Strangers, however, whether favored with the "dock on the floor" or less fortunate with a seat in the delusive galleries, can hardly complain of their accommodations from a House which has not accommodated itself.

It is a literal fact that there are not seats enough in the House of Commons to seat its own members should they all attend at one time. In this House there are six hundred and seventy-eight members, and there are seats for but four hundred and seventy-six. By the usage of the House, therefore, no member is entitled to his seat unless he is in at prayers,—a rule which has something of a schoolboy sound to us. Indeed, the schoolboy atmosphere of the House, to which I shall again refer, is very marked, and forces itself on one's thought all the time.

The whole matter of seating is very different from ours, and conditions the appearance of the House, the habit and style of speaking, and, to some extent, the usage and course of procedure. In truth, the political parties sit in line of battle. I will attempt to make it as clear as possible.

In the first place, there are no desks or tables for the members,—nothing but long rows of red-cushioned benches, four tiers, I think, of them rising from the floor.

These benches run along the two sides of the room in straight lines. The room is a long rectangle, with the Speaker's and clerks' desks at the one end of it, the general door at the other. The rows of benches start from the upper end of the room, "right" and "left" from the Speaker's desk, running down almost to the door. An imaginary line drawn from the lower end of the benches across the room is "the bar." These long parallel rows of benches are divided again in the middle by a narrow aisle running up from the lower tier to the highest, for purposes of access. This is called "the gangway."

The members of the Government party always sit in

the tiers of benches to the right of the Speaker, and are known as "the Right." The members of the Opposition party all sit in the benches to the left of the Speaker, and are known as "the Left." The party forces are thus always massed on the floor and face each other. These grand parliamentary divisions of "Right" and "Left" are further brigaded by the "gangway-line," the regulars sitting "above the gangway" and the irregulars of either side sitting "below the gangway." For instance, to-day the straight-out Conservatives, who have the government, sit on the right above the gangway. The independent Conservatives, on whom they can generally depend, but not always, sit below them,—*i.e.*, on the right side below the gangway. The straight-out Liberals, or Opposition, sit on the left above the gangway, the extreme Liberals, or Radicals, just below them,—*i.e.*, on the left below the gangway.

This custom divides the floor to the eye into four distinct political divisions, and one can always see at a glance how a vote at the moment would stand. It certainly has this advantage.

The leaders of each party, again, always sit on the front bench of their respective sides "above the gangway," and thus face each other. Thus, to-day, on one short bench on the right, sit Sir Stafford Northcote, Colonel Stanley, secretary of state for war, Mr. Cross, etc., leaders of the Right, who, of course, are the Ministry, and facing them, on another small bench, the Marquis of Hartington, the official "leader" of the Opposition, William Ewart Gladstone, Mr. Foster, John Bright, Robert Lowe. The election which took place as these sketches were being prepared for publication has just reversed these seats.

Between these two "benches of leaders" is placed a large, substantial, square office-desk table with solid sides and drawers to the floor. This is strictly the clerk's table, but as the clerical officials of the House

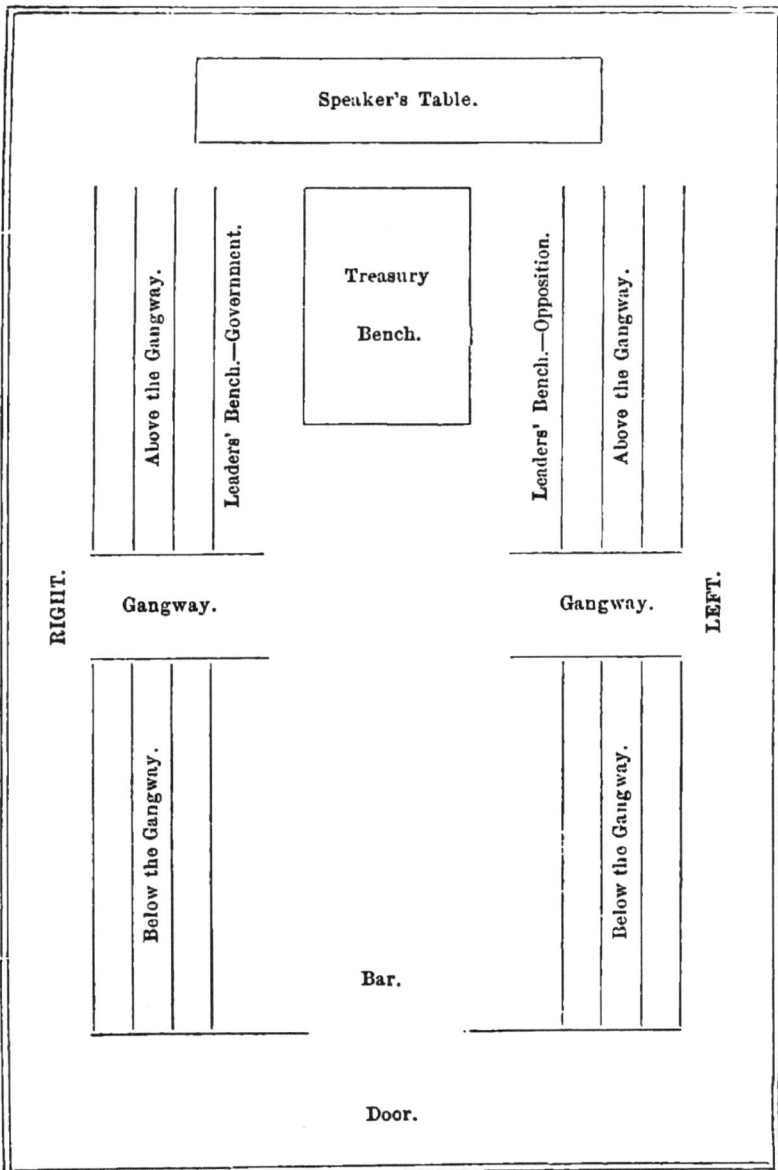

UPPER END.

Speaker's Table.	

Above the Gangway.

Leaders' Bench.—Government.

Treasury Bench.

Leaders' Bench.—Opposition.

Above the Gangway.

RIGHT.

Gangway.

Gangway.

LEFT.

Below the Gangway.

Below the Gangway.

Bar.

Door.

LOWER END.

are not conspicuous, and the right at least of this table is occupied by the ministry, with their secretaries and papers, this section of the floor is popularly spoken of as the treasury bench, although that designation in strictness belongs only to the short front bench where sit officially the leaders of the Right.

The space on the floor between the two tiers of right and left benches is perhaps fifteen to twenty feet, and stretches the entire length of the room. Its uppermost boundary is " the treasury bench," its lowermost limit " the bar." This is the arena, or clear floor, into which our members are so fond of getting when they want to make a speech and give the nation a full view of themselves. No member of the English Parliament, however, dare speak from this space, which is always kept clear. It is an established rule of the House, come down from the centuries now, and a usage stronger than any written regulation, that no member shall address the House save from some spot where, if he sat down, he would sit down on something. So every member must stand to his bench, and most unsatisfactory, awkward, and uncomfortable places are they to speak from. This is undoubtedly a " survival," as is everything you meet here.

I furnish a rough draft or diagram which gives at a glance a bird's-eye view of the political topography of the House of Commons. The knowledge of this, although apparently an incidental and ancillary matter, is very important for a familiar understanding of English politics, as the ordinary political phraseology is based on it, and in speeches and newspaper articles the bulk of references to parties, sections, or members is made to them not by name, but to the location where they sit.

Sitting on long benches, or pews, with no conveniences of table or desk, the members, when in the chamber, must attend to public business. They cannot write private letters or do their committee work during the session, as at Washington. Nor can they adorn the furniture of the House with their feet. They can, however, when bored, read newspapers and sleep, although the position for sleeping is not a happy one, and gives the sleeper rather a drunken and disjointed air.

The members sit with their hats on,—another historic survival. This usage comes down as an assertion of the dignity and sovereignty of the House that it did not have to uncover before any one. As a matter of fact, now only about one-half of the House wear hats at one time, a member relieving himself apparently by sometimes wearing and sometimes removing his hat. This custom in this century results in anything but an effect of dignity, particularly when the House is half-asleep. In fact, it often gives a rowdy, bar-room appearance or tone to the whole room. It has, perhaps, one advantage. When a noble lord is undergoing a severe attack from the champion of the other side, he simply thrusts both hands away down into his trousers-pockets, jams his broad-rimmed silk hat far down over his eyes, projects his motionless crossed legs stiffly forward, and in this statesmanlike intrenchment no movement or play of his features can betray him.

In front of the Speaker's table, on a lower desk (not in the diagram), used by the clerks, lies a huge golden club. It is the mace,—a substantive historic survival, and the outward and visible symbol of the power of the House. When the House goes out of session and sits in committee of the whole the mace is removed and slung on rests under the table.

Whenever a division is taken in the House of Commons the members are all told off bodily by a most clumsy proceeding, a custom which evidently comes down from a very ancient and primitive time. All the members get up and leave the floor, deserting the cham-

ber absolutely. They are literally poured out into a
hall, where they separate themselves into two lobbies,
the "ayes" going into one lobby and the "noes" into
another. From these lobbies they file out, each lobby
pouring out its contents through its own door between
a pair of tellers. The vote is thus counted, and there is
no other way of taking it if the yeas and nays are called
for. Calling for a division, therefore, is a very serious
matter in the way of delay. Half a dozen counts may
consume a whole afternoon or evening session, especially
if any of the members choose to loiter in the hall or
lobby.

By another curious formality, whenever a division
was called we "visitors of the House" were removed
from our private dock to an outer chamber, and when
the ceremony was over brought back again. The
reason gravely given for this usage is "lest any stranger
might get mixed with the members and counted."
During one night I went out thus three times to avoid
the danger of being pressed in as a British legislator.

The description of these arrangements—the machinery of the House of Commons—has consumed so
much space, that I postpone to another letter some description of the appearance of the House itself and of
its ways and modes of doing business as compared with
ours.

I conclude with some explanation of a human instrument of machine politics which we do not have on our
side of the water, in just the same shape, at least,—the
"whip."

It is the duty of the "whip" to see that the necessary party "vote" is always on hand in case it should be
needed either to carry a measure or to prevent an adjournment. An adjournment can always be had here
if there are less than forty members in their seats and
any one chooses to call for a count.

In this land, where parliamentary attendance is so

very negligent, the duty of the " whip" is no light one, and requires a large amount of tact, knowledge of society and the different social relations of the members, prudence, judgment, and sagacity. He must not be nervous and detail the members for duty when they are not needed. He must not be reckless or over-confident or let himself be misled or deceived on the other hand, and be found without any forces when the vote is called.

Everything over here if once tried and accepted works itself very quickly into shape and becomes an institution. The " whip" is now a recognized and well-established cog-wheel in British machine politics. He is always one of the under-secretaries of the treasury,—I think, the second under-secretary. His real work is not the treasury business, of course, but the party management and engineering. He has a special office-room in the Parliament building, one of the treasury-rooms, fitted up for his particular uses and work, with telegraph, messengers, clerks, etc. By courtesy the whip of the Opposition has also a room allowed him in the building, similarly fitted up, to do his party work in, which, to say the least, is very generous of the party in power. However, the taxes of the people pay for both the rooms.

When the Opposition come into power their whip is, by now-established usage, entitled to the post in the new Ministry of second under-secretary of the treasury, and thus the machine works smoothly on.

LONDON.

CHAPTER XIV.

PARLIAMENT (CONTINUED).

House of Commons—The Written Constitution and the Unwritten Constitution—Two Systems of Representation—The Representation of Numbers and the Representation of Interest—National Construction and National Growth—Society in Parliament.

WHILE the English Parliament and the Congress of the United States are fashioned after the same general shape,—the former serving, in fact, as the model of the latter,—there are essential and fundamental differences between them that make all hasty comparisons misleading and render the study and practice of English politics something very different from that of American politics.

Both bodies are divided into two Houses, an upper and a lower; both bodies are elective (in the English Parliament the seats of the English peers are hereditary, but the Scotch and Irish peers are elective); both bodies divide the work in much the same way between the two Houses, the lower House controlling the supplies. All these general features of resemblance, however, only serve to hide the radical differences and mislead the superficial observer.

I shall endeavor briefly, in a running parallel, and in the simplest language possible, to point out the fundamental and radical divergencies which exist between the Governments of our two great English-speaking countries, as administered by their national legislatures, and to show in passing how these differences illustrate themselves on the floors of Parliament and Congress in diverse customs, habits, and modes of procedure.

To begin with, the controlling organic difference be-

tween the two nations is the difference between a
growth and a *construction.* This difference underlies
everything,—government, politics, law, social structure,
and every-day habit and usage. England is a growth,
—we are a structure. You see this in everything you
look at or consider here, every day and every hour.
And wherever there is a difference in the habits, manners, or customs of the two people you can nearly always
trace it back to this source and determine it by this as
a rule.

First, of course, this comes out in the constitutions,
—the bottom and foundation law of both countries.

We all know that ours is a pure construction, a plan
traced carefully on paper by political draughtsmen for
the use of political architects. We know that every
word has been carefully studied and every clause and
sentence thoughtfully adjusted,—or tried to be adjusted.
Every word is plainly written, so that every citizen may
know it. Many of them have been made the subject
of legal interpretation,—even the punctuation has been
so considered. Our Constitution in this feature of absolute and entire construction does not differ from a
written contract, an insurance prospectus, or a railway
company's charter.

Our own Constitution being thus rigidly framed and
fixed on paper, we unconsciously assume that all others
are also. We hear of the " unwritten Constitution"
of England and assent to it, but I presume the average
American, nine times out of ten, thinks of this phrase
loosely as a figure of speech, meaning something,—he
does not exactly know what.

As a matter of literal fact, the Constitution of England—the fundamental and greatest and determining
law of the whole country—is absolutely unwritten.
Nor is it anywhere or in any way divided into chapters
and sections and division of topics, as ours. Nor is it,
of course, indexed. It is a vast body of customs and
usages, most of which are rights *which have grown up,*—

rights of the crown; rights of the Church and of special Churches; rights of classes; rights of Parliament and of each House; rights of persons; rights of colleges, village vestries, abbeys, counties, etc., etc., etc. In the chapter of this volume on Westminster Abbey there is noted a striking illustration of one of these early personal usages grown into a right of national proportions.

The whole body of these rights and usages which have grown up from year to year, and from century to century, and which are growing yet, is the English Constitution. They have never been gathered together, they have never been recorded; some of them have perhaps never been definitely reduced to rigid words. No one in England would do all this for them if he could, and no one could, for these rights and usages are living things, changing and growing every day, just as our own bodies grow by constant hourly change.

One can think out for himself how this needs affect the daily life and work of the courts and of the legislatures, and of the politicians and the statesmen, and how it must make their work diverge from ours.

While the English House of Commons and our House of Representatives are both elected by the people, they are elected in an entirely different way, and so as to represent in an entirely different way the body and interests of the nation. Here, again, it is growth and construction.

We choose our representatives to represent purely the principle of numbers or population,—if that is a political principle at all,—each male over twenty-one years of age, and not convicted of infamous crime, be he good or bad, educated or uneducated, cultivated or vulgar, with property or without property, a valuable citizen or a worthless citizen, counting one, and being equally represented in an infinitesimal fraction of the member he sends to Congress. We represent only the individual, not what he is or may have been. We elect our representatives, too, by a very simple and easy method, and in mathematical proportion to the numbers of the population, everything accurately "constructed," like logarithms or the tables of a life-insurance company.

The English system of representation, on the other hand, is very complex and very involved, like the unfolding leaves of bud and flower and tree. It is a growth, various interests and classes having achieved representation from time to time as they have forced themselves forward into notice and power. It is also changing every few years,—*growing*. It could not begin to be described in detail within the limits of a letter, being elaborate, complicated, and not in any way reduced to a simple rule, as ours. There are features in it which seem to us to work great inequalities,—at least if we take our principle of numbers to be the true one.

The great difference between the two systems, however, may be stated thus : That while we represent directly only the individual, the English system undertakes to represent directly a large number of the higher interests of the country. The voter does not vote merely as an individual, but for what he is worth to the community as nearly as that can be ascertained.

For instance, education is represented when the universities send members to Parliament; the Church is represented when the bishops sit in the House of Peers; classes are represented in the same way ; counties are represented when they send members as counties ; boroughs are represented when they send members as boroughs ; and, finally, property is represented in the property qualification, nearly always attached, of the voter. As a matter of fact, too, the army and the navy, great and important institutions and interests in this country, are always well represented on the floor of the House,—this by the personal choice of the voters, however, and not by any direct provision. Labor is represented also in the towns which it has built up,—

Manchester, Leeds, Birmingham,—and which send members *as towns* and not by reason of population.

It will be seen that the members of Congress and the members of Parliament go to Washington and Westminster in a very different way and represent very different things.

The duties and labors of the English Parliament are very vast and onerous as compared with those of the Congress at Washington. Our legislative functions have been distributed by *construction* to the State governments and other bodies, while in the gradual *growth* of centuries all the burdens of the whole nation, and latterly of an empire, have been piled up on Parliament. Our simple distribution of legislative functions is familiar to every one at home. Parliament does, or undertakes to do, everything. It debates on the construction of a bridge across the little Thames one day, and the reconstruction of the Indian empire or the conduct of a foreign war or the peace of Europe the next. In this respect the machine seems to have broken down at present. Everybody, Conservative leader as well as Liberal, admits that the business of the House of Commons is at this moment hopelessly in arrears. It is in the condition of a court with an overburdened docket, —back, not for terms, but, as is variously estimated, from ten to fifty years.

All these great differences—of organic law, of structure, of functions—show themselves clearly, work themselves down in the appearance, in the manners and usages, and in the mode of proceeding of the two great Houses.

When you first look over the House of Commons and contrast it with our House of Representatives, two things strike you at once. You see, first, that the average of years of the representative is higher than with us; and, second, you find a larger proportion to

the membership of distinguished men than with us,—
men of known ability as soldiers, statesmen, thinkers,
scholars.

The first fact is simply the general tendency and
result of a more highly organized and mature community. We send older men from Philadelphia and
Boston than from the Kickapoo and Oshkosh and
such-like districts.

The second fact—the larger presence of strong men
—is directly traceable to the English system of representation and one of its usages. In the first place, the
average grade of the voter in England is higher than
with us, which, of course, raises the grade of the representative. Under the system prevailing now, the
very ignorant man or the man without any property
interest in his country at all (unless he have a high
educational qualification, as on the university lists) is
pretty surely excluded from the ballot-box. No Tammany legions can be marshalled and marched to the
polls here; and that is the reason, perhaps, why they
march in New York rather than in London or Dublin.

Then it is the happy usage of an English constituency to select for their representative the ablest and
most distinguished man they can get in their kingdom,
whether he is born inside the parish lines of the district
or out of them. They want to be represented, not to
satisfy the claims of Little Peddlington or this or that
cross-roads section. For instance, in 1865, Mr. Gladstone was returned from South Lancashire, and while
serving for that district became the leader of the
Liberal party, succeeding Palmerston. In 1868, South
Lancashire failed to re-elect him. He was not lost, however, either to England or to the party. Greenwich
immediately asked the honor of his candidacy, returned
him, and in December, 1868, he was prime minister
of England. In our country the whole nation would
have suffered for the ignorance of South Lancashire.
Again, the Marquis of Hartington, the new leader of

the Liberals, at the recent election, stood in a different
borough from that which sent him to the previous Parliament.

This judicious "selection of the fittest" can be made
in Pennsylvania under our laws, but it is not the custom, and the petty feeling of local prejudice is against
it. The wildest and most barren and meagrely educated district in our mountains can send the most distinguished lawyer or scholar of Philadelphia to represent them in Congress if they want. Had Thaddeus
Stevens been rejected by Lancaster, the Chester or the
Bradford or any other strong Republican district could
have sent him if they had wanted to; but I suppose
they would rather have left the House of Representatives in the crisis of war without its great leader than
to have done so.

Another incidental feature of the House which
immediately strikes an American is the number of
dress-suits scattered over the room,—the men who have
been to dinner or are going; for "society" here is
always distinctly represented in Parliament. I suppose we might say that in our country it is not only
not represented in Congress, but positively excluded
and disfranchised. Here, however, politics is really
fashionable.

The differences of home structure explain this diver-
gency again. There is a great deal of loose talk about
the duty of American gentlemen going into politics,
and the example of English gentlemen devoting their
lives and energies to political work is held up as a
conclusive argument. Of course, they should, as a duty,
but there is no incentive outside of that. There is no
analogy at all between the two cases. The English gentleman goes into politics because he has his class interests at stake and must defend them. His lands depend
on the stability of the present laws, and he must support them. He is "holding the fort" of his position.

Moreover, he has a distinct representation in Parliament,—his position, his class, his education, his property,—while with us nothing is represented but the individual,—his existence as a unit of population. Under the English system not only has "the individual" a certain representation, but also all that he has been able to add to himself of moral or intellectual worth, or even material wealth. The American gentleman in politics, on the contrary, has only the same quality and force as the American blackguard,—one vote. The American scholar in politics has only the same quality and force as the American hoodlum—one vote. The American millionaire in politics has only the same quality and force as the American communist —one vote.

The bottom reason why the American gentleman, the American scholar, the American property-holder, do not go into politics, and are so infrequently seen in Washington, is because education, cultivation, and property as such are not represented in our suffrage system, and there is no constituency, therefore, to send these men. We represent only the "individual," and, consequently, as a rule, "individuals" go into politics, and "individuals" are sent to Washington.

The dress-coats, I may mention in concluding, are this year mainly on the Government side, although the Marquis of Hartington, the leader of the Opposition, frequently addresses the House in full dinner-costume. Still, Liberalism in some way seems to tend strongly to sack-coats and felt hats and ready-made clothing.

LONDON.

11*

CHAPTER XV.

PARLIAMENT (CONTINUED).

House of Commons—The Cries of Parliament—The School-
boy in Parliament—Fair Play—Individual Independence—Etiquette of the Floor—The Speaker of the
House—"Politician" or "Statesman"—Dignity of the
House—Decline of Oratory—Speaking in the House
of Commons—Cicero on the Treasury Bench—The
Agent.

I HAVE mentioned the school-boy atmosphere which
often marks the House of Commons.

English life, or at least the life of the upper, and so
far controlling, classes, begins at the public schools—of
which Eton and Rugby are examples familiar to us—
and receives there an impress which never leaves it.
Looking over the floor of either House of Parliament,
you can see there the Eton boy and the university man
all the time. They are the foundation of English public life, not merely intellectual, but moral.

There is no more forcible illustration of the surviving
force of this boy-education than the cries of Parliament,
which sound so strangely to a foreigner, but which he
soon sees are a real part of the process of legislation,
just as regular and just as effective as the speech-
making. Sometimes I thought them more so. These
cries, so unusual to our ears, are a kind of low inter-
mittent chorus with which the house at times accompa-
nies the speaker, each political section, "right" and
"left," "right above the gangway," "left above the
gangway," etc., bearing its part. Unlike the Greek
chorus, this accompaniment is not used to explain the
plot of the speaker, but it does serve admirably to explain the effect of the speech on the audience and on

each part of it. Usually, of course, these cries are confined to staccato explosions of dissent or approbation at the ends of sentences or at the point of some startling facts or figures. Sometimes, however, a speaker is accompanied from beginning to end with a kind of monotonous chant, rising, swelling, or sinking from time to time and sung in two or more parts. Mr. Edward Jenkins, who is especially distasteful to the Conservatives, generally speaks to music of this kind.

These cries are exactly such as might be heard from a school-room of boys anxious to put down a speaker, who by a natural reaction is supported in his turn by his friends, who come up to his aid with an opposing volume of sounds. Singularly enough, these sounds are often—generally, I think—given more or less furtively. You see before you a body of dignified, rather elderly gentlemen; you know them to be perhaps the strongest legislative body in the world; you see among them some of the greatest thinkers, writers, and statesmen of the time; you recognize some of England's noblemen of high rank; some gallant officers of her army, perhaps an admiral, too, or distinguished author; suddenly you hear a low, rising swell of sound that carries you back to your callow days of spelling-books and popcorn and mint-stick candy,—O-o-o-o-o-h; Ou-oo-oo-oo; Ah-a-a-a; Whoo-whoo-wh; Eeh-eeh-eeh-eh; Boo-oo-oo; Err-r-r-r; Oh-ah-ooh-bah; Umm-m-m-m-m; Ay-ay-ay,—all the vowel-sounds of the alphabet with every conceivable intonation and form of expression. It is these old gentlemen assisting in the making of a law of England.

Watching closer, you will see, perhaps, a nervous sexagenarian member sitting squarely up in his seat and looking straight into the eyes of the speaker with a severely-dissenting frown. His stern, grave features never move, but from his open mouth your ears detect a steadily-flowing stream of guttural bass. Another one intones openly his chant of derision or dissent.

You see hats go up before mouths, heads turned away, a legislator or two suspiciously close behind a column, and other venerable but franker old gentlemen in boyish abandon giving way openly to the jollities of the hour. Then up from the other side comes a counter-wave, bearing on its swell the sense of injury and a protest,—indignation and the determination to stand by its spokesman ; and so this battle, which is not on " the order of the day," and which is not recorded in the next morning's papers, wages from night to night.

Some members, by practice and experience, perhaps by constitutional adaptation or perhaps from having worked hard at school, attain great proficiency and ability in this mode of parliamentary tactics. One evening two portly old legislators with broad, cheery faces, white whiskers, and generally a fine, responsible, conservative air, who sat for the moment on the bench just in front of mine, opened fire at the same time, evidently by preconcert. Not a feature moved ; their lips were just apart and apparently in rest; the bland, kindly expression of countenance never changed, but from these stout, smooth-shaven throats a strong volume of derisive sound flowed steadily and in smooth current, without a waver or break, for at least some minutes, a chorus sufficient to disconcert a pretty self-reliant speaker, the more so from its being so well masked and conveying a mysterious opposition.

The custom has some practical uses. Although the sounds are mostly simple vowel-notes, you soon learn to understand their meaning, and are able to mark the immediate effect of a speech in all parts of the house. It is, in fact, an almost instantaneous and continuous vote, enabling the speaker and his friends or foes to follow the effect of his argument from moment to moment. Where there is a political topography of the floor, and the House sits in party platoons, as it does here, the feeling and condition of the body at any given moment are very clearly traceable in this way.

While these school-room cries are rather a boyish kind of warfare, they are generally used with a boy's sense of candor, fair dealing, and fair play. They seem to be largely the spontaneous utterance of individual opinion, and not a mere partisan game, directed and organized. The cry "Oh!" is the general note used to express derision, disapprobation, and opposition; "Hear!" to express support, sympathy, or to call especial attention to any fact or opinion. "Hear!" might be called a kind of emphasis underlining contributed by the audience. It is also used ironically at times. The several cries frequently greeted a speaker from all sections of the house at one time, showing that they were individual and not mere responses. I have more than once seen a member while speaking applauded from the opposite side of the house, and I have also seen derisive cries on either side silenced by counter cries from the same side.

This sense of fairness on the floor of Parliament, and aversion to partisan tactics, is a marked feature. The individual legislator has full freedom, and he is often allowed even to abuse it rather than that the right of free speech should suffer in his person. There is no "previous question" in the House in the sense of our rule, and I have heard members talk platitudes far into the morning and repeat each other wearily without rebuke or remonstrance, although the floor must have had its patience well worn out. Certainly the foreign visitors had. The chairman, too, allows the widest latitude in speaking to the question. This generous worship of fair play will be recognized as a well-known British school-boy trait.

I never saw it violated in the House save on an occasion when Mr. Edward Jenkins arose to speak on the "flogging-in-the-army" debate. Then the entire Conservative side—gray whiskers, bald-heads, dress-suits, army and navy officers, lords, statesmen, white hairs and all—set up a concerted symphony of disturbance

i

entirely drowning his voice. Mr. Jenkins faced the in-decorous storm with great composure, speaking for four or five minutes,—the usual length of the speeches then being made,—although he was entirely unheard from beginning to end, an occasional detached word, sentences apart, being the only sound intelligible. His compo-sure, as I afterwards learned, was perhaps like that of the eels which got used to be skinned, as he for some time past has always spoken under such circumstances. This gentleman, better known in the United States as " Ginx's Baby," has made himself especially obnoxious to the Conservatives, who allege that his assaults on the Government and its officials have been ungentlemanly and offensive, and placed him outside of the pale of gen-tlemen. Mr. Jenkins's friends, on the other hand, claim that all his movements have been legitimate and neces-sary ; that some of the abuses of English administra-tion are so involved with vested interests and hereditary claims that it is impossible to attack them without seem-ing to become personal. The question is therefore a debatable one inside of the House, and this treatment of Mr. Jenkins to an American view appears indefensible and hardly worthy of a great party. It is, in a sense, however, a strong tribute to Mr. Jenkins's power, as it proves that he has struck a blow or blows somewhere where they have hurt.

The sibilant " hiss" of popular assemblies is, I be-lieve, used very little or not at all in Parliament. I do not recall hearing it.

In addition to this admonitory refrain of dissent or assent, members are constantly subjected to another species of boyish training by " calls." Does a speaker indulge in some loose assertion, some wild generalization or inexact statement of fact, he is immediately reined up with sharp calls of " Date ?" " Date ?" " Name ?" " Name ?" " When ?" " Where ?" " Time ?" " Place ?" " Year ?" " Day ?" or positive cries of " No !" " No !"

if any one wishes to personally traverse his allegations. The educational influence of this usage is very great and very valuable. Careless declamation, vague rhetoric, cowardly innuendo, rapidly shrink under this treatment. There is little speaking for effect in the House of Commons: a man must speak to the facts. There is no chance, either, under this rule of indulging in the unmanly habit of making loose and sweeping charges in the expectation that they will go to the country unanswered and do their work before an answer can come. Nor is it possible, under this regimen, to make foolish speeches and vainglorious threats to be read at home by your constituency, safe in the sure knowledge that none of your fellow-members will be silly enough to notice them. In short, in these respects the floor of the House of Commons is very much like a ring in a boys' schoolground. Any boy may fight in it, but he must strike fair.

It need hardly be added that these habits conduce to the habitual display of great personal independence on the part of the members. The personal independence of the English politician, his ready assertion of his individuality, is a marked fact which soon strikes the political observer from America accustomed to the ready subserviency and machine drill of our own men of this class. The English political leader starts, as a rule, with social position, education, and an inherited income. He is not dependent on his political exertions, therefore, either for his standing in his community or for his means of livelihood, and has, besides, social and intellectual resources within himself which preclude the need of his seeking occupation or mental activity in politics. Fortunate thus in his triple armor, he need never sacrifice his individual opinions or his self-respect under the coercion of circumstances. So far, happily for England, the professional politician—the man who makes his living by politics—has not appeared, but I fear, with the social transition in progress, he is coming.

There are, of course, men who will cringe and crawl
under any circumstances, and England has her share
of them, but as a class her public men are independent and courageous in the expression of individual
opinion to an extent which contrasts most happily with
the sad reverse in our own country. They are so by
reason of their education and assured social position.
I heard the Marquis of Hartington, the Liberal leader,
one night in the House, and from the leaders' bench,
make a speech disclaiming and rebuking the action of
a section of his party which I feel sure no leader in our
House would dare to make. And it created no especial
surprise or commotion here. It seemed to be expected
that Lord Hartington would do it,—that he owed it to
himself. He owed it as a leader. With us, unfortunately, the leadership of a party too often consists in the
collective sense of the average and commonplace majority of its membership.

There is much about the landed system of Great
Britain—the "great-families" system, based on primo-
geniture and entail—which a republican cannot but
consider bad for the state and for the human individual, but this great tribute must be paid to it,—that
it does secure independent and educated politicians for
the administration of the affairs of state. The syco-
phancy of England so far is social rather than political,
and as such comparatively harmless to the state.

In fact, the very use of words shows the difference
in the moral grade of the two countries on this point.
"Politician," a depreciated word with us, is here an
honorable one. It means here about what "statesman"
means with us in the popular acceptation and use,—*i.e.*,
one who administers public affairs as a trust. Unconsciously, with us politician has come to mean one who
is working for his own personal ends, and we seek in
the word statesman to express some higher conception.
People may not consciously acknowledge this, but I
believe any fair man will admit that when it is ordi-

narily said of any one in our land, "X is going into politics," it means that "X" is beginning to look for personal political employment. Politics means working for office. Statesmanship means government or the administration of the public interests. Now, the English popular mind does not so degrade its political men as yet. Politics means, in popular acceptation, the administration of the affairs of state, and politicians the men who administer them.

In fact, the popular sense of propriety does not admit that a politician—a member of the House, for instance—should busy himself about his election. The machinery of election, the science of elections, are something below the legislator, and which he must not touch. I do not mean to say that many members of Parliament do not busy themselves most earnestly about their elections and watch with most efficient care the whole process, but they must do it within-doors, with carefully-concealed hand, and not ostentatiously and so as to offend the conventional and traditional feeling of their constituency in this matter. Votes, voting, and the active direction of the canvass must be left to "the agent."

While the beggarly seating of the House of Commons, its boyish cries, and the wearing of hats by the members give an undignified and almost indecorous air to its exterior, it is at bottom a most dignified and substantial body. The sense of the House of its own dignity is something far surpassing anything of the kind known in our Congress. It is an historic evolution. The House of Commons represents, and means, and *is*, "the people of England." It never forgets that. Every privilege it has has been wrested from reluctant power. They have come at long intervals,—generations apart. Many of them have been paid for with blood, offered on the scaffold and shed in battle. Many of them have cost life and property, long years of merciless imprisonment, and cruel confiscation. No wonder that this treasure, this trust for the nation, is so sacredly and jealously guarded. Every offence against the dignity of the House from without or within is an assault on the liberties of England. Hence the extreme sensitiveness of the Englishman to the rights of the House, and the honest feeling that an attempt to coerce or bribe a member is the highest kind of treason to the people. For instance, this month a citizen, a lawyer-lobbyist, was committed to the tower of Westminster by Parliament for merely saying that he could influence a parliamentary committee. It was generally admitted that he did not believe that he could do so, and that he lied to his client when he said so, but Parliament considered its honor involved by such a statement even from a comparatively irresponsible man, and he went to prison by a unanimous vote of the House, the leaders of both parties vying with one another to punish the impertinent falsehood. I was present when the motion for commitment was made. The facts having been established by a report of a select committee, there was no debate at all, the House seeming to disdain to soil its hands with such a discussion, and the whole affair was a matter of only a few moments.

In previous letters I noted several traditional usages and observances which illustrate how zealously, even in petty things, the House guards its dignity and privileges.

There are also some habits and traditional formulæ of speech which, although seemingly of small moment in themselves, act as efficient mechanical aids in preserving the dignity of official or political intercourse. Names are never used. One member always speaks of another as "the honorable gentleman and member from ——." This is inexorable, and is only the first step. All members are "honorable gentlemen," and must be addressed as such. If they are or have been in the Ministry, they must be addressed as "the right honorable gentlemen." If a member is also a lawyer, he must be addressed as "the honorable and learned gentleman." If he has served in the army or navy, he is addressed as "the honorable and gallant gentleman." If he is, further, a peer, he is to be addressed as "the honorable gentleman" or "right honorable gentleman and noble lord," or "most noble lord" if his rank is high enough. A member may readily be a "right honorable and gallant gentleman and noble lord," and, if he is, must be so addressed every time he is spoken to or of on the floor.

This usage, although a mechanical form, acts as an effectual barrier to indecorous or impertinent familiarity or to bad manners, which may be unintentional, the unfortunate heritage of early vulgarity. It would be impossible, for instance, under this rule for one statesman to speak of another as Johnny Sherman, or Andy Johnson, or Abe Lincoln, or Tom Corwin, or Zach Chandler. The habits of good society thus acquired in the House, if not attained before, are carried on to the stump,—or hustings, as they say here,—where the language of the speakers is, with rare exceptions, that of gentlemen.

Every idea in England must have a personal embodiment or conception. She is much nearer the "idol" stage of thought than we. She believes in a personal sovereign as necessary to localize and animate the national sense of loyalty. This sovereign, too, must have a golden crown and a sceptre like any monarch in Afghanistan or Persia or Zululand or the fifth century. She believes that her judges need robes and wigs to express the majesty of the law, invisible here, but which is so clearly visible in the pine-table court-rooms of the backwoods of Pennsylvania and Minnesota.

So the power and dignity and authority of the House of Commons centre in the person of the Speaker. He

sums up in his official presence centuries of history.
And in this case there is a dramatic and historical propriety in the political nimbus which encircles his figure.
He it was that for hundreds of years was first arrested
when the crown moved against the people of England.
He it was who rotted in the dungeon and died on the
scaffold.   And he represents to-day a popular strength
and is looked up to with a respect and kind of loyalty
which in no way attaches to the office in our country.

His authority inside the House is correspondingly
respected.   His slightest movement seemed to command
attention and respect.   The rude accessory of the hammer is entirely unneeded.   I listened to one debate
which Englishmen of long parliamentary experience
seemed to think almost unprecedented in its heat and
disorder, and one distinguished member frankly expressed his mortification that I should witness the same
and carry it away as an impression of the British
Parliament.   Feeling certainly ran high, although
the language was always guarded and, compared with
our legislative *emeutes*, moderate.   The Irish members,
however, were openly engaged in the work of " ob-
struction," and, with their English friends aiding and
abetting, the night was far spent, and the situation was
unquestionably trying.   The speaking was brief, but
quick and spirited, and the floor always contested, half
a dozen or more members often striving for it at once.
In all this evening the Speaker's decisions—which were
manifestly impartial and honest—were never contested,
and when a surge of feeling or cries seemed about to
overwhelm the room and sweep away everything, a
simple wave of his hand without moving from his seat
instantly calmed the rising storm and restored tran-
quillity and order.   The noisy pounding of a hammer
or the frantic ringing of a bell, as in Italy or France,
would be resented in Westminster.

The Speaker, Mr. Brand, it is fair to say, is, however,
an exceptionably able man.   He is a Liberal, and his

discharge of his office under the former administration was so acceptable and satisfactory that he was re-elected to his position by the new Conservative House,—by a unanimous vote, in fact, I think. This evidences a very marked contrast between politics in England and America.

The salary of the Speaker of the House is £5000, about $25,000. The members receive no salary for their services, or compensation of any kind in money.

There is no system of standing committees in the House, as with us, nor is there any call of the previous question, in the sense of our use of it.

The most marked difference, however, by all odds between the legislatures of the two countries is in the style of speaking and general conduct of business,—the demonstrative " oration" on our side and the quiet, business-like statement of a few sentences here. It is commonly known, I suppose, that there is no such thing as "oratory" in Parliament, in either House. No member ever " makes a speech" in the conventional sense of that phrase, as known with us. Some of the usages I have described are clearly incompatible with the traditional custom of forensic declamation or pompous and pretentious argument, and are sufficient to account for its absence. Many writers ascribe the death of oratory in the House to the uncomfortable benches and limited accommodations,—a clearly superficial and thoughtless view, as in the palmy oratorical days of Pitt and Burke the accommodations were no better, and most likely worse, especially in the auxiliary point of retiring-rooms, wash-rooms, closets, etc.

The cause of the decline of forensic declamation is deeper and historical. The days of the Pitts and of Fox and of Burke are gone forever in England, because she is too far advanced in thought and education. Impassioned oratory, I take it, is an ingredient of immature civilization and dies before a higher condition of general education. Demosthenes was possible only under the crude and simple conditions of Greek society. Cicero and the brilliant school of contemporary orators were the product of a slavocratic republic, where the mass of the people were unlearned and untaught. Chrysostom spoke to congregations of Christian converts densely ignorant and rude in their manners, as his own reproofs of them show. When Bossuet and Bourdeloue swayed all France with emotion and passion, common France was in a state of mental and religious tutelage. England, when she was proud of Pitt and Fox and Burke, had a class of country gentlemen she will never be proud of as men of intelligence and intellectual calibre, whatever else may have been their merits. Even Clay and Webster represent a very crude and provisional stage of civilization in our own country, while Patrick Henry and the Revolutionary orators were the outcome of our cradle-hours. The rule holds good in the United States even at this moment. Wherever civilization is highest and scholarship compact and influential, there the pyrotechnic "orator" flickers out. The "mountain eagles" of our Alleghenies and Cordilleras, the "silver-tongued clarions" who thrill courts and stump and legislatures on the prairies or in the Mississippi bottom, cut a sorry figure if ever they get before the Supreme Court of the United States or of any Eastern State. Oratory is, in fact, only a means of impressing simple or half-educated people which fails when the people get beyond that way of receiving impressions. The civilized world of to-day has pronounced against it. Bismarck declares parliamentary oratory to be "a mischief." England suppressed it a generation ago, and we are going in the same direction.

The speaking in the House of Commons to-day is extremely severe and simple. Members usually speak only from three to five minutes even on the most important subjects, and their language is studied in its simplicity and avoidance of rhetoric. Of course there are times when both the occasion and the matter demand elaborate and more lengthy treatment and a minister or member may speak for an hour or hours, but this is very rare. The habitual mode is for members to rise only for a few moments, delivering themselves straight to the point in a rather conversational style, but every word weighed, guarded, and carefully chosen, very much as an experienced merchant might speak in making a contract. The British legislator has a sense of personal responsibility for every *word* uttered on the floor which does not exist in our legislative bodies at all. In fact, the conduct of business in Parliament resembles rather the consultation of responsible merchants in a counting-room or the meeting of a small board of railway directors than anything like our popular conception of a legislative discussion. The usage of "interrogating the Ministry" also leads directly both to brevity, a conversational style, and caution and precision in the selection of words.

The substance of parliamentary speech is generally substantial and good, and the scene would be impressive and dignified were not the whole effect marred by a hesitation and labored awkwardness in speaking which, if it is not affectation, has all the appearance of it. But whether an affectation or an infirmity, it is a serious blemish. There is observable throughout all the English higher classes a cultivated diffidence and tendency to self-depreciation, which is perhaps in the start a recoil from the self-assertion and pretension of the vulgar and new-made classes. It has been carried, however, to an extreme which verges on effeminacy, if it is not that already. This mannerism of halting and hawing is its development on the rostrum, and it effectually disposes of all forensic grace and a good deal of forensic efficiency. The far remove of the British Parliament from all the traditions of the forum is best illustrated by reporting one of Cicero's speeches as it would be delivered from the treasury bench to-day : *Quousque —ah—tandem — ah-a-abutere,— Catilina — hem-m-m— patientia, n-nostra ? Quamdiu nos etiam—haw-aw— furor—hem—haw—ah-h-h.* Yet this is the exact way in which a British legislator grapples with a question of state, and to get the force of what he is saying you have to disabuse your mind absolutely of the vice and ungracefulness of its delivery.

Nevertheless, taken as a whole, the general impression made by the House of Commons when compared with the leading legislative bodies of the world is good. Its dignity is well sustained, and there is a thorough and conscious power in the membership which inspires confidence. There is no attempt at producing effects or making a personal display, and the body keeps pretty steadily to the work in hand, although, for reasons already mentioned, it is not either skilful or successful in producing results. The work of legislation is fearfully behind, by common admission. It is to the high credit of the membership, however, to be able to say when you look over the floor and listen to it you feel a sense of its integrity. You believe that the bulk of the body is honestly at work trying to make laws,—not talking to the distant county of Buncombe or manufacturing issues and records for the next campaign.

In fact, legislation—the administration of public affairs—here is one thing, the function of a gentleman, and getting elected is another thing, and public opinion so far jealously enforces their division. That is at least the traditional feeling, which as yet the politician dare not offend. He must not conduct his campaign personally, but through an agent.

Hence has arisen in English political life " the agent," —a distinctive cog-wheel in the political machine to which we have no direct equivalent. The agent is a kind of political attorney who has made votes and the science of voting a study. He has the records of many elections for many years. All elections here are very local,—in boroughs, counties, universities, or some restricted limits. The agent knows the past history of all these votes and the characteristics of the sections. He can calculate political " probabilities" and give estimates, and, having this fund of special knowledge and this special bent of mind, he is regularly employed by the candidates to control their campaign and is paid in money for this service. The nominee is presumed at least to be above this kind of work. Thus votes and voting are one thing here, and politics—*i.e.*, statesmanship—is another, and the man of votes cannot presume to be the politician.

This distinction is severely maintained clear down to comparatively minute details. For instance, paid canvassers, clerks, managers, or watchers, under an act of 1867, are not allowed to be polled, and lose their votes by reason of the nature of their occupation.

It is needed to be said, greatly to their credit, that the English laws in their provisions for guarding the integrity of the polls are very strict. Gratuitous refreshments in all forms have long been forbidden. Charities distributed in a borough by a man who afterwards contested it have been held to be corruption. This rule, although its intent is honorable, might at times work great hardships both to the poor and to liberal gentlemen.

Looking over the House of Commons, even a stranger can see clear evidence of great changes at work, for under the healthy law of the British Constitution the House must change with the changing social structure of the kingdom. And these changes follow our lead.

LONDON.

CHAPTER XVI.

PARLIAMENT (CONTINUED).

THE HOUSE OF LORDS—A HISTORIC SURVIVAL—THE THRONE OF ENGLAND—SAILING OF THE "MAYFLOWER."

THE House of Lords has less interest for an American than the Commons, for it is a lost form in the machinery of government. Like our electoral colleges, the life has gone out of it, and only the shell remains; but it is a very handsome shell. The hall itself is a gorgeous flood of gold and color flushed with soft light and walled in with Gothic oak and stained-glass windows. Around the wall in solemn niches stand the statues of the bold barons of Runnymede. The stalwart barons of England, however, have long since abandoned this floor.

There is no special difficulty in seeing a session of the House of Lords, as the order of any peer will admit one, and not merely to a caged gallery, but to very good seats just in the rear of the floor and on a level with it. From here one can see all that is to be seen, which, in the way of parliamentary procedure, is not much, and what there is of it is dull and spiritless.

As the American visitor walks through the peers' corridor on his way to that portion of Westminster Hall which contains the chamber of the House of Lords, he experiences for a moment the slight shock of a complimentary sensation in seeing as one of the eight great frescos of the walls "The Sailing of the Mayflower," a companion-piece to the interminable "Landing of the Pilgrims," which forever stares one in the face from bank-notes and legislative halls throughout all the confines of the United States. But

it certainly makes one feel suddenly at home, and with
even a pride of kinship in the place, to find the English
end of the story told with such honor, and almost at
the footsteps of the throne. An odd sight which strikes
one passing through the lobby or vestibule to the floor,
quite a small and cramped chamber, is a number of
rows of common pegs, such as might be in the closet
of a boys' school-room, but over each peg the name of
a peer of England,—all the dukes and earls and barons.
These pegs are crowded close together, and are for the
hats and coats of the members,—a peg to a peer. The
provision is not a whit better than that of many a common school-house in our land to which barefoot boys
come with ragged felts and perhaps no coat at all, but
it is all there is for these lords, who drive up to the
door with a brace of footmen, perhaps, and from a
palace. The custom, however, has some historic sanc-
tion, and they stick to it. It will probably last as long
as the House of Lords.

Inside of the main hall the seating and general appearance of the interior are about the same as those of
the House of Commons. At the head of the room,
however, where the Speaker's desk would be in our
Senate chamber, you see "the throne of England."
You feel an absurd sense of suffering a disillusion when
you see only a chair,—a very profound achievement
of upholstery, no doubt, but still a chair. The American republican knows in his heart that a throne must
be a chair; still, as it is associated in his mind with fairy
tales and myths and all the wonders of childhood, it
has grown into something grand and stately and impressive, and he suffers a pang to find it only a piece
of furniture replaceable from any cabinet-shop. The
throne is one of those things which, on the whole, it is
best not to see. When it is resolved into a commonplace chair there is a shattering of faith as sad as when
the beanpole of Jack the Giant-Killer vanishes into
the thin cold air of experience and science. In front of

the throne some little distance, and at its foot, is the celebrated "woolsack." It is a capacious, heavily-cushioned footstool. On this sits the Lord Chancellor of England, who presides over the sessions of the House of Lords.

By the law and theory of the English government, the House of Lords is something more than a co-ordinate body of the national legislature, like our Senate. It has an absolute veto on all legislation by the House of Commons. Not only is this power utterly unused, but it has ceased even to deter. It will never be claimed. Politically, the House of Lords has ceased to exist, its functions in the government having passed to the Cabinet, or Ministry, which is practically' the Upper House. Even the family influence of the peers, to yield political results in this day, must be wielded through the House of Commons.

As a historical picture, however, the House of Lords still survives in good condition. A nominal number of peers attend its daily sessions during Parliament season, and mechanically pass all the bills and go through all the forms of legislation. On state occasions this venerable relic solemnly "summons" the lower House into its presence, and the House comes. The crimsoned hall, too, serves as a splendid stage, where the queen occasionally gives a grand spectacular political tableau something like one of the gorgeous religious functions you see at intervals in the great churches of Rome.

It is worth while dropping in on the House of Lords as often as possible just to study the *personnel* of the body, and see that type of man which a privileged class, carefully tended for centuries, and draining the blood and soil of the land,—its education and culture and power and wealth,—evolves. That is about all, although it is a good deal. You will see nothing of debate or action in it, learn nothing of politics. The House of Lords in our day is an interesting social study, but it has ceased to be a political one, save as an antique or remain.

CHAPTER XVII.

FOREIGN SERVICE.

THE OLD AMBASSADOR AND THE NEW—A NEWSPAPER PLENI-
POTENTIARY—THE OLD-WORLD AMBASSADOR WITHOUT USES
IN THE POLITICAL MACHINERY OF THE NEW—EDUCATIONAL
FUNCTIONS OF THE SERVICE—HOW BEST TO CONSERVE IT—
ROTATION ON THE DIPLOMATIC LIST—TENDENCY OF THE EU-
ROPEAN LIFE TO DE-AMERICANIZE THE REPUBLICAN CITI-
ZEN.

IT is one of the anomalies of the present transition
state of society from old ideas and usages to newer ones
that, while our government sends fifteen ministers to
Europe at salaries of from $7500 to $17,500, to represent us and, speak for us, the incessant, effective representation is done by a modest journalist in Philadelphia,
Mr. Joel Cook, the American correspondent of the London *Times*, whose voice is heard every day, not only in
one but in all the courts of Europe, and not only by
the official governments, but by the people. He is by
far the most omnipresent and influential envoy extraordinary that has ever gone from this country.

While the London *Times* has not the circulation of
many of the papers of Europe, it has a weight and influence which none of them have. It is taken by every
foreign minister of all countries, and in all countries its
dispatches are accredited as authority. They are quoted
in Parliament and at the dinner-tables and official desks
of ambassadors. What Europe at this time from day
to day thinks of America and the American people is
decided, not by the communications of our diplomatic
force, but by what says the London *Times*.

There is a grave and growing doubt in the public
mind whether our foreign or diplomatic service is worth
its cost to the republic since the introduction of ocean

cables and newspaper correspondence and the absolute adoption of the Monroe doctrine as an article of popular political faith. A look over the ground I think justifies the conclusion that it has little meaning at all for us any more in the old sense, but that possibly it can still be put to better and higher uses than it has ever served, and that without change of form. It is better perhaps for the present to let the shell of the old institution remain, but to gradually give to the service itself a new character and function.

"The ambassador" is the survival of a European condition of society which never was transferred here. His functions belong to a machinery of government which never was put in motion on this continent. His work, in the natural revolution of our new social growth, has been taken up and is discharged on a larger scale by a new personage,—the special correspondent.

Prince Metternich, in his gossippy memories of Old-World and old-fashioned diplomacy, just given to print by his son, relates that he once asked a brother ambassador "how he contrived to have a letter to send to London every post day." There were two a week.

"You will see no difficulty in it when I tell you my secret. If anything comes to my knowledge that may interest my government, I tell it; if not, I invent my news, and contradict it by the next courier."

Now, that is exactly the trick of the lazy or unreliable newspaper correspondent of our time ; but it illustrates forcibly how exactly one of the functions of the old ambassador has devolved upon the new international envoy. The ambassador reported to his government all that he could of the social and political movements in foreign countries ; the correspondent reports exactly the same, only a thousand times more fully, to the people, which *is* our government.

The Old-World ambassador had three grand functions which were the meaning of his office and the reason of his being :

I. To represent in his person the relations, whatever they were, which existed between his own Government and the Government to which he was sent.

II. At times to act for his Government on his own responsibility according to his best judgment.

III. To keep his Government constantly advised of all the news.

For the American situation the Monroe doctrine has done away with the first of these functions, the telegraph with the second, and the newspaper with the third.

We have no foreign relations in the sense of European diplomacy with any power in Europe. When it is necessary for a minister to act now, he receives specific instructions by telegraph. He can even cable a conversation. The diplomatic reports are always far behind the public information of wire and type.

As a matter of fact, our entire diplomatic list could be swept away with entire safety. Our only real relations with foreign countries are commercial ones, and these are handled by the consular department. As far as my judgment goes, however, I would not advise its abolition, but strongly urge its retention for the present on broader grounds of national utility. There is no more broadening education than the comparative study of foreign nations, their governments, social structure, and systems of thought and religion, and there is no education more needful at present to our own national wants.

The diplomatic service affords an admirable school for this. It may be made, in fact, a national free college for this kind of education, and its uses in this way are twofold. It serves to educate personally the men whom we specially select for this elevated tuition, and, if their selection is judicious, they in turn become teachers of the whole people. A James Russell Lowell in England, a Motley or Bancroft or Bayard Taylor or an

Andrew White at Berlin, a George P. Marsh at Rome, do something more than answer all our meagre official uses, or than even to train and strengthen themselves. They serve to translate and send over something of England and Germany and all Europe to us, and Bret Harte and Eugene Schuyler, at their consular desks, are worth a good deal more to the American people and literature than all their possible service as registrars of shipping entries. Nathaniel Hawthorne, consul to Liverpool, is doing good service to the whole nation yet, although the Government and the men that sent him are long ago gone with him into the grave. It is by the adoption of this principle of appointment—the selection for diplomatic posts of men of high character and of scholarly rather than of an average politician's abilities—that we can best conserve our diplomatic department under an altering condition of things, and obtain its fullest and highest uses for the whole nation.

At all events, as it stands at present, our diplomatic service is thoroughly illogical and unsatisfactory, and no change or experiment even could much impair its illusory efficiency.

The salaries of the several embassies are extremely inadequate to do what they are supposed to do, and it is impossible for the ministers living on them to represent our country as other countries are represented. If it is the idea of the government to perpetuate the old-fashioned system of diplomatic representation and communication, then funds should be supplied our representatives to act their part decently, according to the requirements of the old-fashioned code.

Again, according to the established law of diplomatic usage and etiquette settled long before we came on the stage, an ambassador is one who represents the *person* of a sovereign ruler and always outranks a minister plenipotentiary, who only represents the *government* of a country. Now, we know nothing at all of the doctrine of the sanctity or superiority of the person of a sovereign, and, when it is explained to us, look on it only as either political heresy or silliness ; but we are forced all the time to impliedly admit it in our diplomatic relations. At any court of Europe in any question of rank or precedence, any ambassador representing a toy king (of Greece, for instance) or a burlesque emperor (of Hayti, for instance) will always take the lead of the republican representative of fifty millions of American citizens. No American minister, no matter what his years or influence or seniority of service, can ever be the dean of the diplomatic college at any capital where there is an ambassador present. This is the very case now at one of the prominent courts of Europe.

But there is another and more serious consequence resulting from this fundamental diplomatic law. An ambassador as representing the person of his sovereign may always demand and have a personal interview with the sovereign of the country to which he is accredited. A minister plenipotentiary may deal only through the ministry. In a crisis the foreign sovereign of his own pleasure may grant him an interview, but the minister cannot demand it as a right. We are therefore in this false position, that should our relations with any European court at any time become critical, our minister at that very court would not have equal facilities for action with the ambassadors of other powers. For instance, the empire of Russia is an autocratic government. The pleasure of the Emperor is supreme, and his word is law. Should this imperial person meditate a huge war involving the interests of every first-rate power on the earth, the ambassadors from England and Germany could see him and talk with him at their will ; but the minister plenipotentiary of the United States at St. Petersburg could not,—not even if the threatened war was with ourselves. Could any position be more false than this, and what is the propriety of recognizing a system which forces us to accept it?

13*

Lastly, the men whom we do send on this important service, which may be made more important every year, should be real Americans, fresh from the soil, and not those who have lived long enough abroad to have de-Americanized themselves. The European life inevitably tends to lessen one's respect for the human person and to weaken one's trust and hope in the people. This moral change is sure to come, and it comes so slowly and insensibly that the victims are not aware of their own transmutation. It must needs be when the vast mass of the people are looked down upon, are classified to the bottom, are used, when perhaps they have lost respect for themselves, that one comes to feel unconsciously contempt for them, and that manhood fails to command the respect which is given to class and privilege. Yet an instinctive reverence for humanity, no matter what its mask, and faith in the people are two of the foundation-pillars of the republic, and he who has lost them does not any more represent the American people.

There is a sound, healthy democratic principle at bottom in the usage of rotation in office on foreign service. Jefferson held, I think, that no man could represent us abroad with usefulness longer than eight years, and he was about right, although no fixed term can be intelligently laid down, for men are not alike. Some men travel in Europe only during a long residence of years. Others begin to live there from the moment of their landing on its shores.

CHAPTER XVIII.

COMPARATIVE POLITICS.

CONTRAST BETWEEN THE POLITICS OF ENGLAND AND OF THE
UNITED STATES—THE COMPARATIVE MAGNITUDE AND RE-
SPONSIBILITIES OF ADMINISTRATION—EVOLUTION OF THE
EUROPEAN STATESMAN—THE EDUCATED FORCES OF EURO-
PEAN POLITICS—THE INTELLECTUAL REQUIREMENTS OF GOV-
ERNMENT ABROAD—THE ENGLISH STATESMEN.

THERE is nothing in all Europe that challenges one's
profounder respect than the strength of her statesmen,
and nothing that is more of a revelation to a New-World
stranger than the gravity and intellectual range of
her politics. Government abroad is a science, here it
"runs itself;" and there could be nothing better calculated to repress the "spread eagle" of the average citizen
than an honest attempt to master the political system
of one of these "effete monarchies," and to gain some
definite conception of its practical workings. The
problem of government in Europe is so vexed, the
dangers so imminent, so fixed and hereditary, the relations with all neighboring powers so involved and entangling, the internal interests so conflicting, the people
so poor and discontented and burdened, that our own
troubles and questions of state seem poor and childish
in comparison.

Studying the range and demands of European statesmanship, one sees readily how it has produced the educated statesman, so unfamiliar to us, and why the conduct of government abroad calls for a breadth of
scholarship and a trained intellectual force that have not
yet been a necessity in the United States. The " log
cabin" and " mill-boy" and " horny-handed" statesmen

of our prairie reputation would wreck any European ship of state irretrievably in three months, perhaps in twenty-four hours. In viewing the field of foreign governments one sees a new wisdom and safety in the Monroe doctrine. Perhaps its framers foresaw even in their early hour that our crude political leaders would never be able to meet in equal combat the intellectual giants of the Old World.

To illustrate more clearly the disparity between the magnitude of the burden of European government and the simplicity of ours, I propose to etch a running parallel between the political systems of Great Britain and of our country,—in the briefest outline, of course; but it will serve to suggest the wide difference between the requirements of statesmanship in the two nations. I select England because the similarity of her institutions admits best of direct comparison, but nearly every European government faces all the troubles and dangers and responsibilities of England; some have them intensified; and some have special problems of their own.

I. Perhaps the initial and commonest form of national self-glorification with us is the boast of our space of territory,—the eagle that rests on Rocky Mountain cordilleras and laves his wings in the Atlantic and Pacific. Now, extent of territory is in itself not necessarily either a danger or a source of power, although it may be both. Judea and Greece have been the mightiest forces of known civilization, and the Roman empire managed to govern the whole world without steamships, railways, or telegraphs. But, as far as magnitude of dominion tests statesmanship or is evidence of national power, we with one segment of a continent do not begin to approach Great Britain. The British rule to-day extends over one-third of the surface of the globe, and over one-fourth of its population. We are but a modest principality in comparison.

Again, the territory of the British empire is not

compact and contiguous as is ours (with the inconsiderable exception of Alaska), but lies in every quarter of the globe, separated by seas and continents, and on it dwell people of every race and of nearly every language, speaking in different tongues, thinking by different modes, inheriting diverse systems of thought and religion and political tradition. We are one people.

II. In England the structure of society is a rigid stratification of classes; in the United States there is but one homogeneous class. The people of our country are one mass of molecular atoms, each atom politically alike. The English legislator legislates for many classes, each with defined limits and vested rights fixed by law and sanctified by inheritance. These rights and the interests of the several classes from time to time jar and clash. He must legislate for many kingdoms in one. The American legislator, on the other hand, simply passes one law for all, because all are equal before the law and in the eye of the law. By virtue also of this homogeneousness of the people, political ideas travel rapidly and equally, permeating a common mass. In England they cannot, by reason of the sectional and class barriers. A given view of politics or of some special question of policy may be accepted and adopted by some one class long before it reaches another, or it may linger long in some certain locality for historical reasons. The Scotchman and the Welshman and the Irishman do not fuse mentally with the Englishman, do not think according to the same modes of thought. Even the Yorkshire man and Lancashire man stand apart, and the man of Surrey or Devon from him of Northumberland. Nor, for that matter, do the farmers with the gentry, or the clergy with the laborer, or the professional man with the peerage, or any of these classes with the others. The body politic has neither the constant internal circulation nor the uniform molecular composition of ours. Everything in England is fixed to the soil in small local centres by fastenings

of society and of blood, and there is not that mobility
in the community at large by virtue of which, with us,
a national idea travels rapidly and uniformly over the
whole nation.   Each county has different customs,
usages, and habits of thought which differentiate it from
the rest of the nation as a whole and in all its social
strata.   The great family estates, covering compact
territories, transmit family peculiarities of living, of
thinking, even of farming and working, and operate
as a barrier to national impulses of thought.   In our
country a wave of thought moves rapidly and evenly
over all the land and through all the people.   The
whole country feels it at once.   Witness not only the
passage of political emotions over the national mind,
the rapid transit of a new party issue, or of the thoughts
of a great speech, but of social or mental sensation, as
in the sweep of the praying-band or spelling-bee excitement from one ocean to the other.   In England it is
not so.   Men do not travel, ideas do not travel.   It is
but thirteen hours from London to Edinburgh, but it
takes more than thirteen years for a political idea to
traverse the route.

III. Our government is a simple republic, a federation of a body of equal and co-ordinate States, each
State peopled by a population of the same race, the
same language, the same history.   All the States have
the same rights, powers, and obligations, and all these
are defined.   The administration of the government,
even, is by a written chart.   Everything is laid down
on paper.

Compare with this simplicity the tremendous imperial system of Great Britain,—a system that has an
illustration only in Rome under the Cæsars.   A little
class of great families dominate, first, their own order
and through it England, and, controlling social England, elect their own Parliament.   Through this Parliament they govern allied kingdoms and an empire
stretching through Asia, Africa, the Americas, Europe,

Australasia, and the islands of the sea. The imperial standard of this great dominion floats over colonial nations of all races, spanning even the great gulf between the Aryan and Semitic bloods; over people of every religion and creed, the regnant faith of Christianity being in the minority; over all latitudes, all colors, all languages, all traditions, all forms of government. The British empire of to-day, morally and physically, is grander than ever were those of Greece or Rome, and its rule is far more conscientious and beneficent. And these principalities and powers and provinces and distant kingdoms of the seas the imperial Parliament governs, not on one simple and uniform plan, but by ever diverse and varying machineries,—by legislatures, by armies, by imperial decrees, by proconsuls, by military governors, by civil governors, by unpretentious "political agents," or by regal viceroys. The name is nothing, the power is always there. The heart of this marvellous body politic throbs at Westminster, whence its currents of blood are impelled to the uttermost ends of the earth. The brain is the premier of England. Contrast this with our ready-made work at Washington.

IV. Our provincial statesmen groan under what they call the burden of national patronage. When they affect liberal political culture, they tell us that the unparalleled magnitude of this patronage is a grave danger to the republic. When they simply claim to be strong politicians, "leaders," they struggle and wrestle and raise mighty tempests about the distribution of a few petty clerkships and evanescent post-offices. The whole government patronage of the United States is but as a flea-bite to that of England. Whatever we have England has on a grander scale. What are our petty post-offices, with New York at $8000 salary and Philadelphia at $4000 heading the list, to the limitless range of public offices necessary to administer the vast and imposing imperial machine? Consider the endless civil-service list; the post-offices; the telegraph-service, which, in

Great Britain, is governmental; the army and navy commissions for colossal hosts and fleets; the swollen pension-lists, not only military, but civil, literary, and political; the Church preferment; the court patronage to tradesmen; the immense foreign service; and, finally, the dazzling rewards of titles, orders, and peerages. Consider alone the patronage of India, with its state railways and public works, an army of four hundred thousand men, and a parental government over a population of more than two hundred millions of souls.

On this question of patronage I will instance just one item to illustrate what its splendors and magnitude and tempting prizes are under the English government. It is an item to which we have no equivalent at all, like the titles and orders and peerages and telegraph- and railway-service and foreign civil list, and other departments. The bishoprics of the Church of England are in the gift of the government. There are twenty-eight of them and two archbishoprics. The Archbishop of Canterbury receives $75,000 a year and two official palaces for a residence, and holds office for life. The Archbishop of York gets $50,000 a year, and a palace and his office for life. Either of these positions, in the way of worldly emolument, is better than the Presidency of the United States. The twenty-eight bishops receive salaries ranging from $20,000 to $50,000 a year (they average over $25,000 a year), a residence, a seat in the House of Lords, and they have all this for life. The whole higher-class patronage in the gift of the United States, the Supreme bench, the Cabinet, the Vice-presidency, and our entire European diplomatic list, does not begin to approach in splendor or dignity or money value to this one item. The whole body of these great offices of our state are less in number than these bishoprics; their salaries range but from $7500 to $17,500; there are no official residences attached, and they are not held for life.

V. This ecclesiastical item of patronage suggests one

of the ugliest of all the problems of European politics,
—one which is a danger and burden to every European
Government to-day, but from which our country happily is and always has been entirely free,—the vexed
question of Church and State. The Established Church
of England, a Church embracing a minority only of the
people, is a part of the Government of England. The
head of the Church is the head of the State; its
bishops, by virtue of their mitres, sit in Parliament; its
clergy are necessarily a kind of national police. The
Church is in the very Constitution. Its interests enter
sharply into every party platform and struggle. They
fought over the Irish-Church disestablishment a few
years ago,—they are going to fight soon over English
disestablishment. As a consequence, the clerical interest goes actively into the political campaigns in a way
that rather shocks our American sense of propriety.
The clergy assist at the nominations, and the Church
vote at the polls is cast on as purely selfish and grace-
less principles as would be the Irish or negro ballot in
our cities. The alliance of the Church and liquor interests—" beer and Bibles"—is one of the open scandals
of the recent elections. Further, this marriage of
Church and State makes an appeal to religious hatreds
and fanaticism, the most dangerous and wicked of all
passions, an effective political weapon always on hand
and useful. A vulgar anti-popery speech that, in the
United States, would hardly be tolerated, is acceptable
and effective on most English hustings. Thus it comes
that premiers and cardinal-princes are writing hotly on
questions which we have removed entirely from the
field of popular passion.

While the situation of Church and State in England
is indecorous and embarrassing to Transatlantic view,
it is only that, and not a danger, as it is to most of the
other European nations. In Italy the Church is a vast
octopus, with its dank, flaccid arms sucking at every
pore of the State. The fight of Germany with Rome

is historic and inherited.   At this very hour the inflammable question of French politics is the expulsion of the Jesuits.   Even Japan has just got through a gigantic civil war to decide this very question,—the supremacy of Tycoon or Mikado.   We alone of all nations have not inherited in our politics this brand of discord, which has been the occasion of more wars in Christendom than any one other cause,—perhaps of more than all others combined.

VI.   We have no foreign relations, no entangling alliances, no responsibilities or obligations outside of ourselves.   With every European people this is the main field of politics.   The nation itself is but the starting-point of government.   The real work is ramified and spread all over the continent, perhaps all over the world. Not a step can be taken without consulting other nations and understanding their interests.   Europe is as we would be were all the States of our Union independent, antagonistic, and with inherited animosities of blood, race, and faith, with diverse languages, modes of thought, and political traditions, and with the quarrels and revenges of a thousand years to settle.   It is this that makes the minister of state so important a personage in European government and so often its head.   Following traditional forms, we have made our Secretary of State the head of our Cabinet, but it is only a survival.   He is but a shadow, for happily we have no foreign affairs.   It is this also which produces the broad scholarship and intellectual supremacy of the European statesman, and drives the demagogue and the half-educated out of the field of politics.   Our Monroe doctrine is a political blessing, but it necessarily limits the range and powers of our public men, because it limits the demands and the strain on them.   It deprives them of the comparative study of politics and history, which European politics, on the other hand, enforce and necessitate.   And comparative study has been the law of all advancement in thought and science in this century.

The general elections of 1880 in England were fought on issues almost entirely outside of England, and they involved an intelligent knowledge not only of modern continental politics and history, but of the Greek, Ottoman, and Asiatic civilizations. Just imagine the statesman of Kentucky or Nebraska being called on for this kind of work! Or how many members are there in any State delegation in Congress whom we could trust to vote for us on such questions when the consequence of an ignorant or reckless vote might be war?

VII. Finally, the critical responsibilities of government in our country are a mere nothing compared with those which immediately and forever confront the European statesman. We never feel them ; they are never brought home either to the people or to the legislator.

The European statesman legislates with a sword suspended over his head. He deals with armed nations ready to strike. Vast camps of populations surround his own, in fatal readiness to move at a signal. A false vote, and before it was circulated through the kingdom hostile bayonets would be swarming across the frontier, and hostile artillery thundering over the land. Within twenty-four hours after a declaration of war by Germany or France or Italy or Russia, the cavalry would be over the border. A legislative debate in Europe may be like brandishing a torch in a powder-magazine.

The European statesman, further, has absolutely no margin on which to make mistakes in home affairs, either. He deals with a discontented people, a burdened people, a suffering people. With the utmost wisdom and prudence, the average lot of the people will not be a pleasant one. Imprudent or ignorant legislation will bring suffering to many and sure death to some. How different the situation from ours where the land, from one end to the other, is one happy field, with a whole nation garnering smiling harvests, or at

cheerful and contented work in its shops and factories!
We have an illimitable margin for legislative mistake.
No blunder costs us either blood or money that we feel.
We are living like spendthrifts on accumulated capital.
This country would have been wrecked a dozen times
within living memory by its ignorant leadership had we
had the same narrow margin to go on for errors as
have the European nations.　When that time comes in
which a foolish word may precipitate a war, an indiscreet tax raise a riot, or a blunder of political economy
result in national convulsion, then we will begin to
appreciate the value of education in government, and
of the scholar in politics.

Let me recapitulate briefly, in such form that the
eye may take it in at a glance, some of the main points
of this imperfect contrast between the involved politics
of the Old World and the simple field of the New.　So
shall we better see the different manner of public men
that the two fields call for:

England.	*The United States.*
One-third of the globe and one-fourth of its population. The empire scattered over all the continents.	A moderate and contiguous territory.
A social structure of many classes, with unlike interests and vested rights.	One homogeneous people.
An imperial government, administered through the Parliament, of one kingdom, and using all known kinds of political machinery.	One simple form of government, with uniform machinery.
Distribution and control of enormous government patronage. Civil service, immense foreign service, military, naval, Church, titles, orders, peerage, public works, railways, telegraph, etc.	Moderate government patronage.

England.	*The United States.*
Church and State,—infinite political and religious complications.	None.
Established and involved foreign relations. Responsibilities in common. The nation only a component part of the continent.	None. Monroe doctrine.
No margin for political or legislative mistakes.	Wide margin.
In the midst of armed powers with colossal armies. Huge standing armies.	No armies without or within.
An increasing national debt.	A decreasing national debt.
A discontented people. Emigration.	A contented people. Immigration.
A people taxed to their utmost capacity.	A generous margin for taxation.
Ignorant lower classes.	A general common education.

Is it any wonder that European politics evolve a stronger order of men than do ours? When you meet or hear or read the English statesman, you feel the immediate contrast, and a little study of the country shows how different are all the conditions of his life and work.

The English statesman must be an educated man, for he deals with educated forces and with history.

He generally springs from the upper classes, and has that knowledge of society which comes from looking from the top down, and not from the bottom up. So far—and it strikes the American with a strong impression—the higher culture of Great Britain governs it, although it has little in common with the mental or religious life of the body of the people, and no sym-

pathy at all with their social life. But this is changing :
the governing power is passing every year farther
down the social scale.

The English statesman, finally, is mostly a man of
means.   He has leisure to study for his work, and
independence to do as he thinks best.   Politics is not
with him a means of making a livelihood.

London.

LONDON.

CHAPTER XIX.

WESTMINSTER ABBEY.

A Sermon in Stone—The Peace of the Grave—How a
Grave in Westminster Abbey Comes—A Monumental
Epitome of English History—England's Worship of
Courage—Our Country in the Abbey—The Birth-Spot
of the "Shorter Catechism"—"The Elect of Eng-
land's Dead."

It was my good fortune to be shown the treasures
and beauties of Westminster Abbey by its scholarly
and accomplished dean, whose reputation and fame are
as broad in all our land and in all the learned world
as his own broad sympathies and the generous gospel
he preaches so boldly in the first of English churches.
I shall not attempt a picture of this historic fane, which
rises so stately here, and which stands perhaps in still
statelier and more unattainable proportions in the imagination of all read and cultured Americans. I will not
even speak here of the sermons I heard of two of its
greatest preachers, Dean Stanley himself and Canon
Farrar, reserving the opportunity to touch on them in
a later letter on the London pulpit, when a larger comparative hearing of its eminent men shall have qualified
me to write of it with more information and judgment.

I would not write with the rapid pen and flow of
newspaper work of Westminster Abbey, which centres
and sums up in itself all of English history, and which,
year by year, gathers to its bosom the best and greatest
of England's men. Its picturing or treatment demands
long and special study, and any other treatment is an
injustice alike to the spot and to the reader. I suppose, indeed, that many of my countrymen to whom

the venerable pile is familiar by painting and engraving and the allusions of literature may feel somewhat disappointed at the mention of its name without an effort at its description. There are those, however, whose lives have been a labor of love in its service, and who have written fully, authoritatively, and responsibly. To their works I refer all across the water who would see or know the best that pen and pencil can do for the abbey. Or, better yet, come and see it.

"*They sleep with their fathers.*" It was a noble instinct, worthy of illustrating its age, whatever that age was, which first conceived the idea of making the churches of England the tombs of its great dead, and Westminster Abbey has been highly favored of history and of England in becoming the shrine of the nation. "Let us here praise famous men and our fathers that begat us." It is the one thing which I most envy of Europe, this wealth of its great men and the noble and beautiful use which it may make and does make of their graves, by which it carries down through the centuries what is best of them, keeping their memory green and imperishable, but, more than that, transfusing, as it were, their virtues into the daily life and generation of the hour. Here they lie in stately tombs all over England, the men who have deserved well of their country, who have served their fellow-men, who have honored their race,—the soldiers, the philanthropists, the teachers,—a lesson, a stimulus, an inspiration, to all that come after them. And it is alike to the honor of England, and convincing evidence of her moral vigor and integrity and of long national life yet to come, that this recognition, these great honors, are open to all. Riches will not buy a tomb in Westminster Abbey, nor a life of ostentation and luxury and display; but its walls are free to the young lieutenant, the young clergyman, the sailor or private soldier or drummer or cabin-boy, who does his duty, and dies in doing it.

Perhaps the distinctive feature of Westminster Abbey to a thoughtful stranger is the wonderful catholicity of its tombs. We unconsciously think of it as an aristocratic burial-place of the Established Church of England,—words of limitation. We find its consecrated crypts open to humanity,—literally, to all the world. It has been eloquently called the "temple of silence and conciliation," and this language is the literal truth. Variances of faiths, harsh judgments on personal lives, the asperities of politics, the rancorous struggles of ambition, the bitterness of parties,—all are forgotten in its still and passionless chapels where side by side sleep friend and foe. The clangor of arms and the damnatory clauses of old creeds are hushed in its hallowed and silent aisles. Here, walking among its graves, eloquent in their mute and voiceless expression, one comes again and again on tombs or monuments of men almost startling you by their associations or the dramatic contrast of their lives with their last resting-place. You find in a place of honor "John and Charles Wesley," their tablet legended "My parish is the world,"—the founders of Methodism in the pantheon of the Anglican Church. You pause involuntarily at the name of John Bradshaw, the regicide judge, and president of the fatal court. Cromwell and the two Charleses and General Monk sleep near together. An English mob, in unhappier times, once rifled the tomb of the Puritan statesman and soldier and scattered his dust and bones, but the empty grave and its inscribed slab are still there in memory and honor of the man. John Dryden, the Roman Catholic; Isaac Watts, the nonconformist; Mrs. Siddons, the actress; Kemble, the actor; Congreve, the play-writer of broad freedom, to speak gently near his ashes; Casaubon, the Frenchman; Spanheim, the Swiss; Theodorus Paleologus, the Greek; some of the family of Louis Philippe,—all lie peacefully in the resting ranks of the noble army of its dead. It might be easy enough to lay most of these men here now in our better and gentler times, but think of the bitter passions of older days when statesmen paid with their heads for political mistakes, think of the merciless and ignorant hatred which so short a time ago passed for religion and faith, and you can begin to gauge the strength of mind and moral courage and nobility ahead of their generation of the men who dug some of these graves, and who recognized in advance of their time the peace of the grave.

Honor to whom honor is due. The honor for this great service to humanity is due of recent history ultimately to the dean of Westminster (and in earlier centuries, I suppose, to the abbot), who is finally responsible for every tomb, monument, or inscription in the church, and whose veto can exclude anybody, living or dead, and any tablet. Let me explain a moment how a grave in Westminster comes, how the greatest honor England can bestow is given. It is so thoroughly illustrative of the interior of English life, of a power of tradition and usage of which we know absolutely nothing, and which we can hardly understand or comprehend at all, that time is not lost in learning it. This great honor, for which kings hope and prelates strive and soldiers die, rests in law to-day, entirely and absolutely, in the hands of one man,—the dean of the Abbey. He can bury any one in the Abbey he pleases and he can close its doors against any one he pleases, and there is no power in the land that can force or control his judgment or discretion in the matter, save, of course, the special action, in a special case, of Parliament, which, unlike our Congress, limited in its power and field of action, is "supreme, irresistible, and uncontrollable" in all things and over all men in England. It is one of those instances continually arising out of the fortuitous historical development of England in which enormous powers or public trusts or franchises have come into the hands of some

one man or class, who are responsible for their use only to
their own honor and conscience and the general sense of a
whole people, which generally in some way enforces its own
will. And a vast body of such usages, powers, vested
rights, and franchises, ecclesiastical and civil and political, which no one has ever attempted to enumerate or
define, and which no one here would define if he could,
and of which there is nowhere any written or authoritative record, is the Constitution of England. Compare
this condition of things with the carefully-written paper
which is our Constitution, and you have some idea of
the organic differences of the two Governments,—the
one a growth, the other as yet a pure construction.
This fact is the great and foundation difference between
English and American politics, and the reason why
the acts of one are often no precedent for the other.

As a matter of fact, Dean Stanley, as any strong man
would in a similar position, feels bound to act as the
prophet and interpreter of the English people in the
discharge of this unique and singularly high trust, and
does, as have the deans of Westminster before him.
While the exercise of such sole and irresponsible power
looks dangerous to the American mind, accustomed to
the careful distribution of responsibilities and the delicate balance of powers, it has many advantages apparent
at a glance. The popular feeling generally obtains its
will, but it is regulated, restrained perhaps for a time,
by the sounder and truer judgment of an educated and
cultivated man, who can also by his power of veto not
only prevent indecorous burials, which might be forced
under temporary impulse or immature sentiment, but
save the building from the profanation of crude inscriptions, born of ignorance, passion, or bad taste. Indeed,
the present dean has done an acknowledged service,
not only to England, but to the English language, in
the regulation of the mural legends and inscriptions
which have been placed in the Abbey during his long
incumbency. As a whole work they show a marked

force, elegance, and good taste that in future times will be noted and remembered to the credit of our century.

A stroll through the aisles and cloisters of this great church awakens the echoes of history and starts associations almost at every step which lead one to the outer confines of our knowledge—political, religious, and social—of ourselves.

Here, in the ancient Chapter-House, a perfectly circular room, on rude stone benches continuous around the wall in three tiers, without arms or railing or rest of any kind, for three hundred years sat the Parliaments of England.

Here, in the Jerusalem Chamber, a modest kind of vestry room, storied in legend as the death-scene of Henry IV., juggled by a prophecy, was framed and published "The Shorter Catechism," that famous compendium of Presbyterian belief. How many of our American Presbyterians ever think of the "Assembly of Westminster Divines" as assembled and working at this historic Anglican centre?

In this same room sat and worked the men who produced the revision of the Book of Common Prayer in the form in which it is now used in England. And, to keep up the chain of historical tradition in this line, the modern "Committee for the Revision of the Bible" is to-day sitting in this chamber invested with such distinguished ecclesiastical associations.

Here once was the "treasury of the kings of England," and here now all the official gold and silver standards of the coin of the realm are under royal lock and key.

Here, too, opening out of the dean's private study, is the simple closet, now disused, but which once served for the keeping of the crown jewels and regalia, of which the dean and chapter are still the legal and constructive keepers, and which, on the eve of the coronation-day of every monarch, are yet brought to the Abbey and kept there over-night, that they may be ready for the ceremony of the morning; for the coronation of every king or queen of England takes place in this church in front of the Chapel of Henry VII. These jewels are the gorgeous collection of crowns and coronets and sceptres and royal swords and gold and silver and diamonds familiar to all who have visited the Tower of London. Although in the constructive keeping of the Abbey, these regal valuables are by statute in the actual charge as deposits of the constable of the Tower, who is supposed to have the safest place in the kingdom either for state prisoners or state property.

Here, in silent admonitory state, among the dusty tombs of the sovereigns who have sat in it, stands the coronation chair. Under its seat, and part of it now, is the famous "Stone of Scone," the rude throne of the old Scottish chiefs, and which Scottish tradition and relic-worship assert to be the very stone on which the patriarch Jacob rested his head for a pillow when he slept and saw his glorious vision of power and long life and God's protection,—"the Shepherd and the Stone of Israel."

Here, by a dark and narrow stairway, you ascend to the small, rude, touching Chapel of Henry V., swung in the air, the solid stone steps worn almost into cups by the feet of devoted worshippers, who for centuries have climbed its hard, bare way to hear mass and pray by the body of their dead, loved king, the saddle and the helmet of Agincourt keeping solemn guard over the warrior at rest forever. On the Continent I saw many impressive altars in crypts and corners and dramatic situations, but I remember none in the unique position of this one, raised high into the air, on a level above the main altar of the church, and looking down on all around it.

But why lengthen out detached pictures where every foot is illustrative, where every stone is eloquent, where

every aisle and corridor and archway is tremulous with
the memories of centuries?

Westminster Abbey, with its picturesque Old English
architecture, so thoroughly ecclesiastical, so rich, so elegant; with its cloisters and venerable aisles, shadowy
with the associations of legend, history, and tradition;
with its stately tombs, the grand records of England's
glories, learning, and faith; with its historic chapels and
crumbling stones and time-stained walls hung with
dropping banners or crowded with suggestive inscriptions, is one of those places which, like Niagara, cannot
disappoint. One need not fear to see it lest the sight
should dissolve cherished dreams or beautiful images.
No matter what one's range of reading, no matter what
one's fund of learning, no matter what one's sweep and
realm of imagination, the fair fabric of fact stands forever, grander than dream or fancy, a living sermon in
stone.

I could not help thinking, whenever I passed this
historic spot, of the riches with which England is
dowered in this single church, and my mind reverts to
the reflection again and again as I think how long,
long, long it must be before we can be equally favored.
It is a foundation with which no college can ever be
endowed,—a perpetual lesson and education. "Remember the days of old; consider the years of many
generations."

Wandering through Westminster Abbey, as in all the
churches of England, there is forced on one a sense of
the great honors which England pays to her soldiers.
I think that in the cathedrals and churches of the
kingdom a larger proportion of soldiers lie buried in
state, or have their names recorded in memorial legend
if they have died on foreign fields, than any one other
class, not even excepting the clergy, whose homes have
been these buildings, and who themselves in former
times have played so great a part in history. At every
step their stately tombs or eloquent tablets arrest you;

their still stone effigies rest under the gathering dusts of every century; "their good swords rust" on every wall: "their souls are with the Lord, we trust."

It is this cultus of courage and force which has made England, and it is these honors which make her men soldiers. While there is something in her present military organization and structure which seems to produce deficient generalship, or prevent the development and coming forward of the real military genius which is surely in her armies, the soldierly qualities of the body of her officers are something wonderful and worthy of the highest admiration,—their fidelity, their personal chivalry in moments of danger, their perfect willingness and readiness to die. Her gentlemen leave homes of loveliness and cultivation and refinement unequalled on the face of the globe, and die every year, every day, almost, old and young, on the plains of Asia, in the forests of Africa, in fever-swamp and desert-sands, cheerfully and uncomplainingly. Hardly a country home in England but has its soldier's grave somewhere in the uttermost parts of the earth where England is pushing her imperial arms. And that all this sacrifice is made in the face of a general sense of uneasiness and want of confidence in the ability of the directing power makes it all the more wonderful. "Somebody blundered" at Balaklava, just as they did at Braddock's Field and Bunker's Hill, and before the cotton-bales of New Orleans in 1812, and among the kraals of Zululand, and in the cañons of Afghanistan this fatal year; but still the British soldier, gentleman and yeoman, is ever ready, with his life in his hand, to go forward. It is these tombs in the old cathedrals.

Passing from the ancient abbots' palace, now the dwelling of the dean, by private entrance to the church, just before we entered the transept of the main building Dean Stanley, to whom my presence started recollections of Philadelphia, said, "Stop a moment; I want to show you something that will remind you of home," and ascending by a side entry three narrow steps, into a little chapel shut off by an open railing from public entrance, we stood suddenly before the handsome memorial window of Mr. Childs to the two English poets, —a grand blaze of illumination, covering almost an entire wall of the chapel. It is a beautiful and costly work of art, in the conventional ecclesiastical style of glass-painting, rich and impressive.

It is the usage in the Abbey to inscribe on all monuments the incident of their erection, and the story of this one is very simply and frankly told in a single line:

" *D. D.* Georgius Gulielmus Childs. Civis Americanus.*"

This is the first appearance of our country in the historic Abbey. There are a few other American names,—some loyal refugees in the war of 1776–83, some colonial worthies, some British soldiers killed in the Revolution and French wars,—but this is the only inscription which distinctly places the new nation of " the United States of America" in the monumental archives of Westminster.

LONDON.

---

* Donum dedit.

CHAPTER XX.

THE LONDON PULPIT.

DEAN STANLEY IN WESTMINSTER ABBEY—CANON FARRAR AT ST. MARGARET'S — ST. PAUL'S CATHEDRAL — CARDINAL MANNING IN THE PRO-CATHEDRAL AT KENSINGTON—REV. MR. HAWEIS AT MARYLEBONE—THE ENGLISH CLERGY AS PUBLIC MEN.

To an American imagination there is no preacher in all the world who has a grander pulpit than he who speaks in Westminster Abbey. It is an inspiration to stand there. The scene of an ordinary afternoon service is itself a dramatic one. From the little pulpit at the corner of the transept the preacher sees a living sea of heads stretching out every broad aisle as far as the voice will reach. The wave of his audience overflows even the generous provision of the seats and surges up and over the tombs of the historic dead. On the confines of the seated congregation throng dark clouds of standing listeners, moving restlessly for some coign of vantage, pressing forward anxiously and expectant as when some great speech is to be delivered in a Parliament. This, at least, is the scene which every Sunday greets the eye of Dean Stanley, who is one of the most popular preachers in London. This popularity comes solely, too, from the spirit and tone of his sermons, for their delivery breaks their effect rather than adds to it. The dean reads his sermons, which is the murder of oratory, and few voices if any can reach the outer edges of the vast audience which gathers in the spacious graystone halls of the nave and transept. It is the exquisite English of these sermons and their gentle catholic spirit which draws all London and all the world of travel to hear them. Dean Stanley's spare form and

kindly features are so well known now in our country
that the American traveller does not feel as a stranger
when on entering the church he sees the familiar face
in the reading-desk or pulpit.

London is the vortex of the world, Westminster is
the heart of London, and its preacher is so thoroughly
in all the currents of modern life that one loses in every
sermon of Dean Stanley's the more delicate touches, the
keener allusions,—the more effective because so deftly
veiled,—if he is not thoroughly familiar with all
the higher movements of the hour.   Here in a very
striking sense "the parish is the world," and Dean
Stanley has all the tact of a born journalist in harness-
ing the events of each day to the chariot of his work.

When I first heard him the text was a clause of Scripture,—"the service of the sanctuary." The theme, however, was strictly "the Book of Common Prayer," its
historic associations and growth, its spirit, and mainly
and practically the question of the expediency or propriety of its emendation now.   However scholarly or
critical the treatment of this subject,—and this sermon
was both,—the theme, in such a temple and before a
Church-of-England audience, must of necessity involve
panegyric, and that it might not lead to narrowing
opinion or the nurture of prejudice the preacher with
fine tact prefaced his discourse by recalling as appropriate to the subject and the day that this very Sunday
was the anniversary of that historic occasion when the
service of the Established Church of England was read
for the first time and the last time in the national
Church of Scotland.   Then, in perfectly impartial and
dispassionate words and in a tone and voice colorless of
the slightest trace of feeling or judgment, he related
the story of that famous scene in Edinboro' when Janet
Geddes threw the footstool at the dean of Edinboro's
head just as he began to read the collect for the day,—
the same collect in which we had all joined that very
hour,—the uproar and confusion, the broken and ended

service, and the historical consequences of the event. That picture, drawn so calmly, all the passions of the time faded out with the years, as lifeless and departed as if veritably entombed with the dead of centuries that lay all around us, made its own argument. The audience stood at once on the catholic plane of the preacher.

On the question of amendment *now*—the practical body of the discourse—the dean was direct and explicit. Noble as was the book, grand as were its associations, it was a living growth and must change. It had defects, the legacies of times not so fortunate or blessed with light as ours, and they should be amended; the sooner the better. The specific changes suggested and pointed out as desirable were one and all in the line of broadening the Church and opening wide its doors,—wide and loving as the arms of its Founder. Among those instanced were the expurgation of the sweeping damnatory clauses of the Athanasian Creed; also the abolition of that rubric which forbids the burial prayers of the Church to be read over the body " of a man of the purest and most blameless life if he belonged, say, to that most excellent and pious people, the Friends, instead of the Established Church," or " even over the most innocent of little children, those little children of whom Christ Himself said, ' Of such is the kingdom of heaven.' " Another change urged was the wording of those special prayers for rain which seem to assume that the favors of nature are sent upon the just and its disfavors upon the unjust, contrary to the now clearly acknowledged teachings of the New Testament.

In Westminster Abbey the service is rather a medium between the High Church intoning of England and the severely plain enunciation demanded with us. When it was over and the sermon finished the congregation slowly dispersed, not with a rush to the streets, but lingering kindly and lovingly in the cool gray shades of the tombs and arched aisles, and there were no impatient vergers or janitors hanging around to hustle out the last lingerers and close inhospitable doors.

In the yard of Westminster Abbey, a solid pavement of flat tombs, stands the parish church of St. Margaret. St. Margaret's Parish is the first parish in the kingdom, for in its bounds rise both Houses of Parliament, and, I think, the official residences of all the government. The Speaker of the House of Commons, the Speaker of the House of Lords, and most of the great officials of state are always members of this parish. Until within a very few years the House of Commons was accustomed to attend this church in state, as provided in the Prayer-book.

Westminster Abbey, although it fills so large a space in London in American imagination, has no territorial jurisdiction. An abbey is something to which we have no equivalent in Protestant America. It is a college of priests,—a point or foundation purely for worship of God, unclogged by any congregational cares or limitations. It has no congregation in our sense. There is regular service and it is free to all, but it goes on whether any persons from outside come or not.

Dr. F. W. Farrar, whose name as a popular author is so familiar on both sides of the sea, is the rector or pastor of St. Margaret's, and he is so by virtue of holding a canonry in Westminster Abbey. St. Margaret's, too, is a stimulating house in which to preach. It is part of the fabric of the English Constitution; the strongest legislation in the world throbs at its very side, and the congregation must always hold some of the ablest and most influential men living. Add to this that there is not a Sunday but when, in addition to the permanent congregation, there are to be found among the hearers distinguished men of all peoples,—statesmen, thinkers, writers, soldiers,—who come as strangers and travellers, unknown and unseen, but none the less critical and observing. In fact, they are making up the verdict of the world.

The interior of St. Margaret's is very plain. It was the ordinary rectangular American church or meeting-house, with four white walls, and the entire floor filled with plain wooden high-backed pews. Fine stained-glass windows and some historic names graven on mural tablets,—Sir Walter Raleigh lies in.the chancel,—relieve the room from absolute sameness and furnish that rest ·to the eye which one finds so grateful in the churches of Europe, and which he so soon learns to look for.

The conduct of the service was correspondingly simple. Both the prayers and the psalms were read so that each word was intelligible. There was neither in-toning nor drawling. Going to St. Margaret's with the consciousness that I was seeing one of the high-places of the Church of England, it was something of a sur-prise to hear the first hymn given out,—

> "Come let us join our cheerful songs
> With angels round the throne,"

and to have it followed by—

> "How sweet the name of Jesus sounds
> In a believer's ear!"

two hymns in common use by every denomination in the United States. And both were sung to airs famil-iar in all Presbyterian and Congregational churches, and the singing was by the entire congregation.

Dr. Farrar, a dark, brown-faced man with a pleasant countenance, preached from Galatians, the first verse of the fifth chapter,—"the liberty with which Christ hath made us free." It was the broadest of broad-church sermons, the special dangers to Christian freedom from the side of ecclesiastical organization being the drift of the discourse, and at times the argument seemed to press certain practical applications on home issues not immediately discernible to a stranger. I could only quote from recollection, and should be afraid to attempt for fear of being charged with misquotation, but it is sufficient to say that Canon Farrar was as latitudinarian as St. Paul himself, and would probably have been pronounced unorthodox on the Church question from many a Baptist, Lutheran, or Presbyterian pulpit in the United States. He went the length of accepting literally the sayings of the New Testament, translating them into the language and applying them to the situation of the day. He is out and out a disciple of St. Paul. Indeed, it is observable how thoroughly Pauline preaching is the rule in the Church of England, which is suffering a kind of recoil from theological disputation, and to-day sees the old doctrinal lines broken at many a point without apparently thinking of even an effort to defend them.

I have mentioned that this sermon seemed to be bearing on some home question of church government or policy not entirely clear to a passing visitor. It is worthy of remark that nearly every sermon I heard in London bore directly on some imminent matter,—some great question of modern thought or action,—and that the preacher spoke as a lawyer before a bench of judges or a jury does, directly to the point, with the view of convincing some person or persons on a given issue and at that time.

I was not fortunate enough to hear Canon Liddon, of St. Paul's Cathedral, who is ranked by many at the head of the London pulpit in the way of combining both scholarship and popular oratorical power. He was sick and off duty during my three visits to London.

St. Paul's, although dwarfed in American interest by Westminster Abbey, is to Englishmen probably the greater church of the two, and it is always and for any one a most impressive house of worship. It is the cathedral church of the diocese of London and the most prominent building in all that huge city, being in size the third largest church in Christendom. It is the great monument of its architect, Sir Christopher Wren, who got $1000 a year for building it. The bishop of London now gets $50,000 a year. The dean of St. Paul's also now receives $10,000 a year, and a staff of canons $5000 a year each, for conducting service in it. Then there are also archdeacons, prebendaries, minor canons, and the usual equipment of lesser officers,—chancellor, register, and clerks of many kinds.

St. Paul's Cathedral stands now right in the heart of business London. Its once cloistered walks are busy marts, and it is a dramatic surprise to pass in a few steps almost, out of the Bank of England, heated, panting with the pulses of the trade of the world, into the cool, calm shades of a still cathedral where the service of worship is nearly always in progress. There are, I think, four services every day, and perhaps more on Sunday, but it would be, it struck me, a glorious assertion of religious life if they were made continuous day and night, and this magnificent temple, right in the heart of the dominion of Mammon in this world, were constituted a place where literally "prayer is made to God without ceasing." This idea flashed on me like a wave of emotion within ten minutes after I first entered the great cathedral. I suggested it afterwards to an English clergyman, but could not impart to him my enthusiasm. He thought it would "kill the clergy." I would say, "Kill them." If men can die for their country on a desolate and barren battle-field, why not for the glory of God in a comfortable cathedral?

The service of St. Paul's is a great work of art conducted with all the highest accessories of music and ecclesiastical stage effect. It was entirely intoned, and not a word of the priest was intelligible, at least to a non-English stranger. For one not accustomed to the traditional stage delivery of the English altar the tongue might just as well have been Latin or Hebrew. The preacher and reader, however, were perfectly heard.

The ablest sermon I heard in St. Paul's was by the senior canon, Rev. Mr. Gregory. The bishop of the diocese had ordered prayers for good weather in all the churches, and Canon Gregory on this day preached to the order, taking for his theme the whole question of prayer for the specific direction or suspension of the laws of nature. The marked feature of this sermon was the extreme candor and fairness with which the preacher stated the position of his opponents on this matter in all its strength, without the least disposition to contort it or to blink the danger. He fairly admitted that the ground had shifted since the days of mediæval thought, and made not the least attempt to hold it by appeals to transmitted ignorance or prejudice, but grappled with the issue in a way that showed a masterly study of the whole range of modern reading. It was the work of a strong man who knew there was a fight ahead and was ready for it.

Like nearly all English clergymen, Canon Gregory preaches with a vigor, physical and intellectual, which tells of the broad foundation of the university and of generous and conscientious care of the body from youth upwards. He is a large man, of hearty address and that rare honesty of expression and manner that inspires immediate confidence and trust. The close of St. Paul's, in which these canons live in low-roomed old-fashioned houses, with wrought-iron extinguishers and hooks for the link-boys' torches yet attached to their doors, is a most quaint old place which I despair of describing to those who have not seen it or something like it, but it is one of the best living reminiscences of Old London. It is in such out-of-the-way places not in the guide-books, or out of the reach of tourist curiosity, that one gets his freshest and best conception of past England. An old castle with the family still in it, their comfortable every-day life blending through the slow succession of centuries with the half-barbaric magnificence of their ancestors, a dark gray close with a deanery full of girls inheriting the substantial club comforts of a line of dead abbots and their bachelor monks, are worth all the routine ruins and well-trodden ivy walls in the island.

I first heard of the Rev. Charles Haweis many years ago, when I found his "Music and Morals" in the meagre hut of a miner in the Rocky Mountains of Colorado, into which I had been driven by stress of weather to pass the night, and the singular contrast of the incident kept his name fixed in my attention. In London, Mr. Haweis is a very popular preacher, and his church rather a fashionable one in its own stratum of society.

St. James of Marylebone is an old-fashioned church building such as you see yet in old parts of Philadelphia and in many of the interior towns of Maryland and Pennsylvania. The old architectural interior has been religiously preserved,—low, long galleries, quaint pillars, high wooden pews,—but all the plain walls and woodwork are now done over in the glory of modern decorative effect, in gray and red and gold and glass. Indeed, it rather looks as if an energetic æsthetic club had been let loose on all the walls and wooden fronts. The rear end of the church, which serves as a background for the altar, looks something like a huge illuminated title-page, so elaborate is it in pictured glass and gold and neutral-tinted panels, all blazoned over with ecclesiastical and religious symbols. The altar itself was a narrow ledge against the base of the great window. On it rested an elaborate cross in opaque glass or some similar material revealing itself very prettily with a kind of subdued brilliancy out of a wealth of flowers. Above the ledge arose a large rigid old-fashioned square arch or triangle, thus: ∧. Inside of the arch was a perfect circle of scroll-work of some kind; inside of the circle a Greek cross, its four even arms touching the circumference, while its centre was a great garnet-colored stone or piece of glass, which burned or glittered like a fiery eye, and more or less recalled the Shah of Persia or one's boyhood recollections of the " Arabian Nights."

The congregation was apparently of the middle class, wealthy, comfortable, and uneducated. It was the most congregational service, however, I have ever seen. The Confession, Lord's Prayer, Creed, and most of the prayers were said by the whole people so well and spiritedly that the voice of the priest was never heard at all save when he sounded the leading note. The psalms of the day and the hymns were sung by the people, who carried on the whole service. In fact, the whole congregation seemed one body, a living being throbbing and pulsating with worship. It was a congregation very easy and pleasant to preach to, if one was its choice. It was harmonious, very earnest, and entirely satisfied with itself. Without knowing anything of them, I should venture the assertion that the body of the people are of the same class of society and have a high opinion of their own " culture."

Mr. Haweis is a good specimen of the popular preacher toned down by the social limitations of the Church of England. He has all the elements of a stump-speaker, but has never learned to sink the pulpit below the level of the stump, which is the usual work of an American sensational preacher. Mr. Haweis does not even approach this, for neither his education nor Marylebone would suffer it; but somehow his manner suggests that under less fortunate conditions of cultivation he might have drifted that way. He has the best elements and force of the sensational preacher, without his vulgarity. In person Mr. Haweis is a dark, average-sized man, with black side-whiskers, and of a sanguine, bilious-looking temperament. His elocution is very English, apologetic, and with a great deal of hem-ing and haw-ing and aw-ing. His tones are also somewhat nasal, which is not English.

The Roman Catholic pro-cathedral, which is said to be a kind of provisional tabernacle until the Church can make good its claim to St. Paul's or Westminster, is situated away out on the Kensington road, one-half mile by underground railway from Portland Place, and the aristocratic section of which that place is the centre. It is a fairly capacious but very plain church, with pews, little decoration in the way of painting and statuary, and looking not at all in its interior like the Roman churches of Ireland and Italy. Here I went to hear Henry Edward, Cardinal Manning, Archbishop of Westminster.

Cardinal Manning is a tall, spare man, of feeble frame, with an emaciated and almost pallid face, rendered still more wan by hungry, cavernous eyes,—the true ecclesiastical type. He called up at once the political ecclesiastic of the sixteenth century. His wasted features are refined, scholarly, and intellectual. A movable scalp, causing his red skull-cap to move up and down, imparts rather a sinister effect and mars the general impression of his appearance. The thin figure and meagre, fleshless face suggest the mediæval anchorite, the sharp, severe outlines the Middle-Age inquisitor, a man who would be honestly cruel,—cruel to himself as well as to others.

And Cardinal Manning has been cruel to himself, mercilessly honest to his convictions, in leaving the green pastures and pleasant waters of the Established Church of England for the arid and unintellectual wastes of the Roman Catholic Church in Britain. There was no fashion at the pro-cathedral, no good society, no university, no influence, no cultivation. There were ignorant, new-made wealth and dull credulity and heavy mediocrity, but nothing better. It was a real sacrifice of the highest kind for this cultivated, learned, able man, the flower of English education, to be there.

Cardinal Manning's sermon, as indeed was to be expected, was masterly and powerful. It was very earnest, and full of the wisdom of an old and wise man. It was severely plain in language and often very practical, but the whole interior train of thought and argument was entirely above the very inferior congregation which listened to it. They undoubtedly got good from it, but they never knew the perfection of the work. Indeed, it sometimes seemed to me that the great preacher was preaching two sermons simultaneously,—one in the spirit to himself and any stray hearer that chanced to drop in, and another in the flesh of the word to the pitiful audience of the pro-cathedral. I think no educated man could have witnessed this scene without regret, no matter how widely he might have differed from every word and conclusion of the ex-fellow of Oxford. The text of the sermon was the words, " Gold, frankincense, and myrrh," the subject, " Offering,"—the dedication of everything to God ; one's whole self in every part, estate, body, mind. The treatment revealed a great deal of patristic reading, and the language recalled at times the late papal syllabus, " The characteristic of the XIX. century is mental aberration," and the remedy of the cardinal was simple and mechanical : Offer your mind as a sacrifice to God,—*i.e.*, to the Roman Catholic Church.

Cardinal Manning's delivery is very defective, and keeps one on the stretch all the time. Owing to loss of teeth, perhaps, one word out of every eight or ten drops out entirely, and, as his sermons are of that unusual order that one wants to hear every word of them, the loss is very serious. In speaking, Cardinal Manning clenched the rail of the pulpit-box with both his pallid fists, like an English statesman on the hustings, and ejected rather than delivered his words, as if half embarrassed. He wore a scarlet cap and scarlet robe. In quoting Latin, it was rather significant that he used the continental pronunciation, abandoning the English system of his own university training.

The pro-cathedral is not the first Roman Catholic

church in London. That is St. George's Cathedral, across the river from Westminster bridge. In this pro-cathedral, when Cardinal Manning preached, the pews were guarded and a sixpence demanded for an ordinary seat, a shilling for the better ones. The sermon was preached for a charity, and the money thus secured went to it in addition to the special collection taken up. The force of priests at the altar was not strong. Mass was more reverently gone through than in the perfunctory Italian style, but with less regard to the scenic proprieties, and with an utter want of the sense of dress and drapery that was thoroughly English.

The preachers with a Transatlantic fame of other churches were not as conspicuous in the winter of 1879–80 as some years before. Irving, the leader of the famous apostolic movement, was dead. Spurgeon was in Italy in search of health, perhaps of life. The great orator of the Congregationalist denomination was in the divorce court. And so it happens that the view of this letter is confined to the Roman and English State-Churches.

In London the pulpit is a much stronger social force than in any city in our country, and the men who fill it take a much greater and more influential share in the general public life. There are reasons in the structure of English society for this.

The bishops sit in Parliament, and thus have a direct political influence. Again, the entire body of the clergy is a definite class, entitled always to be heard in a society which rests on a basis of class and is itself only a federation of many class-interests. This priestly class, in its highest rank too, reaches into the peerage. It requires a personal knowledge of English life to know how much this means.

Once more, the English clergy have a better and happier education than the main body of ours, which, indeed, they share with the leaders of thought of all England, but it works out special advantages in their profession. Owing to a greater breadth of learning, and as its resultant a larger freedom of thought and expression, many of the great intellectual and social questions which are fought outside of the Church with us are fought inside of it here. Then the good fortune of a university education in England is a great blessing which widens with the years. All the best life of England goes to school either at Cambridge or Oxford. Until more recent years this has been the case almost without exception. The graduates of these two universities divided among themselves all England, and have done so for hundreds of years. Their alumni have been simply a club formed of the leaders in the state, in the Church, in society, in the army, at the bar. England is a small place, where men constantly meet one another. The young university clergyman starts with an acquaintance embracing all that is best in the kingdom, and that will last for life if he is worthy of it. He has, therefore, a much more intimate association with the whole life of the nation than the American clergyman, who starts from the first in the seclusion of a denominational college and further segregates himself by finishing his education in an admittedly sectarian theological school.

Finally, the Established Church itself is an alliance with the politics and good society of the kingdom, and its leaders have necessarily intimate relations with and responsibilities to these interests.

There is another solid reason why the clergy of London should stand to the front of their calling. All England is behind them. The men who preach in St. Paul's and Westminster, at Smithfield or the Temple, and who live at Lambeth Palace, would be less than mortal did they not draw strength and inspiration from the historic theatre of their work.

CHAPTER XXI.

THE PLAY AND THE THEATRE.

The Primitive Inn-Yard Stage of Old England—Disappearance of the English Drama of the Soil—The Saxon Play and the Modern Theatre—London Theatres and Law-Court Rooms—Henry Irving at the Lyceum—The Sceptre of Fashion—Sara Bernhardt over from the Theatre Français.

SEVERAL ancient London inns, with spacious interior court-yards surrounded with galleries in the shape of a continuous porch running around the second story, are still pointed out as the rude and simple play-houses of Old England. The stage here was the pavement of the court-yard. The spectators gathered on the upper porches, or perhaps could even sit at their chamber windows and see and hear the play, as I have done this year in a provincial Italian town, and seen good acting. The servants of the inn and hangers-on clustered in the corners of the court-yard, standing on the ground, or maybe indulging in the kitchen-stools and stable-benches. It is, perhaps, in survival of this tradition that in most of the London theatres of to-day the best part of the house is called the pit, and that seats in it are sold at a cheap price and fashion rigorously shuns it. The modern pit is the survivor of the old inn court-yard, and the flavor of the stable and kitchen still clings to it. Many of the plays of Shakespeare were brought before the people on just such simple boards, some of them in some of these very inns. This was in the days of Merrie England and of strolling players,—the time when England was a play-going nation. She was then Catholic and monarchical in heart. To-day she is

Protestant and republican, and her native drama is
gone.

There is something in democracy and Puritanism
which drives the theatre out of a national life. The
people have risen to higher interests. When the Puritan
became ascendant in England he closed up the play-
houses, burnt the plays, branded the poor players, and,
perhaps, drove them with cropped ears out of the land.
They have never come back. England has her theatres
to-day, but they are no more an institution of the people.
They are simply a conventional amusement of the higher
classes common to the world. They flourish only in her
cities. The "play" of English literature has disappeared.

A popular love of the drama among the humble
body of the people only exists in that condition of civilization where there is a high development of the dramatic element in Church and State. Wherever there
are elaborate rites and forms in the Church, and scenic
displays in the Government, there the heart of the
common people is really moved by its drama, which,
however humble it may be, answers to and satisfies a
popular craving. A drama of the soil flourishes best
when the High-Church principle rules in the Church
and the monarchical principle in the State. In Italy
to-day, where the people are born actors, the daily service of the Church is always an impressive picture, and
it flowers all the time in imposing "functions" in
grand cathedrals so built that the chancel railings
enclose a magnificent stage where a hundred or more
priests and acolytes can countermarch, intone, swing
censers, and group themselves in effective tableaux.
From the England of the play and play-houses come
down scenic coronations and spectacular openings of Parliament, which are performed yet to-day, but to irre-
sponsive audiences. The whole order of life of the peerage is, in fact, a colossal play for the amusement and
impression of the common people. When the people

get behind the scenes then comes democracy. Democracy has come for England, and the drama as a native institution has disappeared before it. The old name, even, is gone. The Saxon " play" of the people has given way to the Latin *theatrum* of fashion. The English theatre of to-day does not differ from the American. The same plays are acted in the same way, and the same kind of people go to hear them,—viz., the well-off world of fashion and the very dregs of the cities. The vast body of the people have no more interest in them than have ours.

The theatres of London, therefore, although good in their several ways, offer no field for the study of English life except incidentally. The houses themselves were not materially different from ours, and they seemed to grade themselves fashionable, middle class, low, much as ours do.

In this similarity to ours they resemble every other institution whose development in England and our country has been under similar conditions. I took a stroll one day through the law-courts of London under a barrister's guidance, and was surprised to find how little they differed from ours. Even the men in them were the same. There was the little, withered-up, old lawyer, the portly, substantial, prosperous one, the hurried, full-of-business advocate, the hungry, shabby attorney, who has given up the race, and haunts the court-room by habit; the judge who tried the case himself, and did all the talking; the judge whose docket was always behindhand; the barrister with unclean linen and unbrushed clothes. They were all there just as they are sitting in the court-rooms of Pennsylvania to-day. It may be that Pennsylvania, accepting the common law in full and the old English system of pleading, and changing very little of anything until within this generation, has carried down something more of the detail of the English court-room than other States, but it is not much. The controlling reason for the likeness is

that for three hundred years the law, always a conservative profession, has advanced with equal steps
and under nearly equal conditions in England and this
country.　The American lawyer has added to his professional labors the burden of politics, which, in England, has been generally shouldered by another class,
but that is about all the difference in their lives.　He
threw away the wig, also, and that is about all the
difference there is in the *coup d'œil* of an English
and American court-room.　And that is a difference
to our advantage.　I failed entirely to see the dignity
and impressiveness which, to the English mind, lies in
a horse-hair wig.　They give a slovenly and unclean air
to a whole room.　Few were well kept, none of them
looked fresh, and many were nasty.

All theatre-going London, in 1879, was divided in
its worship of Henry Irving and Sara Bernhardt, both
of whom are promised to America, and both of whom
have made conquest of the world of fashion as well as
of the stage.

Henry Irving has unquestionably achieved a wonderful success in holding the sustained attention of London.　His plays are mostly of a high order,—mainly
Shakespearian.　His Merchant of Venice has held the
stage for hundreds of nights, and there are no symptoms
to show that the interest is flagging.　One must go a
week beforehand to secure seats, and this has been the
case for several years.　His theatre is the Lyceum,—
on classic ground just off the Strand.　Mr. Irving is a
spare, rather fine-looking man, with an intellectual face
and the carriage of a gentleman.　He has the sem-
blance of a bend in his shoulders greater than the
reality.　When acting you see Henry Irving all the time,
but it is not offensive.　He blends with his character,
but he never loses himself even to the incidents of
his appearance.　There is, for instance, a certain melo-
dramatic air about him, recognizable plainly in his

photographs, which never forsakes him and leaves on
one a suspicion that he is forever posing. He wears a
"melancholy mien," as one who carries around from
hour to hour the burden of a great grief, a secret
mystery, perhaps even a delicious crime. This manner,
however, is one of chaste repression, and the highest
finish of subdued refinement. There is not the least
suggestion of the possibility of a scene or of anything that
might violate the minutest conventionalities of good
society. It is an air eminently calculated to charm and
interest a sympathetic woman with time on her hands
and plenty of money.

This charm Mr. Irving has worked, and it is the
danger which confronts him now in coming to our
country. Although an excellent, conscientious, and
scholarly actor, Mr. Irving owes his sovereignty of the
London stage to the stamp of aristocratic endorsement
set on him personally. Society, in a country where
society is thoroughly organized, has approved him. It
has taken him up, it has opened its drawing-rooms to
him, it has made it the mode to go to the Lyceum.
Bishops hear him, the clergy of good society discuss
him with *religieuse* peeresses; the journal with social
ambition hymns his praises. It is very meet and right
and proper now in England to hear Henry Irving.

Now in this country we have nothing at all to answer
to the direct and powerful influence of the English
aristocracy in general society. It can take up a pet of
any kind, for a mere whim, perhaps, and his fortune is
made. And it does take up these pets all the time, and
in the most capricious way. Sometimes it is an actor,
sometimes it is a clergyman, sometimes it is an artist,
sometimes it is a beauty, sometimes even the whim may
be to buy at a certain shop or patronize a certain tradesman. Whatever it is, the success of the pet is assured.
All London kneels at the feet of the beauty, throngs the
theatre of the actor, buys the pictures of the artist, or
crowds the shop of the favorite tradesman. Perhaps

society even tolerates or half invites a mild and cautious snubbing from its pet. This is the perilous position of Henry Irving. He is the pet of London society, and specially of that wing of it which affects to be non-worldly. He stands at the head of the English stage, but how far he owes that position to an arbitrary degree of fashion, and how far to a genuine mastery of his profession, it may take the verdict of an American public to decide.

When Sara Bernhardt first comes on the stage you see a meagre-looking, rather impassive soubrette, with a plain thin face and a body that looks like an uninteresting fabrication of whalebones and corsets. You are looking anxiously at every entrance for the great actress to make her appearance, when it breaks on you with a disappointment that this inferior young woman is she herself. It can hardly be, it cannot possibly be, but a moment or two and the inexorable caste decides. Yes, it is she, certainly. Soon the "divine skeleton" begins to breathe, the eyes of the soul light up the sunken face, and the worn body clothes itself with flesh and grace.

There can be no question as to the Bernhardt's right to her throne. Disendowed with a body carrying which many a rustic girl would give up the village race, she has placed herself at the head of the actresses of her day, flooded the capitals of two continents with her face, and dictated the mode in dress and adornment of the civilized world. And this resistless power of hers which holds London and Paris at her feet, and sends her fame wherever there is written language, is the more strange that it is so purely intellectual. With none of the sensuous charms of physical attraction, she has nevertheless always made men the slaves of her body. On the stage it is the passion of the soul which achieves her triumphs. You see forever the fiery mind flaming through the frail body. Her power is that wondrous

Hebrew force in civilization which flashes out all through history, and which in our own day we confess in a Disraeli, a Gambetta, a Rothschild, and a Rachel. Almost any woman with Sara Bernhardt's body would look like a faded little seamstress all her life and feel like one. She has set that body on a throne and made all the women in Christendom do homage to it. The experienced modern eye will see modes of dress and little achievements of feminine embellishment in every town of the United States, which were conceived and brought forth solely to rectify certain lines in Miss Bernhardt's physical frame or to draw off attention from certain others that would not be successfully rectified. What greater triumph is open to woman than to thus chain her whole sex to her chariot wheels?

When Sara Bernhardt came to London success was immediate and assured. The commission of the classic *Theatre Français*—the first stage of the world—had, perhaps, made this a sure thing, but nevertheless society undertook her cause, and made it a social necessity to have seen her. Under the ægis of His Royal Highness the Prince of Wales the comparatively Puritanic drawing-rooms of London were opened, with some qualms it is true, to "Miss Sara Bernhardt and son," and Matthew Arnold in the elaborate pages of the *Nineteenth Century* paid the compliments of the world of scholarship and higher letters.

As an actress, there is no doubt of her power. Her very presence grows on one with a fascination he cannot understand. There is a finish, a consummate grace, a trained force in every movement and position that throw around her the real histrionic nimbus and establish her divine right to the succession of the sovereignty of the stage. Her genius is a perfection of simulation of which, perhaps, our heavier Saxon race is not capable, and therefore admires the more.

The special circles which respectively chaperoned Henry Irving and Sara Bernhardt represent rather

antipodal elements of London society, but it is all a
matter of the upper classes. The people of England
know nothing and care nothing for either of the stars
that reign in the theatrical firmament. They have
nothing to do with the London stage of our day, which
is not English. It may be cosmopolitan, electic of the
world, better than all England ever did or could afford,
but it is not national.

LONDON.

CHAPTER XXII.

THE LONDON TIMES.

IN THE FORTRESS OF THE THUNDERER—MECHANICAL PLANT
AND MANAGEMENT OF THE ESTABLISHMENT — PRESSES —
TYPE-FOUNDING—ELECTRIC LIGHT—ELECTROTYPING-SHOP—
THE CANTEEN—TELEGRAPHIC SERVICE—PRINTING BY EAR
—NIGHT-WORK—THE PAPER OF THE FUTURE—AMERICAN
AND ENGLISH JOURNALISM.

PRINTING-HOUSE SQUARE, which sounds so grandly
from across the seas, is in London so modest a place
that one can readily pass by it unwittingly, as I did,
even after having fixed its general locality from the
map, and started out to find it. This, however, is not
because "the Square" is an inconsiderable structure,
but because of the magnitude of London, which is so
immense that one only comes to a conception of it
slowly and by experience such as this.

The Times building is really a massive pile of solid
brick of fair architectural effect, which in New York or
Philadelphia might be one of the features of the city.
In London it is simply lost,—crowded away among
square miles of similar structures densely packed and
pressed together.

Printing-House Square, the castle of the modern

Thunderer, stands on the reputed site of an old Norman fortress. There is something dramatic in this coincidence which makes the spot the suggestive vignette of whole centuries of history, and starts a thousand poetic and philosophic dreams on the local correlation of force.

I had had no acquaintance with *The Times*, but a note of introduction sent by kind thoughtfulness of a leading New York editor opened widely and hospitably its doors, and I spent a portion of a day most profitably in an exhaustive inspection of its plant and watching somewhat the process of its daily work. Let me tell of some of its wonders.

In this letter I shall confine myself chiefly to the mechanical features, as being of most popular interest and best picturing the establishment to the non-professional world. The editorial side is of professional rather than public interest, and, besides, why should the arcana of the profession be laid before those eyes which see not?

I shall avoid also the familiar figures which simply prove a colossal business, and which would be equally impressive in recording the results of a pork-packing or brick-making establishment, and attempt to briefly outline some of the features which are distinctive to *The Times* and characteristic.

Solidly established for years, founded on the strong bases of the University and the governing classes of England, conducted by men every one of whom is an expert and veteran in the business, *The Times* enjoys an income that now comes in of itself, and stretching out like some of our great railway companies, it now employs a portion of its surplus revenues every year in buttressing itself, by extending its works out to the permanent manufacture of its own supplies. These things are permanent investments, not expenses, and, although costly in the start, in the long course of years save money.

17*

Let me enumerate some of the most important as
illustrative of the scope of the plant. *The Times*—

    I. Manufactures its own presses.

    II. Founds its own type.

    III. Provides its own light—electric.

    IV. Feeds its employees on the spot.

    V. Has its own electrotyping-shop.

    VI. Has its own telegraphic service and wires—in
the main ; and

    VII. Repair-shops for all these different machineries.

All these great shops and offices are under one roof, and
the cluster of them, with the other ordinary departments
of a newspaper-office,—editorial-, composing-, proof-,
stereotyping-, making-up-, press-, business-, advertising-,
and distribution-rooms,—form *The Times* building.

The Walter presses are made here for the market as
well as for the proprietor's own paper, and in these
shops I found the workmen in the busy clatter of
turning out great machines, as in any great factory or
foundry.

In the press-room of the paper stand eight; six go
every night and two stand by as a reserve brigade.
Each press prints a whole copy of *The Times*, both
sides, sixteen pages, and at the rate of twelve thousand
per hour. The edition, therefore, goes off at the rate
of seventy-two thousand per hour. These presses are
ranged in three columns in an immense room on the
first floor of the building, the enormous weight supported by arches. The paper-room, another large space,
is just below the press-room, the paper being hoisted up
by a lift (American elevator) into the centre of the
press-room. In the spacious paper-rooms below you
wander through long avenues of huge rolls of paper,
each roll four miles long. I watched at one of the
presses the four-mile run of one of these rolls, and it
was striking to see how quickly it was done.

Much of the mechanical interest of *The Times* centres in its type department. I brought away with me

some type made under my eye in the founding-room. But that is only the beginning of the wonder. Following this type into another department you see it set by machinery. All publishers are familiar with the history of the long effort of Mr. Walter in this direction. Here is the result:

One-half of *The Times* every night is set by machinery. One machine does the work of six to eight skilled compositors. It cannot correct, however, and here is its weak point, or the whole paper would be set with it. As it is, the work is about divided. Doubtful copy and all revisions are done by hand, the steady, regular work by machinery.

A young man sits before what looks like a piano-board, with four or five banks of keys all lettered. He plays on these keys with forefingers of each hand rapidly, and the type are as rapidly shifted into a kind of minute steel galley, the exact width of the body of a type. There is no system of fingering as with piano music,—only the two paws fly like lightning.

The distributing-machine just reverses the process of the setting instrument, and in the last stage each letter of the alphabet is rapidly shunted off on to its separate side-track, where they stand like long trains of freight cars in the yard of a colossal depot. It is a wonderful machine, but there are others, I think, now surely approaching perfection of much more interest and importance to newspaper property.

The last permanent investment of *The Times* has been the manufacture of its own light on the electric system, using carbon points. The cost for the plant of this has been very great, but it is so far successful, and the cost of now producing light is very moderate.

The entire building is lighted by sixteen electric lights, each light of from eight hundred to one thousand candle-power, far more than is needed. Sixteen wires, each starting directly from a battery, are used to distribute the light, and the battery is worked from a solid and powerful steam-engine. This engine had to be built expressly for the electric battery, and its power cannot be used for any other purpose; the light would waver and be unsteady. Quite thick porcelain globes are used to temper the fierce power of the light, and the dark shadows are in part corrected by reflection from white bowls. I see no reason why the new Edison light should not be attached to this plant, if desirable.

This electric manufacture has been an advertisement for *The Times,* but so far it is not an economy. They have more light than they need or want to have, and the cost of the plant is the capital of a gas company, not a legitimate expense of a newspaper establishment.

The employees of *The Times* are fed in the building, —a great saving of time to employer and employed. The canteen consists of a fine large kitchen and two dining-rooms. Food is supplied at cost rates to the men,—"everything except beer, on which is charged a little profit, which saves the canteen always from loss, and the margin of profit, whatever it may be, is always turned in to an employees' relief fund which we have," it was explained to me.

"That is very excellent; but we do not call beer 'food' in America."

The canteen is a very good and saving institution. It supplies a kind of cheap club to the men, but there could be no better illustration of the difference of habits and manners on the liquor question between the two countries. Here was a careful and conscientious employer furnishing liquor to his force; and, more than that, long rows of bright, burnished pewter ale-mugs, each with "The Times" proudly engraved on its beaming face, greeted my vision as one of the embellishments of the canteen.

The electrotyping-shop is a well-appointed room, equipped with all the modern appliances of the trade, where are made the plates for the weather diagrams published daily in *The Times,* and also maps, charts, etc. So well is this shop perfected that a moderate-sized plate can be turned out in a few minutes. Practical newspaper managers will recognize the economy and desirable use of this attachment.

The Times has its own wires over much of England and most of the continent, and its own service of them by accomplished correspondents,—men of ability and influence. It uses Reuter (the Associated Press of Europe), but only partially and as an incident, its page or more of telegraphic news being generally exclusively its own, and the Reuter news coming in only in a supplementary way. It is a common expression among newspaper men in our country that we only use the telegraph largely. I think that the special telegraph service of *The Times* exceeds that of any American newspaper, saving, possibly, the New York *Herald* and the Chicago *Times*. It does not strike the popular and uneducated eye, perhaps, so strongly as ours, because it does not deal in criminal news, small fires, petty accidents, sensations, etc.; but every morning *The Times* does have a despatch from every capital in Europe from a "stick" to a column and a half or two columns in length, giving the political situation of the day and the great business and social features,—the matter that statesmen and scholars and leaders read and talk about. They are its constituency. Its telegraphic service of special matter averages, I think, about a page a day, and a page of *The Times* is equal in superficies to over twenty per cent. more than a page of the New York *Herald*.

It is all solid news, too,—no padding or whipped cream.

The reception of the telegraphic news of *The Times* is something unique. The lines from the continental capitals, Berlin, Paris, Rome, Vienna, etc., all, of course, converge in one room, and the despatches are received over an instrument that prints. The printing, however, serves merely as a record. The despatch, as it is received, is *read off* by the telegraph operator to the operator of a type-machine, who plays it off by ear, and the despatch, thus reduced to written form, is supplied to the editors in printed proof. Of course, only the work of responsible correspondents, likely to need no alteration, is honored in this way. It would be too expensive to treat thus matter requiring editing.

The type-setting-machine compositors are, of course, a class to themselves, or, rather, to *The Times*. Every ordinary compositor going on *The Times* obligates himself to abandon all Unions or outside organizations.

Indeed, in many things the office is exclusive in this way. It does not employ men who serve on other papers, and those who work on *The Times* are protected in many ways from outside affiliations. As a curious instance of this feeling, I was shown, in a distant portion of the building, a rather desolate, cheerless-looking room for casual employees or temporary contributors, " persons that we don't want to mix up with our own men, you know."

But all this costly mechanical plant did not make *The Times*. It was before all these things were, which are but its menial equipment. The being of *The Times* is in the brain-power and character of its founder and directors. It is a power and an authority and an influence because of their strength and social force. So high is the personal character of the direction of this paper, so judicial and scholarly its editing, so careful and judicious its expression, that it has, at home and abroad, all the responsibility, standing, and influence of a living and responsible man. It has, in fact, the social position, political weight, and personal character of the best-born, best-educated, and highest-minded man in Britain, and in its circulation, therefore, has just the association, relations, and influence which such a man would have. And it has all this and keeps it just because it is owned and edited by just this class of men.

A marked feature of the place is the large amount of hard work and unremitting attention bestowed unceasingly on *The Times* by its proprietors and editors.

Here is an old paper, perhaps the best established in the world. Every man on it holding any responsible position is an expert in the business. The experience of some of them is hereditary. Every employee on the paper is of the highest grade of scholarship or business training, but the managers and editor are working as hard and closely as if they were starting a new enterprise. Let me give some facts:

All the editorial work is done at night, the editors not coming down at all in the daytime.

Mr. Chenery, the editor, sees the first paper off the press every night.

Mr. McDonald, the managing publisher, sees the whole edition off the press every night.

The paper goes to press at 3.30 A.M., but these men know that from midnight to 3 A.M. is the quarter-deck in action of a morning paper, and they are on it. Mr. Walter's (the main proprietor's) own house is adjoining and runs into *The Times* building; is substantially a part of it. The dwelling of Mr. Delane, the late editor, stood quite near the office, between Printing-House Square and The Temple. He, too, always was on deck at night until the paper went down. Both of their dwellings are far down town; infinitely farther from the social life and rest of London than would be Third and Chestnut from that of Philadelphia. But the night is the life of a morning paper.

The Times having no long railway routes to travel, as all England is covered in a few hours, and running off its edition at the speed of seventy-two thousand an hour, can afford to wait until a later moment before going to press than a paper of Philadelphia or New York. I may say here, the editors of all kinds each have a room to themselves, and work under all the advantages of seclusion and silence. These rooms, nearly every one of

which I visited, are spacious, often about sixteen by
sixteen or twenty feet, and substantially furnished,
have high ceilings, are well ventilated and comfortably
lighted. They have, in fact, something of the comfortable air of a university chamber.

Another marked feature is the watchful economy
practised in the daily management. While all the first-
cost or investment expenses have been on the most liberal and solid scale, the daily running expenses are very
closely guarded. The story of the rags in *The Times*
composing-room, I suppose, is familiar to all interested
in the newspaper business, but I saw other things quite
as remarkable. For instance, I saw in a comparatively
small package the entire waste paper of the previous
day's seventy thousand edition of *The Times*,—*i.e.*, the
sheets of defective paper or paper spoiled on the press,—
and it was not as large as often is the waste of a Philadelphia paper. Per contra, it is to be said the paper is
of better quality and less likely to tear or break. The
same economy—the child of thorough knowledge of
the business—ran through every department of the establishment, editorial and manufacturing. There was
no waste, no splashing, and close saving. The cost of
specials and of travelling expenses is much better worked
down than with us,—indeed, this is so on all English
papers. The composing-room is closely watched,—no
union rules, of course, interfering. Repeat advertisements are not distributed and reset as in one of our
American newspapers, but held as long as the type remains in good order. When I mentioned the custom
of a New York journal on this point to *The Times*
manager, he was unaffectedly astonished, exclaiming,
C'est magnifique mais ce n'est pas la guerre.

The distinguishing characteristic of *The Times* is
solidity.

The editorial department, like everything else of influence and weight in England, rests squarely on the
university, and what that means it takes some insight

into the English life to understand. The paper addresses the leaders and thinkers and statesmen of the world, and it must have the best trained power to speak to them.

The solid paper that it is printed on is equal to book paper in grade. Three of the sixteen-paged numbers of *The Times* go to the pound of printing-paper.

The proof-reading is perfection,—more scholarly and faultless than that of the average American book.

Of the solidity of the manufacturing plant this letter has amply spoken.

But while everything is solid and perfected on *The Times*, while every man on it is trained and tried in his profession and there is no experimenting in the business of the establishment, there is no cessation of mental energies or invention, for these men are veterans, standing ready to hold their paper abreast of the times and to seize first the vantage-ground of any new discoveries that might affect the property or the newspaper life. *The Times*, indeed, has always been a college of invention and discovery in the newspaper world, spending large sums of money in reaching after new processes and improvements in machinery or management. Among the achieved results of its labors in this way are the Walter press and the type-setting machine,—two enduring monuments. I was rather startled to find in this connection that among the problems revolving in the fecund womb of *The Times* office was one to which I have for several years given a good deal of thought and some practical labor,—viz., the publication simultaneously of a great daily paper in a dozen cities. That is certainly the newspaper of the future, and the future may be near at hand.

There is no excitement or nervous hurry in *The Times* building,—nothing, perhaps, that would impress an unskilled visitor,—but the mental atmosphere is very stimulating. In fact, one feels tired and exhausted— that familiar experience of our Centennial Exposition

—after inspecting honestly its plant and workings, so great are the achieved results, so limitless the range of the thousand suggestions which start themselves in reviewing in the sympathetic companionship of its own management the first newspaper office of the world.

In such a visit one's mind constantly tends to running a parallel between the English journal and the American, but such a contrast is fair to neither, and very illusive. In the first place, the functions or uses of the two papers are very different. As *news*papers we undoubtedly excel; but the English papers do the thinking for their communities in a way that our journals do not, and, as a consequence, their conductors have a higher influence and stronger standing in society. Then, the English idea of "news" is something very different from ours, and the Continental conception is something different again from either. And the English journals, like English society, are divided by classes between which there is a wide gulf such as does not exist with us. The leading papers are very strong, dignified, scholarly, and powerful; the lower papers are very low, and the classes do not grade into each other by insensible shades as with us.

In fact, the papers of a country are the outcome and development of its life. What that is they will be. A comparative study of the great papers of the world, say *The Times* of England, *Independence Belge* of Brussels, *Gölos* of St. Petersburg, *Figaro* of Paris, and others of like representative character, will lead one more and more to this conclusion just as far as he gets a real insight to the representative journals themselves, their editorial direction and work, the character of their news and the methods of its presentation, and, finally, the reception and support of the journals by their respective communities.

LONDON.

CHAPTER XXIII.

HISTORIC TAVERNS.

In the Haunts of Shakespeare and Ben Jonson—The English Inn—The Tavern Clubs of the Seventeenth and Eighteenth Centuries—The Somerset Tavern and the Junius Letters—The Rainbow Coffee-House—Doctor Johnson and the Mitre—The Cheshire Cheese—The Cock—History and Politics in the Inn Names of England.

ALL through English literature there come down to us certain names of homelike London inns, which, although familiar by their oft recurrence and the flood of associations which sweep through them,—the memories and recollections of Shakespeare and Ben Jonson, of Goldsmith, Burke, Garrick, Dean Swift, Pope, Sir Joshua Reynolds, Gibbon, bluff old Dr. Johnson, Boswell, Pepys, and a host of worthies,—are yet mostly thought of by us only as pictures, as something utterly gone and passed away, like the silent forum or the desolated mansions of Macænas.

It is, therefore, a pleasant surprise to find many of them here in the flesh, and they are quite worth visiting and picturing, as in addition to their intrinsic interest their existence to-day is thoroughly illustrative of an inside phase of English life. Many of these historic taverns·exist now almost exactly as they did in the days of Dr. Johnson and Goldsmith, less changed in their outward appearance than would be the doctor or the deathless " Vicar" if living now, while in their inner life and traditions they are essentially the same as a century or more ago.

The English tavern never dies. Landlords may come and go, servants grow venerable and pass into local traditions, barmaids bloom and fade into but

toasts and memories, but "the inn" goes on forever.
Heirlooms accumulate on its time-stained walls; corners
and seats grow famous as the men who once claimed
them reveal themselves in history; the *genii loci* gather
with the centuries; but the inn is fresh and young and
warm and cheery forever. I have already mentioned
that at Stratford-on-Avon an inn at which Washington
Irving rested in 1830, I think, and mentioned in his
published letters, still lives on his genial recommendation and deserves it. At Waltham I found an excellent country inn reputed through the kingdom, which
dates from A.D. 1260, an undoubted case of Bonifacial
succession. The Four Swans blazons to-day this ancient
date on its quaint signboard, and confidently appeals to
a respectable ancestry of six centuries as its best claim
to the patronage of the travellers of 1880–1900.

So it is with the London taverns of literature. Some
of them, it is true, have yielded up the ghost under
the inexorable hand of Time, demolished by Boards
of Public Improvement, or reconstructed into gilded
modern meaninglessness by vulgar enterprise, but many
of them yet live, respectable just as they were respectable of yore, and sober and responsible, with the character of centuries to maintain. "The Somerset Tavern,"
the "Cheshire Cheese," the "Rainbow," the "Mitre,"
and the "Cock," every one of which is grandly illustrated in English literature and history, are all here yet,
living and moving and having their being in the daily
life of this our nineteenth century, but bringing down
to us in hourly detail something of the daily life of the
England of two hundred years ago, and perhaps more.

All of these that I have mentioned are found in Fleet
Street and along the Strand, and quite near together.
They all stand now, however, off the street in courts, or
what were once courts, and are reached either through
dark archways or by extremely narrow and modest
little alleys which a stranger would readily pass un-
noticed. Consequently, they are saved from the pro-

fanation of vulgar and ignorant custom. The customers
of these inns have mostly come to them by inheritance
or congenial introduction. These courts were likely at
first gardens, such as stand around the country inn now
in most villages. In time, as the town choked the
fields, they were built up close around to the very
palings of the little garden ; the roses and pansies and
marigolds gave way to flagstones and solid pavement,
and the hard-stone court was thus developed,—the evolution of the city. Carpenters' Court in Philadelphia,
inclosing the Carpenters' Hall, where the initial Continental Congress sat, is a good American illustration of
these still old English courts.

The Somerset Tavern stands out clear in the memory
of every student of constitutional law and English history. Through the humble hands of its barmaid passed
the MSS. of the famous Junius Letters before they
saw the light of print. This seems to us a very in-
secure and fortuitous mode of communication, but it is a
thoroughly traditional English one, and is yet largely
used. At many an English inn I have seen stuck in
a glass behind the bar or placed upright against the
shelf or decanter on the sideboard broad, square letters
addressed in the modern conventional English hand to
" Mr. Harry Chauncey," or " William Henry Howard,
Esqre.," frequenters of the hostelry, who get their home
letters here just as their fathers did in the seventeenth
century. This unconventional post-office is generally
in charge of the barmaid, who is, in fact, an institution
of the place, and the " next friend" of everybody who
comes about it.

The MSS. of the Junius Letters were left at this
Somerset Tavern, addressed to " Mr. Woodfall,
printer," who probably ate his midday meal or spent
his evenings here. His shop, still here, is about three
minutes' walk from the tavern and behind it. It is
now as then a printing-office, and the name boldly

painted on the wall is the same,—Woodfall. The letters were left at the tavern by a boy.

As a picture this inn is the least interesting of those mentioned. The old house is the same, but it has been remodelled throughout within, after the style of a modern hotel, and a drinking-saloon of the ordinary pattern pushed out so as to give a street entrance. Historically it is a mere shell. The old "interior" and the charm of the old life are both gone.

"The Rainbow," No. 15 Fleet Street, is consecrated with the elusive memories of Shakespeare. Here, too, it is said, came Ben Jonson and Beaumont and Fletcher and Donne, and flashed wit and jest and story with the London actors of that long-ago day. The Rainbow, in early history, stood probably in a garden between the Thames and the Strand. The garden possibly became a court; but if so, now the court—gone after the garden—is built solidly over, and the Rainbow, away off the street and enveloped in a solid mass of building, is reached by a long and very narrow passage—a mere right of way—which opens on Fleet Street almost unperceived.

The Rainbow has kept pace with the times, carefully preserving the old features of the place, the old characteristics, and the old life. The comfortable building is the same. The old-fashioned bar is still there with the little office,—for the Rainbow was and is a spacious hostelry,—the two together presided over still by that remarkable young woman who, in the English inn or hotel of average size, does civilly and agreeably and thoroughly the duties of three conspicuous American officials,—the hotel-clerk, the barkeeper, and the book-keeper and cashier. The pleasant fire in the open chimney-place and the shining pewter are still there. The perfect but unpretentious service is the same which Englishmen shared with you two hundred years ago. The heavy spotless linen, the clear-cut glass, are prob-

ably of our own day. Here you get a good modern
London dinner, based, however, on the old English
tradition of two or three plain courses. The wines are
traditionally known and excellent,—solid in body and
in price. Old usages, too, are as far as possible scru-
pulously observed. Your haunch of mutton or great
roast of beef is wheeled up to your table and your cut
taken off in your presence and under your own direction
if you are particular. The custom of this place, as I
saw it, was of a high and most reputable kind, solid
bankers, merchants, and lawyers, apparently doing business in that locality,—the same class of men who for
two hundred years have been using it in midday and
afternoon. In the evening there is probably more
smoke and wine and clinking glasses.

The Rainbow has a further and better-authenticated
historical interest as having been a "coffee-house," a
younger institution in English history than the tavern,
and one that passed at once and largely into literature.
The first house opened in London for the drinking of
this new beverage was in 1650, the second was in 1652,
and was the Rainbow. It figures as a fashionable resort
in the *Spectator*. The drinking of coffee instead of ale or
canary was considered rather a swell thing when it was
first introduced. It was decried by the common people
as effeminate, an affectation of fashion, and a sign of
degeneracy on the part of Englishmen, and the coffee-
houses were denounced by the lower classes, and looked
on very much as our most exclusive club-houses are
now.

Previously to the opening of the coffee-house the
Rainbow seems to have been a book-stand. "At the
Signe of the Rainbow in Fleete Streat, near the Inner
Temple," is an imprint of the early part of the seventeenth century. It is probable that it was in this
connection its name became linked with those of Shakespeare and Ben Jonson.

The Rainbow is an excellent hostelry of this day, as

well as of two hundred years ago, and the American traveller who delights in clothing himself with the wealth of the associations of the past as he travels will serve himself well by putting up here, if he chooses this locality of the town, instead of at the common run of hotels advertised in the guides and time-tables. He will be thoroughly comfortable and well fed, and will see at once an English " interior." He will be inside of a real old English inn, not merely honeycombed in a cell of a mammoth modern caravansary.

The Mitre lives in tradition as the special haunt of Dr. Samuel Johnson and the brilliant group that clusters around his rude, strong person as its central figure, —Burke, Goldsmith, Garrick, Boswell,—and I suppose it was, for you can see at once the reason of it being chosen as a stated rendezvous. It was a case of natural selection. Goldsmith lived immediately back, in Mitre court; Dr. Johnson just across the way, in Bolt court; while Burke had his chambers in the contiguous "Temple," and, I presume, Boswell, too. From the central point of "The Mitre" they could all stagger home at midnight, covering the least possible distance, and with comparative safety. Sir Joshua Reynolds, who perhaps joined them sometimes, on more formal occasions,—for he moved more generally in a society in which Johnson did not go,—lived quite near, first in St. Martin's Lane, and then in Leicester Square, then a very fashionable neighborhood.

The Mitre Tavern is found somewhat off Fleet Street, in Mitre court, a quiet, retired little recess or eddy. In front rolls down from the Strand the troubled current of London life, in the rear the busy waters of the Thames, but the Mitre is as still as a cloister. The suddenness with which in a few feet one can turn, in London, from the surging roar of the noisy, driven streets into absolute stillness is one of the dramatic surprises of the city. Oliver Goldsmith's grave, close by the fa-

mous Norman Round Temple, the altar of the old cru-
sading knights, lies only a few hundred yards from his
homely tavern, in the hush of a country churchyard.
Shut your eyes, and you would almost fancy the fragrance of the fresh grass and English herbs and expect
to hear the birds sing. You look around you and see
not a green blade or tiny flower or a solitary spot where
one might spring,—nothing but stone and crumbling
effigies and tottering buttresses and high gray walls.
Again, out of the thronging precinct of Westminster,
throbbing with the pulses of the Parliament of an empire, you pass in a few steps into the peaceful cloisters
of the Abbey and plunge at once into the Middle Ages.
And so the close of St. Paul's and dozens of places.

In a part of the spacious building, by the way, shut-
ting off the Mitre court from Fleet Street, but fronting
on it, and known as the Mitre property, are found the
London offices of the New York *Herald*, an historical
succession worthy of being noted as something more
than a passing coincidence. As the representative of
the most advanced journalism of the time, *The Herald*
is the legitimate successor of *The Rambler, Spectator*,
and the *Idler*, and occupies, with something of right,
the abandoned tribune of Dr. Samuel Johnson.

In the interior of the Mitre, which evidently stands
now much as it did a century ago, you can readily trace
the outline of the scenes which passing allusions in
literature and tradition have made so famous,—the
dimly-lighted room dedicated by long pre-emption to
private uses, the smoke-laden atmosphere, the brandy
and hot water, the white-clay pipes and tobacco, the
MSS. and current pamphlets, and the long table from
whose head, night after night, the stout old Bohemian
Tory preached ponderous philosophy, or railed at the
Scotch and hurled angry invective against the American
traitors making history at Philadelphia and Lexington.
A bronze bust of Dr. Johnson fills a niche above the
spot where his chair familiarly stood, and placidly re-

gards to-day those nineteenth-century customers of the
Mitre who have curiosity or influence enough to find
their way into the little back bar-room, which is the
arcanum of the house.

It is fair to say that there are several other Mitre
taverns in London which claim the honors and prestige
of those distinguished literary connections, but the
weight of evidence and the argument from localities
incline to the one I am describing, and whose cheer I
have tested.

Contemporary authority of the best kind fixes the
Mitre Tavern of Mitre court, Fleet Street, as the site
of the traditional Johnsonian symposia. I have no
doubt, however, that if the other claimant taverns were
in existence at that time Dr. Johnson and his friends
gave them a visit.

"The Cheshire Cheese," another favorite haunt of
Dr. Johnson, well known in history and literature, is
perhaps the most unchanged of all these taverns, and
gives one the best idea of the life of those old times.
It is very plain, and all the marked features of the old
style are preserved with fidelity. In fact, it is not
preservation, but continuance. I sipped some canary
here for a half-hour one night with a friend distinguished in journalism and politics and deeply versed
in the scholarship of English literature, and spent
some time watching the custom and incident of the
evening, and I am sure that our eyes beheld the very
same sights and objects which of old met the vision of
Burke and Goldsmith and Garrick,—the same men
and the same things. It stands in Wine-Office court,
just across the street and nearly opposite to Mitre
court.

One-half of the large room is fitted up with plain,
bare, wooden tables of the simplest kind of construction, that would seat four to six persons. Each table
stands in a kind of stall, formed by the high, upright

backs of the straight, hard, uncovered seats. The whole looks like the great wooden pews in our old-fashioned churches. The seats are about as uncomfortable as they can be, but the English—as their Parliament House and the church pew (their evolution) attest— have little idea of the luxury of rest. A large open space of sanded floor, with arm-chairs and a small table or two of freer position, complete the room. An open chimney-place, with a burning grate, on which fizzled away a kettle of boiling water, gave a cosey and domestic air to the room. At the right-hand corner of this fireplace stood the chair of Dr. Johnson. Long white earthen pipes, fresh, and some pouches, evidently private, of tobacco, lay on the mantel-shelf. Two good but somewhat smoke-discolored oil paintings of old servants of the inn hung on the walls. Their legend recited that they were contributed as a mark of respect by gentlemen who frequented the inn, and they were dedicated as special heirlooms to pass with the tavern property.

The Cheshire, contrasted with its famous fellows, is "poor but respectable." Everything was extremely plain, simple, and almost coarse, but all was neat, clean, and honest; the quality both of food and wines good for the cost. In this it is, as it has been probably for centuries, thoroughly solid and English. The cheaper inn in England is not a mere dirty and pretentious imitation of a higher class of house. It has its own character and is proud of it, and as far as it goes is solid, good, and honest; and, as a rule, this holds good with other English things than inns, and also with the people.

It was from this tavern one day, when Goldsmith was confined in it by the landlady for his score, and watched by a bailiff outside the door, that Dr. Johnson went out and sold a MS. for him for sixty pounds. The MS. was the " Vicar of Wakefield."

" The Cock," 201 Fleet Street, a tavern of the same

age and general character and uses as the Rainbow or the Mitre, has more modern associations, its sponsor in literature and chiefest treasure being Alfred Tennyson,—

"O plump head-waiter of the Cock!"

The plump head-waiter is still living and on duty, and the junior bar of London assure you that the best "bitter" in the town is to be had in this most reputable hostelry, which bears a diploma from the Poet Laureate,—

"To each his perfect pint of stout."

You sit in old-fashioned stalls, as at the Cheshire Cheese,—the floors are wooden and uncovered, as at all these taverns,—your quarters are rather contracted, but your company eminently respectable. There is some old oak carving over the mantel-piece, and the whole interior is said to be unaltered from the time of James the First. The Cock is nearly opposite the Rainbow, and, like it, imbedded in a conglomerate mass of masonry, representing the resistless encroachments of centuries, and you reach it now only by an inconspicuous alley-way. It is now, too, a retreat. It was to the Cock that Pepys was wont to take Mistress Knipp and give her little dinners, much to the distress of his wife. "Thence to the Cock Alehouse and drank and eat a lobster, and mightily merry;" it was a Mistress Pierce this time, and Pepys faithfully relates the domestic explanations which were necessary to explain these tavern outings, to which he was apparently fonder of treating his neighbors' wives than his own.

The Whyte Harte, where Jack Cade's peasant army disbanded, and in whose court-yard Shakespeare's plays were probably acted, is still an extant house. It was burned down in 1676, but was rebuilt in the old style, wooden balconies and all. It was from these interior wooden balconies that the frequenters of the inn watched the open-air performance below on the rude flag-stoned pavement of the court-yard. It was a rude stage, but a common one, in the simple fashion of those days.

George's Coffee-house, at 213 Fleet Street, was frequented by Shenstone, "who found his warmest welcome at an inn."

The dead centuries take form and flesh and color and grow wonderfully near as you sit in one of these old hostelries and see the life of London flowing through it very much just as it flowed a hundred years ago,— the same walls, the same furniture, the same cheer, the same order and service, and much the same manner of men.

It is a little difficult for us to understand in our day the conspicuous part the tavern played in the lives of men whose names now sound so grandly, and whose forms, swelling to historic proportions, are so imposing. We must bear in mind, however, a number of things. Life was certainly somewhat ruder than it is now, and, again, the inn of those days was relatively higher than it is now. It was certainly much higher than our American conception of a country tavern, which, with its "bar-room" and noise, has nothing in common with the quiet, home-like English inn of to-day,—the inn of Shenstone and Coleridge.

Again, there were no clubs in those days,—none at all in our modern sense, and but few of any kind,—and the tavern was the club of the community. Here men of all kinds met and gathered in circles, according to their several tastes,—sometimes in the private apartments, sometimes in the common room. The "private bar" is now, perhaps, a survival of those usages. Dr. Johnson and his friends frequently, according to tradition, sat in the public room, dominating it both by their numbers and by the power and brilliancy of their conversation. A stranger would probably have been a

little crowded down unless he chanced to have been a
congenial mind. Here came from evening to evening
the young barristers from the adjacent Temple and law
inns, the worthy tradesmen of the neighborhood, who
lived above their shops and banks (the famous "Childs"
bank was close to the Mitre), the writers for the
meagre journals of the day. Perhaps a stranger from
the country counties occasionally dropped in, or per-
chance an adventurous traveller from Penn's far-off
Sylvania or Mary Land. The place was the primitive
"Saturday Night Club" of a century or more ago, in
London, and of a rather humble class.

For these great names, we must remember, were
not in good society at this tavern stage of their existence. Shakespeare was, in early life at least, something
of a vagabond. Ben Jonson was a bricklayer; some
of his work stood very near the Cheshire Cheese.
Later down, Dr. Johnson was to the last a congenial
Bohemian. He was the old man of the party, who
gathered around him young Burke and Garrick and
Goldsmith and other young men, unknown, or who
had just come up from the country to try their fortunes
in famous London town. Boswell was, perhaps, the
nearest to the gentleman of the crowd. The fine gentlemen of London did not come to these taverns, nor
did Burke, likely, and many of the others when they
had made their mark and won fame. Tennyson does
not now frequent the "Cock." These tavern days that
have gone into literature, and by which we know them,
were the days of their youth and poverty and obscurity.

It is a striking reflection on the eternity and immor-
tality of the human side of our existence, and of the
littleness or nothingness of business or fashion or co-
temporary success, that what lives of these men is the
hour they gave to rest and the play of human feeling.
The point at which they dropped their routine toil,
their daily life of publishers and business and briefs
and writs and fees and wages, was the point at which

they touched fame and the common heart of generations and nations yet to come.

A few hundred years ago the tavern was the club and the newspaper of the community. But it was also something more. Public opinion not only was formed at these houses, but passed into tradition and was perpetuated by them. One can read the history of all England to-day in the names of its inns. When our English ancestors wished to honor a cause or a man they wrote their names on a tavern signboard and swung it out to posterity.

Thus, the St. George and the Green Dragon record the familiar mythic legends of our earliest history ; the White Horse was the victorious standard of the Saxons when they invaded England,—the battle-flag of Hengist and Horsa ; the Angel is a mutilated survival of a favorite old sign, the "Salutation of the Angel" to the Blessed Virgin, recalling a time when the *Ave Maria* was the evening song of England ; the Saracen's Head is a record of the crusades ; the Mitre comes down from the old days of Church and State, and the Church first. Even as late as the last century Boswell, writing of the Fleet Street "Mitre," says Dr. Johnson approved the "orthodox High-Church tone of its name." In the "Cross-Keys," which is still a familiar sign in many towns of Pennsylvania, few of us will recognize the crossed keys of St. Peter, but that is just what they are,—the very same sign that may be seen on the front of the great St. Peter's at Rome. The White Swan is the device of Edward of Lancaster and the White Hart of Richard the Second. The humble Blue Pig is a survival of the Blue Boar, the crest of Richard III. The Rose is the badge of the Tudors, and the rose and the portcullis will be found blazoned alike on cathedral and tavern all over England. The Bear is the emblem of the Leicesters, the Antelope of the Bohuns, and, indeed, the family arms of all England are carved and painted over all the land on its inns,—the rude Herald's College of the people. When once one becomes a little familiar with these crests, it is always easy to tell in what part of the country one is by looking at the village inns. This adoption of the family crest as a tavern sign is very natural, as these country inns are generally kept by retired servants of the great families of the place,—a fact which, in turn, accounts largely for their comfort and excellent service.

This political nomenclature of the inns is proof that they filled the office of clubs in our communities. There were no Union League and Tammany clubs to gather up and organize political opinion, but the politicians of every faith did have their special taverns, where the men of each cause could meet, strengthen each other, and propagate their ideas. The old English feeling had its White Horses, the Church party their Cross-Keys and Mitres, the Nationalists their Crowns and King's Heads.

It is solid evidence of the social advance of our land that we have dropped this usage of naming taverns or hotels as an expression either of popular esteem or of political honor. There are a few Washington and Jefferson and Lafayette houses, that have come down from the Revolution, and a scattering Jackson tavern, but the habit about ended with the rude time and life of which Jackson was the last distinguished exponent. We have Lincoln Universities now, but no Lincoln Hotels, and there are no Grant or Sherman or Stanton or Hancock Taverns, although we have just passed the throes of a civil war.

The tavern is no longer a factor in American society.

LONDON.

SCOTLAND.

CHAPTER XXIV.

ENTERING SCOTLAND.

THE SCOTCH BLOOD IN THE UNITED STATES—STRONG STAMP OF THE SCOTCH CHARACTER ON OUR NATION—THE ROMAN CATHOLIC AND PRESBYTERIAN CLANS—MARGARET WILSON.

As you travel northward from the heated and murky fogs of London a change comes gradually over the scene. The smiling harvests of grain and corn give way to slatternly-looking turnip-fields; the trains and coaches advertise to run on " lawful days;" the children by the wayside grow barelegged and barefooted; green hills and meadows are replaced by brown and red ranges, whose infinite lines, stretching out one beyond the other, sweep out against the sky; the hats of the men diminish to rimless cloth caps; the petticoats of the women shorten and thicken; bright shocks of flaming red and fair blond yellow hair vary the rather neutral sameness of the English head; the naked knees of the men emerge; whisky redolent of peat becomes the regular station refreshment, taken with a serious and solemn air; old ladies appear in the cars reading " The Christian Herald," and seeming to find great satisfaction therein; the faces at each passing railway station become more and more reflective, lined, and joyless; red heather, black-footed Cheviot sheep, tartan plaids and half-military kilts greet your eye for the first time on their native heath : you are in Scotland.

I have made a pretty thorough tour of this country, which has done so much for our land, and which is itself so crowded with incident in the history of freedom. Starting from Edinboro', I have travelled by the great

Highland Railway—the backbone of Scotland—to Inverness, the capital of the Highland region; thence downward by the scenic Caledonian chain of lakes,—the Rhine of Scotland; thence from Oban out to Iona and through the Hebrides and back; thence across-country by stage and rail to Aberdeen; thence back again by a lower route to Stirling; and then by the classic Lochs Lomond and Katrine into Glasgow, and from there again into Argyllshire.

It is interesting and instructive to see how thoroughly the Scotch mind has stamped itself on our country, on our manners, speech, and habit of thought. Although the pure Scotch migration to the United States has been comparatively small as weighed, for instance, against the German or Irish, it has impressed its force more definitely and lastingly than either. It almost seems to be the substratum of our national character.

In Scotland one meets all the time customs, usages, tones, inflections of speech, incidents, and little things of all kinds which recall the interior country life of our own land, and show how thoroughly we have been cradled in these hills. It is from these cold, bracing mountains that we get, first and last, and best of all, that unquestionable love of liberty and sense of personal independence which has made us what we are,—which may be uncomfortable or unpleasant in some of its manifestations and inimical to vast undertakings, but which is the salt of true political and social advancement. Scotland is a land of small undertakings, of small businesses, and of small fortunes, because the Scotchman is not a ready tool or executive instrument for the uses of others; but then he is free,—the head of his own little home, the master of his own movements.

While we have secured this strong bone and sinew of the Scotchman as the framework of our new national life, we have clothed it with a much more generous body. We are essentially eclectic and able to take and assimilate the best of all other nations, peoples, and races. Now, the Scot is a Celt, and the Celtic blood by itself has never attained very great things. It is, however, the very best flux to mix with other bloods. Even crossed with itself it improves. The Scotch-Irishman is a much stronger man and race than either the Scotch or the Irish by itself. It is through this fortunate blending that it affects particularly our national character.

The old distinctive characteristics linger longest in the individual. My own blood in one line comes directly from Argyllshire, and I was interested, of course, in studying the characteristics of this especial people, whom I do not think the lapse of the one hundred and eighty years since I left them have much changed. Manners, of course, have softened, ideas have broadened and liberalized, but the old essential fibre and characteristics are there yet. It is said of this people that " they never forget a benefit or forgive a wrong," and this rule of blood, whatever may be thought of it as a rule of morals, is admirably adapted to perpetuate race instincts and individuality.

And this is certainly so here. The friendships and hatreds, the loyalties and enmities, of hundreds of years ago are all extant forces yet and part of the common life of the people. Often the remembrance is but sentimental, as in the feeling for the Stuarts, but it is there still in that form. The Scotch of this day sing and play the old Jacobite songs with a spirit and feeling and power of emotion that in Celtic Paris would surely evoke a revolution.

Families, although they do not murder each other any more, retain the old traditions of feuds *in piam memoriam,* and the old political divisions are still perpetuated in a variance of faith and Church allegiance. The old loyalist Scottish clans are Roman Catholic yet, —staunch and devoted and true. The Protestant ascendency in Church and State has not swerved them, and in many parts of Western Scotland you still find small districts—the clan territories of the old Stuart lieges—

P

which are thoroughly Roman Catholic, high and low, poor and rich, for they are all of one family,—the chief and his followers.

These little sections seem quite an anachronism in stern Presbyterian Scotland, but they serve to show the undying tenacity with which the Scotch blood follows a friend or fights a foe.

On a little steamer on one of the Highland lakes I fell in with a young Roman Catholic priest,—a gentleman of education and of gentle birth,—an Englishman, but on duty in the snows of Scotland.

I told him that " I thought he looked rather cold up here, and was afraid he was sowing seed on pretty rocky soil."

He replied, laughing, " that faith would remove even Scotch mountains."

Another priest, of more years and with his enthusiasm tempered by larger experience, summed up the situation more practically with the candid statement that " it takes more money to convert a Scotchman than he is worth."

When we got to the end of our journey the young priest showed me, with a good deal of pride, quite a noble pile of buildings which were going up as a monastery and school, and to which he was attached as one of the brothers. I did not think it right to dampen his religious ardor and hope, even if I had had the heart to do so, but I am very sure that he will not get a Scotch boy in his school save from the old Royalist clans, who are already Catholic, and would remain so without schools or care. As he was an English gentleman, however, his own faith was probably a matter of descent and family pride,—I mean in the good sense of that word.

It is very curious, indeed, to observe how all along here a man's religion, or his Church relations rather, follow as an obligation to certain family traditions or to a family's position. Even the head of a great house does not presume to lead it or dictate to it in this matter. He simply accepts the situation to which he has been born, respects the collective sense of his tribe or clan, and puts himself at the head of it. Said a very large Scottish landowner of high rank to me one day walking over his estates : " Two-thirds of my tenants go to the kirk, and I think, therefore, I ought to go, too. Don't you think so ?" I unqualifiedly said " Yes."

This gentleman's taste, in all probability, would have led him to prefer personally the highly-finished and artistic service of the Established Church of England, but duty, as the head of an old historical family, led him every Sunday to the bare walls of the little village kirk. Now the country kirk of Scotland is something " bluer" than the old-fashioned Seceder congregations of Pennsylvania in early days, — harder benches, longer psalms, just as disjointed tunes, longer prayers, longer Scripture readings and more of them, and a sermon utterly unrestrained by any sense of time.

For the same reason, many of the Scotch nobility are Liberals in politics because their family and clan have been Whigs in past times.

Scotland, politically, belongs to the " Liberal" party, lords and people naturally inclining that way by reason of their blood and history. It flows naturally from their almost fierce sense of independence, which shows itself everywhere.

I have often talked with very humble members of the " Free Kirk of Scotland," the people's Church.

" Is not the difference between you and the Established Church only one of church government ?"

" No ; it is something a great deal deeper than a question of government when the queen or the government can send down a minister to us against our will."

" Would such a thing ever be done ? Has it ever been done ?"

" I don't know. It is enough that it can be done. We will never allow such an authority. It is not right."

And the feeling with which such words were always uttered showed that it was a real matter of principle and belief, for which the Scotch peasant or croftsman of to-day would sacrifice comfort and advancement, or fight, or, if needs be, die, just as he has done again and again for generations.

The memory of these humble martyrs or affiants for the truth is cherished everywhere in Scotland in memorials often touching in their rudeness. Janet Geddes, who drove the Established Church of England out of Scotland with a three-legged stool, is remembered with a good deal of warmth in the popular heart. In this town of Stirling, the central feature of the fine park cemetery which lies grandly on a castellated hill, is a monument to Margaret Wilson, whose story is a household legend in Presbyterian America, and whose death is one of the most wonderful of martyrdoms. This young girl in her teens, tied to a stake in the Solway tide, died bravely and calmly rather than acknowledge the Episcopal supremacy as a governing power in the Church. She surely did not understand the full scope and grasp of the question,—could not by reason of her years and want of education. She only knew that the Stuarts were forcing it on Scotland, that it was a threat to the liberty of her country and a danger to freedom, and she willingly gave her testimony against it, even unto death.

The monument which commemorates this grand fact and this great national characteristic is, I regret to say, in the very worst of taste. Some marble figures are inclosed in a glass case on a stone pedestal. The colorless glass is bordered with strips of the same material in deep blue and light green, while the whole body of the monument is plastered over with texts and multitudinous Scripture references too bulky for any particular appositeness. This when the whole Bible and all history is ringing with single grand words that fit the occasion !

The main inscription begins with a gush about "the virgin martyr of the ocean wave," and ends with the information that she chose to die " rather than own to Erastian usurpation." This heroic grave is one of the worst instances of the Scotch want of taste and uncouth tendency to obtrude theological technicalities everywhere.

While I was looking at this tomb three young Scotch soldiers with kilts were slowly working out the cumbersome inscription, and one, familiar with the story, was trying to tell it to his comrades, apparently recruits. He naturally found some difficulty in this, as " Erastianism" was not a garrison word. He struggled bravely with the trouble, however, and summed up the whole matter by asserting that she was right anyhow, and died because she was. And with a hearty oath the two new boys confirmed the statement—" Yes, and —— ————, she was." And the story and its lesson went rudely down to another generation.

I noticed the entire evening I spent in this old graveyard that this grave was surrounded by humble, plain people, reading its barbarous inscription sorrowfully, and honoring in respectful silence the martyr. Being Scotch, they could not lay a flower on the tomb or kneel in prayer at the grave, as French women or men or Italians would have done at the shrine of their saint; but they were taking it all in, nevertheless. Margaret Wilson died in 1685. Her grave and her memory are as green as if the relentless waters had gone over her young body only yesterday. They are *the facts* of Stirling remembered in the common heart before all the deeds of the hundred chieftains who have fought around this citadel and made it the central point of Scottish history. Her grave lies in sight of twelve battle-fields of Scotland, but she is the greatest warrior of all.

We owe much to Scotland, but this legacy of personal independence and determination, this unwillingness ever to yield, ever to submit to a wrong, ever to compromise, is her best and greatest gift.

STIRLING, SCOTLAND.

CHAPTER XXV.

SCOTTISH NOTES.

THE LOWER SIDE OF SCOTCH LIFE—SCOTCH WHISKEY AND ITS REIGN—THE HARDNESS OF SCOTCH POVERTY—HIGHER SCOTLAND—SCOTCH THRIFT—SCOTCH NEWSPAPERS—SCOTCH HOTELS—RURAL SCOTLAND GOING FORWARD—THE THEOLOGICAL SCOT.

LET me throw together some observations on certain phases of Scotch life and some Scotch institutions as seen in a pretty extended tour of six weeks over all the kingdom. It is a land of sharp contrasts and salient features, the old and the new existing yet side by side, sometimes fusing but sometimes standing apart.

I had heard much of the bad condition of the lowest classes in Scotland, but was hardly prepared for the appalling truth as exhibited in the streets of their larger towns. There is a misery and degradation here which is perhaps unequalled in any civilized land. There is a dirtiness that I think surpasses the filth of Italy, and it is unrelieved by bright eyes and smiling faces and beautiful forms and graceful movement. Scotch poverty is simple, sullen, vicious-looking degradation. Instead of song and music and pleasing lying, the Scotch lazzaroni are given over to the beastly vices of drunkenness and prostitution, which are fearfully prevalent and whose results are clearly visible on the lower streets of every town of any size in Scotland. Begging, too, is prevalent, and the squalid mendicant, with brutal slouch and rum-burnt visage, stoutly curses and swears at you when you refuse him.

So degraded and unclean are the herds who swarm even good streets that in Glasgow, for instance, after night, I have left the pavement and taken the middle of the street rather than run the risk of being brushed against by beings reeking with the marks and odors of disease, filth, and uncleanness.

But the saddest feature of Scotch degradation is the way it seems to harden the individual and drive out everything that is softening or gentle or relieving in human nature. The faces of the poor are pinched, meagre, calculating; their voices hardened and harsh; their tones angry and impatient; their eyes sullen and vicious. Everything of light and hope is gone even from the little children; all is ungracious and unlovely. The little things start life with this dreadful heritage. Some days since, on the outskirts of Stirling, being in some doubt at the forks of a road, I asked my way of a little girl who, with bare legs, uncombed hair, ill clad, and no bonnet, was swinging alone on the fence, and gave her a few pennies. The child seemed confused at being kindly spoken to, and I fear the gift was an entirely new revelation. After recovering from the surprise the little thing, with a look of wonder still on her face, and extremely grateful, began to explain the way, offering to go along, and very anxious to do something in return. It was painful to see her evident attempt to speak in pleasant, gentle tones and the inexorable failure. Her voice was already hard and set, and against her will and to her deep mortification and distress the words would only come out in the old harsh, ungracious, ugly tones,—the only sounds she knew.

Again, this morning in Glasgow, in one of the low streets leading to the great cathedral, which now stands in a dismal and dirty quarter of the town, I heard a squalid, degraded woman, who was carrying a wretched, meagre babe in her arms, both half naked, address it thus: "Shet up your cryin', will you? I'll choke you ded and brek your hed against the wall. Whust now!"

The woman was not drunk.   It was her own child, and
the words, although spoken in a rude and rigid tone,
were not unkindly meant.   They were, in fact, a
Glasgow lullaby, the "sounds from home" of this
quarter.

  Much of this utter lowness and degradation of Scotch
poverty comes from the frightful habits of drinking
which prevail among the poorer classes of men and
women, but this will not account for it all, for the
drinking itself is, in part, only a result of the degradation.   The Scotch people are making an earnest and
desperate fight against intemperance all over Scotland,
and well they may, for a more shocking exhibition of
national drunkenness, I suppose, is not to be seen the
world over than that which protrudes itself everywhere
on the traveller in this land.   You see drunken men
reeling in the streets, and, women, too, in broad day-
light, and often quite early in the morning.   And it is
not confined to what might be called the lowest classes.
I frequently see venerable-looking old men with white
hair, and whose countenances indicate that they have
led fairly intelligent and industrious lives, staggering
blindly, or, as is more often the case, attempting to
hold a drunken argument with any passer-by they can
fasten.   To-day I saw in this town of Glasgow a very
respectable-looking young woman of about thirty, very
neatly and quite well dressed, apparently the wife of a
well-to-do mechanic, reeling for half a square in midday through a crowded street.   Old women, gray-haired
and bent, their faces bloated and burnt flaming red with
years of drink, meet you everywhere, and are to an
American stranger the marked and most repulsive
feature of the begging class.

  It is needless to say that drinking-shops and small
retail shops of liquor "not to be drunk on the premises,"
abound in all the streets.   Their number is something
ghastly; they are low, dirty, dingy, and squalid, and
in front of them hang around all day squads of vicious,

criminal-looking young men with that villainous slouch and sullen gait so well known in the police and quarter sessions courts.

The drunkenness of Scotland, like its poverty, is something hideous, unrelieved by a single softening feature, even in the way of glamour. There is no attempt to mask it or excuse it or commend it. The gin-shops are not palaces of gas and light, as in other lands, to allure and tempt. They are foul dens, which, in most countries, would repel and disgust, but here they are sought. The Scotch drunkard evidently drinks to be drunk, shamelessly, from the lowest and most brutish of purposes; and it is this which makes his case so hopeless, and so warmly enlists one's sympathies for the men and women who are fighting the up-hill battle for the redemption of their land from its greatest curse.

The cause or causes of the wretched and debased condition of the poorest classes of Scotland is an interesting and very difficult social problem, covering a vast range of inquiry, into which there is not time to go in a letter, or perhaps even in a single book. I aim here only to present the facts, not to account for them. Independent of its interest as a study in social science, this question has a deeper importance for us Americans, as there is a strong family likeness between our two civilizations, or conditions of society. Scotland, as we are, is a land of churches and Bibles; a land of schools and newspapers and common education; a land of reading and a general diffusion of average and commonplace information (even the drunken Scotchman is argumentative and ludicrously hortatory); a land "Liberal" in its politics, and the Liberal party here stands to the Tory as the Republican does to the Democratic in our country, the party of advanced ideas and progress; yet, in one of the first and fundamental trusts of the Church and of the State—the care of the poor—it has made a complete and terrible failure. I believe, deliberately, that it is far better to-day, better for soul and body, to be an Italian peasant, ignorant, in rags, trodden under in politics, image worshipping, and lying, if you will, but happy, full of the human emotions, with grace of body and movement, able to sing and to speak kindly and lovingly, with the power to enjoy the beautiful in nature and art, than to endure the brutal degradation of Scotch poverty as seen in her cities,—a degradation which breeds coarse and debasing vices, crushes the light out of the eyes of its victim, self-respect from his face, and hope from his soul; which not only leaves him nothing to enjoy, but takes away even the power of enjoyment; which robs even childhood of its birthright of love and careless pleasure.

But let us turn to something more pleasant.

Rural Scotland presents a pleasant contrast to the towns and cities. If there is suffering there at least it is not concentrated. Drink and its attendant evils there are. Country Scotland, with its new granite farmhouses, looks solid, comfortable, and prosperous. Indeed, large portions of it look like a new country, so thoroughly has rebuilding or new building been going on within the present generation. The old thatched mud cottage, rudely built and very humble in appearance, is giving way to neat new small buildings of solid masonry, the gray granite looking not merely thrifty, but quite substantial. In many places you see the old quarters still standing, abandoned, perhaps, or used as temporary shelter for cattle or animals, and the cluster of new buildings, trim and comfortable, rising from some better located site on the farm. This is the Scotland that is going forward.

There is a curious, raw-boned, theological cast to the Scotch popular mind which crops out everywhere, and the disposition to obtrude theological technicalities into common life is very marked, and sometimes produces odd effects. I have mentioned how the dramatic martyrdom of Margaret Wilson is blanketed on her

tomb as the death of one " who would not own to Erastianism." On the gravestones in the cemeteries, instead
of a salient clause or effective word from Scripture,
are copious references to passages simply by chapter and
verse, thus: Deut., c. xxxv., v., vi., or 1st Kings, c.
xxiii., v., xviii. Often a stone is fairly covered over
with these references, in part to verses and sometimes
to whole chapters at once. A favorite mortuary inscription is a very positive " Covenant" reference im-
plying indirectly that this stone evidences a completed
contract, and sometimes with a kind of baldness that
rather jars on one's sense of delicacy, to say nothing
of reverence. To get the proper effect of an average
Scotch cemetery one must go through it Bible in hand,
and then it would be several days' good work. Again,
in a country Scotch church, when the minister announces
his text, reads it, and alleges that it comes from a certain chapter and verse, the whole congregation picks
up its Bibles and refers to the place to verify their pastor's word or satisfy themselves individually on some
other point.

In the bookstores and stalls there is a distinctly theological coloring to the volumes and prints exposed for
sale. In Edinburgh, for instance, they do not seem to
have gotten over the Reformation yet, and are still
fighting it out with polemic treatises and newspaper
articles. I have noticed also one or two popular peri-
odicals which announce a weekly " prophetic" article as
among their attractions. In Glasgow I passed a poor
blind beggar, who stood by the wayside begging in a
rather common and crowded street, and to attract attention was laboriously reading word by word by touch
out of a Bible printed in raised letters. He was tugging
away in the dust and dirt at a chapter from the Epistle
to the Hebrews by way of catching the popular ear.

There is one institution in Glasgow worthy of note,—
the Great Western Cooking Depot. This famed phil-
anthropic institution is something like the excellent

Philadelphia model coffee-houses,—its object is to supply cheap food, well cooked, for the poorer classes. It does supply a good plain breakfast, substantial enough for a hungry workingman, at a cost of six cents of our money, and a dinner, soup, meat, potatoes, and pudding, for nine cents. Now, Glasgow is a city which imports food from us, grain, pork, canned meats, live cattle, dead cattle, dead sheep, tallow, lard, butter, and cheese, and many other articles. If Glasgow, importing from us, can feed workmen at fifteen cents a day, what ought we not to do?

Indeed, in every way the prices of common things seem to be very cheap in Glasgow, and from a superficial look at the streets, I should say that the workman making a dollar a day here was as well off as one making say one dollar and forty cents a day in Philadelphia. I cannot speak as to rents, and base my estimates only on food and clothing.

The Scotch newspapers resemble the American nearer than do those of any other country. In the Scotch towns the multiplicity of papers and of readers is quite marked in contrast with England. You see it the moment you cross the line. Towns like Glasgow and Edinburgh, and even much smaller places, all have their crop of dailies, morning and afternoon.

On the other hand, these papers tend continually to average and commonplace level, and do not have the weight or influence of the English. They are "snappy" and smart rather than thoughtful and strong, of the terrier rather than the bull-dog style.

The reason for this similarity of the Scotch and American paper is a similarity of social structure. There is in Scotland the same vast mass of crude half-education diffused through all the community as with us.

I am not speaking in condemnation of the Scotch papers. They answer a very useful and respectable purpose. They supply the kind of food that is wanted for a large lower- and middle-class population of superficial intelligence which is numerous in Scotland. In England there is no such class, the lower strata of society being very ignorant, and not readers of anything. The papers of England, therefore, appeal solely to the upper and governing class, which is a class of education, the class of the universities, of prestige of birth, of wide experience of men and travel. They are written by that class for their own class. The Scotch papers necessarily, with some few prominent exceptions, are not.

Scotland shares with us the fortune or misfortune of leading in the drift of modern civilization, which in its present stage is a movement towards the apotheosis of the average and commonplace. Good men of both parties, the Liberal and Conservative, tell me that there is a growing tendency the same way in politics,—*i.e.*, to the evolution of commonplace men, the men who make an impression on the crude and half-educated mind.

The Scotch hotels of the better kind—the large and newly-built houses—are more like the American ones than any I have found anywhere in Britain or on the Continent. They have our spacious public provision for comfort nowhere found on the same scale in European hostelries, generous wash- and retiring-rooms, billiard-rooms, writing-rooms, reading-rooms, public parlors. While they thus approach the virtues of our system, they also share its vices,—defective service, hurry, and a mechanical routine.

It is worthy of remark that Scotland, from which we took so much one or two centuries ago, is now taking back from us the new institutions which we have developed under our new condition.

I close with a Scottish note of to-day, which illustrates how thoroughly the old Scottish spirit of integrity, the spirit which willingly sacrifices itself for right, the spirit which utterly refuses compromise or half-way settlement with wrong, is alive and burning in Scotland to-day. It is one of the principles of the United Presbyterian Church not to accept money for sacred uses from unclean hands. They decline to take for God, and as His agent or minister, money that, as far as they can see, has not been honestly made.

When the great Glasgow Bank failure took place here some of the directors were members of the United Presbyterian congregations of the city, and one or more of them were large givers,—almost the support, I am told, of their particular churches. When, by the judgment of the civil courts, these directors were declared to have been guilty of systematic fraud for some years back, their liberal donations were all returned to them, although it more than crippled the congregations who did it.

This fact was told me not by any of themselves, but by a learned clergyman of the Established Church of Scotland, who bore honorable testimony to their devotion to principle, and their own profession.

GLASGOW, SCOTLAND.

CHAPTER XXVI.

TOWARDS THE HEBRIDES.

THE HIGHLANDS AND THE WEST COAST OF SCOTLAND—HOME OF THE CLAN CAMERON—PRESBYTERIAN SCOTLAND OF TO-DAY—A SABBATH EVE IN ARGYLESHIRE—A KIRK FAIR—THE APPLES OF OBAN—AT A SCOTCH KIRK—THE TROOPER CLAVERHOUSE IN SILK ATTIRE.

I STARTED for " Iona's holy fane" from Inverness, intending to give a summer's month to the bracing storms and sheeted vapors of the Hebrides, seeking health and youth in the shadowy land of Ossianic tradition, that land whose song and legend are born in one with Highland blood, and which the descendant of Celtic ancestry visits, not as a strange country, but as one going back into the mists and vague eternity of childhood. It is wonderful how human existence, through these nebulous vapors and the cloudy sweep of storm and wind and spray, seems to almost tone and merge itself into the infinite life of the universe. Clouds here encircle the form of our fathers, their voices ride on the winds, and the whole spirit and imagery of Ossian is as real as the rocks and the waves.

Inverness is a central part of departure on the northeast coast of Scotland, although almost in the centre of the northern counties, the great Moray Firth here breaking into the shore for a hundred miles or more. It is a kind of base of supplies for the tourist undertaking a campaign against Hebridian fogs and tempests, —a place where you can buy stout hunters' shoes and sailors' headgear and waterproof and wondrous Scotch tweeds with yawning flaps and capotes.

From this point the best road to the west coast lies through the Caledonian canal or water-way, cutting right through the Highlands, and which is formed by connecting several long, narrow lakes by short canals. It is something like the old military water-line in provincial times of our own country, formed by Lake George and Lake Champlain. This route is known as the Rhine of Scotland, and is always thronged with summer travel. It is wild and beautiful, every hill replete with legend and incident, and to a Scotch-American every town and name recalling home associations.

Along here is the home of the Camerons, who are pretty thick in their own section,—a thin-faced, active, aggressive race, lords and liegemen, with a common type of feature, like that of the distinguished Pennsylvanian family. I also found the Buchanan family face a very marked type through Scotland. You see on this route a modest stone shaft, known as the Royal Charlie.

It is a granite pillar which marks the exact spot where, in 1745, the Clan Cameron, seven hundred strong, raised the standard of Prince Charles Edward,—an act which was more plucky ·than long-headed, as seen in our light, but which might have been a fair political risk one hundred and fifty years ago. Here, also, they show you the dramatic wreck of the house of Lochiel, —the very spot on which the last of the name knowingly accepted death and ruin and the extinction of his family name to save his honor and make good his pledged word by a desperate and hopeless conflict.

Of a weather-beaten, kilted Highlander, who stood near me at the time, I asked,—

" Have you many Camerons about here now?"

" Yes ; a good many."

" Do they go much into politics over here ?"

" Well," laughing, " we think a good deal of them in this part, and one of them is our member of Parliament just now."

" What's his name ?"

" Donald."

In London I looked over the Parliamentary roll, and sure enough the member for Inverness is Donald Cameron. This Donald Cameron is a Conservative, while the general political drift of Scotland is strongly Liberal. But the individual Scotchman, as I have before said, never forgets a friend or a foe, and the Clan Cameron of 1879 is staunch to the tradition of 1745.

You end the Caledonia Canal route at Oban, "the Charing-Cross of the Highlands," where you make ready to take the seas. It is a remote Scottish village, situated beautifully on a bay, the inland extremity of which its streets encircle very prettily. I got here on Saturday and remained over Sunday, engaging passage in a coasting vessel for Monday to Iona. I was anxious to have an interior view of modern Scotch village-life, and very glad of the opportunity to see it here in its simplicity, away from the influences of any "great house."

We have a conventional idea in many parts of our country that in Scotland the Sabbath begins on Saturday evening at sunset; that the aged cotter at that time gets out a ponderous family Bible, collects a cleanly-clad, serious family around him in a picturesque tableau, and begins the devotions, which continue, with slight changes, for twenty-four hours. I had long since given up the "cleanly-clad" touch of this picture, but I held on to the main design.

I dined in Oban at six o'clock, and went out on to the streets of the little village at about eight. It was wet and drizzling, of course, but the children of Hebridian mists pay not the least attention to such light discomforts as rain and mud and darkness. Through the leaden, vapory sheets of mist and the obscured clouds I could see the faint lights all around the circular line of the street and hear coming out of the dense fogs the sounds of lively music at different points. Pushing out along the water front, all the shops were open, the windows lighted, the streets full of young men and women. Bagpipes were going in one place, and farther off a horn and violin band were playing "Over the River to Charlie" with vim and spirit enough to have started a French barricade. Some young couples strolled with locked hands rather aimlessly from one centre of sound to another, steering expertly between the squads of more or less drunken men. Generally the town was *en fête*, although after the heavy northern fashion. Barring the drunkenness, with the fishermen and the sailors and the shepherds and the girls and the music and dreamy lights on the sea, you might have fancied yourself in Italy had there only been a little moonlight and a few Madonnas.

At the far end of the village stood a rude, frame school-house, decked with limp, wet flags, illuminated through the chinks and cracks of the planks, and from

which the music of fiddles rang merrily Scotch reels and
the stirring old rebel Jacobite airs.   To all appearances
things had gone so far that the Covenanter youths of
Scotland were having a Saturday-evening dance just like
the simple peasantry of Bretagne.   It was not quite so
bad, however.   Entering, there was no dancing or provision for it.   It was only a kirk-fair.   The village
kirk-house was in need of repairs.   The repairs were
being made, and the maids and matrons of the kirk
were raising or helping to raise the funds.

The scene within was quite animated, and had the
ordinary features of a country church-fair in our land.
The girls, being Scotch, were pretty and lithe and bright;
the articles of sale as utterly impracticable and valueless
as if they had been exposed on aristocratic tables in a
city charitable bazaar.   There were some matters of
detail a little different from our customs.   The refresh-
ment-table, for instance, had a generous supply of wines
and certain gurgling-necked bottles, which, from their
familiar national character, I presumed to contain
whiskey.   It would be unfair, however, to look on this
incident as we would on whiskey sold at an American
fair or bazaar.   Its use is the general habit and custom
of the country, and there was no unseemly drinking or
noise in the hall.   Had you gone into the private house
of the clergyman of the kirk whiskey would probably
have been offered you as a common mark of hospitality,
and I observe that Americans, when in Scotland, however
they may moralize at home on the evil consequences,
generally take the whiskey.   It is an incident of the
Ossianic mists, and has been so from the times of the
Vikings.

The prominent and popular feature of the kirk-fair,
however, was the lottery.   Everything was offered in
chances and shares, and raffling was evidently the most
successful "ways and means" of the enterprise.   My
companion and myself, assailed on every side, earnestly
remonstrated with these enthusiastic young Covenanters,

representing that we had been raised as Presbyterians, and could not conscientiously indulge in such practices, even they bring the fair temptation; further, that in the far-off provinces from which we came all lotteries were criminal offences; that we could not break the laws of our own country, even in a foreign land, and especially so near to the Sabbath-day. But the young women, as usual, were not amenable to reason. There were half a dozen young male Americans of Puritan training and descent at this village fair that evening, and I fear they all ate of the apples of Oban.

Next morning, however, Scotland was herself again, and the Sabbath morning broke upon an Oban as stiff and silent and decorous as if there never had been a violin or a kirk lottery or a Saturday evening *fête* within its precincts.

I went to the Established Kirk, where the old faith and the old worship hold the fort, strong and safe. It was in the main a very familiar scene. The faces were just the same as you would see to-day in any country Presbyterian congregation in the Cumberland Valley. You could pick them all out, elders and deacons, and the men that expected in time to be,—the stern, rigid faces that accepted nothing on trust, and weighed every sentence of their preacher in the balances. The sandy features were perhaps in the predominance, but there was a strong infusion of the old " black Celt." Even here the old race characteristics assert their individuality and refuse, closed up together for centuries, to blend or mingle. Everything was intensely Scotch in look and sound and custom. A McDougall was the chief man of the congregation, the head of the clan on the bay; an unregenerate young Campbell, who kicked lustily, was forcibly baptized during the services. I sat in the pew of Duncan McGregor. The " local color" was all an artist could pray for.

The services of the morning did not differ materially from those of an ordinary Presbyterian or Congrega-

tional congregation in our land, save in the quantity.
I give the order: singing of a hymn, prayer, reading
from the Old Testament, singing of a hymn, reading
from the New Testament, singing of a paraphrase, the
sermon, prayer, singing-of a hymn, baptism, singing,
benediction,—twelve separate exercises. The baptismal
services, which was an interpolation in the order of the
day, possibly added something.

There were some differences in the service and scene
between the old Presbyterian usages of our land worth
noting. The church building was in cruciform shape,
and the saints and angels looked down on you from
rich stained-glass windows. The hymnal was a modern
collection of two hundred good hymns, many of them
those in use in our congregational bodies. The Two
Hundredth, however, was the ordinary English version
of the *Te Deum Laudamus,* closing before the Kyrie
Eleison clauses. The Apostles' Creed and the Lord's
Prayer were introduced in the extempore prayers, and
the Creed again in the baptismal service. The choir
sat in the apse.

The preacher was a young man, with red hair parted
in the middle, whiskers, and a moustache. He wore
the black gown and bands and a purple university
hood. He preached a vigorous and able sermon, Old
Testament throughout in tone and imagery and train
of thought. His delivery was demonstrative and sten-
torian, markedly in contrast with the quieter and more
scholarly tone of the English pulpit. It was, however,
well suited to the place and the audience, to whom, I
think, his effort—scholarly and thoughtful in its way
—was very acceptable. He fired a shot at the pope,
of course.

I think there are many just such congregations in
Pennsylvania to-day, and all through the country, even
out in Alamosa, where, three years ago, I saw the
atoms of organization arranging themselves,—just such
bodies of people listening to just the same doctrines

enforced by just the same argument. The preacher
here was, as his hood betokened, a university man,
and his sermon gave evidence of greater scholarship
and force of trained thought than the average American pulpit effort. The stained-glass windows and the
definite ecclesiastical architecture showed a broader
sense of power and a larger freedom of culture than
holds in many of our villages, but they have come in
the cities and will spread down.

Time was when the saint in the window and the
cross of nave and transept was a political emblem,
much more than anything else, and the sturdy Presbyterians of Scotland were perfectly right and logical in
tearing them down. We are reaping the fruits in our
civil freedom and religious liberty now. But the time
is past when such things are to be feared, and there is
no reason now why all the beauties of art and established æsthetic principles should not adorn the temples
of any faith in our land or England.

These changes in the æsthetic development of the
form and plan of worship have not weakened the vigor
or power of the faith. The old soul was there in the
kirk of Oban just as resolute and true, and a good deal
broader, and, consequently, stronger than a hundred
years ago.

It was very interesting to me to trace these simili-
tudes or divergencies between the Presbyterianism of
the old land and of our own. They mark and record
the mental and historical development of the two
peoples. There are Presbyterian corners of our land
that are to-day perhaps more Scotch than Scotland.
We brought over the Scotland of 1700, and hold it
there unchanged still, while the General Kirk of Scotland, changing with history and life of a people, has
gone on to something different. On the other hand,
there are spots in Scotland which have never changed
for a hundred years, and will not for a hundred years
to come. The general religious life of both countries

is, however, I think, under somewhat different conditions, moving forward much alike, and with very equal step. The Presbyterianism of our country and of Scotland to-day is much alike, although it is very different from what it was either here or there a generation ago. But the race holds together in its march.

I may mention here a little incident of interest in this connection which I came across during the summer at another point in Scotland. In the drawing-room of the Earl of Strathmore at Glamis Castle there hangs with the family portraits a full-length painting of the famous dragoon Claverhouse, whose name was once such a terror to the Covenanters, and whose memory yet is recalled only with unuttered imprecations by their descendants. Much to my surprise, thinking of him only from the conventional conception of Covenanter tradition, I found the portrait of an entirely different manner of man. He was sumptuously dressed in a wealth of rich colored silk that in our time would be effeminate, and his form and carriage bore the unmistakable impress of a man accustomed to good society and trained to its amenities. His face was refined, pleasing, and almost gentle,—very much the same face as those which gather at the castle to-day, with ladies and flowers and music, for luncheon and lawn-tennis. In this mild, amiable, gentlemanly officer it was impossible to see the rough and merciless mosstrooper of Scottish tradition. There is nothing at all vindictive or cruel in the face, and little that is indicative of force. I can only infer that Claverhouse was not the motive-power of his own action. He was probably an amiable kind of man, receptive to the impressions of a stronger will, the ready tool of a firmer hand and more cunning head,—one of those men who are good for instruments and to work under and for others. He had even, possibly, a strong religious tendency, which exercised itself in following ignorantly and unthinkingly the instructions of any ecclesiastical authority to which he professed fealty. I do not mean to say that he had ecclesiastical instruction for his savage forays on the Scotch conventicles, but he was probably taught by his Church, after the unchristian spirit of those times, that it was doing God service to crush out heresy by violence, and he was honest enough to practise what others only preached.

Let us be thankful for our gentler and better times, which enable us to think of this man without anger, and to judge him dispassionately.

At this point of Oban I left the mainland for Iona, which, with its traditions, as the early seat of our Christianity, the northern ark, when all the world was in chaos under the flood which swept away the Roman Empire and civilization, and Staffa, with its grand "temple not made with human hands," and Ulva's isle, I must leave for another paper.

OBAN, SCOTLAND.

CHAPTER XXVII.

IONA.

THE AURORAL LIGHT OF NORTHERN CHRISTIANITY—A STORM OFF THE WEST COAST OF SCOTLAND—A RUDE WESTMINSTER —THE FUNERAL CORTEGE OF FORGOTTEN LINES OF KINGS— MACBETH'S GRAVE—A DOVE OF THE CHURCH—THE STORY OF ST. COLUMBA—THE IRISH SAINTS MILITANT OF OLD—IN GÆLIC LAND—THE HOME OF THE MACLEANS—IONA OF TO- DAY—THE HOLY PLACE OF DRUID, PAGAN, CHRISTIAN— SAILING THE SUMMER SEAS OF SCOTTISH ROMANCE—FIN- GAL'S CAVE, THE CATHEDRAL OF THE SEAS—LORD ULLIN'S DAUGHTER—THE HIGHLANDERS OF THE SEA.

> "The Hebrid Isles
> Placed far amid the melancholy main."

MONDAY morning broke with a fresh, whistling gale sweeping along the west coast of Scotland, but as that is rather the rule and calm weather the exception on the Hebridean seas, our coaster boldly put off from the black, slippery dock at Oban, and headed for the lowering and leaden skies. After a rough passage, with no worse disaster than the relentless ravages of the *mal de mer*, which took down a goodly proportion of the passenger-list, the staunch little craft anchored off a reef some distance out from the inhospitable shores of the Holy Island, and we visitors were taken aground in some little fisherman's boats. The coaster, which, in summer-time, makes daily trips to Iona, lands its passengers in this wise, and after driving them through the main ruins of the island, much as you might conduct a herd of cattle, sails away again, all in an hour. This seems to have been the unsatisfactory routine from the time of Wordsworth, if I read aright the complaint of some of his verses. Taking heed from the poet's disappointment, my brother and myself concluded to lay over the night in a humble inn which is found on the island, and, after a day spent at leisure among the Druidic and Christian remains, to take a fisherman's boat and meet the coasting vessel at some farther point out on its next day's trip, when it was to come down from the north instead of up from the south.

This plan, which is the only one by which one can see the place intelligently, and which I would adopt again were I visiting Iona another time, in this instance cost us four days' solitary imprisonment on the little island. The storm grew only more furious as night came on, and the next day seemed only to increase in rage. Until Thursday not a vessel ever came in sight, or even put out from Scotland, as we afterwards learned, and not a fisherman dare leave the shore. All the time the entire seas around were lashed with foam, ceaselessly breaking and charging on the giant rocks and deadly reefs with demoniac fury. Sometimes the angry waters seemed forced through clefts or caverns in the rocks, and would shoot up into the air columns of foam and spray apparently several hundreds of feet high. It

was a supremely magnificent spectacle, and it moved
all day long and all night to the rhythmic thunders of
the mighty surges rumbling awful basses away below
the range of the human scale.   During the second day
the torn and mutilated body of a little boy was washed
ashore, utterly unrecognizable and unknown.   From
the clothing and other indications the fishermen believed it to be some shepherd lad from one of the
neighboring islands, snatched from the earth by the
angry sea in one of its frenzied inroads.

The venerable religious and race associations which
centre in Iona are familiar to the educated world.   It
was, stretching back into remote ages whose antiquity
cannot now be told, holy ground,—a kind of Mecca, or
Jerusalem, or Rome, for the savage clans of our forefathers who rode the northern seas.   Scandinavian, Pict,
Scot, Irish, Celt, Gael, revered its soil, worshipped at
its altars, and buried their great in its consecrated earth.
Dr. Johnson calls it "this awful ground."   During the
sixth century, when the world was breaking up in the
convulsive dissolution of the Roman Empire, this little
isle held the light of Christianity and civilization for
the new race that was coming on to the scene.   It was,
undoubtedly, a rude faith and a very meagre civilization, but it held the spark, such as it was, and kept the
flame alive.

Perhaps the most touching, certainly the most impressive, of all the remains of Iona are its rude, kingly
graves.   In the universal wreck and plunder which
marked the savage warfare of our Norse ancestors, all
peoples seem to have respected "the Blessed Isle," as
it was reverentially called, and the bones of the great
and the good were carried there from afar, that they
might be safe from spoliation, and await in peace and
under holy guard the morning of the resurrection.

Tradition says that for centuries the kings of France,
and Ireland, and Scotland, and Norway, and of far
isles were buried here.   Here, also, were brought the

bishops and lordly abbots of legendary memory. The cemetery of these royal tombs is shown, and the traces of many graves are clearly visible. They lie in long rows, many of them under monumental slabs of an enduring slate, rudely etched with crosses, croziers, and shields and swords and Runic symbols. These slate tombstones have a hard, polished surface, and seem almost imperishable, and much of the etching is bold and spirited. A great Runic cross stretches its protecting arms over this sacred enclosure. It is evident that there has been some restoration in the arrangement of the graves of this yard, and some of the royal tablets are certainly over the wrong bodies; but the general fact of the long sanctity of the spot and its kingly occupancy is undoubted and established. It is the rude Westminster of the unrecorded history of our race.

This was the burying-place, also, of the Lords of the Isles, sung by Sir Walter Scott. Here, too, Macbeth is buried and his murdered sovereign.

Rosse.—" Where is Duncan's body ?"
Macduff.—" Carried to Colmekill;
　　　The sacred storehouse of his predecessors,
　　　And guardian of their bones."

I should have stated before that the ancient name of Iona—the name of mediæval legend and history— is I-Columb-Kill, the island of St. Columba of the Church.

By the aid of a rude monkish chart or map preserved on the island, and giving the contour of the shore in its historic days, my brother and myself traced the whole outline of the land, and found the tiny bay or cove which tradition asserts to have been the landing-place of these sad processions. It is a narrow, rock-walled entrance of several hundred feet, terminating in a few yards of smooth, sandy shore covered with white and richly-colored pebbles worn almost purely round by the endless wash of the waves. I

hear yet the grating rattle of these sounding stones
ceaselessly rolling alone for centuries. In good weather
small row-boats might land here with comparative
safety and in decent quiet. Once on land, a level and
sheltered stretch of ground affords an appropriate spot
for a temporary halt and any preliminary services.
This favored landing is, however, on the opposite shore
of the island from the cemetery and ecclesiastical buildings,—the cathedral, convent, and consecrated ground,
—and in a diagonal direction. They bore, therefore,
the bodies of their kings in stately procession a distance
of some two miles or more, and over the mountain
range, which is crossed by a moderate pass, through
which an imperfect road now winds.

It was from this far shore of the island that came
the precious green stones, which, in the Middle Ages,
properly consecrated and blessed, circulated all over
Europe as holy amulets.

Our enforced confinement on the island, although
involuntary, was a pleasant and gainful episode. Four
days of the storms of the Scottish seas are a substantial
investment in the way of health, and in no other way
could we have so entered into the life and spirit of the
place. Shut out from the world, its solemn traditions
came slowly back out of the ages, and were part of the
hour and moment.

With this time at our disposal we traced out the
whole plan of the primitive ecclesiastical establishment
as it stood in the eleventh century, and probably in the
sixth; for the later, or restoration, buildings seem to
have been faithfully erected on the site of the ancient
sanctuaries built by St. Columba and his disciples, and
destroyed by the pagan Danes, A.D. 807, when the
whole island was pillaged, the inhabitants slain, the
priests sacrificed, and every stone razed to the ground.

Of St. Columba, whose name is the savor of this
spot, and whose work gave it a place in history, it is
difficult to speak truthfully at this time without con-

veying an erroneous and damaging impression, the
lights of his age and ours are so different. He comes
down, of course, in the tradition of the Church, endowed with all the Christian graces; a priest burning
with love; the "Dove of the Church," as his legendary
name tells; a worker of miracles; a teacher of civilization; and the legend always closes with the hal-
lowing shades of a venerated death-bed, when, full of
years and honor, and in the odor of sanctity, the saint
went up in peace and joy to meet his God. These are
the shades, and this the coloring of the picture drawn
in the convent and mellowed by time and the softening
distance of ages.

Viewed nearer, the lines are much harsher and less
romantic. We now know St. Columba to have been a
saint militant of the most aggressive and pugnacious
kind, for whom even Ireland was too gentle and peaceful a land. We know that his record there was one of
strife and trouble, and that he finally left it by the
advice of his ecclesiastical superior. Even when he
had settled Iona, reared his triumphant crosses on its soil,
erected his convent and set his matin and vesper bells
a-ringing over its waves, his life then was probably
nearer that of our Indian frontier than of a modern
missionary. He had foes within and without; wars
with the pagan clans of the North seas and with preda-
tory monks of his own faith, eager as he for conquest
and adventure. On one occasion some Irish saints of
a rival order, having landed, gained a footing in Iona,
and built their convent and chapel on the far shore of
the island; the dove-like Columba, after some inef-
fective controversies, moved in force, with a detach-
ment of his saints, against the invading brethren, drove
them out, and razed to the ground the offending sanctuary, "as was the law in such cases," gravely annotates
the faithful chronicler. Every trace of this fated
mission is now gone, but from the old chart one can
exactly locate its site, which is, in all respects save a

commanding sweep for its tower and bells over the seas, better than that of St. Columba's. Again, the simple biographer and disciple: "Now a question arose between St. Columba and St. Comgar concerning a church near Coleraine," and it, too, was finally decided by a pitched battle between the fraternities of these pious leaders.

I found on this lonely island an old monkish chronicle, written in rude, mediæval Latin, of the life and adventures of St. Columba, extremely interesting and picturesque when read on the spot. Of course, one now can hardly believe in the accuracy or literal truth of much of it, but, like Pompeiian frescoes or Middle-Age tapestries, the whole gave a wonderfully vivid and life-like picture of the daily existence of the time,—the habits of the saints, the atmosphere of simple credulity and childish ignorance in which they habitually moved and thought. Everything was rude and humble and primitive, their surroundings and accommodations of the very simplest and most limited kind.

St. Columba worked miracles daily and endlessly and on the very slightest provocation, but they were all of the rudest and most humble incident,—exorcising the devil out of a milk-pail carried by one of the brothers, holding on a wooden wheel on a cart without a linch-pin, or protecting the working brethren from the cold and snows. The little road from the brothers' house and stables to the church—hardly five hundred yards long, and now marked at its angles with a fine Runic cross, the reverent offering of later centuries— was a perfect theatre of spiritual manifestations, the angels dividing daily its poor and meagre accommodations with the brethren. Jacob's glittering ladder was hardly so grand a roadway. It was a condition of life and thought we can hardly understand, and perhaps cannot do justice to at all. The cold, rude rocks of this barren islet, with their ruder people, were a theatre of the warmest fervency of faith and devotion. This place was, for these simple, half-barbarian Christians, the very gates of heaven, and they lived from year to year in a kind of sluggish, arctic ecstasis.

But this we do know of the heroic saint whose force and fervency of character has thrown his name out of dark ages far into the light and brilliancy of future ones: he was a man of his time and a historic leader. However rude some things may sound to us now, he had all the education and advantages of his period,— the education of the schools, of the monastery, of travel, and, I think, of arms. He was also a man of good birth, and had the power which always comes from high social relations and experience. He was qualified for his great work and the time in which he did it. His labors were given, not to his own advantage, but for his fellows, and his name still lives.

In the very darkest of the Dark Ages, about A.D. 563, Columba, an Irish monk of noble blood, left Ireland, and, sailing northward, sought an unknown island and founded there a monastic home. He brought with him, tradition says, twelve disciples, brother-monks, and his avowed mission was the conversion to Christianity of the Northern pagan kings and the spread of civilization among their tribes. He did convert first Connall, king of the Dalriads, a name even that is lost now. Successively he brought under the standard of the cross the heathen Picts and the Scots, and the savage clans of the Orkneys and even of far-off Iceland. From this little seat of learning and faith the auroral lights of Northern Christianity were shed in this early century even thus far out toward our own unknown continent.

The force of faith and love which St. Columba had centred in this aggressive mission projected itself far out for hundreds and hundreds of years, and its memory will never die now so long as Christianity endures. Columba himself died before the century was out. He had entered, by human acclamation, the goodly fellowship of the saints long before death came, and the legend of his departure, as told in the simple Latin of the old chronicle, is a very beautiful and touching story. For three years he had prayed God without ceasing for release, and at last, advised in the night-time that his prayer was granted, he repaired at once, unattended, through the inclement blasts and snow of a boreal winter, to the simple stone altar which had been his life-work and whose future was to be so great, and there, in the act of prayer, ascended to heaven. His body was immediately enshrined in this holy place; the saint was beneath the altar.

For two hundred years the fires of faith burned brightly in Iona, illuminating the northern horizon. During the chaos of Europe this little island was the lamp of the world. It kept alive in its slender flame learning and civilization and Christianity. At last, but not until a new civilization was emerging in Europe from the chaos of the old, its flame, too, was extinguished in a dramatic tragedy. After hopeless struggles, from time to time, with the Scandinavian pagans, long years of fluctuating vicissitudes, of pillages, of escape, of plunderings, of martyrdoms, in 807 the Danes swept the island with ferocious vengeance, destroyed every vestige of building, murdered or carried off the defenceless population, and offered up the priests of Christianity on the triumphant altars of Odin. Then there was night in Iona.

Generations after, when quieter times came, Iona was repeopled by Christian converts, her fanes rebuilt, her altars re-established. It was then she became famous as the remembered cradle of British Christianity. It was then that her very soil came to bear the flavor of sanctity, and that the kings of warring tribes respected it as a common sepulchre. It is the ruins of these times that we now see, some of them as late, probably, as the thirteenth century,—that wonderful epoch of cathedral-building all over Europe. It is from this period that come the impressive monolithic crosses, the slate and granite tombs with kingly helmets and lordly mitres,—the emblems of princely abbots at a time in British history when the abbot was a far more important and powerful personage than is the bishop of this age.

The Iona of to-day is a straggling fisherman's hamlet of a dozen or so houses, with a few more huts for shepherds at solitary points over the island. Everything is rude, and, like the island, meagre, poor, and scanty. The houses are low, but built of tremendous thickness of walls, to stand the constant sweep of the wind and the periodic break of tempests. These poor, rude dwellings are covered with thatch, and the thatch secured by a strong network of rope extending over the entire roof, and held to its place by large, heavy bowlders fastened to the ends.

Inside the houses everything is simple and primitive: stone flags for floors, and sometimes only mud; a peg or two for the nets and fishing-tackle, a plain stool, some humble kitchen utensils, are generally all the furniture. The cleaning up seems to be done by the ducks and pigs, which have the freedom of the house.

So small and confined is the settlement, and the life of the island so much in common, that the animals seem to have lost their fear of mankind, and move around like citizens conscious of their "equal rights." Even the dogs which ran out to meet us in the village and over the bare, heathered hills never plunged out angrily, but came forward for the first time with wagging tails, friendly bark, and every demonstration of pleasure, glad to greet a new form.

There is no coal on the island and no wood, the barren hills growing only heather, gorse, and nettles. This alone adds fearfully to the poverty of a place that is cold and wet nearly all the year round. I make this note September 2d, and we are having fire every day, and all day, in our rooms, and outside the poor farmers complain of the lateness of the season. Buttercups, too, are blooming now—September—instead of May, as with us.

This island, three miles long by one to two wide, has an area of two thousand acres, only six hundred of which are capable of cultivation. It yields to its owner, the Duke of Argyll, a rental of four hundred pounds,—just a dollar an acre for all the land, good and bad. At least one-half of it is rock, and none of it would be tilled at all by the average American farmer, who would not consider life worth living in its wet sands.

When we remember that we can buy in Kansas or Colorado the best wheat-lands in the world at less per acre than the rental for one year of a bleak Scotch sand shore, inaccessible and inclement, we can judge how much better is the lot of the poor man with us than here.

Nevertheless, the place has charms of its own for men of this race. The family we are staying with came here five years ago as a matter of choice, and I made the acquaintance of a Scotch stranger on the landing who afterwards told me he came here many summers from the love of the place.

The language of the island is Gaelic, and the people speak it in a thick, guttural tone, and with a shy, half-alarmed manner that prevents your even getting at all the real sounds. Seeing no one at all save some tourists for a few weeks in the year, the children run around like young savages, barelegged and barefooted, and with thick, black horse-hair falling from their heads and over their faces, like our Indians. There is no beauty among them, either of face or form. Life is too hard. Little children with hard, unlovely faces follow you on a trot over sharp stones or through coarse wet grass, dirty, unkempt, and almost unclad, to sell their meagre treasures of shells or pebbles.

The little girls we saw wore commonly a short petticoat, not reaching to their knees, and that generally partly torn away by exercise and long use. The color of this garment was indiscernible; the color of their skin was a dark, ruddy red, almost that of our savage. Although the ground of this island is hard and stony, the winds sharp and cutting, and the soil productive of generous crops of thistles, nettles, and thorny plants, its inhabitants go about with bare feet and legs with impunity, less protected even than the sheep or pigs.

There is no corn-mill in Iona, and the scanty crop of grain is carried over to an adjoining island to be ground. When this support fails by reason of continued storms or absence of the men fishing, resort is had to the "quern," or hand-mill, the same as mentioned in the Bible. There are two of these primitive mills on the island.

Iona is the home of the Macleans, a stalwart tribe well known in Scotch-Irish America. A few generations ago every soul on the island bore this name, but with the dying out of the clan system this has disappeared, and there are several varieties of family names in Iona to-day,—all pure Scotch, however.

The ruins of Iona as they stand to-day are very moderate and modest compared with those of other centres of attraction in this way,—the falling walls of the old cathedral, in which you can still trace transept, nave, and the usual chapels, the convent, the consecrated burial-ground of the kings, another cemetery immediately around the church, the unique crosses at these different points, and the staunch, towering campanile from whose open windows the Christian bells hundreds of years ago rang out over the fierce Northern seas. The interest of these modest remains is not in themselves, but in the vast body of associations which they call up and marshal in lengthening hosts that extend back through centuries.

In the middle of the island are found some Druidic

remains of traditional interest. These are not seen at all by the visitor who trusts himself to the one-hour tour of the vessel's guide, as they are not on the routine programme, their distance being too great from the landing. Before the times of St. Columba, Iona was a famed centre of Druid worship, and the traces of the familiar contour of a Druidic holy of holies are yet visible to patient search,—the central mound and the circle of stones, the seats of the angels. We discovered their location after a good deal of labor, for much of it is covered with the drift of a thousand years; but, once ascertained, you can quite definitely locate the tumuli and understand their former relations and uses. The central mound is quite a hill,—a sharp, green knob of uniform curve.

Later researches, it is claimed, prove that these stone circles all over England were not, as is popularly supposed, built by the Druids, who were Celts, but are the work of a far anterior race,—the men of the Stone Age. The Stone Age came to an end in Europe about two thousand years before the birth of Christ. Its shortest duration is estimated at a term of two thousand years. This calculation would place the erection of these primitive temples, say, about three thousand to four thousand years before the Christian era. Other chronologies of the Stone Age would place it still farther back.

Iona is one of those remarkable spots which, from prehistoric times, seem always to have been held as sacred localities,—points where God came in contact with the world, and where He was worshipped and revealed without regard to creed or chronology of Church speaking "in divers manners in times past." In spite of the rudeness and simplicity of its modern face, of the meagreness of its remains, of its bleak and forbidding location, it is well worth visiting and study. Few theatres of human history are more impressive. It is one of " the places of the earth." It is a splendid page in the militant history of Christianity. There the

bloody altars of Thor and Odin have smoked, tended by
our Northern ancestors.   There God at sundry times
in the twilight of the ages spake to our Druid fathers.

On Thursday, when the winds were calmed and the
angry ocean had quieted down to comparative reason,
we hired a fisherman's sail-boat, and, with a pair of
small but sinewy Gaelic seamen at the oars, pulled off
for a cruise among the neighboring islands to explore
the classic seas of school-boy legend and memory.
Our morning's destination was Staffa, with its wondrous
columnar formation ; our hope, that we might be able
to enter with our little boat the surging portal of the
grand nave of Fingal's solemn cave.   Every wave
this morning was crested with associations and story,
—behind, the campanile of Iona, with Oronsay and
Colonsay, twin islets of saints and mediæval miracles
and sacred tradition ; ahead, the frowning masses of
Mull, the famous stronghold of the Lords of the Isles,
and "Ulva dark" and the broader lands of the Lords
of Ullin.

> 'Oh! I'm the chief of Ulva's isle,
> And this Lord Ullin's daughter.''

We skirted the shores of the tragic escapade, and
sailed over the spot where the "waters wild" went over
the fated lovers.

Fingal's Cave, with its strange basaltic columns, its
curiously ecclesiastical effect of Gothic roof, pillared
nave, and choir of thundering surges, with its dim
religious lights of green and purple and gold reflected
from the waves below, is a most impressive and unique
sight, but it hardly deserves its relative rank among
the wonders of the world gotten from our crude geog-
raphies, written at a time when the modern world was
unexplored, when America and Australia and Africa
and the great table-lands of India and Central Asia
were unknown.

This picturesquely imposing cavern is a great cleft in the primeval rock, two hundred and twenty-two feet long, forty-two feet wide at the entrance, and in height sixty-six feet at mean tide. The bottom is always a flood of roaring water. The sides are nearly parallel, and rise up perpendicularly, closing away up in a vaulted roof. They are not plain walls, however, but solid masses of pentagonal and hexagonal columns of wonderful symmetry, and many of them monoliths. They present the effect of innumerable corridors of columns,—aisles and aisles of them. As a picture, the cave most resembles the mighty nave of some great cathedral arched in the foundation-rock. Into this grand church the waves, with a noise far below the range of any human organ, grander and deeper, surge forever forward and backward, singing unto each other in eternal antiphone.

Staffa's Island is but a little bit of grass and soil, just enough to respectably cover the basaltic ribs of its great wonder. You can climb to the top of it and get a grand view of the entrance of the cave from over-head. You can climb around the side over hundreds of broken pillars washed down during the ages by the ceaseless violence of the waves, and enter the cavern, finding your way from one rude pedestal to another along the edge of the columnar wall until you reach about where the altar would be in a church, and here the spot where the thunderous surges break against the massive rock foundation of the island with a noise mightier than that of the waves, and with deep resounding bass echoes that never die away.

Unfortunately, the condition of the waters was such that the Gaelic fishermen would not attempt to put their boats in, and we had to be content with this kind of view of the cave, landing on the rear of the island and clambering around over the slippery bases denuded of their shafts.

This rude Gaelic land of the Argyllshire coast and

the Hebrides is known as part of the Highlands of Scotland, although, of course, it is on the level of the sea. Highland is now an ethnological rather than a topographical distinction. The people here, too, rude and meagre as is their life, have all the fierce spirit of freedom and the strong self-respect of the clans of the hills. They prove their blood. The only man, woman, or child in all Europe who ever refused a gratuity at my hands was a little Highland boy of Iona, and I put it on record to the credit of his land. One who has travelled in Europe will know how much it means.

The Scotch have certainly acquired all the world over an unfortunate low-grade reputation for being "canny," and canny, in the way it has come to be applied as their national characteristic, means only selfishness and cunning. It certainly, however, does not come from the Highlands. The Highlanders to-day are mostly poor, and they always have been so. They are not a money-making or a money-loving race, and they have always been 'ready to sacrifice their property for their principles, their reputation, or their vengeance.

Iona.

NORTHERN ITALY.

263

CHAPTER XXVIII.

VENICE.

St. Mark's Grand Grave—Gracious Influences of the
Sea—A City Set as a Stage Scene—Street Life in
Venice—The Lares and Penates—Church and State—
The Sacred Birds of Venice—Venus Aphrodite.

VENICE blazons as her city arms the Lion of St.
Mark,—the winged beast of the Apocalypse,—and the
selection is appropriate, for in a certain sense the city
herself is apocalyptic in being like to no other place on
the face of the earth or in the waters under.

This lovely city, that floats like a picture on the sea,
is in fact and in spirit the splendid mausoleum and
monument of St. Mark, the humble shoemaker-evan-
gelist. They bore his remains here one thousand years
ago from Alexandria, and his worship, the honor of his
name, the glory of his legends, became at once the civic
life of the town. It was a quaint, mediæval habit, suggestive of the historic life of those times, for all the
cities to take to themselves some saint as a local deity,
and their existence thenceforth took life and color from
his name and spirit,—was bound up with it. The city
and the saint went on together when once their fortunes
were thus joined. He prayed for his people in heaven
above, and sometimes came down with spear and shield
to fight their battles below. In return they glorified
his name on earth.

St. Mark sleeps his final rest in the grand cathedral
which bears his name and fronts the magnificent piazza
San Marco. The cathedral is one of the great churches
of the world; the piazza is unique in brilliancy and

splendor and pleasing life,—a picture that, perhaps, no other place can offer. The whole city to-day is crested and carved with the images and legends of its patron saint. His lion crouches and sleeps and rears and flies on column and porch and palace and church and pavement, and the loyal artists of Venice have faithfully wrestled on canvas and in stone with the kindred beasts of the Apocalypse to do him company. St. Mark is fortunate in his apotheosis. His is the city of poetry and splendor.

Just think what Venice gained over the cities of the earth when she was taken under the protection of the sea.

No grimy locomotive, breathing smoke and soot, can ever go groaning and shrieking through the streets, leaving a trail of black dirt in its offensive rear.

No wagons rattle and rumble, no horses clatter with dissonant noise, over her streets and stones. Her sounds are all of music.

Washed forever by the slowly falling and rising waters, there is no dust in her streets or on her marble-floored squares: one leaves windows up as safely as in country groves.

Being no dust, there is comparatively little dirt. Even rough work hardly soils the clothes of the toilers, and her gondoliers—the stable-smelling hackmen and cabbies of other towns—do their work to song and in bright, clean linen.

Finally, the cool sea-breezes forever sweep her stones, and there are freshness and bracing salt air in-doors and out from morning till night, and till morning again.

It is these softening and gracious influences of the sea on its daily life and being that give to Venice her peculiar charm and distinctive beauty. It has been my good fortune to see the city in the splendor of pure sunshine by day and under the mellowing softness of moonlight by night. It is a picture—a dream—something one feels too lovely for the prosaic life of mortal men.

The life of all Venice converges and centres in the grand Square of St. Mark's, and in the evening,—it seems then a perpetual scene set for the representation of some grand spectacular opera, only that the properties, instead of being pasteboard, are the finest palaces and architecture in the world, and the music is human life and pleasure. You think the curtain *must* fall. It does fall towards midnight, but it rises again next evening.

Imagine a vast space say in length from the Union League House to the Academy of Music in Philadelphia, and in width perhaps three times that of Broad Street, paved smooth with marble and blocks of trachyte, shut off from the noise of wheels or horses. On the one side the floating domes of the great Byzantine cathedral and its grand arched fronts, with their golden mosaics lustrous in the night-time, on the other the famous Palace of the Doges, wasteful in magnificence; the towering shaft of the Campanile, with its colonnades of white arches fluttering in the air, and up to whose very pinnacle you could ride a horse, so wonderful is the engineering of the interior ascent; the three tall red mast-like spires draped with the colors of Italy,—columns so ancient and strange that tradition can hardly tell their origin,—and all around a continuous chain of stately marble palaces, stained with age and time. Imagine all this, and you have the faint outlines of St. Mark's piazza. Around three sides of the square there runs a covered archway lined with shops and supported by a corridor of columns, on which rest the fronts of the palaces. In the evening these shops are brilliantly lighted, a glittering line of fire encircling the piazza. In front of this corridor of columns, when the falling shadows draw towards sunset, hundreds and hundreds of chairs and little tables are set out before the cafés. At these tables citizens and strangers gather in families and parties to eat ices, sip coffee, *eau sucré*, light wines, drink beer, and smoke,

children, women, old men, young, middle-aged, and all.
In fact, Venice does its visiting at these tables, and one
can pick out the belles of the city at a glance by the dark,
bee-like clusters which surround their mothers' tables.

On to this grand stage the whole city throws itself
every evening,—all classes, all ages, all the world of
Venice.   A large military band of many pieces takes
its station in the centre, and there is good music all
evening for everybody,—free.   In the mean while, those
people not sitting, or who do not come to thus enjoy
themselves, promenade under the brilliant corridors or
down and up the long aisles formed by the masses of
chairs, filing, passing, returning, all the evening.
If you sit in the front rows of chairs you can see, thus
at rest, the whole life of the city stream before you, and
it is this scene which is so irresistibly operatic in its
effect,—the whole town moving and living for an evening to music.

All classes mingle and jostle, and in such a setting the
sailors of all climes, gathered here from East and West,—
sufficiently rough and prosaic elsewhere, here all washed
and clean,—look like wandering tenors, disguised noblemen, lost heirs.   There pass before you Venetian
dames stately in black-lace veils, and demoiselles with
wondrous blond hair and the open slipper dear to the
heart of feminine Italy; swarthy Lascars in white cotton; water-girls "with rings on their fingers;" flower-
girls (somewhat mature,—another theatrical touch);
merchants of the Orient all-brilliant in slashed scarlet
robes and fez caps; gay gondoliers in blue and white;
the *dé bonnair* officers of Italy's army in blue and
gold; naval officers from the ships in port of all nations; Greeks with their clear-cut cameo-like profiles;
beggars happy for the evening and avoiding "shop"
for the moment as a point of honor; the handsome men
of Italy, lithe, active, dark; travellers of all tongues
and lands, labelled with red books; and the ever-present
British female tourist with stout boots,—all the world.

This is the every-night opera of Venice,—music, flowers, costumes, statuary, columns, arcaded vistas, moonlights, star, legended trophies, golden paintings. Do we wonder that, with all this luxury as an inheritance and education, the Venetian of to-day has grown somewhat indolent, and takes his exercise in sleeping in a gondola or inhaling the fragrance of a flower in some arched and grated palace window?

This brilliant panorama lasts till about midnight. At ten o'clock the shops begin to take in their glittering wares and close ; at half-past ten o'clock the music ceases, and the ladies then begin to leave. Shortly after eleven o'clock the place is abandoned to gentlemen. Then the waiters begin to stack up the chairs, the lights one by one go out, and shortly the dark shadows of the palaces fall on an empty square.

Venice goes to bed as early as Philadelphia or Boston or New York, and earlier than Paris or London, notwithstanding all the fascinations of sea-air and moonlight that might well tempt her to stay up all night. It is a commonplace of travellers, and sometimes even of the guide-book, yet to assert that the Venetians turn night into day. There was a time long ago when they did, when the city was powerful and rich, and was lived in and ruled by a class of wealthy and luxurious nobles. Then all this grand square was lined with gambling-rooms and houses of pleasure, and men ate and drank and played and lost their fortunes, and the whole place was a blaze of light until morning.

Now, Venice, like the rest of Italy, is poor, and her habits are simple. One of the most marked features of an evening on the piazza is the innocence and extreme simplicity of the pleasures of this people. They will spend a whole evening with almost no expenditure of money or movement. A tiny cup of coffee will last a gentleman the whole evening, and he appears to be always busy in its consumption. A very small saucer of ice or a small glass of water colored by a drop of

anisette does the same service for a lady. A single
"pony" glass of beer and a two-cent cigar employ an
officer of the army for an hour or two. I do not think
the average visitor at these cafés spends ten cents a
night. For this he has a table and chair all the evening, a cool seat, excellent music, the view of the promenade, the opportunity to make calls or receive visits,
rest, conversation, moonlight, flowers.

The flower-girls are a feature and a part of the en-
tertainment. They circulate among the chairs with a
basket of flowers, giving one to each gentleman for his
button-hole and to the ladies with him. This is a gift
offered with all the coquetry and compliment in the
vender's power. The stranger, who is addressed in
French, returns his gift at once in money. The Venetians do not, but at intervals, and not at the tables, give
their flower-friend some gift. She, in return, regularly
decorates them every evening with a little bouquet.

There is music all the evening, but, with the national
inclination to inaction, no dancing. I have remarked
this all over Italy. On the fête-days and in the evenings in the villages there is always good instrumental
music, but the people never dance, only move gently
around from place to place, half walking, half standing.

Venice's great impression is its street life,—so brilliant, so highly colored, so unlike that of any other
city. The commonplace shows of the guide-books are
flat and disappointing,—the prisons, dungeons, Bridge
of Sighs, and so forth. The school-girl glamour thrown
over these places is mainly traceable, I suppose, to
Byron's sentimental verse.

The daily picture of all Venice, however, is something of which one never tires, and which changes ever
with the hour. Gondola life is something deliciously
dreamy and luxurious in the soft light of day or under
the sheen of moon and starlight. Let dark night come
and rain, however, and these long, narrow, deep, black
boats, seen mysteriously from the faint point of light

on their prow, take to themselves the likeness of floating coffins steered by the shades. The effect is indescribably sepulchral. You seem to be alone in the waters of Hades among the spirits. The gondolas are all of a funereal black,—painted black, carved in black, with black draperies over the dark cabin. Many centuries ago a Venetian law ordered this pattern and color, for a good reason of that time. The laws in Venice do not change, and the gondolas are all black and ghostly to this day.

The streets are very narrow and blaze with light. Their narrowness—sometimes not over three feet—makes a very little light serve to brilliantly illuminate them, and the jets in the shop windows, kept open till late at night, keep them bright and blazing almost without the out-door lamps. Through them the people surge in constant streams,—all nations, all classes, all colors. You study the world, but even the Venetians themselves present some strong contrasts, for they in time are made up of the blood of many people. One striking contrast, which you soon note, is that the Venetian men, as a body, are dark, their women blond. The sounds, too, are polyglottal, and everything is international. Venice will likely be, for instance, the tourist's first experience of Greek money, which is current coin here.

At every corner you come are the little shrines and altars to the Virgin and the saints, built in dwelling-houses and over the shops, with lamps burning before them. These bright-colored shrines, with their glass frames and swinging, censer-like lights, produce a very picturesque effect, especially when the niches are reflected by the water. You feel with a new meaning the poetry of the litany, *Ave Maria, stella maris.* Indeed, the sea is very gracious and beneficent to Venice, in that it doubles all her beauties and splendors. She has her stars in the heavens and under her feet, her palaces above the earth and under the waters. Her beautiful bridges span their solid piers and tremble in the waves below them. Everything has a double form of grace and beauty,—a life of marble and a life of motion.

To return to the shrines : their images are here, as elsewhere in Italy, the *Lares and Penates* of the modern Romans, and this domestic worship, perpetual and hourly, and the devotion and love and apparent faith of the homely service, is something very pleasing and touching. It is only a pleasant illusion, however. The *cultus* of these shrines is, I fear, but an inherited habit,—a custom, a usage,—not an intelligent act. I regret to say that no amount of shrines or altars in an Italian shop will prevent your being shamelessly treated there. I do not think a Madonna on the very counter of daily fraud would protect you.

In Venice they sell fresh water on the streets in bottles and by the glass, and people are constantly drinking it. I have not seen so much water-drinking in all Europe, and the habit seems to be a confirmed one. There may be an useful hint for temperance societies in this little fact.

The cathedral church of St. Mark is perhaps the central architectural feature of Venice; at all events, it divides the honor with the rich Palace of the Doges. It is the great triumph of Romano-Byzantine architecture, and in its profusion of ornament and wealth of decoration mingles the splendors of two civilizations, —of the East and of the West. In its shrines are the most precious workmanship of Constantinople, costly gems, rare marbles of Europe, pillars from the temple of Solomon. Under the great altar rests the stolen body of St. Mark. Its treasury of relics contains some of the most precious memorials of faith,—a piece of the head of St. John, a fragment of the sacred column of the Passion, a vial of the blood of Christ. Its pictures of the masters and its old statues teach tradition, history, and religion to the people, whose thronging, treading feet for centuries have worn the marbles of its floors uneven and fluctuating like the waves of the sea. It is a temple,—an eternal monument and lesson to Venice.

In the vestibule of this cathedral, itself a stately hall larger and grander than most of the churches of our country, they show three great red, flat stones, forming a broad stairway, as the spot of the historic reconciliation between the Emperor Frederick Barbarossa and Pope Alexander III., an affair in which the conciliation, as was the fashion of those times, was all on one side. *"Non tibi sed Petro"* ("Not to you, but to St. Peter"), said the dishonored emperor when he knelt, probably feeling that he was doing something wrong, although he may not have known how great was the magnitude of the trust he was betraying, and which he had better have died to protect. *"Mihi et Petro"* ("To me and Peter"), said the modest pope.

And so it is everywhere in Europe. There is hardly a great church on the Continent which, in some shape or other, in painting or marble or brass or ostentatious relic, does not contain some deliberate and insolent affront to the civil authority,—some perpetual assertion of the claim of Rome to supreme political power. St. Peter's, the first church of the world, is full of them, and they are repeated so systematically everywhere that their presence seems to be the result of a policy and an order. Remember that in Europe the churches are the common schools of the people, who frequent them daily from childhood, studying their pictures, carvings, statues, bronzes, columns, and receiving their first and most lasting impressions from them. I do not wonder any more at Bismarck's relentless and uncompromising warfare on the ecclesiastical organization of Rome. I only wonder that any strong men who have ever attempted to found a state or been intrusted with the keeping of the civil liberties of the people have not made the same war, and made it more bitterly.

Every one knows the story of the civic pigeons of

Venice, and meets them like old acquaintances when
he goes there; and the birds meet all the world in the
same way. They belong to history and legend, and
have been translated from their lower life and taken
into the fellowship of men. Within an hour of my
coming one of these pigeons looked in at my window
facing on the grand piazza, and after a few moments'
cautious reconnoitring was trustingly and fearlessly
feeding from my hand. Seeing what was going on, a
whole flock came swiftly trooping in from all sides, entirely bankrupting my limited commissariat provision
in a moment or two.

Many hundreds of years ago some pigeons "assisted"
at a great victory had by the Venetians over Candia,
I think, by carrying very important despatches. The
victorious general sent them home with the news of his
triumph, and grateful Venice adopted the birds as the
"wards of the nation." To this time their descendants
are fed every day in the great square of St. Mark, at
the expense of the city, and no one in Venice ever
touches a pigeon. They rest at night in the eaves of
the palaces and the cornices of the great cathedral, on
triumphal columns and arches, and in the airy arcades
of the *campanili.* They nestle with the winged lions
and dart noiselessly through the churches. They brush
the sacred altars and the tombs of kings and doges and
bishops. They walk the marble pavements in groups
and in hundreds, unmolested among throngs of passers.
They play with the children and fly up on to your café
table for their share of the cake or water. They do
just what all other birds and animals would do if man
only treated them with humanity,—but gave them their
"civil rights."

Venice is a mirror in which you study the influence
of the sea on the human race,—on its physical, political,
and intellectual development. It has conditioned and
determined the physical appearance, the daily life, the
history, the art, of this people.

They were sailors, of course, and became a naval power, and their whole outside history and political relations started from that point and have been conditioned by it for ten centuries. The cleanliness and ease of transportation induced luxury and magnificence, a wealth of coloring and costume, which the daily life of no other city could support. One can go anywhere over Venice in a soft dress shoe. The pavements are smooth as floors and spotless, the gondolas are carpeted. The protection to dress is as great out-doors as in. The gorgeous costumes of Titian and Tintoretto and the Venetian school are but the legitimate development of the social life of a class of nobles in a city built as this is, and drawing on both the Orient and the Occident for treasures of sumptuousness, luxury, and display. Their pictures, of course, breathe the luxurious and color-loving spirit of their time, for they, too, are part of its development, but they are also portraits, faithful copies of the very picture of the city.

More directly in the famous glass of Venice you see imprisoned the elusive colors of the sea itself. Art has simply taken its lesson from the waves.

Again, the moment you enter this town you meet everywhere, at random among all classes, perhaps most noticeably among the poorer, that beautiful female face which is the glory of Venice, and which her painters have made immortal,—a soft sea-shell complexion of delicate loveliness, Titian eyes, and a wealth of golden blond hair,—a kind of Venus Aphrodite face. It is the sea again.

And so you may trace endlessly its visible influence here at every turn and every way you look. The old traditional ceremony of state when the new Doge, on behalf of Venice, in solemn form, celebrates its nuptials with the sea and casts into its waters the wedding-ring, is something more than a legend. It is history and fact. Venice—the Venetian race—is the child of Man by the Sea.

CHAPTER XXIX.

GENOA.

The Great Dead and the Little Living—Five Hundred
Years without Sunlight — The Cross of Malta —
Poverty, Want, and Wretchedness that we call the
Picturesque — Priests and Soldiers — San Lorenzo—
An Italian Sunday-School—The Practical Side of
the Italians — Railway Management — The Marble
Wealth.

A sort of dreamy listlessness falls over one in Genoa,
which it is hard to define, and harder still to resist.
The weight of the centuries seems to come down, and
repress individual action or vigor by dwarfing its
results in contrasting them with the movements of
ages. Men have lived on this spot—in this town—for
twenty-five hundred years of recorded history; have
worked, loved, fought, died. What is one human
atom, however brilliant his momentary position or
achievement, in all the vast stream of life !

I think this feeling must unconsciously oppress this
people, and bar the way to that individual energy and
vigor whose sum makes human progress. At all
events, they act so. For thousands of years life has
gone on quietly or stormily, and the Genoese of to-day
live and act as if they had thousands of years yet to
come, and a day, a week, or year was of no account.
Why hurry, with whole centuries yet of time ?

For this very reason, perhaps, Genoa is such a
picturesque and pleasing city. Spared largely from
the destructive rush of travel, it preserves somewhat
of its mediæval flavor, and retains the charm of distinctive sight and sound which all European cities are
losing so fast.

It is hard to describe Genoa and its unique life and ways to the American mind used to regularity and construction. You live here from tradition; your houses, your streets, are all handed down from centuries. You only accept them; you are not responsible for them or expected to account for them. There is no city surveyor with a whole digest of brand-new municipal ordinances. No two streets run parallel, and no one street runs for any length in one direction. No two houses stand on the same line. No wall even stands perpendicular. The windows appear where they have a mind to; the doors are mere holes in the wall at any place, behind a buttress or around an angle. I chose for my temporary residence "the Hotel of the Cross of Malta," an old historic pile, consecrated as the headquarters, hundreds of years ago, of the Knights of Malta, who gathered here to plan their campaigns and embark for the Holy Land. Hardly any two rooms have exactly the same level. The floors are hopelessly involved, and strange doors tempt you to mysterious passages at every corner. The place is yet lordly in its lowered uses. Corridors of marble stairways lined with exotic plants and flowers greet your entrance. You dine and read and smoke in noble rooms twenty feet high, frescoed by great artists, and whose walls are heavy with historic pictures. Statues of great men in bronze and marble look down on you from pedestals and niches at every turn. As a matter of fact, Scipio Africanus was the first figure which met my eyes as I entered this hotel, and he presided, grave and thoughtful, while I watched the transfer of my baggage and bargained for rooms.

This communion of the great dead with the little living is a feature of Italy. At the railway depot in Turin I awaited the lazy pleasure of the custom-house officials in a magnificent hall thirty feet high, frescoed with lovely Cupids and grotesque Bacchuses, larger than life, lit with clusters of handsome chandeliers, and

paved with marble. The other side of the picture was
that this ducal palace of a depot was cold and chilly.
But one-sixteenth of the jets were lighted, and the
place was so dismally gloomy you could hardly read
your ticket. A guard stood at each door of this room,
and at every possible entrance or doorway in the really
vast station-building, and effectually prevented any
rapidity of movement.

The streets of old Genoa range from three feet to
twenty in width. Of course, sunlight never strikes
the flagstones of the three-feet avenues. They must
be delightful summer resorts, but at this time are rather
chilly, even when some parts of the town are bright
with warm sunshine and redolent with exotic perfumes.
My own room in this aristocratic old hotel has probably never seen the sunshine for five hundred years.
When I want sunlight I do as I suppose the old
Knights of Malta did,—go out and find it on the hills
or open piazzas, where the Genoese eat confections and
drink the Falernian wines so thoroughly advertised by
Horace.

In these narrow streets, which close in on each other
like Colorado cañons, and where the houses, which,
kept at a formal distance on the first floor, kiss each
other at the roofs, fountains splash dreamily all day,
and the venders of small wares transact their business
in song, exactly as in the representation of an opera.
All day long and far into the night tenor, baritone, and
chorus snatches float into my room, now swelling, now
dying away in faint echoes. It is the work of Genoa,
the rhythmic labor of Italy, the chant of the poor people working hard for their daily macaroni. It does
not seem to us as if work thus set to music and carried
on by refrain could be very onerous, and perhaps it is
not; although it is certainly ceaseless, but it does not
matter much. There is very little work to do, and very
many to do it, and the man who hurried through a day's
work in an hour would only be idle the rest of the day.

Out of the window just opposite mine, and only a few feet from it, all day long there lolls an Italian girl, beautiful, dirty, lazy, badly dressed, and always eating something. Priest and soldier and beggar and donkey and tourist and sailor flow on beneath in a steady stream to slow music. She gazes listlessly on the human current forever, but takes no human interest in it, and shows signs of intelligent life but about once every half-hour, when she retires to a cupboard to fill her pockets again with cake. It is Italy,—only the bulk of the people do not have cake, and get along with garlic.

There is everything in Genoa to make the place quaint and grotesque. Not only do the dark and narrow streets refuse to run anywhere with certainty, and curve and wind and twist with labyrinthine complexity, but they run under and over each other. Occasionally a great church tower or spire serves as a landmark or beacon for a few minutes, but it, too, is soon lost behind a hill or under some huge mediæval wall, and the situation is more hopeless than ever. It is useless to attempt to know the streets or find one's way. The Genoese do it by tradition, but for a stranger it is lost time. When I go out I only walk and walk and walk among sights and sounds ever new and shifting, and when I am tired hire a small boy or a large man —it is immaterial which—to lead me back to my hotel. This service, from boy or man, costs exactly five mills. In fact, five mills is a very respectable sum here, and with a pocket full of copper centesimi one feels rather princely.

In truth, it is very sad to see what a copper coin will do in Italy. It is the only money many of the people ever see. I have had small shopkeepers refuse to take gold because they did not know what it was. We in America—in Colorado, Nevada, and California —decline daily to take in change the sums which would support a poor Italian in comparative comfort. Could there be any stronger contrast?

In fact, amid all the quaintness and picturesque effect of Italy, so pleasing to the passing stranger, it is a depressing reflection ever recurring that it is all the result and evidence of an awful poverty,—a poverty which the average American is so fortunate that he cannot comprehend. For the unhappy Italian, however, of the lower class, it is his only inheritance and the only legacy he can hope to leave his children. Yet, withal, he sings through life like the plantation negro of American tradition, but his song, as the slave's was, is largely a moan, a minor monotone like the endless current of the ocean. Better a thousand times the crude, prosaic comfort of our prairie settler than the poetic squalor of Italy,—the hopeless slavery of misery and want.

It is strange, however, how the result of centuries of ignorance and poverty and oppression is to make a land outwardly picturesque and beautiful. In all Genoa there is hardly a point from which every view is not a picture. You stand anywhere in the old streets, turn in any direction, and you wish you had the painter's pencil. There is a poetic effect of the lines of the buildings as well as in the movement and pose of the people, and when you add the skies of Italy and the fruits, flowers, and perfumes of the Mediterranean, life is a poem, and you feel as if it might be better to live here in bodily poverty than to exist elsewhere under colder suns and a less sympathetic nature.

Nevertheless, this loveliness is all on the outside. An army of priests hold the land in spiritual subjection, and heavy siege-guns frown on all the walls. Genoa, in fact, is a huge fortress, compared with which our heaviest fortifications in war times were but toys. Here, as all over Europe, you see heavy artillery mounted in the parks, sweeping the beautiful fields and the busy streets. Between cathedrals and cannon the people have had a poor chance, and their condition after centuries of this kind of guardianship proves it.

Cardinal Wiseman, in his writings of years ago, claimed especial credit for Italy on the point of her free schools,—conducted by the Church, of course. Last Sunday I saw in several churches what we would call a Sabbath-school, and the sight was so novel and different from our own that I thought its description would be interesting.

Hearing music in the cathedral church of San Lorenzo—the great church here—as I was passing it about four o'clock in the afternoon, I entered. It was so dark you could hardly distinguish human figures at first, the wax lights being mere fire-flies in the vast vaulted arches, and the long rows of columns interfering with even their feeble light. Slowly the eye, however, adjusted itself, the shadowy forms became visible, and one could find his way about. Some fifty priests and choristers were chanting a low, wailing music, and with them, out of recesses from every side and aisle, joined the voices of the congregation. The service here is, so far as I have seen, largely congregational, and the Italians being good singers, the effect is artistically pleasing, as well as devotional.

During this service, which was just closing, I discovered that a general interest seemed to centre in the middle of the church, where a crowd was gathered. Moving over to it, I found some thirty children ranged on two lines of rude wooden benches, facing inwards. At each end on chairs, and facing each other, sat two teachers, elderly gentlemen of benign countenance and in priestly vestments. Around the children, who were all of the poorer class, knelt or stood a crowd of their relatives and friends, their mothers, their grandparents, their sisters, their cousins, and their kindly neighbors. Some private soldiers in uniform were among the group, and other soldiers, with their swords on, were kneeling praying near us. A vender of soap and matches had brought in his basket of wares and knelt by it, praying half audibly. Three ladies, well dressed and of Italian face and figure, came in, took the group in at a glance, casting a momentary look of curiosity at the foreign-dressed stranger, and then dropped down on their knees in the outskirts of the crowd, with their backs to it, however, and facing some minor altar, and in a moment were deeply absorbed in their own prayers. Near by, a black-eyed baby was dabbling its little hand in the holy-water fountain, its sister and nurse, a laughing girl of about fifteen, trying to teach it to cross itself properly.

As the singing ceased and the altar force marched out in procession—an ecclesiastical military company—the teaching began. The children stood up and answered such questions as were put to them. There were no books used. One of the teachers seemed to be a superior of some kind inspecting the work, and what was probably the stated teacher frequently prompted his pupils. In answer to some question, one of the little ones made some reply which I did not understand. Both the priests, or teachers, smiled kindly, and a good-natured laugh broke out from the entire crowd. This crowd, some kneeling, some sitting on the floor, some standing, as was easiest, and a number of them women with infants in their arms, took the liveliest interest in what was going on. A murmur of applause often rewarded some of the children for good and ready answers, and when a child could not answer or was confused, a look of mortification and wounded pride always came over the little group of friends and supporters at its back.

The instruction was thoroughly conversational and kindly, but intelligent and earnest. The scene was picturesque and pretty, and you felt the work was doing good. You could not but wonder, however, at its small scope compared with the population and the dignity of the machinery. Genoa is a town of over one hundred and sixty thousand souls. San Lorenzo is its cathedral. Attached to this cathedral there is

an ecclesiastical force which no Protestant church ever
has, yet the Bethany Sunday-school in Philadelphia
every Sunday brings more children under instruction
than are taught in all Genoa for a month, if last Sunday
was any metre. There were about thirty in the
cathedral, and from forty to fifty more in each of two
other churches I visited.

There is something inexplicable to us in the devotion of the Latin mind. No incongruity of outward
circumstances seems to disturb or affect it. There is
no consciousness of sight, sound, or smell when once
the Italian drops down to pray. Things that would
affect us as physically intolerable, or that we would
resent as profane intrusion, they do not seem to be even
conscious of. Children play on the floors and creep
around among the groups of worshippers, or right
under the pulpit, while the priest is preaching. Men
and women come and go, mutter half-audible prayers,
kneel and pray in all directions, facing the altar of
their choice; but as long as there is no very loud noise
and intentional display of irreverence, it seems to disturb no one. We would insist on better outward order
at a political meeting.

In this beautiful and picturesque city, where every
view is a scene striking with arches and terraces and
statuary and ruined walls; where the air is redolent
with the perfumes of almond and magnolia and orange;
where brilliant flowers flash from half-concealed gardens
and droop down from balconies and towers; where
light-hearted people, clad in the brightest of colors, go
singing all the day long; where the altars of the
churches are set with stage effect, and in them music
rolls and surges from morning to night; where the
streets, crowded with priests and soldiers in contrasting
uniforms, with ragged muleteers and laughing children,
present the effect of a continuous carnival, you cannot
for the life of you avoid the feeling that the whole
thing is a play, an elaborate and well-produced opera,

whose scenic effects will dissolve, and whose music will hush with the near tinkling of the call-bell as the curtain drops. Nevertheless, these people have been living this life for centuries, and their fathers, who were like them, have done some great things. The Italians of to-day are great grown-up children. They have the happy carelessness of children and their outward abandon,—their love for the beautiful, their enjoyment of the moment, their unselfish kindness and sympathy.

It is hard for us, perhaps, to understand them or give them due credit for what they can do. With all their immense superiority to us in politeness, in thoughtfulness and personal culture, they reveal, at times, a practical side which, under equal conditions, might prove them to be our equals in even that practical development of which we are so proud, and which exists with us along with so much of coarseness and vulgarity. They have an excellent and efficient army, the result of discipline and organization. Their railways are so much better administered than those of France that you feel the difference the moment you cross the border. · I have not often been in a better-managed or more thoroughly well-ordered hotel than that in which I write to-day, and regret to leave to-morrow. In all these matters of physical achievement they are our equals. In the higher culture of mind and heart, in the thousand amenities of life which make human association pleasant and agreeable, they are immeasurably our superiors.

In all their common life they carry out the desire to please in a wonderful manner. The railway depot at this place, for instance, is not an altered palace, as are many public buildings here, but was built by the company for its own use. Its conception, however, is not that of a shed as is the conventional American mammoth depot. It is a noble hall. You sit in waiting-rooms twenty-five feet high or more, frescoed and panelled with excellent painting, and the front of the building, in the effect of its rich carvings and marble columns, is more imposing than the Academies of Music and opera-houses of our large cities. It is, too, very spacious, thoroughly well arranged and adapted for its special use. In many of the banks and buildings for business offices you find interior courts of most artistic effect, well lighted, warm with rich flowers, cool and musical with sparkling fountains, and elaborate with carving and statuary.

As it is a gateway into Italy, one of the most striking impressions of Genoa is the profusion of statuary and carving which here begins to meet you. Most of the old palaces have fine work on the fronts, and it becomes more elaborate and imposing inside, where magnificent halls and massive stairways, whose entrance is very frequently a pair of colossal, crouching lions, lead from room to room and floor to floor. In the streets, the very walls of the common houses, particularly at the corners and over the doorways, at odd angles and in curious niches over little shops you find the images of an innumerable army of saints, the effigies often set up in the fashion of a little altar. Through the hotels and banks, and public buildings of every kind, are the statues of great men, modern and old. All this besides the churches and parks and cemeteries and public gardens, which are crowded with rare and costly works. It is this wealth of marble, pure and white, and shaped with exquisite art, that has justly won for this city its well-merited title, "Genoa la Superba."

GENOA.

CHAPTER XXX.

PISA.

ENTERING INTO TUSCANY—TUSCAN CIVILIZATION—QUATTRO
FABBRICHE—THE CIVIC REPUBLICS—NATIONAL BAPTIS-
TRIES—GROTESQUE CARVING AND FRESCOES—THE ARTIST'S
LICENSE IN THE CATHEDRALS—PISA OF HISTORY AND OF
TO-DAY.

AT Pisa you enter on the Tuscan civilization, the
glory of modern Italy,—and modern here means the
last thousand years, for these Italians were learned and
accomplished people when our Saxon forefathers were
rude savages,—when England was a forest filled with
warring tribes, and the Howards were "hog-wards."
It was to Italy that Milton came for travel and polite
education when his own country was so rude that it
was a question whether to write for it in its own tongue.
It was from Italy that Shakespeare borrowed plots and
thoughts when he would seek a higher plane of civilization than Tudor England afforded. In fact, until
within a very brief time English literature has regularly
fed from the crumbs of the table of Italy. It has been
the school of letters, manners, and art for the modern
world.

Pisa is a railway junction where five roads centre.
This is equivalent to about ten in the United States,
and consequently the traveller need take no thought of
how to get there. He will be coming to it all the time,
and can always have half a day there and will often
be forced to stop over several hours. Happily the
railway restaurant is very good, carriages abound at a
franc or two an hour, and the wonderful Quattro Fabbriche are very near. Time need never hang heavily
on one's hands, and the beautiful cathedral, with its

close of glittering white architecture, looks handsomer every time it is seen.

Pisa itself is rather a modern-looking town compared with many of Tuscany. It has no city gates, for instance, nor massive encircling walls, but lies open on the plains, while at Sienna, Orvieto, Rome itself, and many others you enter through huge gates, with ponderous doors which swing heavily open or shut, and are in real use. At Rome the gates remain open until toward midnight, but in some of the country towns they close at eight or nine o'clock; and once shut for the night they never open till morning. Should any one linger without until after this hour he stays out. Fortunately there is little outside of the walls of an Italian town to tempt a stranger either to ramble or linger.

It happens for the ease and instruction of tourist and student that all that is best in Pisa is summed up in the celebrated Four Buildings, which are grouped in one spot,—a miniature quadrilateral of architecture,—and which, taken together, afford an admirable introductory study of Tuscan art and architecture, as they are representative and finished specimens of the style.

These buildings are the great Cathedral of Pisa, the famous Leaning Tower, which is a detached tower of exquisite symmetry, raised for the purpose of swinging the cathedral bells; a huge Baptistry, and a walled Holy Field, or cemetery. All the buildings are of pure white marble, of faultless design and masterly finish, and together constitute a group which is without equal in the world. They illustrate well, too, the wealth which, in the Middle Ages, was lavished on church-buildings, and the splendor and elaborateness of their establishment. Of this splendid group, each one of which is a masterpiece, taking rank among the great buildings of the world, the Cathedral is, of course, the centre; all the others are mere adjuncts to it.

The Leaning Tower, or Campanile, is simply a detached belfry. This was the customary way of building them in the Middle Ages. There are many such in Italy, and one, at least, is now extant in England,—at Elstow. The Baptistry is a colossal font under its own separate building. It was a mediæval usage that all the baptisms in the Republic should take place, not in the several churches, but at the Cathedral. Hence arose rather a necessity for a separate building for this special use, and very naturally an imposing provision for the rite. Specimens of these national fonts remain at Florence and Pistoja. The Campo Santo is but a graveyard, but this one is walled with costly statuary, and the burial-ground made with numberless shiploads of earth brought from Jerusalem. At Florence there is the same magnificent equipment for the cathedral church there,—the Campanile,—a square tower, ranking as the first of its kind in the world.

And when this wonderful endowment of a single cathedral is considered, it must be remembered, too, that Pisa is a small place. It has but twenty-six thousand inhabitants, and is the centre of a district of about fifty thousand people only. Nevertheless, the Pisans, although a little, have been a mighty people. They were great soldiers and sailors in their day, and their physical energy was always animated by the force of education and high culture. There was, therefore, little of lost power in their development, and thus they carried their arms into all parts of the world, and their name into history. At one time they dominated Italy, and through it the world, displaying military and executive genius of the highest kind. The Bonaparte family was of Tuscan descent, and although Napoleon came on the field when the glory of Pisa was but tradition, he seems to have only gathered up and renewed in himself what was once a common inheritance of Tuscan blood.

It is no wonder, therefore, that the Pisans are proud of their city and its history. Indeed, Italian history, up to to-day, is but the record of a brilliant constellation of civic republics. There has never been a na-

tional growth. Its life has been municipal, and therefore limited. This spirit exists yet. The Pisan, the
Genoese, the Venetian, the Milanese look on each other
as foreigners. They have been fighting with each
other for a thousand years, and Italian unity to-day is,
therefore, a conception rather than a growth. The
Pisan's instinctive allegiance is to Pisa, the Genoese to
Genoa, just as with us the Virginian's first impulse is
to Virginia, the Carolinian's to Carolina. The greater
idea of a nation is yet to come. Moreover, our State
rights doctrine is but the fruit of a hundred years of
rude, provincial existence. The city independence and
individuality of Italy is the growth of a thousand years
of culture, power, and glorious tradition. We must
recognize this historic fact when we would appreciate
properly the wonderful political ability which has brought
about the unification of Italy and made it a nation.

The Pisa of to-day sleeps in rest and beauty after
the toil and achievement of centuries. A summer's
sunlight floods the town, and the calm of the clear
Arno spreads from street to street. The quiet of a
New England Sunday broods over the place, and the
picturesque inhabitants, poor but robed with a Tuscan
wealth of color, hardly seem to move. They stand
around like artistically-grouped figures in tableaux.
Indeed, the worship of the tortoise seems to have pre-
vailed at Pisa at some time. On the bronze doors of
this church, rich in rare and costly work, the tortoise
figures again and again, the legend, "*tardo sed tuto,*"
engraven over his elaborately-recorded exploits. It is
hard always to trace in their time-stained and quaint
figures the incidents of the long story, but the bottom
of a door generally winds up with a complacent, self-
satisfied tortoise, sitting or sleeping calmly some paces
in advance of a very demoralized and apologetic-look-
ing stag. In the shop-windows, too, all over the town
are alabaster and marble figures of the contented deity.
What the legend may be I do not know, but the moral

N   t   25

has worked its way into the life of Pisa. The worship
has had fruition, and the Pisan of to-day has been
absorbed into the soul of his divinity.

On entering Italy one immediately begins to come
on traces of that singular marriage of impiety and
religion which so strongly characterizes the Middle
Ages. A traveller tells of finding in an old shop a
solid carved crucifix of costly work and worn and
stained by long use. On touching a concealed spring
there shot out from the long arm of the cross a mur-
derous knife. It is mediæval Italy all over. It was
in this town of Pisa, I think, that a verger, unlocking
the chancel-railings, took me to the rear of the great
altar and showed a nude Eve, of life-size, tempted by
the serpent. The picture was a fine painting, but so
impure and suggestive that it was considerately kept
covered where only priests could study it.

This shameless profanation of the churches, which is
not uncommon, seems to have been, in part, owing to a
singular license enjoyed by the builders and artists, who
were allowed to carve or paint almost anything they
pleased, and who used this freedom to its widest stretch.
Often their work took the form of satire, often it is
merely grotesque and vulgar. Sometimes the entire
meaning is lost for us. On a famous church door at
Verona there is carved a figure of a pig clad in priestly
canonicals and reading out of a breviary. In the judgment-hall at Pistoja, facing the seat of the judges, there
is a fox robed in the judicial ermine. Much of this
satire is coarse in the extreme, even to obscenity, but,
after reading the literary efforts in this direction of Eras-
mus, who was a polished and cultivated man of his
time, one need not be surprised at anything from
unknown and nameless lampooners.

What is stranger to our sense is the use of the cathedral for such purposes. It was, evidently, the *Punch*
or *Puck* of those ages, where, among saints and angels
and by noble tombs, the comic artists of the day carved

their satire, their censure, and their fun; and all of it
very rough to our gentler life. That there were some
limits to this strange license is seen in the fact that
these odd extravagances are generally partly hidden,
being, as a rule, found in dark recesses or under the
capitals of columns, or only traceable with difficulty in
the secondary lines of frescos, and not visible at all,
perhaps, to the careless observer. A favorite field for
these grotesque carvings is under the carved seats of
the stalls in the choir.

Although sleeping in a century that has no more
meaning for it, Pisa itself, outside of its marble wonders,
is a place full of quiet beauty and picturesque attraction
for the American stranger. Here, travelling from the
North, he, probably for the first time, comes on a town
where all society is strictly classed, and the classi-
fication emphasized by uniforms on the street. The
women are all dark and béautiful in their black lace
and veils. The priests are those of Northern Italy,
intellectual in their countenances and looking clean
and gentlemanly in their black-silk stockings and
silver shoebuckles,—alas, how different from their
Southern brothers! The gentlemen wear cloaks in
brigand fashion. The laboring-men are picturesque
in clean blue blouses, and their wives in all the bright
colors of the rainbow. Then comes the army, the
handsome infantry-officers in soft blue and white, and
the swaggering *bersaglieri* (sharpshooters) in their
rolling bandit hats and plumes of black-cock feathers.

In the great cathedral at Pisa hangs a massive bronze
lamp—a group of four figures suspended at a vast
distance from the ceiling—which, tradition says, gave
Galileo the hint of the pendulum. It is not an ecclesiastical relic, but is a shrine of a good deal of interest.
My guide told me, with only half-repressed irritation,
that the English people always asked after it, and he
seemed to regard this conduct as an eccentricity hardly
excusable, even in the barbarian *forestieri*. I think he

knew the whole history of Galileo, and considered him yet a dangerous man. But, in spite of his qualms of conscience, he had learned that not an altar in all the cathedral was so prolific of barbarian fees. So he took the heretic silver, and balanced his account with an extra prayer or two.

The corridors of grand pillars in this splendid house of God are trophies of war brought away by the Pisans in their conquests in many lands when Pisa was mistress of the seas and her ships brought tribute from almost every foreign shore. The cathedral itself is a monument in honor of a great naval victory had near Palermo, and most of the churches commemorate triumph by sea or land against Turk or rival Italian cities. The idea of building a church as the monument of a field of blood is something that has passed out of our American civilization. We could hardly consecrate a cathedral of Gettysburg or a church of the Holy Field of Shiloh, or dedicate an altar to Our Lady of Stone River, but all Europe is full of just such monuments. And they could build their temples with pillaged columns and marbles, adorn them with plundered statues, and, if need be, sanctify the altar with the stolen body of an apostle.

CHAPTER XXXI.

SIENA.

An Enchanted Town of the Middle Ages—A Living Tomb of the Past—The Fourteenth Century in the Nineteenth—A Mediæval Survival—Siena's Grand Cathedral—A Broad-Church Temple—The Vanished Sibyls Sleeping with the Saints—Socrates and Hermes Enshrined in a Christian Pantheon—The Golden Age of Tuscany—The Lost Republics of Italy—And We Too?

All through the interior of Italy there are interesting cities—towns of from fifteen thousand to forty thousand inhabitants—which are more striking in their general effect than Rome, or Genoa, or Naples, or Milan, or any of the cities of travel, and more really instructive in the way of picturing vividly the mediæval life of Europe. These towns have been kept unspotted from the world. The eager currents of modern life have never poured through them, and they stand the spared monuments of ages gone by.

Of all this group of quaint towns, there is none more curious or picturesquely representative than Siena,—a name which is to many, perhaps, only a vague recollection, the faint memory of a footnote in some history of art or dictionary of dates. Nevertheless, it was once a grand factor in European history,—a centre of art and civil freedom which died out together; then a theatre of fierce passions, intestinal wars, tragedies, tyrannies, and endless and bloody revolutions; then the lifeless quiet of exhaustion.

As the modern railway carries you out of the dreary sepulchre of the Roman Campagna, and into the garlanded and smiling fields of Tuscany, that pleasing land flowing with oil and wine, you see afar off what seems to be a huge fortress, throwing out its battlemented turrets sharply against the sky. As you draw nearer the heavy walls lengthen and broaden and divide into the lines of a town. It is Siena,—a solid mass of masonry set on the steep, sharp crest of a hill bristling with bastions and frowning towers. Nearly all of the mediæval towns are so placed. They were simply fortified camps, and in times when warfare was carried on by hand-weapons the natural site of a fixed camp was the highest hilltop in the neighborhood. From that point it commanded all the country in sight. This was the origin of the castle,—*castellum* meaning, etymologically, a little camp,—and in time, by the law of the survival of the fittest, the best-located castle became the city.

As a consequence of this hilltop location, the railways in Central Italy usually do not go into any town, the grades being simply impossible, but land you at a depot bearing the town name, and sometimes some four miles away from it. The hill itself is often shaved down on all sides, so that its native rock may form not only the foundation, but part of the outer walls, of the town which crowns its crest. The smooth face of this wall may thus be one hundred feet in perpendicular height, and one often cannot tell what part is built masonry and what part natural rock.

In the case of Siena it is a little better. The train, by a powerful effort, backs up a zigzag something like the celebrated approach to the great St. Louis bridge in our country, and lands you within a mile of the town.

At this outside depot you are received in state. The daily ceremony of going to this station, by which Siena touches the outer world, is, I think, a solemn form observed with religious care. I was the only hotel passenger on the express train, and I am inclined to think the arrivals of that day were a little above the average. Two four-horse vehicles, stately and black, were drawn

up in line at the gate of the yard. The force of guards
and porters and station-men were far more rigid in
their demeanor and less cheerful in their manner and
movements than a body of average Italian priests and
ecclesiastics officiating at mass. When I approached
the gold-laced and uniformed official in charge of one
of the funereal wagons, handed him my baggage receipts,
and told him I was going to honor "The Grand Hotel
of the Royal Black Eagle" with my presence, he
seemed staggered and stunned at the unwonted sound,
and by the magnitude of the responsibility so suddenly
cast upon him. Recovering from the shock, however,
he very soon directed some one else, who in turn ordered
still another, to go and get my trunks, and in due time
everything was accomplished decently and in order. I
entered my hearse-like carriage of state, the empty omnibus drove off slowly in silence and dignity, three
officials mounted my wagon, the procession moved de-
corously up the hill towards the town, the gates of the
train-yard were softly closed, the station-men sank
back in repose, and the quiet of a Sabbath fell upon
the Siena depot.

About half a mile up you enter the walls of the
town, and as the great iron gates close behind you this
world is shut out,—the nineteenth century, the life
that you know. You are shut in with the fourteenth
century. You feel an unknown sensation in which the
whole life of the mediæval times envelops you,—takes
possession of you. You are in an unburied Pompeii of
the Middle Ages.

It is, indeed, a most singular and wonderful study.
Here is a massive city, full of stately palaces, grand
churches, softly-splashing fountains, spacious squares
paved with fine stones and ornamented with beautiful
columns, its streets thronged with people,—children are
at play, men move in their shops, soldiers stand guard
before the palaces, priests silently steal along the ways,
—but the city is dead, absolutely dead, to all that we

call life and to all that we know. It has, so far as we can see, no meaning or place in this world now. It exists—these people live and move and have their daily being—solely by the impulse of a force originally projected in the Middle Ages, and which, never renewed, is lessening every day.

Siena is a segment of the Middle Ages projected into the nineteenth century, and held there like a fly in amber. Let us look a little more closely at the wonderful picture. Siena is to-day an inland town of some twenty-three thousand or twenty-five thousand inhabitants,—about the size of Lancaster, in Pennsylvania. Hundreds of years ago it had a population of over one hundred thousand souls,—busy men of action, soldiers at a time when arms was the great profession, artists of first fame in the world, learned priests and scholars, powerful citizens, merchants trading over all the seas, architects, builders, workers of every kind. These people built their city and their houses for defence and for eternity, with walls from three to twenty feet thick, and they are all there yet. Consequently, the Sienese of to-day live in castles and palaces almost for nothing, and the town remains a perfect mediæval picture. It is more than a picture: it is a survival.

Once inside of Siena, closed in its narrow streets paved with smooth, flat stones joined as regularly as the masonry of the walls that rise up abruptly almost within arm's-length on each side of you, one never sees the green fields or the sky, except as a thin line of blue or soft gray directly overhead. In the night-time there is seen likewise only a segment of the stars. It is a gloomy, sombre city of heavy shadows and cool, moist atmosphere,—an atmosphere that breathes forever over stone and cold marble. You see no woodwork in the streets, save, perhaps, an occasional ponderous door,— a modern injection and anachronism. The palaces join each other and face on the narrow, irregular streets in long lines as do our houses, but every house is a fort-

ress, built of massive masonry,—sometimes buttressed,
—its walls capable of resisting cannon. The great
stones are firmly set one on and in another till the
whole looks like a natural rock. Solid stone benches
often stand along the front of the house in the street-
way. There are no windows, but only apertures covered with immense wrought-iron grates, and these are
very sparing. To the side of each window and door
on the lower floor are fastened huge iron spikes, from
each one of which hangs a great ring, also of tough
wrought-iron. Intelligent Italians of this day could
not tell me the ancient use of these fastenings, and for
a time they were mysterious puzzles. History seems
to show that they were used to stretch great chains
across the street in times of fighting.

It is impossible to describe the monumental appearance of old Siena, or how these ponderous, castellated
dwellings call up the life and legend of mediæval time.
These houses have seen tragedies within and troubles
without. Men have scaled and stormed them; men
have been flung dead and living from their frowning
windows; seditions, revolutions, and riots have streamed
around their base. But through all changes, conspiracies, revolts, plunder, confiscation, barbarous revenges,
depopulation, crime, and fierce passions within, lawless-
ness and violence without, their great walls, gigantic,
gloomy, severe, have stood passionless and impartial,
like the gods of the classic pagans. Every stone seems
to tell of the frightful tragedies, the play of ungovern-
able passion, the wild license, the desperation of humanity, in the dense darkness of the night of superstition, which make even the reading of mediæval history
so stifling and oppressive.

Siena seems to have been forgotten of history, and
allowed to stand untouched in the stream of time as its
currents washed out almost all over Europe the traces
of the worn-out feudal life of the Continent. Until
within a few years no railway came near it. The lines

of trade had changed, and it was left out of the world of commerce and human relations. A new art, a new religion, a new system of government, had come up, and the world knew it no more. It had nothing to give, and dropped out of human care or thought. It was a two days' journey by horse or carriage, through an undefended country, and men did not come near it. So it remained unchanged. Even now its isolation is curiously strange. It has lived so long out of the world that with a railway at its door it cannot come in. It has no sympathies with our modern life, and our blood will not flow into its corpse. There are but two great hotels,—that is, hotels for the use of strangers. I was the first guest for a week at mine. I came alone, ate alone, sat alone in the empty chambers, went away alone. At Rome I had unfortunately left my *Baedeker*, covering Central Italy, and was entirely without any detailed information as to the history of the place or local points of interest, only knowing of its great cathedral and its importance as an early school of art. I went out to buy anything that would help me through, either one of the standard guide-books or any local publication, but I could not find even a book-store. I have reason to believe from what I have learned since that there is now such a store in the place, but it is certainly not conspicuous. All along the rather brilliant shops of the Corso or main street I searched for it in vain, and had to come away as poor as I entered. Again, in the stone-covered porch of the side entrance to the grand cathedral there were posted on the church walls, as is the custom in Italy, public notices,—some civil, some ecclesiastical. There were in all but some six or eight on the wall, and one of them was dated as far back as 1870. Only one, I think, bore date of this year. Time has no more any meaning to Siena; a day is as a hundred years.

It is the cathedral which the travellers that find Siena

come to see, and it is one of the great churches of
Europe, whether you view it in itself or in its relation
to the history and development of art. This noble
edifice was built in the thirteenth century, in the early
Italian-Gothic style, in many respects the most effective
order of church architecture. It made on me a much
stronger and more pleasing impression as a church than
St. Peter's, which has something of a polytheistic character,—a pantheon for the modern mythology of Rome,
—or than the handsome ball-room effect, inside and out,
of the graceful Madeleine at Paris.

In this remarkable church, which exists now just as
it did five hundred years ago, whichever way you look,
long aisles of Gothic arched columns stretch away like
the trees of the forest. Under them kneeling groups
cluster, or entering worshippers move noiselessly forward like ants. So great is the grand nave, so wide
the dark aisles, so high the fretted ceiling, that you do
not hear the feet of rude men and wooden-shod peasant
women as they tramp the marble floor. The noble
dead of mediæval ages sleep in their stone coffins about
you in peaceful and eternal rest. The organ rolls, the
clouds of incense float upward, and by their tombs the
same rhythmic prayers ascend that these men heard
here in their lifetimes. All around in niches and
chapels stand fine statues, not the morbid and ascetic
work of a later period, but after the more human fashion of the antique, rejoicing in the beauty and loveliness
of the human figure. In front, against a dark background of ancient, rich wood-carving panelling the
walls and covering the stalls of the choir, stands out
the great main altar, splendid in its mass of silver and
its hundred lights, glittering with jewels and gleaming
crosses, and the gold-worked robes of the priests, and
you think of Jupiter come down to see Danæ. The
time has passed when religion can be taught or enforced by dramatic effects. The æsthetic fable of classic
legend, and the lower theatrical splendors of the

mediæval altar, have both had their day,—have both
served, perhaps, a useful purpose, and are both equally
useless for good in this day and generation.

In this old cathedral, where every quaint corner is a
study, there is one very curious and striking feature
of rare historical interest. We all know that in the
earlier history of the Christian Church there was a
peculiar veneration and honor for the pagan sibyls.
They were held in great esteem, and perhaps something more; but just what were the honors paid them,
or how far the respect.verged on something higher, is
not clear. A great saint, in a great hymn yet used in
the burial-service of the Catholic Church, did not
scruple to write,—

"Teste David cum Sibylla."

Did they rank with the prophets? Were they a
little lower than the angels?

Here they are all in the great cathedral of Siena
with the saints and martyrs, and their presentation is
on such a large scale as to make them one of the distinguishing features of the church. On the broad
pavement of the two great aisles which flank the nave
I found them all in colossal form. Their representation is in fine and almost imperishable etching,—the
etching done in white stone, inlaid in a surface of black
marble. The designs are spirited, free, and strong, and
the general effect very impressive. The sibyls themselves—ten or twelve in number, as I remember—are
all fine, large, comely women, most of them apparently
about thirty-five, of full form and rounded contour.
The figures are colossal,—about four times human size.
Each sibyl has a brief legend in old script set in the
black ground, giving her shadowy credentials; sometimes it is a sentence from an old classic, sometimes a
monkish rescript, reciting the substance of her prophecy
or foreshadowing. I much regret that I did not copy

these. Often they ran about thus: " The [Thracian] sibyl concerning whom [Epaminondas] wrote." And that is about all we know of most of them. There they live in marble, the dead goddesses of two religions, and men have to-day only the faintest and most elusive traces of their being.

The spirit of that easy-going catholicity of classic Rome which accepted and assimilated the gods of all people lingered long in Italy. In the goodly fellow-ship of this impressive temple are Moses and Samson and Socrates, Solomon and Judas Maccabæus, and on the pavement near the door, Hermes Trismegistos,— that mythical personage whose name carries one far back into the shadows of the morning æons. Hermes —Mercury—Thoth—the Logos of Egyptian tradition.

In fact, this grand old cathedral, out of the world now, sleeping in the cool shades of history, is the most hospitable pantheon I have ever seen. It is a broad-church temple of mediæval faith, whose doors opened wider and more freely than anything in Anglican England to-day. There are no national limitations to its honors, and it has leaped the bounds of any one religion. The gods and the heroes, the popes and the philosophers, the saints and the martyrs and the leaders, of many times and many people are gathered here ; and they rest among civic crests and municipal standards and flagstaffs and crucifixes carried in battle by the victorious Sienese six hundred years ago.

If possible, a visit to this place should cover the sixth day of May, which is the *festa* of the great St. Catharine of Siena, when her head is exposed for the edification of the faithful, and the whole scene affords an excellent " interior" of Italian life which it is getting harder to see every year. St. Catharine is one of the larger luminaries of the Roman mythology and the divinity of Siena, remembered here and throughout the Church after the popes and the princes of Sienese splendor have been long forgotten. She is one of the representative saints of Europe, and her curious story one of the best illustrative studies of mediæval society and the mediæval Church. And nowhere can it be studied to more advantage than in its natural setting, this quaint old town.

Historically for the student, politically for the thoughtful American citizen, Siena is a point of instructive study, its rise and fall a lesson pregnant with interest. Hundreds of years ago, before the present states and governments of Europe were, it was a centre of learning, art, and civilization,—and it was a republic! From the eleventh to the thirteenth centuries Pisa and Siena were the brightest stars in that brilliant historical constellation—the lost Republics of Italy.

At that time they were the centre of a wonderful revival of art, the seats of a school of painting and sculpture, and particularly architecture, of fine characteristics and great promise, whose sudden appearance and equally sudden and complete disappearance have never been yet philosophically explained. It is one of the vexed problems of history. This period has been felicitously called "the Renaissance before the Renaissance." We know little of this interesting time, and cannot trust that, for it has been written by priests and monkish chroniclers who came into power over its ruins. This we do know,—that these little republics threw the morning rays of art and learning and prosperity and modern civilization over Europe. Men built great cities, carved grand sculptures of force and originality, painted great paintings, traded with distant lands, grew rich and powerful, and governed themselves. There was freedom and glory and prosperity, but weakness somewhere, for in a brief time the priest took the place of the statesman, and night fell upon Europe. Then came the lethargic stupor of the Middle Ages, unbroken until the Reformation and the Renaissance.

This strange episode of this time is a social and political tragedy,—a catastrophe in the evolution of human advancement.

There is one record which remains to tell of the life of this fated people,—its architecture. That, fortunately, is impartial, accurate, and unimpeachable, for it is itself the product and result of the national life, and it cannot be altered or tampered with. It is here that the cathedral of Siena becomes of historic value, as well as that of Orvieto and the wonderful group of buildings at Pisa, of which I have before written. The Pisa of to-day sleeps and is meaningless, but on its confines, in the little field which holds the famed cathedral, baptistery, campanile (Leaning Tower), and Campo Santo, the Pisa of history still lives in beauty and speaks with eloquence.

The architecture and sculpture of this time, as it comes down to us, has a positive and distinctive character. It is instinct with life, and freshness, and youth. Its material, pure white marble relievos, or the outlines emphasized sometimes in black, gives the work a peculiar delicacy and attraction, and not only admits but seems to demand the graceful ornamentation and richness of finish which characterize the buildings of this period. They abound in airy colonnades, superimposed, one row on another, in ranges of arches and arcades often raised into the air in light and graceful columns multiplied and repeated and rejoicing in charming Corinthian capitals and an affluence of leaves and flowers. The façades of some of these churches are a wondrous mass of elegant figures, covering the whole front like a delicate veil of marble lace-work. In all this exuberance and wealth of ornament there is, of course, occasional crudity and immaturity, as there always must be in everything which has yet the power to grow, but you lose it all in the feeling of life and joyousness and freedom. The people who developed this style of architecture were in the youth of their

political state, strong, active, buoyant, and full of the
conscious pleasure of life and the sense of progress.
There was freedom of individual action and civil liberty.

They had a pleasure in the life and strength of the
human body; they delighted in depicting the beauty
and symmetry of its form.   Their art was the child of
Greece as well as of the hardy Gothic North, and there
is often a curious simplicity in the mixture of classic
and Christian legend in their sculpture.   Their churches
are bright with statuary fashioned after the antique,
light and graceful with an architecture of delicate lines
and tracery that seem to float and carry up the buildings into the air.   They are lavishly dowered with
ornament.   All that is beautiful in art, all the treasures
of wealth, have been poured into them without stint or
measure,—lovely statues, precious stones, rare paintings,
curiously-carved pulpits with whole lives of legend
told in marble on their panels, altars that are solid
masses of silver.   The people who built these churches,
so white and pure and delicate, had a cheerful religion,
a faith of love and trust and hope.   It was something
that was the natural outgrowth and development of the
sunshine and smiling fields of Tuscany, lustrous with
the rich foliage of their olives, and wreathed and festooned and garlanded with grapes.   It was the natural
incense of happy Italy ascending to heaven,—something
very different from the slavish superstition and morbid
religion that hang like a pall over this land to-day,
when men have lost their sense of the living Christ in
the worship of His dead body and of death.

What might have been the future of Italy and of the
Continent and of the world if this auspicious aurora of
freedom had not been quenched!   How different might
history have been if the republics of Tuscany instead of
Rome had guided Italy!

And we too?   It is the tragic fate of these early
Italian republics which is the European argument
against republicanism.   Men of learning and experi-

ence in the conduct of affairs meet you with it all the time when you challenge a discussion of our free institutions and form of government. The dead republics of Italy — dead in their youth — were relatively as powerful as we are ; they carried their arms and commerce over the known world. Their people were as prosperous as we are; they had more of learning and cultivation and higher education. But—it is the verdict of history—their institutions and popular form of government tended to develop and bring into power the average and commonplace man. The state fell under the control of this class of men, and went rapidly to pieces. Now, says the European statesman, "Are you in America not travelling the same road?" And it is a pretty hard question to answer.

SIENA.

CHAPTER XXXII.

ORVIETO.

THE HILL-SET CITIES OF TUSCANY—ASHES OF THE MIDDLE AGES—A PALACE WAITING AT TEN FRANCS A DAY—MEDIÆVAL CRIME AND PAGANISM—DEVOTED SERVICE—THE LEGEND-FAÇADED CATHEDRAL OF ORVIETO—THE EUROPEAN CATHEDRALS—SHARP CONTRAST BETWEEN THE BUILDINGS AND THE WORSHIP IN THEM—VIN DU PAYS OF ORVIETO—THE WINES OF ITALY—A GOOD BISHOP'S DEATH—EST, EST, EST, OF MONTE FIASCONE—THE FALERNIAN FIELDS OF HORACE.

ORVIETO, like Siena, is the fortressed and castellated crown of a hill frowning with defiant bastions of solid rock, and with great gloomy gates that look treacherous and inauspicious. One almost fears to enter their black and yawning shadows, and recalls instinctively the venomous ferocities and merciless passions that

scorch the pages of mediæval Italian history.   But the
gateways are unguarded now, the threatening parapets
empty of helmet or weapon, the ditches dry and dusty
and unclean with the foul refuse of a modern Italian
town.   To violence and the unbridled play of lust and
fierce passions have succeeded exhaustion, extinction,
ashes.   Only the harmless form remains like the skeleton fibre of a dead and worm-gnawed leaf.

These hill-set cities, so distinctive and suggestive, are
one of the charms of the lovely landscape of Tuscany,
and Orvieto is one of the most picturesque and striking
of them all, not even excepting Perugia.   Its walls are
steep and precipitous, sheering down for hundreds of
feet, the solid masonry growing into the hewn tufa rock
so that it cannot be seen where the one ends and the
other begins.   Its battlemented outlines stand clear-
cut against the sky, grim walls and clusters of dungeon
towers and open *campanili* and ascending masses of tall
Italian dwelling-houses forming a fine gray setting for
the white marble relief of the famed cathedral.   At sunset, when the slanting rays fall across the valley, light-
ing up the gray tops with a glory, and flooding plain
and stream below with glowing color, it is a perfect
picture.

> " The splendor falls on castle walls
>   And snowy summits old in story;
> The long light shakes across the lakes.
>   *   *   *   *   *   *   *
> ———They die in yon red sky;
> They faint on hill or field or river."

There is a shadowy, elusive sketch of Orvieto by
Turner in his collection in the National Gallery in
London, all slanting lines of sunset and dissolving
landscape; and it is very like, for the whole spirit of
the scene is the spirit of Turner's genius.   It is Tur-
neresque : that best describes it.

The picture of Orvieto, however, is all from the outside. Once inside, the streets are narrow, dirty, meaningless, and hot. They are commonplace, too, for Tuscany, devoid of legend and special monument, full of smells, wretchedness, and uncleanness. The historic cathedral, brilliant in black and white, is the sole modern attraction. There are other churches in plenty, but they are shabby, uninteresting, and wanting in any special significance.

Few strangers find Orvieto, for it is not a halting-place on the modern lines of travel; nevertheless, the accommodations for the traveller are very good. He can have a whole palace to himself if he wants it, and a whole train of servants, at very little cost. Orvieto was once a powerful city and the home of the Guelphs, a family who built their houses as strongholds and sorely needed that style of residence. It is now a desolate town of a few thousand souls, but the strong rock-walled houses are all there yet, and the dwindled Orvieto of to-day resembles a small boy struggling in his father's ulster. This effect is very general over all Italy.

My hotel was a palace of past generations, desolate and pathetic in its sunken fortunes, but grand yet. The rooms were spacious and stately in height and proportions. The walls were pictured in bright color and moving design from top to bottom,—a great serial story in fresco that ran through halls and chambers; a tale of lords and ladies, of love and wars, of olive-groves and stormed fortresses, of banquets and knightly halls and fountains and blushing gardens,—a reminiscence of Boccaccio, in fact. Along the solemn stairways, in the silent corridors and vast dining-hall, stood marble statues, looking so shut up and lonesome that it seemed as if they must speak at the dear sight of a human face. It was a whole lordly palace waiting for one, and glad to see its lord at ten francs a day.

My bedchamber was a grand apartment on the first floor, so nobly high that you lost the demeaning sense

of there being any one domiciled above you, so long
that when you placed your two wax candles in one end
of the room you could not see the other. A glory of
romantic frescos, too, ran all around the spacious walls.
It was well appointed, also; everything was clean and
neat and fresh, and my assiduous retainers were only
happy when they were bringing in continuous cans of
hot water. The baronial floors, however, were all of
marble and bare stone, innocent of carpet, rug, or
matting, and there was no lock on the doors,—that had
gone with the centuries,—although some huge wrought-
iron clamps and hasps showed that one of no little
strength had once been necessary. The stone walls,
however, were four or five feet thick, and gave an eminent feeling of security.

The table was full and good, and even elaborate,
while the service was excellent. It was more: it was
devoted. The traditions of the centuries of the grandeur and state of the house seemed to come down upon
the dignified, stately old servant who officiated as butler and footman and garçon, and he did his best to
meet the accumulated responsibilities. He struggled
manfully to supply in himself the services of a whole
retinue and conceal the deficiency of the troops of
servitors that once lined the hospitable halls. At my
private apartments he announced in stately form, "The
dinner is served, signor," and bent with grave obei-
sance as I passed through the solid stone doorway. He
disappeared deftly, and as I approached the great door
of the old dining-hall there he was again, drawn up in
the shadowy similitude of two invisible lines of solemn
footmen. I walked between him in serious state, and,
lo! he was behind my chair as I made ready to sit down
to my solitary dinner, served under courtly frescos and
statuary and a wealth of drooping flowers. The efforts
of this ancient servitor to support the departed glories
of the house, his simple fidelity to the name and blood
and dignities that had drifted away hundreds of years,

was almost touching. It never relaxed for a moment during the twenty-four hours of my stay, every meal being served with equal state commensurate to its rank in the service of the day. And when on leaving I played my American part in the comedy by giving from the parting "good-hand" a five-franc note, I think the old fellow dreamed for a brief moment that perhaps the good old days of princes and Cencian ladies and brigand cardinals had come back again.

In-doors Orvieto was very pleasant and comfortable. Out of doors the sun-baked town is unattractive and worse than comfortless. The whole place, perched on a high mass of rock and forever exposed to the beating rays, is parched and heated. The whole life of the place is dry and miserable. The sweet breath of the fields never blows here. No fragrance of fresh leaves and flowers ever reaches this parched town swung high in the hot air. The streets glare, the walls are the home of the glittering lizard. The whole impression of the place is disappointing, it is so unlike the soft and gentle wine of Orvieto, famous even down to Rome, or the graceful tracery of the cathedral,—the two associations of the spot.

In solid Siena, with its comfortable bourgeois existence, you seem to feel even at this day something of the real life of the Middle Ages. It is passionless and still, but living yet, although without relation or meaning to our time. Orvieto is dead,—an extinct volcano, —an ashy residuum of mediæval crime. There is nothing in the history of society more appalling than Italy in the fourteenth and fifteenth centuries. It is hard to conceive of it now,—impossible to reconstruct it even in imagination. We are all somewhat familiar with the Borgias and the Cencis, whose annals blister the history of Rome and are conspicuous because of that theatre, but all interior Italy was filled with just such great families, of whom the world now knows nothing,

but who were just as wicked, just as passionate, just as
defiant of God and man.   They plundered and fought
with each other.   They poisoned and intrigued and cast
each other into merciless prisons.   Their very love was
defiant and criminal and shameless.   The struggles of
these families, dissolute, abandoned, and unrestrained
by any conventions of society or religion, were the politics of the time.   They made popes and added the
prostitution of the headship of the visible Church to
personal and private vice.   It was an age of delirium,
—a kaleidoscopic whirl of guilt,—an age of ungovern-
able passions, of barbarous ferocities, of vicious pleasures indulged in openly as by pagans.   The picture of
that day is a confused panorama of morbid superstition
and measureless crimes; of masses and miracles and
murders; of poisonings and appalling incests; of fla-
gellants; of conspiracies and treacheries; of dungeons
and tortures and atrocious cruelties.   This was the Italy
of Orvieto.

The modern renown of Orvieto is its beautiful cathedral, another of those magnificent Italian Gothic structures, all clad in white and edged in black, after the
striking fashion of the Pisan, Sienese, and Florentine
work.   The whole façade of the front is covered with a
white net-work of miniature statuary,—the history of
the world, apparently, according to mediæval tradition,
in a series of tableaux.   There are thousands of figures.
The pictures begin with Adam and Eve.   Many of
the scenes are recognizable, but quite a number are
evidently legends that are now entirely lost.   All the
designs are intensely realistic, and many of them exceedingly quaint.   In the Creation of Eve, for instance,
Adam lies in a dead sleep on the ground while God,
a venerable old man with a carving-knife, is making a
slit in his side with one hand, while with the other He
drags out Eve, whose well-coiffured head and shoulders
are just visible.

The building of this cathedral itself is a curious ·

illustration of the wonderful contrasts of its time. It
is built in commemoration of a miracle establishing the
dogma of transubstantiation. There was a sceptical
priest who doubted the truth of this doctrine. Once,
when offering mass, he tempted a physical test of the
sacred wafer, when it immediately bled in the five
gashes, the great drops of blood falling upon and stain-
ing the napkin. The fact of this bleeding is perfectly
well authenticated by such evidence as attests the mass
of mediæval church history. It was officially attested
by Pope Urban IV., and a cathedral ordered to be
built in its honor. Now, the wonderful contrast is
between the coarse conception of the miracle and the
refined, artistic conception of the cathedral, the bloody
thaumaturgy of the altar and the pure and delicate
work of the temple. The miracle tells of a barbarous
condition of mind and society ; the cathedral, although
of the same age, is a work of the highest order of art.
And this strong contrast between the men who built
the cathedrals and the men who conduct the worship
in them confronts one all the time in Europe. The
architecture of the buildings is of the highest reach of
art, always dignified, and sometimes approaching a
sublimity that cannot be transcribed in words. The
altars are nearly always tawdry with tinsel or barbaric
riches, while the devotional decorations are coarse and
puerile beyond conception,—ghastly, writhing images,
grinning skulls, dried human limbs or whole corpses,
wax figures gorgeous in green and yellow hues and
encased in cheap glass fronts, marble images with tin
crowns or clothed in silk and cotton skirts. Sometimes
the altars are furnished with imitation ornaments—
counterfeit candlesticks and tin splendors—and from
the rear they look as shabby, fraudulent, and dreary as
the " behind the scenes" of a second-rate theatre. The
builder seems always to have been educated and vigorous, the priest ignorant and vulgar. Were the builders
an unknown order of men who have disappeared, or

was the Church of the thirteenth century something immeasurably superior to the Church of the nineteenth century ?

At Orvieto you touch the finest wine-growing district of modern Italy. The wine of Orvieto itself is a gentle, straw-colored liquid, much esteemed both for its delicate flavor and soft acidulous properties. It is known at Rome and is good there, but, like all the Italian wines, should be drank in its own district. They are all of them so delicate as not to bear transportation even for fifty miles. The districts are also very limited, so that one changes his wine nearly every day when travelling in Italy. Even if the wines of Italy were strong and rough enough to bear transportation, the vineyards of any one grape are too small to establish any given brand in the markets of the world.

At Montefiascone, a few miles south of Orvieto, the traveller tastes the queen of all the wines of Italy to-day. It is the Montefiascone, or wine of the country,— a Muscatel, the finest brand of which is popularly known as Est, Est, Est. Its name is flavored with a legend. Many hundreds of years ago a princely bishop of Bohemia (the Bohemia of geography and not of letters) was travelling to Rome in state. Before him a whole day's journey always went a tried retainer, who tasted the wines of the land and left for his lord a report, writing "Est" on the doors of that inn where the best was to be had. When the lord bishop came to Montefiascone, on the doors of the village hostelry was written, "Est, est, est." So good was the wine that the bishop never got any farther, but died there shortly afterwards. Sir John Evelyn, travelling in 1644, says that he saw here the tomb of the bishop, with this inscription :

> "*Propter Est, Est, Est,*
> *Dominus meus mortuus est.*"

The modern story is broader, and relates the inscription as—

*"Est, Est, Est. Propter nimium est,
Dominus meus mortuus est."*

Evelyn, in his quaint and simple diary, seems to confound this wine with the Falernian of Horace, confusing, most likely, Falerii, the modern village of Civita Castellana, near Montefiascone, with Falernus. What is given one now in Italy as Falernian wine is rather poor stuff, but red and powerful as Horace sings it. The modern Montefiascone is a very mild wine and light in color, its flavor so delicate and elusive that it needs quite a cultivated taste to judge its virtues. At first trial it feels in the mouth almost like pure, soft rain-water, but the full benediction of its blessings comes in time. The Horatian Falernian fields had grown poor and harsh in Pliny's time, and it is probable that they have entirely disappeared now. But, in drinking the soft and limpid Montefiascone, one begins to understand what may have been the generous inspiration of the warmth with which Horace sings the wines of his country,—a warmth which an experience of the modern wines of Italy hardly justifies.

CHAPTER XXXIII.

PISTOJA.

The Local Color of the Italy of To-day—A Roman Pretorian Palace—A Mediæval Hall of Judgment and
a Modern Court-House—The Feast of Corpus Christi
in a Rural Diocese—The Miracles of Provincial Italy
—A Dying Faith—A Touching Peasant Bambino—An
Italian Provincial Inn—The Smiling Fields of Tuscany.

Pistoja is another of those picturesque Tuscan
towns so interesting as having had their day in the
early ages of the lost republics of Italy,—that aurora
of art and freedom in Europe, but a morning that
never saw the fulness of noon. It is full of the art
and architecture of the Pisan and Sienese school, and
abounding in quaint remains of the feudal times of
mediæval Italy.

It is in these hidden cities rather than in the mod-
ernized towns that one can best study the past and see
the present life of Italy. Here you find the native
manners, the dress and costumes, of the different classes,
and, most interesting of all, see the every-day life and
faith of the people. Here are the open-air altars; the
provincial festas; the miracles of the soil; the quaint
old churches, with their mediæval legends graven in
stone, their feudal tombs worn and dusty; the curious
black Madonnas; the beasts of the Apocalypse in all
their grotesque ugliness; the devotional wax-works for
the peasants, dressed with beads and crown and satins,
male dolls as well as female, and framed and protected
in glass cases; the Bambinos, rude but often touching in
their earnest homeliness; in brief, the local deities and
the local color of Italian religion.

Pistoja is an idyllic country town, and looks very lovely under the summer foliage and in its provincial festa dress. It is the feast of Corpus Christi when I am in it. Although bright with the life of this time, it is a very ancient place. Catiline was killed here before the time of Christ, and it must always have been a fighting-point, as it is just at the foot of the Alps and commands one of the passes into Italy. Nevertheless, although abounding in picturesque and imposing palaces and mediæval buildings, it has not the narrow streets and gloomy aspect of the ordinary Italian town whose foundations were laid and conditioned either in the feudal ages or the earlier times of imperial or republican Rome. It is light, cheerful, airy, spacious,—a little Italian Paris. In the Middle Ages it had repute for its manufactures of arms, and tradition says the pistol was invented here and took its name from the town.

The distinctive feature of Pistoja to-day, perhaps, is its ancient Pretorian Palace, now serving for a court-house, as it did of old under another name. In the "Hall of the Tribunal" you see yet untouched the massive stone benches of the old judges, and in front of these the great stone table,—a suggestively-gloomy court-room of the Middle Ages. Directly facing the seats of the judges there is a curious picture on the wall of a fox dressed in robes and sitting in judgment,—one of those singular freaks of fancy or satire which you come across all the time in mediæval researches. In fact, this whole hall is remarkable for its wealth of feudal heraldic lore, and is known and prized the world over for its riches in this line of study.

This entire hall, which is vaulted and supported by massive square columns, is wholly covered—ceilings, walls, stairways, and columns—with feudal coats-of-arms graven or painted on the stone; some are set in, others cut in, others frescoed. There is not an inch of woodwork in the whole hall,—nothing but stone and wrought iron,—or, if I remember aright, any windows, the light coming in from an opening in the ceiling. Among the other striking remains is a set of feudal standards, twelve in number, "the gonfalons of the companies of the people," proud memories of republican civic glory. The place is rich also in antique inscriptions. The modern contribution to this interesting historical monument is a large tablet, set in the main stairway, in honor of the soldiers who died in achieving the union and independence of Italy.

There is a quaint mediæval feature in these towns in the constant repetition in all places—on the public buildings, in the churches, in the piazzas, on the fountains, in the streets, on columns and doors—of the figure of some animal, the symbol and popular crest of the town. In addition to all this, each ward is designated by a column surmounted with the "city arms" in shape of the symbolic statue, and numbered with the number of the district. In Siena it was the wolf suckling Romulus and Remus, and the design—always the same—was very spirited and much superior to the carving in Rome. Here it is the lion. You see him everywhere, grim, worn, and stained, and, as some of these effigies have come down from the twelfth century, sometimes he is rather decrepid.

It was my fortune to be in Pistoja on the Sunday of the feast of Corpus Christi. I had seen the procession also in Massa, a much ruder place, a few days previous. The feature of this feast is a procession in which the consecrated wafer—or, as it is always popularly called here on this feast, the body of Christ—is carried by the bishop through the streets for the adoration of the people. The sight of this spectacle gives one a very good idea of the popular religion. In Massa the sacred burden was followed immediately by a brass band, and was preceded by bands of peasants and little children, marshalled by nuns, bearing tapers and singing hymns,

—a rude procession, but rather effective at a distance. Here the ceremonies were more elegant, and the scene in the church very brilliant and in good taste as well as picturesque,—the white masks of the penitents, the long white veils of the girls, the lilies and the roses, the gleaming wax-lights, the bending and kneeling worshippers, the clouds of incense, and the radiating splendors of the altar, a shaking mass of flame and gold and silver, making a very dramatic tableau.

The devotion and reverence was absolute. I have never seen it equalled save once, in the Mormon temple at Salt Lake City, in Utah, when the late Brigham Young was speaking, and after a while bluntly announced in coarse English that the Spirit of God was on him and he was going to reveal. The vast assemblage of devout Mormons then seemed to feel the bodily presence of God in their midst, just as the devout Roman peasant does to-day all over Italy. There is no mistaking the feeling and belief of this people in this matter. It is no question of *trans* or *con*, no refinement of scientific theology, with them. They have a corporeal God, and worship Him just as truly and earnestly and with as simple faith as their forefathers worshipped Jupiter on the same spot. And therein lies the mortmain grasp—the dead hand—of the priesthood of Italy. The whole scene irresistibly reminded me of the insolent retort recorded in history of a mediæval prelate to some civil ruler: "I hold your God in my hands every day." The indiscreet priest who made this famous reply only phrased in other words the "What are you going to do about it?" of the New York political rough. And the situation was very much the same.

Both here and at Massa the bishops had dull, heavy, gross faces,—the faces of men given to overeating and blind following. In fact, in Italy, ecclesiastical promotion depends on mediocrity, for it rests on servile obedience. The Roman bishop, as far as my observation goes, is not the equal, morally or intellectually, of the average American priest.

The absence of the young and middle-aged men and the men of the better classes from these religious ceremonies was marked and suggestive. (Neither at Massa did they take part or still less here.) The whole attendance and participation was by peasants and little children. The better classes were represented solely by women. In fact, the religion of Italy is a shell. Faith is in a transition state, just as in the time of Constantine. The upper classes and educated people do not believe at all in the popular religion, nor, I think, do the higher ranks of the clergy, who administer it as a political machine, and either laugh at the credulity of the common people or defend it as the best thing for them in their ignorant condition. A monk, for instance, in a well-known church of Rome, for ten cents uncovered and showed me the imprint of the feet of Christ, made on a marble slab on a certain occasion when He miraculously visited Italy. The shape of the foot was neither Hebrew nor Arabian. The size was colossal and the contour clumsy. I cannot think that the learned cardinals, many of them men of scientific and historic erudition, believed what this simple monk believed. Nevertheless, they—English and American as well as Italian cardinals—accept principalities in a kingdom whose revenues are raised from the offerings of poor peasants who come to kiss and kneel before just such relics. This relic, too, was quite respectable compared with many of them, and their quantity is innumerable, as well as are the miracle-working images and shrines. I had my rooms in Rome on a short street, about the length of two Philadelphia squares, and situated in the middle of the city. At one end of the street was the decapitated head of St. John and at the other a picture of the Madonna—quite a good work of art, by the way—which has spoken from its frame, and is, in consequence, very much adored. Lights were always burning at its shrine, which I never found deserted of worshippers. I met several Madonnas who had spoken or moved their eyes, and were in consequence objects of special adoration. Indeed, the popularity of certain images in Italy to the exclusion of others apparently equally deserving is one of the curious features of the churches. These inanimate idols of wood or wax or marble have their fortunes just like popular preachers or actresses. In the fine old church of St. Ambrose, in Milan, on a slight metal column in the middle of the nave, I saw twined a brazen serpent which popular belief accredits as that which Moses lifted up in the desert.

Pistoja is strong in mediæval churches, abounding in graven images, odd statues, quaint tombs, curious inscriptions, legendary paintings, and the conventional rural *presepe.* Some of these things are rude, others works of high art and sometimes of great costliness. There is a famous silver altar here on which men worked for two entire centuries, the fourteenth and fifteenth, a splendid and enduring monument of patient and consecrated labor that assuredly deserves its well-known and well-won place in the history of silver-work.

Over the tomb of a great old feudal family—a family that furnished cardinals and warriors in the history of Pistoja hundreds of years ago—I found the following Latin puzzle. The tomb lies in the pavement in front of the main altar of one of the old churches:

Terra Teras Terram
Te Terram Terra
Tenebit.
Terra Trahet Transit
Torrida Terra
Trahet.

This play on *terra* is not infrequent in the mediæval epitaphs.

In another old church there is a Bambino, with its little legs tightly wrapped and swaddled, just as Italian

women swaddle their babies to-day, which is very much
the same way as Indian papooses are bound up in our
country, excepting that boards are not used. The humble homeliness of this representation seemed at first sight
very odd and ignorant, but it probably is the literal
truth. I suppose the middle and lower-class Roman
women in the time of Augustus swaddled their children
in just the same way as the same classes do here now,
and if so, then these provincial peasants, in their childlike simplicity, are right, and the conventional picture
of the Madonna and child, the world over, is wrong,
so far as the accurate representation of fact is concerned.

Among so much that is rude and coarse and ignorant,
one comes all the time on fine paintings, beautiful frescos, and grand carvings and statuary.

At this provincial place I had the experience of a
purely Italian reception. There was not a servant or
attendant of any kind at the inn who spoke a word of
French, German, or English. The table, which was
excellent, was of Italian cooking. The service was
unexceptionable and the rooms were good and clean,
but how these Italian inns exist is a continual mystery.
Here again I was the only guest, enjoying the undivided
attention and service of the whole establishment, which
was complete and full. At Bologna I met an acquaintance who had followed my visit to Pistoja about a week
later and gone to the same inn. He also had had the
house to himself during his stay. Nevertheless, these
inns, though existing apparently on the casual chance
of an occasional visitor, are excellent and often admirable
hostelries,—everything clean and good, the service of a
high order, the table plentiful, even to a fair selection
of wines, and the host cheerful, attentive, and obliging.
The rooms, and halls too, are generally lined with old
oil-paintings and bric-a-brac carvings, and in the evenings there is good music on "the piazza."

Pistoja is a fairly pleasant place to rest in, because

coming from the north you enter here on the lovely land of Tuscany and meet its early charms. Here you begin to see the laughing vineyards, with the vines and grapes festooned in graceful sweeps, until all the fields seem to be dancing like little loves and Bacchuses. Here you find again—after the ashen and leaden gloom of England—the dear blue skies of our own land. Here in this very Pistoja you can sit in the open air in the streets or piazzas (public squares) and drink your wine under groves of blushing oleanders. Here are the golden lemon-trees and flowering almonds, the fragrant orange-blossoms, and avenues of grieving cypress. Here are the dark-green olive-trees, the generous breast of the earth.

Perhaps the most distinctive feature of the landscape of Italy is the human shape which the olive-tree takes. It seems always to be a human form struggling to escape from the imprisonment of a lower life. Sometimes these shapes are of a grotesque and goblin effect, but more often they are writhing, twisted, and contorted as if in pain. In the very fields and hillsides all around him, one reads Ovid again, and all that weird legend of torture and suffering in an outer life so strong in Italian literature. It needs no imagination to see in these gnarled trunks and struggling roots the imprisoned souls of Dante's verse and Doré's pencil. They are there. These ghostly trees inspired the poet and the painter.

Tuscany has always been the native home of beauty. It was the land of the Etruscans, that wonderful people whose sense of form is yet a marvel. It was the "Tyrrhenian shores" of the Greek, but it was never lovelier or more fascinating than it is now.

v

CHAPTER XXXIV.

RAVENNA.

An Abandoned Imperial City—Christian and Arian Ruins—The Cradle of Pure Christian Art and Civilization—The Old Mosaics—The Honor oe Melchisedek in the Churches of Ravenna—Tomb of Theodoric—Dull Bologna.

To get to Ravenna from almost anywhere, as the lines of travel are now arranged, one is forced to go through Bologna, and as the Italian railways connect by what Italians themselves call "coincidences," one has usually some time on hand there. It is a fatal railway centre, to which one comes again and again in seeing North Italy, for Bologna is a dull, heavy town, monotonous from its perpetual arcades, which soon lose their first effect of novelty, and serve only to darken and depress. The place has the gloominess without the picturesqueness of a mediæval-built city, and in its general effect is unpleasing, devoid of lightness, elegance, or cultivated taste. Even its famous leaning-towers are heavy, dirty, and drunken-looking. It is coarse, solid, very substantial, but shapeless,—something like its famous sausages, which are its symbolic product and development. It has contributed some other achievements to the meat-market of the world, which are proudly displayed in its shops. The mass of the people whom you see on the streets are like their town. They have heavy forms, gross, round faces, the lines almost obliterated by corpulence,—the faces and bodies of heavy feeders, well-to-do, vulgar bourgeois.

The architecture is solid, monotonous, and much of it rough. Perhaps the central point of interest which they show one is a singular pile of churches, coming through several ages down from the fifth century, and now all worked into one. These churches, seven in number, were built in a confused kind of way, at different times, on the site of an ancient temple of Isis. They are of different levels, one being clear under the main one and serving now as a crypt, of different orders of architecture, mostly quite rude and early, of different sizes, shapes, and dedications. As they could not all exist in this tumbled-over condition, each encroaching on the other and pushing it into ruin, they have all been restored, made to communicate interiorly, and built or pressed into one conglomerate mass known now as St. Stephen's. It is quite interesting and suggestive, but it is a kind of sausage, too, in its way.

I have been laid over at Bologna twice, and am always glad to get out of it. It is a town where the sense of the predominance of the physical is oppressive and repulsive,—Bologna " la grassa."

From heavy Bologna you run down to Ravenna returning, unless you are going to make the coast-line tour of Italy. Ravenna, once the capital of the Occidental Empire, the city of emperors, exarchs, and regal bishops, though rude and fallen, stripped of its former wealth and possessions, and a very picture of desolation, is a most interesting place.

It is of vast historic significance, as the point where Christian art and social life had opportunities to develop their own growth, free from the dominating intellectual influences of the Roman civilization which they succeeded and displaced. Here Christian civilization flourished on its own soil and was powerful. It could develop freely its own germ and law of society, affected only by the Byzantine culture which it met on even terms, fighting and trading with the East.

The town in its general effect is rude, humble, and inelegant, poorly laid out, and the few palaces yet standing showing little traces of magnificence or luxury. The dwellings of the commoner kind are very poor and coarse, the streets narrow and confined. There are no grand piazzas or promenades, or great, luxurious, open spaces. The tombs of emperors and empresses are solid and enduring, but their decoration rude and primitive. In fact, it is hard to think of Ravenna as an imperial centre. The churches are interesting in their early half-Byzantine order of architecture and their quaint mosaics, picturing rudely the Christian thought and legend of early mediæval history.

They show how strong was the influence of the Old Testament on the thinking and life of the early centuries as compared with ours. Moses, Abraham, Elijah, Joshua, Abel, Melchisedek, Samson, Solomon, Adam, were real men for Europe in that age, whose influence was daily felt and appreciated. The churches of Italy are full of their images. In these churches of Ravenna the influencing force seems to have been the patriarchal and earlier life of the Old Testament. Melchisedek offering bread and wine is everywhere. It is one of the features of Ravenna. The quaint representations of this scene pictured on altar after altar in old mosaic, prove how minute is the change in the daily habits of life here even through the length of a thousand years. Melchisedek, the friend of God and King of Salem, generally stands behind or near a humble wooden table on which are the bread and wine. The stiff little table is precisely such as is found in a common Italian dwelling now. The wine is in a cheap crane-necked flask, just as it is sold in any Roman shop now, and the bread is a pile of the same execrably sodden wads served one in any *trattoria* to-day. The meal of Melchisedek, as set forth in these antique Ravenna mosaics, is precisely that which has been served me more than once this year when I entered a wayside inn in rural Italy and asked for lunch. Next after this scene comes

Abel with his sacrifice of a lamb, and the offering up of Isaac. Abraham entertaining the three angels —the table with the food on it being always conspicuous—and Elijah fed by the ravens occur often. Briefly stated, the sacrificial legend of the Old Testament, and those stories from it which relate the giving or taking of food from heaven, are the *motif* of these walls. The pictures of these scenes generally occur in chronological succession, closing with the life of Christ, —a kind of illustrated historical argument. The actual scene of the Crucifixion does not often appear, as it rarely ever does in the Catacombs, and for the same reason, that the event was yet a matter of deep shame and mortification to the struggling Church. The symbol of the cross does not appear in the Catacombs, I think, at all until the fourth century.

The predominant influence on the early Church at Ravenna was not only the Old Testament, but, very singularly, the first few chapters of it. This is strongly evidenced by the old mosaics. These pictured walls were the church history of the time, and the great bulk of their history does not get beyond the biblical record as contained in the book of Genesis, short of the story of Joseph. Indeed, if a travelling Japanese scholar, ignorant of our history, were to drop down in Ravenna, he would probably think that Melchisedek was the divinity to whose worship these strange old churches had been erected.

This revelation of these almost forgotten walls is an evidence of how insularity or ignorance may amplify any fragment that seizes on its imagination, and perhaps swell it into an imposing fabric. These early Christians, rude and simple and earnest, knew nothing more of Melchisedek than we do, but his brief story, appealing in some way to their hopes or wants, became a vivid reality, directing their devotions and coloring their whole theological thought for several centuries. This name of Melchisedek, which is not named perhaps once a year

28

in a modern Protestant church, was to these Ravenna Christians a name second only to that of Christ.

The Ravenna which we see is the Ravenna of the sixth century, and these old basilicas are therefore not lumbered up with the importunate crowd of mediæval saints who press nearly everything else out of most of the modern Italian churches. They are filled, however, with scenes in the lives of the Christian emperors, who seem to have been held in the Church at that time in much the same honor as a saint in the Middle Ages. Church and state were evidently bound up far more closely than anything we know of now.

The mosaics, for which the town is so celebrated, and which are the specialty of its art, are all, to a modern trained eye at least, conventional, stiff, formal. It took later centuries of half pagan and classic study to give them that perfection and finish which has made them the highest order of painting for churches. The Byzantine architecture, which, with the aid of Roman culture, grew into such glory and splendor under the worldlier influences of Venice, is here constrained, primitive, and humble. There is no splendor, no grandeur, no magnificence, little of luxury and cultivation. In fact, Ravenna, in its social and æsthetic presentment, is the legitimate development of the social ideas and Essenic teachings of the New Testament, which declare war against luxury, refinement, elegance, personal ease, temporal power, riches, all that goes to make up the civilization or, as it is called in the New Testament, "the spirit" of this world.

Ravenna was a stronghold of Arianism, which has left its traces here in Arian crosses imbedded firmly in the walls and in the records of the wanderings of the ashes of some of the dead emperors and leaders who had embraced this faith. The Roman Church, on regaining power, not being, perhaps, honestly satisfied in its own mind of its power to execute its threat of burning their souls, took out its vengeance in violating their graves. Theodoric, however, after some adventures, got his bones carried back to their original resting-place prepared by his daughter, and he now sleeps peacefully in the fields outside of the walls, in a perfect stronghold of a mausoleum. I visited this last castle of the old warrior by moonlight, and, as you entered the vaulted and covered outway and passed the moat and ascended a kind of drawbridge-stairway, now permanent, you felt how savage were the instincts of the Middle Ages, when a distinguished and honored and powerful ruler had to fight for the repose of his ashes against a Church which professed to have the exclusive monopoly of teaching on earth the doctrines of Christ and the gospel of peace.

This tomb is a round tower of solid masonry, against which even a modern cannon-ball would fall harmless. It is surmounted by a single block of stone of enormous size and weight, which answers as a roof. The whole structure looks as if it were carved out of rock, or placed there by giants rather than built by men. Within this dense mass of stone—like the hollow for a kernel in a shell—there is a small altar and a huge sarcophagus. There were no guards to watch the ashes now; no janitor even to break the solemn proprieties of the place by a hungry whining for *pour-boire.* So, finding the massive grate, which opened to let air and dim light into the dungeon of the altar of the tomb, we dropped through its iron bars some lighted matches: the stone floor fortunately was dry; the shadows fell quickly back before the leaping lines of ephemeral flame, and for a moment we had all to ourselves a private illumination of the mausoleum of Theodoric the Great.

ROME.

CHAPTER XXXV.

THE ETERNAL CITY—THE SPELL OF ROME.

WHEN one first reaches the Eternal City it seems almost hopeless to write of Rome. All the centuries, all the civilizations, all the religions seem to centre here, and the mind refuses to grasp in symmetrical conception the mighty whole. Although but a small town now of only a quarter of a million of inhabitants, Rome has a wonderfully cosmopolitan atmosphere, by virtue both of historic tradition and of present fact.

Her ruins are the record of successive strata of civilizations, stretching back into the shadows of history until the shadows are lost in the darkness of total night. Her palaces are built on the seats of lost empires ; her cathedrals on the buried temples of abandoned faiths. As a matter of fact, during what is substantially known history, she has been the imperial city of the world, ruling it either by arms, learning, or ecclesiastical power, and the monuments of her past glories are splendid and instructive even in ruin.

To-day the men of influence of all countries, and of all followings, come to her to learn. And so it has been for centuries. Since the last two or three hundred years, when travel was possible, there has hardly been a distinguished name in Europe that has not in some way left its record in Rome. There is not to-day a better centre to meet the controlling men of all the world, one by one, than Rome ; and it has been so for years and years. Sooner or later they all come, either in the glory of power, or to study in art, letters, religion, or statesmanship, or driven by the stress of misfortune, to die. Indeed, the tombs of Rome are more eloquent, perhaps, than anything else of her world-wide rule and sympathy. You are startled every now and then by meeting the graves of men of distant ages, of far-off countries, of strange faiths. John Lascaris, of Constantinople, found rest here, as did Charles Edward, the young pretender to the throne of England, and his brother, Cardinal York. Daniel O'Connell, the great Irishman, gave his heart to the keeping of Rome. Shelley, Keats, and Howitt lie near together in the Protestant burial-ground outside the walls, where sleep with them brethren from Greece and Russia and America and Asia. In fact, this little graveyard, set apart as an exclusion, has become the catholic resting-place of all the world save those of the Roman faith. Angelica Kauffmann is buried in a chapel only a few houses from where I write. In that magnificent mausoleum, the crypt of St. Peter's, are the burial-urns of the three last princes of the unfortunate house of Stuart, who lost the crown of England; of Queen Christina, of Sweden; the Emperor Otho II., and others of the great ones of earth of every tongue and clime. The central building of the powerful Jesuit order is the grand and fitting tomb of Loyola. St. Peter and St. Paul, or what religious tradition accepts as their bodies, sleep in the very heart of the greatest church of all Christendom, and so all through the city. Great basilicas at almost every corner are the tombs of great men who have founded states or orders, while out the wonderful aisle of the Appian Way generals and senators and magnates of old Rome, and their friends or victims, the kings of forgotten nations, are marshalled for miles and miles in unknown and despoiled graves.

Even in the character of to-day, that present which seems so infinitesimally small in the presence of her endless past, Rome keeps her claim for catholicity and world-wide range of interest and control. The features of cosmopolitan influence and connection are stamped everywhere. On the streets Greek, Jew, and barbarian jostle each other. In the hotels, among the ruins, in the churches, you hear every tongue and see the men of all nations. Not the least of the impressive features of St. Peter's is the seemingly endless succession of the confessional-boxes, each one labelled with a different tongue, until all the ends of the earth are provided for. It seemed a little thing at first, but as you walked until wearied through arched aisles, ever on your left the perpetually-recurring confessional-niche, — *pro lingua Illyrica*—*pro lingua Hispana*—*pro lingua Anglica*, etc., —you felt the force of a claim in greater strength than any words could formulate it.

Then again, in a visible assertion of imperial rule in the faith of the world, is the great institution of the Propaganda, with its massive central building, its polyglottal printing-press, whence issue books in all tongues and languages, and its schools of priests for all nations. There are Roman Catholic churches, too, and colleges for all peoples, not merely of the Latin races, but for those of Scotland, the United States, England, and the essentially Protestant blood of the North. The printing-office of the Propaganda is particularly rich in Oriental type,—an evidence of its wide range and exhaustless scope.

Even outside of the Roman Catholic Church, which for a thousand years has held Rome in its exclusive grasp, the cosmopolitan impress and representation here are strong. Of course the foreign travel is from the whole world. You see not only priests in the national vestments of all nations and of all shades and colors of skins, but you daily meet educated visitors from all parts of the globe. At a dinner-party in good society here one frequently hears four or five languages, and generally two or three. The literature of the bookstores is consequently German, French, English, Italian, Spanish, with a sprinkling of the less frequently used tongues. The servants are forced to know at least French, and the tradesmen attempt bravely to answer in any language in which you address them.

To-day there are Hebrew synagogues and six or eight Protestant churches, German, English, and American. When one remembers that for centuries the Roman Catholic service has been the only form tolerated, and that the traditions of ages have been against any other, it can be seen how wide the doors are already opened, and how the last vestige of mediæval provincialism and insularity is disappearing. Under the reigns of Victor Emmanuel and Humbert, indeed, there is practical liberty of faith. Should a Chinaman now wish to worship God in Rome, in his own way and as his fathers have taught him, I suppose he has the same civil right to do so as he has in San Francisco, and I think he would probably be as honestly protected in that right as in California, nor would there likely be any popular interference with his devotions.

These Protestant churches, of course, are, in the main, for the use of the foreign and travelling population of the city, but so, for that matter, is all Rome. Its luxuries, its best accommodations, its galleries, its ruins, are all now for the enjoyment of the Northern barbarians, who, from far-off countries, press in to-day, —not as of old as soldiers, but peacefully as tourists and occupying the land. Without its travellers Rome would be in eternal sleep.

It is this thoroughly cosmopolitan character—taking in its embrace the whole world of to-day and stretch-·ing back through the ages in one continuous line farther than recorded history—that gives Rome its peculiar charm to men of thought and influence. Hardly a man of power or education in all history who has not been here and left in some way the record of his impression. And in a country whose literature of travel embraces such names as Addison, Ruskin, Shelley, the poet Gray, Hemans, Hawthorne, Hilliard, Howitt, Dickens, Disraeli, Cardinal Wiseman, Byron, Goethe, Bunsen, Niebuhr, Hans Andersen, Ampère, About, Montaigne, Chateaubriand, De Staël, Castelar, Taine, Gautier, and farther back Chrysostom and St. Paul and Cicero, is it any wonder that one feels appalled at ever attempting to write, and hardly knows how to begin, or where?

It is this greatness of Rome, swallowing up time and history, which, like the infinity of the ocean, draws all men to it with an irresistible fascination, as if it were a pleasure to lose themselves in its limitless existence, and which creates that insatiable longing to return, to be forever in it and of it, which every strong man who ever saw the Eternal City has confessed. This indefinable sense of Rome which takes possession of one with a kind of pantheistic force, and often by some odd power of association involuntarily floods his whole being at the mere passing memory of its laughing-eyed beggars, its incense-smelling churches, its corporeal smells wandering from dirty courts, its aromatic Pincian or the sunny, humble Trastevere,—this strange compelling sense is the evidence of the spell of its historic incantation. And those blessed ones to whom it comes are they who have drank of the real waters of the fountain of Trevi.

Rome.

CHAPTER XXXVI.

SAINT PETER'S, AND ITALIAN PREACHING.

The First Church of the World—In the Shade of a
Forest of Marble Columns—Modern Indulgences—
The Pallas Athene of Rome—Italian Preaching—An
Educating Pulpit.

I am not going to attempt a pen-painting of St.
Peter's, the first and greatest church of Christendom.
It would take a volume to merely index its wealth of
present treasure and range of suggestive and historic
association, or picture the outlines of its magnitude.
Even then one could hardly achieve a conception of its
magnificence and grandeur unless he had something to
measure it by, and in our country as yet, unfortunately,
we have not.

Let me suggest, however, a point from which one
might begin to work up to some approximate idea of its
size. Its effect and historical relation are something
entirely apart from that and higher. In all the United
States I suppose the largest and most imposing pile
sprung from a single design is "The Public Buildings,"
at Broad and Market Streets, in the city of Philadelphia.
This great structure has a base of four hundred and fifty
feet by four hundred and fifty feet—a grand square—and
is to be over five hundred feet high. Now, you could
take up this entire immense mass of building and set it
bodily down inside of the piazza or portico which is the
magnificent threshold of St. Peter's; and then you
would have so much room to spare that you could throw
around in the crevices such of our home churches as
those of Holy Trinity at either New York or Philadel-

phia, and they would be lost and hidden in the shade of the corners. Even our longitudinal Capitol at Washington with all its extensions could be placed within this wonderful portico without materially interfering with the passage-way.

This porch or piazza is five hundred and eighty-eight feet wide by one thousand and thirty-four long, and some authorities give even greater dimensions. It is flanked on either side by a magnificent forest of marble columns, arranged in semicircular avenues and roofed. Under these pillars, of which with the massive pilasters there are some three hundred and fifty, there is perpetual shade and coolness even throughout the whole summer's blaze of an Italian sun, for sunlight never penetrates their cool recesses. And this was their intention, as the Latin superscription legended above them eloquently tells: "A tabernacle for a shade in the daytime and a security and covert from the whirlwind and from the rain." And all this they literally are to-day.

More than this, with the immense façade, this noble approach serves to hide all the adjacent and rear buildings of the place, and one draws towards the entrance of St. Peter's without seeing a single other structure in the world. It stands alone in the heart of a great city. Among the buildings very happily thus kept out of sight is the iniquitous "Palace of the Holy Office," or, in English, *The Inquisition.* In the centre of this portico rises the needle-like spire of an Egyptian obelisk, one of the earliest of religious monuments, erected originally to the sun, now a captive adorning the temple of the God who made the sun. Around it play colossal fountains, which cast up massive jets of water that, after reaching a height over that of an ordinary American three-story house, return downward in delicious spray, swept by the winds over a vast area of the stone-flagged pavement of the piazza, keeping it moist and cool.

All this is but the threshold and entrance to a won-

derful church, whose nave is a magnificent sweep of
over six hundred feet in length, in whose transepts you
could place cathedrals, and where the chapels in the
side aisles are as large as a common American church.
Withal, everything within is pleasing and harmonious,
light and beautiful, and so symmetrical that, until you
think and compare, you do not see or feel the awful
size. The baby cherubs that hold up the basins of
holy water are colossal giants when you note the girth
of their limbs and compare them with those of the
human form. The doves are enormous birds, and the
angels recall the far-off shadowy days in the morning
of the world when the sons of God came down to the
fair daughters of men. The surpassing splendor of
this great temple, which gathers up in its walls a vast
congregation of churches, its uncounted wealth of marbles and precious stones, its lofty arches, through which
you ever catch new vistas of cathedral grandeur, its
labyrinth of the tombs of the great ones of the earth,
its storied sculptures, its enduring mosaics, its endless
altars laden with gold and gleaming with sacred lights,
all seem to lift it out of the limited range of the handi-
work of man and up to the proportions of some great
work of nature. In "God's first temple" to-day you
feel "the primeval forest," the mysterious influence of
rock and water and endless nature.

While there is a studied attempt in the interior decorations of St. Peter's to assert and record the sectional
characteristics of the Roman Church, particularly its
claim to temporal sovereignty and its historic struggle
against national independence, still the general effect is
so overpowering and grand that you lose in it the sense
of these blemishes just as you do of all petty details.
Protestants, at all events, ought not to quarrel with St.
Peter's, for it is the cradle of the Reformation. The
immense burden of its construction,—the main building
alone cost over fifty million dollars, and the annual repairs and keeping up now demand forty thousand dol-

lars per year,—the immense burden of this construction at a time when money was more costly than now led to the sale of indulgences as a source of revenue, which abuse was the popular lever of the Reformation. It stiffened up Luther to take the decisive step, and gave him something with which to go before the people.

A word here about indulgences, the profuse advertisements of which over the church doors are one of the first things which strike the ordinary Protestant traveller and give him a slight moral shock. The scandalous and public abuse of the system, which gave birth to the Protestant development, is long since gone here. Indulgences are not any more issued on paper and delivered, except, perhaps, in occasional and exceptional cases. In legal phrase, they take effect, not by delivery, "but by operation of law." Whenever the conditions are fulfilled they inure to the benefit of the sinner. These "conditions" are the essence of the whole thing, and are what are not popularly understood by the non-Catholic world, which commonly looks on an indulgence either as a bare license to sin or an absolute and unqualified remission of sin. The modern Roman indulgence, in its operative clause, is strictly limited in its own terms, just like the "absolution" of the Protestant Episcopal and some other Protestant denominations. It is only an authoritative declaration to those who perform certain acts of devotion that their sins will be forgiven them *on condition of true repentance.* This "condition" is the consideration. Whether the average Roman worshipper understands the condition is another question. This condition is, however, the theory and technical definition of "indulgence" as officially given here to-day, and we can hardly fairly go beyond that. The advantages accrue only to such as truly repent of their sins.

Traces of the old abuse and of the popular misconception, however, abound everywhere. Being an

irredeemable promise as far as the Church is concerned,
—that is, a promise which some one else must pay or
redeem—the thing works out exactly like an irredeemable issue of paper money. There is an uncontrolled
and reckless emission of them of all sizes and values,
from one day up to, I believe, in one case, one hundred
thousand years. Rival orders, rival churches, rival
chapels, compete in granting them, and the whole town
is flooded with them. The devotional element of Italy
not being mathematical, the poor peasants will work
away, repeating prayers, going up steps on their knees,
making pilgrimages to shrines, etc., for a thirty days'
indulgence, when the same acts, differently directed,
would bring them the same results for a thousand
years.

Again, practically there is a commercial flavor to
the whole transaction, and the contract is often drawn up
with such looseness as not only to make it bristle with
problems to a legal mind, but to suggest in equity a
"false pretence." In several churches in Rome, built
under French auspices, you read this official declaration : "Ten days' indulgence to all who pray for the
soul of the King of France granted by bull, or decree,
of Pope ——, A.D.——," many hundred years ago. I
suppose some king of France in former days sold away
the liberties of his subjects or gave away their moneys
and took his pay in this coin. But who is to be
prayed for, the unnamed king who made the bargain,
or the living king reigning at the time the prayer is
offered? And, if the latter, is it a personal boon or a
franchise of the French crown? And, if this, does it
inure to President Grévy now, as successor, or to the
National Assembly, more or less infidel, or to the body
of the French people, the ultimate and collective sovereignty of France? Or has it utterly lapsed, and does
the simple Italian peasant lose his ten days entirely?
Or does it matter at all whether the peasant has any
idea of what or whom he is praying for?

There are some curious phases in the religious life of Rome. The dominant power of the old polytheistic faith crops out all the time. The groups of minor gods displaced by Constantine reappear still in the popular saints. Apollo with his arrows survives in the beautiful youth, St. Sebastian, shot to death by Roman archers near the Colosseum, and always painted or sculptured with the shafts from the bow in his body. I have seen the Virgin Mary in the old churches of the Trastevere and in the ancient city of Pistoja with the moon depicted at her feet, the old symbol of Venus, and thought of Milton's—

"Astarte, Queen of Heaven, with crescent horn."

The divine honors paid to the emperors in the corrupt decadence of Rome are reproduced in the doctrine of the infallibility of the Pope. There are saints, too, for the seasons, saints for cities and provinces, saints for lovers, saints for harvest-time, saints for the horses, saints to be invoked for diseases, just as in the familiar mythology of our school-books, and shrines and special altars for their worship in these special characters.

But the most striking development of this tendency is comparatively recent; at least, its "push" is modern, and of our very time. Rome is to-day as thoroughly dedicated to the Virgin Mary as ever Athens was to Pallas. The Christian Roman of this generation asks of the Virgin just what the patriotic Athenian of classic times asked of Minerva, and looks to her for the same aid and protection. Her churches are far more numerous than those of any other dedication, and her altars in the churches are those most popular and frequented. Her images work the miracles and have the throngs of worshippers.

But the modern worship of the Virgin is not a mere popular impulse which might be apologized for on one hand or explained away philosophically on the other.

The order comes from the Vatican, and is a part of a policy deliberately adopted and boldly lived up to. The Church of the country avows it and glories in it. On the doors of the churches of Rome there appeared in May of this year official ecclesiastical notices, signed by high prelates, speaking of this city proudly as "Rome, the city of Mary, and Rome, the city of Jesus," giving to the woman in written language the precedence which she always has here in the hearts of her worshippers.

The religious Roman art of this generation will go into history, too, as distinctively consecrated to this new deity. Pius IX. raised in the central Piazza di Espagna a towering obelisk in honor of the triumph of the dogma of the immaculate conception. He panelled the tribunal of St. Peter's with a great tablet commemorating its official promulgation by the Œcumenical Council, and recorded on side panels the names of the cardinals, archbishops, and bishops of all the world voting for the measure. He added to the celebrated *stanze* of the Vatican—a suite of state rooms frescoed by the great masters—an additional room wholly devoted to the history of the new dogma, its passage in the council, its promulgation by himself, and the reception of the news in heaven! On one of the façades of the square base of the obelisk just mentioned there is an attempt to represent in marble the very act of the conception of the Blessed Virgin by the Holy Ghost,—a peculiar but characteristic illustration of the morbid bent of the Roman ecclesiastical mind.

Every Roman girl, the Italian women tell me, is baptized Maria. She may have as many other names as her parents choose to give her, but Maria is obligatory.

Did classic Athens ever do as much as all this for her Pallas?

I close with a word on the way they preach in Italy, which has some decided advantages over our usage.

While the sermon has become the central feature in Protestant worship instead of a mere incident, as in the old Catholic service, it is not a little singular that the preaching in the Roman churches should be so much freer and more natural than with us, and, of course, as a consequence, more effective. In the first place, it is more dramatic. In the churches of Italy a platform or scaffolding of some kind is often built in front or out of the pulpit. On this the preacher stands in full-length view of his hearers, whom he addresses all around, facing at will in any direction. On this platform, a little to the rear of the speaker, there is generally a high crucifix, a chair in which he may rest by sitting from time to time as he talks, and sometimes a little table for a glass of water, a Bible, or a handkerchief, but not for manuscript. I have never seen a Roman Catholic priest read a sermon. This platform, which is raised six or eight feet from the floor, is, in some churches, hung with tapestry, illustrating sacred legends. The whole makes a pleasing picture, and gives the speaker a much greater freedom and power of oratorical action than the rigid, straight-line, box-pulpits of our land.

And the freedom of the people is equal. When the sermon is about to begin they all settle themselves around in chairs in the best positions to hear comfortably. The churches are so large that a vast audience can be thus accommodated, each in his chair, but in irregular groups, families or friends together. When the audiences number thousands they become more compact, and around the seated hearers are dense crowds of men and women standing. No one is obliged here by stress of custom or the pressure of respectability to hear a sermon. When the service is over "church is out," and you can go, unless you think the preacher has something to say worth listening to. You are as free as at an American political meeting. If the sermon is dull or stupid you can leave at any moment.

You can go out of the building, or walk through its grand aisles, crowded with sculpture and paintings and historic tombs. At your convenience you can go back to the speaker when he grows more eloquent than the tombs or master-pieces of art. If he is not equal to the situation, you can let him alone.

In fact, the service exactly resembles our political meetings in the freedom and mobility of the audience. The preacher holds his hearers by his abilities and his eloquence and not by outside force. If he has nothing to say, or cannot give his sacred message as it should be given, he has no hearers, and no opportunity, therefore, to discredit his high office, or to make the Gospel distasteful through his own weakness or ignorance. It is just to the discipline of this training that I ascribe the general eloquence of the Roman clergy and the popular impression made by their preaching. They have the same incentive to speak well that the American politician has when addressing his fellow-citizens, or the American lecturer, who must even do more,—attract people to pay for the privilege of hearing him.

Often the scene during sermon-time in an Italian church is a very picturesque one. Women sit nursing their babes in comfortable cane chairs; others are on their knees in silent prayer; little children are playing quietly among the listening groups at the chancels of adjoining altars; squads of ecclesiastical students, in bright scarlet or blue gowns, drop in on their way to or from college to hear the noted orators, and remain as long as their critical judgments are satisfied; soldiers in uniform hang on the outskirts, and men come and go as if the sermon were a thing of life and interest and not a dead body of words. In brief, the hearers listen or the preacher has no hearers, and in either case there is not the loss of a sermon.

The average American clergyman, accustomed to hold his audience by some force outside of himself, will probably object to all this as irreverence, but I do not see that it is. I do not think it is more irreverent for children to play in the house of God than to be tortured there by unnatural confinement on high benches that drive the blood out of the legs. I do not believe it is more irreverent for poor women to nurse their children in the house of God than to stay away because they have no one to nurse them at home. And, finally, it is not more irreverent to get up and leave in the middle of a soporific sermon than to go to sleep. Moreover, if this honest freedom develops a higher order of sermons, it is the very highest kind of reverence. I notice further, on the question of reverence, that when the Roman priest is about to begin to preach he kneels on the open platform for a few moments in silent prayer, and the whole congregation kneels and prays with him.

As a training-school I can think of nothing better adapted to develop the oratorical power and real efficiency of the preacher than this custom. It is a practical use of the law of the survival of the fittest. It is exactly the training which our secular speakers undergo, and those of them who are not speakers soon ascertain it, while the conventional preacher never finds it out.

It is customary for us to speak and think of the Roman Catholic form of worship as rigid and "formal." It is, in fact, in its whole ritual and service, the most flexible in the world, and it is this very power of self-adjustment and adaptation that has given it its great hold on all times, all countries, and all peoples.

ROME.

CHAPTER XXXVII.

THE PANTHEON.

The Oldest House of Continuous Human Worship in the Civilized World—Graves of Raphael and Victor Emmanuel—Old and New—Modern Paganism—Cleaning up the Pantheon.

When you enter the Pantheon, and passing by the cheap adornment of pictures and altars look through the floating dome up to the sky "where God sitteth eternal in the heavens," you are in the oldest place of human worship in the civilized world which yet retains its ancient form and structure. The very building, as it stands to-day, is the one in which the vanished gods of classic Rome were worshipped with sacrifice and incense and prayer before Christ was born in Bethlehem, and it is the only spared monument of the kind that comes down from before the Christian era.

Robbed, plundered, defaced, now closed and voiceless in the transition of faiths, now filled with soldiers, a fortress fought around by rival Popes proclaiming themselves the vicars of a God and new gospel of peace, now given over to neglect and profane uses, the débris of mediæval night and ruin rising around its base and portico and threatening to bury it with the ages, it still stands as it stood before the angels sang the hymn of the nativity in Judea, and men worship God within its walls. In its endless associations and its perfect beauty, which cannot be torn away from it, it is the most effective and suggestive of all the temples of Christendom to-day. In the old days when the fires on its altar were kindled to Jupiter, its dead brick walls of massive masonry were outlined with pure white marble, glittering in the sun and soft in the moonlight. Popes and princes have carried this off to embellish their palaces and enrich their favorites. Its wonderful dome blazed within and without with brass and bronze. Emperor Constantine came to Rome between 600 and 700 A.D., to worship at the shrines and adore the relics which then had found a home in the Pantheon, and balanced his devotion by stripping and carrying off shiploads of its metal wealth. The plunder was completed by Pope Urban VIII., who took what was left to build a gaudy baldachino for a church and cast cannons for the castle of San Angelo,—four hundred and fifty thousand pounds. Benedict XIV. committed the latest spoliation, in taking away all the precious marbles that lined the vast attic.

Nevertheless, so grand is the conception of this building, and so perfect its proportions, that you do not see or feel the loss of these incidents. The temple stands there yet as it came from the brain of its unknown architect. You do not see the mutilation and scars of the warring centuries, just as you do not see the tawdry ornaments and wretched tin crowns and hearts and gewgaws with which modern Italian devotion has desecrated its altars and defaced its walls. The temple crushes out its ignorant priests to-day, as it has defied time itself in the past, and stands sublime in the grandeur of its simplicity.

This most effective of all buildings for worship is, in its interior, a simple dome, supported by a plain, round wall; no corridors, no naves, no transepts,— nothing to break the force and simplicity of idea. There is but one great door, whose massive bronze folds close in with the line of the wall and seem part of it. There are no windows, but the light streams in from a great circular opening in the centre of the dome, twenty-eight feet in diameter, never closed, flooding every recess and every portion with an equal ray.

There is something wonderfully effective in this idea,

which puts the temple, as it were, in direct communication with the skies of heaven, and makes it already the
threshold and vestibule of the other world. It im-
presses one at once as the natural conception of a place
of worship. This world, with all its little noise and
struggles, is utterly shut out and closed from you.
You look up and see the clouds with the birds in them
sail by. The rains of heaven fall on the porphyry pavement at your feet and lie there. They are of God and
come into His house. Or the warm sunshine streams
in and rests on some chosen altar,—a golden pathway
on which the angels ascend and descend. In the night
the moon and the stars look in and watch with men the
still shrines and voiceless tombs.

It is a temple where God is in communion with man
and speaks without a liturgy or formulated ceremony.

There is such a unity of effect, with nothing to dis-
tract or divide attention, it is so light and cheerful
and calm and loving, that you feel you are in the house
of the living God and loving Father, and not the God
of death and the grave,—the feeling which steals over
one in the gloomy shadows of the Gothic cathedral.

It is a humiliating reflection which bears down on me
every time I enter the impressive portal of this wonderful temple that what is grand here, what is elevating,
what is beautiful, is pagan; what is false, what is de-
grading, what is ignorant, is of our time and age. The
religion which is in the building was put in by its
classic builders; the superstition and vulgarity we are
responsible for.

I have attempted to outline the simple grandeur and
majesty of this temple as it sprung into life,—the best
development of ancient Roman art and civilization.
Let us see how the priest of to-day has dealt with the
finest legacy of the old faith.

We will pass by the plunder of columns and marble
and bronze for private uses,—the deliberate mutilation,
the wholesale military profanation of the church by

bishops. They may be charged to the civilization of the time, although a Church that claims the temporal rule of the world should be held responsible for its civilization.

Let us inspect the nineteenth-century contributions to this time-honored temple. As you enter, the first unpleasant sight which is apt to catch the eye is a dirty mass of white and black drapery, fastened up to some pillars just to the right of the main altar. They are the muslin banners and faded, dusty wreaths of some civil and political societies, and an object of much interest to the native Italians who throng the temple. An old sergeant or veteran in a half-civil, half-military uniform and not very neat or soldierly in appearance or carriage, keeps a kind of slouching guard over the spot. This gloomy and rather shabby pile of crape, muslin, and mechanical-looking immortelles, so common in Latin-Europe, is the grave of Victor Emmanuel. It is a great grave in a great spot, but we would make it far more impressive in one of our churches.

Around the niches are paintings of various scenes and quality. The old masters are not here. A ghastly life-size representation of the crucifixion in some kind of dark-red material, with a crown of thorns and a real white cloth around the loins, adorns one panel. A number of the altars have cheap tin votive offerings nailed up around them. Others have small common engravings or prints framed and hung up or placed near them.

The altar which attracts most attention, however, both from priest and people, and before which one nearly always finds some persons in prayer, is that of a popular Madonna,—the third one from the left of the main or high altar. It is a singular fact that certain Madonnas here, sometimes oil-paintings, two or three of whom have spoken, and sometimes marble statues, become popular favorites and the subjects of great adoration, to the entire exclusion of their neighbors. There are several other Madonnas in the Pantheon, but I never saw prayers said to them, whereas I have several times heard mass being said in front of this one, and never saw her without some one kneeling before her.

This statue is the altar-piece of an altar under which Raphael is buried, and was made by a friend and pupil for the tomb of his master. It is a much finer image, therefore, as a work of art than many that are the subjects of popular adoration. Nevertheless, this fine sculpture has a metal crown on its head, a coral necklace on its neck, and a tin heart tied on its arm. The marble babe in the arms of the Madonna has also a gilt crown and a petticoat of embroidered gray cloth around its stone legs. A rude arch of tin shapes—votive offerings sold in the shops for a penny or two—framed the entire altar. Hung up on the side of the niche, over the grave of Raphael, were two or three most wretched daubs of paintings, representing some cures in a hospital-ward effected by the miraculous intervention of the Virgin, and apparently painted by the patients. After saying their prayers in front of this image, the devout worshippers generally kiss its feet. A rude framed print of the image was placed at its base, and I have seen peasant women take that down too and kiss it and teach their children to do the same.

Such is the altar which is the centre of the nineteenth-century worship in the Pantheon.

I must add an incident illustrative of the curious condition of mind of this people, by reason of which no incongruity in the house of God seems to offend their taste or feeling, provided that it is not intended as deliberate irreverence. One day while I was in the Pantheon, mass was being said at this altar of the Madonna, only a half-dozen of worshippers assisting. Inside of the chancel of the main altar, only a few yards off and very near its base, stood an open flask of native wine, half drank. It belonged to some workmen who were cleaning the rear of the altar, and the rasping sound of whose scraping and sanding mingled with the intoning of the priests at the adjoining shrine, and was quite as audible through the church. While the whole thing was grating and offensive to us, it was evidently not meant as irreverence, and did not annoy either the worshippers or the officiating priests.

It is to be said, too, for the credit of the clergy in immediate charge of the church of the Pantheon, and in their behalf, that the decoration of the altars and walls is in better taste and less offensive than that of a large number of the churches of Rome. The altar-furnishing is mainly limited to candles of plain style. There are no wax figures, no glass cases, and no skulls or bones or other horrors. An instinct of reverence, perhaps, has saved it from much of the trumpery and tinsel, and gewgaws and frippery images, and bad millinery which disfigure many other churches here and seem to be the fitting devotional aids to the ignorant and superstitious faith of the place.

Of old the Pantheon stood in an elegant and spacious quarter of the city, and was raised on a slight elevation, which gave its symmetrical form proper effect. To-day it is found in the distant and most squalid portion of Rome—the Ghetto, from which it is not far off, excepted—and below the level of the ground. The flight of steps by which it was originally approached is buried absolutely, and you step down from the wretched modern piazza on to the floor of the ancient portico, the finest of its kind in the world. It is the centre of a network of narrow and confusing Roman streets, many of them not the width of our alleys, lined continuously with high stone buildings, densely packed with people, full of foul smells and offensive dirt of all kinds. Old houses lean up against a portion of the walls and are built into it, and beggars camp all day around and among its Corinthian columns. During the Middle Ages these grand columns had booths and stalls built into them, and vegetables and cheap meats were sold literally in the gates. How has the glory of the old temple departed !

The proportions of the main lines of this building are as wonderful in their simplicity as the building is itself in its effect. The interior, remember, is a pure rotunda, simply covered with a dome.

```
Diameter of rotunda ...............................................142 feet.
From floor to top of dome.............................................143   "
Height of wall of rotunda.............................................. 71½ "
Height of dome........................................................ 71½ "
```

or just one-half of the whole elevation. The diameter is given from inside measurements. The walls of the Pantheon are said to be 20 feet wide. The great dome of St. Peter's is 139 feet in diameter at its base, 3 feet less than the Pantheon, but it is vastly higher, the distance from the top of the cross on the dome to the floor of the church being 448 feet. It was Michael Angelo's boast, in building St. Peter's, that he would swing the Pantheon in the air, and he has done it.

But the Pantheon is a grander church than St. Peter's to-day. It is a wonder, while St. Peter's is an ecclesiastical labyrinth, and, greater than all, it is the place in which God has been continuously worshipped for nineteen hundred years.

Rome.

CHAPTER XXXVIII.

PRISON OF ST. PAUL AND ST. PETER.

Twenty-five Centuries of Dissolving Kingdoms and Faiths on One Spot—The Confusion of Ruin—St. Paul and St. Peter in the Political Prison of Rome—The Mamertine Dungeons—The Church of the Ara Cœli—The Altar of the Capitol.

WANDERING through an obscure portion of the city to-day, on my way for an afternoon dream in the Colosseum, I came suddenly upon a rude out-house of some kind, leaning against and built into a tenement house for modern Romans of the poorer sort, over the grated doorway of which was inscribed in still clear, legible letters the Latin legend, "Blessed are the dead who die in the Lord." It was the entrance probably to the vault of some ruined and forgotten Christian church which, itself, had likely been built over and out of some destroyed temple of old, for it stood near and in sight of the Forum. To-day the cheerful and airy temple of classic faith, beautiful in symmetry, proportion, and graceful Corinthian columns,—the gloomy church of mediæval religion,—heavy, dark, and dismal, with ghastly pictures and the rude votive offerings of superstition, alike are gone, and all that remains of either serves the mean use of eking out the wretched dwelling of an Italian beggar.

It is a picture of all Rome, and serves well as the vignette of a letter which shall attempt to give some faint outline of a group of ruins of mingled religious and classic interest, which in this city of ruins fitly illustrates the way in which the remains of different ages are merged into and mixed with each other.

It is the embarrassing and confusing feature of the ruins of Rome that they lie massed and piled and contorted one on another, and in and with each other. They are the survivals of chance and accident in the wreck of centuries, and hold now neither topographical nor historical relation to each other. You cannot see what you want nor anything when you want, but must take them as they come,—jumbled and piled and mixed, —Pelasgic, Etruscan, Roman, and mediæval, in one disastrous burial blent. There is no help for it now. Imperial Rome, in the splendor and solidity of her works, crushed out all that had gone before, forcing into disappearance even the massive Etruscan masonry. In later times degenerate emperors stole from their greater predecessors, taking their statues and arches and labelling them with their own disgraced names, changing the sculpture, and altering the inscriptions to suit. At times of civil war, too, one party, when successful, razed to the ground all traces of the trophies and power of the other.

But the storm of destruction came in with the establishment of the Christian religion. As this took a political form, it became, of course, evidence of both patriotic and religious fervor to destroy the temples and glories of the old faith, and it is a wonder that as much survives as does. Temples were everywhere converted into churches, and statues of the classic deities into those of the popes, the Virgin Mary, and the saints.

The wanton and inexcusable destruction took place, however, in the Middle Ages, when popes and cardinals built great palaces out of the temples and public buildings of antiquity,—when the walls of the Colosseum itself were torn down to get the iron braces out of them, —and when tombs and palaces and temples were robbed of fine statues by thousands, that they might be burned down for lime. To the intelligent mediæval mind this was the most satisfactory way of obtaining a supply of iron and lime. Two popes at different

times—seized no doubt with an attack of development
—erected manufactories for woollen goods and saltpetre
in the Colosseum and out of its plundered walls, and the
history of all Rome is full of similar atrocities of van-
dalism.

To-day the most interesting ruins of Rome lie in the
dirtiest quarter of the town, and are mixed up inextri-
cably with the commonest kind of dwellings and small
shops, stables and mean out-houses. The same piece
of masonry may be common, or what in modern law
we call "a party wall," to a half-excavated Roman
temple and a squalid hovel of to-day, reeking with
filthy odors, fleas, and young beggars. Ruins, churches,
and hovels, and sometimes inhabited palaces, lie thus
up against each other, one bit of wall or foundation
representing the different uses of successive centuries
far apart. Even the streets have been pushed aside by
the fortunes of ages, and run sometimes over, sometimes
under, sometimes clambering around, a pile of picturesque and traditional brick and marble. When you
add to this the fact that human habitation for thousands of years has gradually raised the level of the
surface of the earth from thirty to a hundred feet,—
that all the Forum, for instance, once the centre of municipal life, is now reached only by *excavation*, and
that you look down steep banks into the halls where
Roman senators once walked and Roman orators ha-
rangued the populace,—you have some idea of how
utter the ruin is, and how fragmentary and piecemeal
are even the best survivals.

Following up the rude grate with its scriptural legend, now diverted to such thoroughly unconsecrated
uses, I found that the house to which it served as an
attachment gradually merged, after about a hundred
feet of "row" tenement buildings on no particular line,
but all closely joined together by a kind of growth
rather than construction, into the well-known landmark, the prison of St. Peter and St. Paul, where they

are said to have suffered confinement for nine months. The entrance to the prison, which was a common Roman house-front, is on the ground, and over the prison-door is now a rude marble carving representing St. Peter with his keys and St. Paul with a sword, looking out of an iron grate,—something like the common bars which form the windows of an ordinary Pennsylvania county-jail.

This humble building, invested with such sacred interest, and which is the entrance into one of the ugliest dungeons of history, horrible in the merciless ignorance of its construction, and frightful with a record of weary ages of atrocious and inhuman cruelties, has been converted, with some of the interior cells, into a chapel or oratory—a low-ceilinged room known as the church of *San Pietro in Carcere.* There is built over it and into the hillside another church—Saint Joseph, of the carpenters—which answers for the guild of that trade something of the purposes of the ancient "Carpenters' Hall," of Philadelphia. As the whole face of the hill is apparently one building, and the entrance to the prison is almost under ground, visitors frequently enter Saint Joseph's Church, supposing they are in San Pietro in Carcere. These ugly dungeons, known as the Mamertine prisons, although chiefly visited now for their religious traditions, have a historic interest reaching back nearly six hundred years before the time of Saints Peter and Paul. They—or at least the first cells—were built over five hundred years before Christ, in the kingly period, and the masonry is said to be the best specimen of Etruscan work of the magnitude extant. Here the Catiline conspirators were executed— Cicero coming out of the prison and announcing it in person to the people on the Forum, which is just adjacent. Here, for a thousand years, the savage punishments of Republican and Imperial Rome were visited on State prisoners, and the list of victims is as distinguished as it is sad.

It is the tradition, and it seems to be a reasonable one, that Saint Peter and Saint Paul were both confined here awaiting death, and that from these gloomy rooms were written the Second Epistle of Saint Peter: "*Shortly I must put off this my tabernacle;*" and also the Second Epistle of Saint Paul to Timothy: "*The time of my departure is at hand.*" Saint Peter and Saint Paul were both distinguished leaders of a new faith, whose followers were bound together by especial ties. Martyrdom was the highest honor of the church, and from the very first the memory and the relics of the martyrs were preserved with jealous fervor and handed down with pious care—the heirlooms of the faith. Moreover, during the early centuries, the management of the church was more honest than in later times. I had rather credit a tradition of the second century than a miracle of the fifteenth. It is in every way reasonable, I think, to accept this tradition, and to think and believe that this was the very spot of the sufferings of the great apostles. And knowing this, the situation becomes intensely dramatic, for when the expected martyrs entered this gloomy prison, or as they came out of it for trial or for death, they faced, and saw grouped around them, within a small centre, the Forum, the citadel of the Capitol, the imperial palace of justice, the great temple of Jupiter, arches, corridors of Corinthian columns, the temples of a galaxy of deities—all the splendor, glories, and power of Rome blazing around them, or frowning on the imperial hill close above them.

Even to-day, from this little point of Christian interest, standing in front of an obscure chapel as plain and modest and unecclesiastical-looking as a prairie Methodist meeting-house, the traveller can see and study the historic citadel of the Capitol, bristling with the legends of centuries, the great Forum, the famous palace of the Cæsars, the Colosseum, the arches of Constantine, Septimus Severus, and that of Titus, with the ark and the golden candle-sticks,—graven trophies commemo-

rating the capture of Jerusalem,—the temple of the sun,
the old Roman pavement of the *via triumphalis* that rang
so often to the returning tread of victorious armies, wind-
ing now like a snake in the sun by the ruined columns
that tell of a dead faith and the open porches of the
sleepy churches of the new, and ruins, ruins, ruins re-
ceding through the centuries—from mediæval to classic
times, from classic to Etruscan, from Etruscan to prehistoric,—the shadowless morning of the world.

Retracing our steps to the old grated out-house which
served as a *point d'appui* for our explorations, it is found
to be at the threshold of a dirty flight of small pebbled
stairs, which seems to lose itself shortly in a bank of
earth and ruined brickwork. Instead of being lost,
however, the staircase only disappears around the base
of a hill to appear on the other side with marble and
sandstone steps, and turns out to be a historic flight.
Up these steps, centuries before the birth of Christ, was
fought many a stout battle for the possession of the
Capitol. On this hillside had cackled the sacred geese
of Juno, and at the head of this flight had stood the
bold soldier Manlius when he defended the citadel.
Here for ages had trodden senators and generals and
high priests. To-day they were hung, not with triumphal banners, but with dirty washing suspended by
strings from dilapidated windows and roofs. Unclean
children, goats, and dogs played together in the sand and
pebbles. Slovenly women sat or idly lounged at the
doors of the hovels which clambered up the hillside
line of the once imperial flight.

Pushing up these steps you come on an entrance to
the piazza of the modern Capitol, flanked on three sides
with historic and handsome marble palaces, and filled
with statuary familiar, and some of it dear, to the art
world. Even the roofs around the entire square are
lined with ranks of colossal statues of the heroes and
great men of Rome, standing like sentinels forever.

Resisting the temptation to loiter here, but going still further on and up the picturesque stairs, worn half into ruin by the use of ages, I came by a sharp turn on a half-hidden side entrance to one of the most striking and historically interesting of the churches of Rome, the *Ara Cœli*. It was a fête day, and as I pushed aside the heavy leathern curtain which masked the entrance a stifling cloud of incense swept out into the air with the prayers and music. Endless wax lights from altars in every direction half illuminated the vast building, throwing moving shadows here, reflecting back there with a half lurid glare from the scarlet-draped columns. More like an English cathedral than a Roman church, this building was crowded with the tombs and busts and names of the great dead,—nobles, princes, cardinals, popes. Every foot of the floor of this church was paved with tablets, effigies, and strangely etched stones covering graves. These etched pictures were mostly worn to barely traceable lines, the inscriptions almost obliterated, and the effigies had generally their noses, faces, and all salient limbs worn bare and flat by the feet of the worshipping multitudes who had trodden there for hundreds of years.

So crowded with religious associations and incident is this church that the altar chapels succeed each other, without interval, all around the three walls, front and sides, and two are erected around the pillars of the nave. Many of the altars are the burial-places of noble families, their niches lined with tablets and sculptured figures. And well might religious tradition centre and cluster here, for this Christian church stands on the ancient site of the great temple of Jupiter Capitolinus —the national shrine of the old Roman State. It was the great pagan temple which crowned the Capitoline hill—the heart of the power and glory of Rome. Founded six hundred years before Christ, it was several times destroyed and rebuilt as a pagan temple, and, somewhere about six hundred years after Christ, was finally transmuted into a Christian church—the church covering the site of the temple of Jupiter, which was comparatively small, as were all the temples, and also, as some authorities say, of the great basilica, or court of justice of the capital, and built out of their ruins. To-day the twenty-two great pillars which form the aisles are of different sizes, shapes, materials, and architecture, showing that they were taken from temple or palace just as they could be had. This great basilica on the Capitol hill—the basilica of the imperial palace —was the judgment hall where St. Paul stood his trial, "an ambassador in bonds," where he was condemned to die, and from whence he went out "ready to be offered." It was down the ruined steps we have ascended that he descended into the dungeon at the bottom of the hill, which was the vestibule to martyrdom. The Christian traditions and interest of the spot date, therefore, far back of its formal consecration to Christian worship.

This church of the *Ara Cœli,* dim and dingy in the fast-fading splendor of centuries, has been the site of human worship for twenty-five hundred years of recorded history. Its history has been the history of religious faith and progress in Rome all that time. The stones in its walls have seen sacrifices smoking and heard prayers ascend to Jupiter for victory. In sight of it in the long centuries a great arch was erected to Isis, and crumbled away. Near by it a temple arose to the sun, and in the course of years was buried under a new city. Almost on its threshold the imperial decrees of Constantine, establishing the civil rights of Christianity, must have been published. To-day it is the home and sacred shrine of the miraculous image of the Bambino, which devout Romans gather in multitudes to adore.

The door by which I entered the *Ara Cœli* was a side entrance. From the front there sweeps down another immense flight of steps, each step a venerable base of worn gray stone. When the *Ara Cœli* was the temple of Jupiter it was up this way that Julius Cæsar climbed on his knees to return thanks at the great altar, smoking with grateful sacrifices, for his Gallic victories. So even the devotion of the Scala Santa has a pagan precedent.

It was in this church—the very heart of the history of Rome, listening to the lazy chanting of vespers—that Gibbon, as he himself tells us, conceived the idea of writing the "Decline and Fall."

The church has a further world-wide interest as being, with the convent attached, the ecclesiastical headquarters of the Order of Franciscans, the barefooted friars, followers of St. Francis of Assisium. The general of the order resides in this convent, and the great sunny steps leading into the front entrance to the church are generally covered over with unwashed, brown-gowned friars, with their bare heads and rope girdles, and still dirtier beggars picking up pennies from tourists and fleas from each other. In Italy this is called poetic and picturesque; in our land it would simply be called filthy, and the crowd driven off by a policeman.

In virtue of the civic as well as religious interest of this site and its traditions the church of the *Ara Cœli* is the municipal church of Rome, and over its doors, along with an image of the Virgin Mary, is blazoned the familiar monogram S. P. Q. R. It is still the altar—be the cultus Christian or pagan—of the God of the Capitol.

Rome.

Q   31

CHAPTER XXXIX.

THE PALACE OF THE INQUISITION.

The Gloomy Palace of the Holy Office—A Deaf Stone Grave in the Heart of a Moving City—An Inhuman Construction—The Inquisition as it Exists To-day—A Prisoner of the Inquisition of the Nineteenth Century.

Just behind that noble grove of pillars which forms the wonderful portico of St. Peter's and to the right as you leave the church, but masked by some common, irregular structures, there arises a gloomy and forbidding pile of massive masonry known to Rome as the " Palace of the Holy Office." This sacred or sacrilegious euphemism conceals a celebrated building which is looked for with much interest by American visitors, and regarded with singular emotion and profound thankfulness that it too now belongs to Rome of the past—the Rome of Caligula and Nero and the Borgias. For reasons readily understood it does not figure very conspicuously in the guide-books.

This accursed building, in which they killed the body, and sometimes the soul, is an immense structure of solid stone-work, nearly four hundred feet in front. It is almost rectangular in shape, the front being the long side, and is a little over fifty feet in height. The outer walls are many feet in thickness, and in places buttressed. There are almost no windows in the entire building. The immense wall of the north end is one unrelieved blank, unbroken by an opening of any kind. The entire north wing has but three small windows, all of them thirty-six feet above the ground, equal to the fourth story of an average Philadelphia house. In the main building there are a few windows, grated with immense iron bars. In the south wing there are no windows excepting at the height of the three in the northern wing, although there are imitation windows on a lower floor, so well constructed and painted as to deceive one at first into the belief that they were real. Built into the back is the rear of a large church, which effectually closes up that side.

For all ingress or exit to this immense and terrible building there is but one visible door, and it gave me a sensation of pleasure to see standing on guard before it, with bayonet fixed, a bright-eyed, red-cheeked young soldier of the army of Italy. The people have confiscated this palace of atrocities, and it is now used as a military station and barracks.

In the Revolution of 1848 the gates of this merciless structure, at once judgment-hall and prison, were opened and the prisoners set free. I marvel greatly that it was not then razed to the ground, for it was a more infamous building than the Bastile, and more justly the object of wrath and vengeance, inasmuch as it had been blasphemously conducted in the name of God. In 1849 the Inquisition, as an institution, was formally abolished by the Roman Assembly during its brief tenure of power, but was re-established by Pius IX. the same year when he regained his authority.

Victor Emmanuel, when he was made king, again cleared out the building, and it may be a matter of some interest to know that military possession was taken of it by the present king, then a lieutenant-general in his father's army. The Inquisition still survives, however, as an institution and court of the Roman Church under Pope Leo XIII. The organization is that established in the sixteenth century,—a body of twelve cardinals with the Pope officially at its head, —and its secret sessions are now held in the Vatican. Its legal title is *Sacra Congregatio Romanæ et Universalis Inquisitionis,*—The Holy Congregation for the

Inquisition of Rome and the whole Church. Its power, however, is greatly limited and confined by the civil law, and it dares no more arrest a Roman citizen. It has full power, however, I believe, over the bishops and priests of the Roman Catholic Church, and probably over the entire population of the Vatican enclosure— that curious little ecclesiastical *imperium* in a civil *imperio*—which is too much. I suppose an American priest or bishop could be imprisoned here if he chose to come over and put his head in the tiger's mouth.

While the lowering Palace of the Holy Office, with its deaf stone ears and voiceless walls, is the representative monument of the Inquisition, designed and specially built for its dreadful uses, it has not been the scene of some of its historic crimes most familiarly known to the civilized world. Galileo did not make within its walls his famous recantation of the movement of the earth. That shameful triumph of brutal ignorance took place in the convent of the Church of Santa Maria Sopra Minerva, long used as the tribunal and dungeon of the Inquisition. Bruno, for teaching the heresy of the Copernican system, was not burnt in its court, but in the Campo de Fiori, a kind of Roman Smithfield, across the river, where the barbarous *autos-da-fe* of that time were customarily held. It is now a dirty market-place, wide and open, filled with foul smells and petty traffic. Savanarola was burnt at Florence.

But although this palace, only erected about 1600, has been spared some of the dramatic horrors of the history of the Inquisition, it is the building which must ever be associated in the public mind with this institution and bear its odium,—an odium that will grow stronger and deeper as men grow gentler and juster and more Christian. It was the official head-quarters of the Inquisition, the seat of the unjust judge, the chamber of torture and of death,—built deliberately and in cold blood for the worst purposes of the institution, when it was at the height of its power and cruelty. I do not propose in this place to enter into any argument as to the nature or character of the secret trials of the Inquisition. I am only describing the character and appearance of the building prepared for its operations,—a building constructed so that human eye cannot see nor ear hear what is going on within it, and which is stronger than a castle. In this building the most appalling tortures, the most atrocious murders might be carried on within twenty feet of a passer-by on the street of a crowded city. It is a building whose plan and construction is unholy—a building literally conceived in sin and born in iniquity, and which has no right to exist.

So much for the outside and the story which it tells. I will let Mr. A. J. C. Hare, a writer whose exhaustive studies on Rome are known the world over, tell in a few brief lines the story of the inside:

"In the interior of the building is a lofty hall with gloomy frescos of Dominican saints, and many terrible dungeons and cells, in which the visitor is unable to stand upright, having their vaulted ceilings lined with reeds to deaden sound. When the people rushed into the Inquisition at the Revolution, a number of human bones were found in these vaults, which so excited the popular fury that an attack on the Dominican Convent at the Minerva was anticipated."

While these things add to the dramatic horrors of the place, they do not essentially increase its wrong. To the Anglo-Saxon mind secret trial is a wrong which cannot be very well made worse. It is unfair; it is a harm to the State as well as to the prisoner. It is in itself a violation of law and a prostitution of justice, and a fit ground for violent revolution. And it is just because this belief is grounded in us we have no bastiles and no inquisitions. And I think the same good day is coming for the Romans. It is customary to charge the outrages, moral and physical, of the Inquisition on the alleged cruelty of the Italian nature. As the Italian people have, however, within thirty years three times driven out the institution, it can hardly with fairness be laid to their doors.

It is said also in its defence that its terrible and inhuman punishments were mediæval, and to be charged to the spirit of the age, and that they could not be repeated now under any circumstances. This is simply not the case. The claws of the ecclesiastical tiger of Rome are cut and his fangs muzzled, but claws and teeth are both there yet. I suppose it perhaps would not do to burn an offender in 1880 in the piazza of St. Peter's for not thinking as you wanted him to, but I have seen a man, yet comparatively young, who, a few years ago, when Pope Pius IX.—who was claimed to have been a gentle ruler—was in power, was arrested without warning, hearing, or being allowed bail, confined in the Inquisition, tried secretly, and sentenced to a punishment of diabolic ingenuity and cruelty. He was chained to the bottom of a flat-boat in the river without a cover day or night, exposed to the glare of the sun and the deadly damps of the night air. When you understand that the Italian never walks in the sun for fear of it, but seeks even the morning shade of the street, never sleeps with an open window for dread of the malarial air from the Campagna, you see the fiendish intent of this punishment. And most of the squad in this boat did die, as they were meant to,— burned to death by the sun instead of the fagot, by slow torture instead of quick torture.

The dismantled palace of the Inquisition is one of the features of the Rome that has gone. It is one of the few monuments that the world would not willingly see restored. It has passed into the dust of history only within living memory, but its sinister walls are already as admonitory a theatre for republican musing as the débris of the Forum or the vanished altars of the Pantheon.

Rome.

CHAPTER XL.

CONSTANTINE'S BATTLE-FIELD.

In Hoc Signo—The Liliputian Face of the Imperial City—The Forum Romanum—Ruins, Ruins, Ruins—The Marble People—On the Via Triomphale—The Red Cross in the Sky.

THIS morning, while out in the saddle for exercise, I rode over the battle-field which, sixteen hundred years ago, decided the fate of Rome and the course of the world's history—that decisive field over which hung in the sky the great red cross, and *in hoc signo* led Constantine into imperial power and made Christianity the religion of the State. To-day a body of Bersaglieri—Italian zouaves—were being exercised in skirmish drill on its skirts, peacefully playing at arms where the fortunes of the world had been staked and won. It is so everywhere here—the tamer uses of the present stand out in sharp contrast with the heroic memories of the past, which seem to reprove and shame them. This great battle was fought in the peaceful fields but a few miles from the walls, and its nearness to the city serves as a measure of difference in strategic movements brought about by the use of firearms and long-range weapons. To-day this field—the centre of the contest in olden times—would be but the outer line of the city defences. Crossing the Tiber on my way into Rome, I passed in by the only bridge across the north of the town—the modest little *Ponte Molle* flowing over the very spot where Constantine threw into the river the dead body of his defeated rival, Maxentius. It was in this battle and at this crossing was lost the seven-branched golden candlestick brought from the temple of Jerusalem by Titus.

It was at this little bridge, too, that the returning envoys of the Allobrogi were arrested and the guilty letters of the Catiline conspirators found on them—the letters that cost Catiline his head and brought triumph and political success and honors to Cicero. Attempting to cross this bridge, too, General Oudinot, a few years ago, met with a severe repulse, and the yellow waters were crimsoned with French blood. It is thus that every inch of ground here has its successive strata of historic associations, and one cannot help feeling, even on a pleasure party or when employed in the pettiest purposes of every-day life, that he is walking among the tombs and monuments of the great. Not a spot here but has been the scene of heroic struggle and achievement and sacrifice.

Perhaps it is this very greatness of its memories, stretching back through time in endless vistas, which so dwarfs the impressions of modern Rome and makes everything look and feel so small and little. You look for a Roman senator—you see a dirty friar. Of course, as regards physical impressions, the American eye, from the grandeur of our continent, its mighty mountains, great lakes, and noble rivers, is set on a large scale and must be readjusted to Europe, where nature has been less generous and has graven the face of the earth in miniature. The seven hills of Rome which rise so grandly on our school-books and boyish imaginations, are really inconsiderable swellings of the surface of the ground. A night or two after my arrival I attended a dinner-party at Minister Marsh's, and left without the least idea that I had been on the Esquiline hill, and that we had been drinking champagne in the classic precincts where of old Antony, and Virgil, and Horace, and Macænas had been content with the more modest brands of Falernus, and thought them good enough to send down to posterity in history and verse. It would certainly be dangerous to fall from the Tarpeian rock to-day, but there is nothing appalling in the baby cliff to an American eye. I have a friend in Colorado who has in his private grounds a much more imposing precipice. The magnificent artificial lakes, too, of classic fame must have been, many of them, mere basins, or perhaps fountains. The old Roman highways, the first military roads of history, are entirely too narrow for the march of a modern army with any safety. Even the great citadel of the capitol—the Capitoline hill of legend and tradition, still crested with palaces and stately with statued flights of stairways—is yet a very modest elevation. The Pantheon is but a small church, as indeed were all the Roman temples, the service being sacrificial and conducted by the priests alone, or, at most, sometimes in the presence of a few distinguished personages of state. The Tiber, which gleams like a golden thread through all the poets, is a dirty, muddy, unpicturesque stream of inconsiderable width, but of some military consequence by reason of its depth and slippery banks. The Corso, with all the glamour which the carnival has thrown about it, although now the leading street of Rome, as in the days of imperial glory, when it was the *via lata,* or Broadway, of the capital, is quite narrow and unimposing, its shops meagre, its sidewalks wretched—one of those places that, if in Philadelphia, would be thrown up as a reproach to Councils, and adduced as an instance of the inefficiency of Republican administration in cities.

The Forum, that magnificent theatre which shines so splendidly in imagination, is a space of very moderate dimensions as seen on the ground. It hardly seems adequate at all to the purposes with which history credits it. It is a lengthy quadrilateral area, narrowing from one base to the other. The extreme landmarks, from the standing arch of Severus to the ruined arch of Fabius, are perfectly well known. This space includes the *comitium,* an open place for holding mass meetings, and the *forum* proper. Its dimensions, as given by Bunsen, are but six hundred feet in length by

an average breadth of say one hundred and fifty feet.
And this area, although probably entirely flagged with
stone or marble pavement, was not an unobstructed
space, but was studded with public monuments, altars,
columns, tombs, statuary, besides the several rostra, the
corridors of pillars under whose shades the orators and
clients walked, and the legion of statues of the great
generals. It is not as large as the central Penn Square
in Philadelphia, in which stands a single solid building
whose foundations are four hundred and fifty feet
square. Yet Penn Square looks of modest size to an eye
adjusted to the American range. And how the Forum
dwindles, too, when contrasted with that magnificent
sweep in Paris embracing the gardens of the Tuileries
and the Place de la Concorde. Much of the splendor
of the Forum Romanum undoubtedly came from the
grand buildings which lined its limits, the shining temples, the imposing basilicas, the triumphal arches, and
the overhanging glories of the Capitol hill; but allow-
ing for all this, it could have never have compared with
the grandeur of modern civic magnificence.

To be sure, it must be borne in mind that the attri-
tion of ages has worn down the hills, and that the continuous wreck of centuries has levelled up the surface
of the ground; but still, the history of Rome is so far
greater than its physical features that the first sight of
them generally disappoints the traveller. The altar of
the world is a small one.

Again, the general impression of Rome which one
gets from the street is one of commercial pettiness.
Everything exposed for sale is in small quantities. The
shops are petty, and meagre almost to poverty. There
is no advertising, no display, nothing of any kind to
indicate that business is being carried on on a broad or
generous scale, or with any amount either of capital or
stock of goods. With the exception of a few of the
leading stores, the shops are such as one sees in Philadelphia and New York in the poorer streets. The

wholesale feature of trade is entirely absent. Men work for small ends in a small way.

In fact, Italy, as well as all Continental Europe, lives by small economies.

It is the lesson which we must learn in America, and have been learning latterly by severe experience; and it is wonderful how much it means for the poor man or person of moderate means. These people here absolutely live on what we throw away. For instance, beef here, wholesale—a dressed beef or a quarter of it—is more costly than in Philadelphia or New York; but the steak raw, from the small butcher-shop, or cooked, from the restaurant, costs less than with us. The saving is in the division, in the consumption of every portion, and in the absence or strict limitation of the profits of middlemen. Everything is counted to the centime (the one-fifth part of our cent), in which figure all petty amounts are kept.

The benefit of this severe economy to the whole community is seen in the large number of Americans and English people of moderate means who come here to live. While residence here temporarily, or for those whose tastes or calling compel them to associate with people of distinction or influence, is as expensive as in most other places, those who come to reside permanently, and to live quietly and rather obscurely, can do so with great comfort on incomes which would not support bare life in America. The things which are lavish here are the luxuries of culture.

There is a profusion of art and ruins, which cannot be described. The heavens seem to have rained down sculpture and statuary on the favored city. There are statues of the great dead of history and tradition, of Christian and pagan, and legendary fame, by thousands and thousands. Whole galleries and corridors are lined with them. Parks and public grounds and fountains and squares and courts are thronged with a marble population, while the hundreds of churches are all stately and imposing, with a wealth of stone effigies, angels and archangels, warriors, popes, cardinals, and princes. Out the Appian Way mutilated statues, like voiceless sentries, stand guard over the unknown dead of unknown lands for miles. You cannot dig the foundations of the commonest house but you come on ruins, and these ruins may be rare and costly marbles. In fact, there are people here who "prospect" the soil for antiques and marbles, just as in Nevada or California they prospect for gold mines. Statuary, a single piece of which in our land would be the central feature of a millionaire's residence, is here found in the most out-of-the-way places, and consigned to the commonest uses. In the house where I lodge, for instance,—not a palace now or ever, but the dwelling of a citizen of the middle class,—the landings on the stone stairways are adorned with old Roman tombs; and all the time, in some new niche or corner, I come on a burial-urn, an inscription, or piece of sculpture; while over the inner court of the garden a bust of Domitian frowns all day, and looks miserable when it rains.

According to an official Roman record preserved, there were, A.D. 540, in Rome 22 great equestrian statues in bronze, of which only one remains to-day, 66 ivory statues of the gods, 80 gilt statues of the gods, of which only one remains, and no less than 3785 statues of emperors and generals in bronze. Now, of these nearly 4000 great bronzes only the very slightest number have survived, while we have thousands of marble statues which apparently were too common to be enumerated. What must have been the marble wealth of Rome, distributed in her 17,097 palaces and 13,052 fountains and 39 theatres and 9000 baths of that date, and in her numberless temples and wealthy private houses! It was a marble population as great as that of many a busy and ambitious American city of our day,—say Hartford, or Nashville, or Omaha, or Denver. And this classic population was not confined to imperial Rome, but was spread over all Italy, even to such purely commercial points as the shipping-port of Ostia. This was the legacy which pagan civilization left to the keeping of the mediæval Church.

It is a curious fact, too, that while thousands of dollars are spent annually in the restoration of classic ruins, the ruin of to-day goes steadily on. Churches are frequently falling into decay. Old arches and gateways and walls that, a few centuries ago, defended their owner's landed premises, are now peacefully falling down around farm-fields, mortified, perhaps, in their decayed gentility at their lowered fortunes. Even the faith of the hour cannot preserve its shrines. Riding, the other day, out the *Via Triomphale*, only five or six miles from the city, and on the open highway, I came on an abandoned roadside altar that, within only a few years, had been one of some pretensions. The bent cross had fallen from the top of the arched niche, the lamp—its light gone out for ever—lay untended and untouched, the once brilliant frescos, depicting in life-size figures the Crucifixion, were being washed out by the rain. The glass and iron which had protected the shrine were bent and broken. There was no sacrilegious hand to mutilate or deface the consecrated spot, but there was none to tend or protect. The service was over, the worshippers were gone; the faith of old had fled, and all this with a church almost in sight and the fallen shrine itself built into the high walls of a pile of substantial farm-buildings. I reined up my horse, to look and think, before a Christian altar, forgotten, as desolate, and silent, and abandoned of human heart and prayer, as if it had been in Thebes or Carthage, and all in sight of St. Peter's great dome.

Yes, in Rome itself, on this spot which has seen the dissolution of the greatest systems of human thought and human power, ruin is at this hour the law and order of the day. The Church, its hold on the confidence and trust of the people gone, is even now but a historic "survival," a picture slowly dissolving in the approaching rays of some new dispensation, and the civil government of Italy, in common with those of all Europe, visibly trembles under the volcanic rumblings of Red Republicanism. The red cross of Constantine is in the sky again.

Rome.

CHAPTER XLI.

OSTIA.

A BURIED CITY—THE LOST SHIPPING-PORT OF THE ANCIENT WORLD—CAMPO MORTO—IN THE WASTE OF THE MAREMNA —ANCIENT ROMAN CIVILIZATION— AN ITALIAN POMPEII—IN THE WILDERNESS AND DESERT ON THE CONFINES OF ROME— MEDIÆVAL OSTIA—THE SARACEN IN ITALY.

THIS week, in company with a New England author held in honor in Europe no less than his own country, I drove down to the buried seaport of Ostia, at the mouth of the Tiber, to spend a day among its ruins. It was our purpose to visit this locality at our leisure, and, by a somewhat careful examination of the ground in person, establish clearly to our own minds the outlines and lost physical features of what was once the first commercial metropolis of the world, and that, too, at that splendid time when its imperial dominion centered in Rome.

This lost and ancient city, now seated in the heart of pestilential swamps, and apart from any line of civilized travel, is rarely visited, although it has been the theatre of much critical study, and vast sums of money have been spent on it, from time to time, in intelligent archæological explorations. It is, however, a most interesting spot, and eloquent with the lessons of history. In fact, its mute ruins give a vividness and color to our conception of the busy life and activities of imperial Rome which you do not get in Rome itself.

Ostia was the seaport of Rome, the Tiber at Rome itself furnishing no facilities for extensive wharfage or the reception of vessels of large draught. At the flush period of the Roman power it was the Liverpool of the world. It was greater than Liverpool, for it was the shipping city of the world at a time when there were no railways or telegraphs. It was, for many centuries, the point from which the great Roman expeditions to conquer, one after another, the countries of the known world debarked. From here Scipio Africanus sailed with his fleet for Spain, and Claudius for Britain, and by this shore long, long before, Æneas had sailed up the "yellow" tide. From here for hundreds of years set out the fleets of many oared merchantmen for Carthage and Corinth and Tyre and Sidon.

To-day this city, once throbbing with the commerce of the world, and floating its triumphant navies, is absolutely abandoned, desolate, and silent. Human life has left it. The degenerate Rome of to-day hardly knows where it is, forgetting it, with its hundreds of other forgotten glories, and even the Tiber has changed its banks and deserted it. It lies under ground and under water in the centre of a deadly waste. This *mal-aria* is known, in the picturesque tongue of Italy, as the Campo Morto; so fatal is its breath that it is popularly believed to be death for a traveller to spend a night at Ostia. And, even before the shades of night fall, the passing stranger shudders—with good reason—as he sees spectral arms of pale mist stretching out from the marsh to clasp him in their deadly embrace. These fever-swamps that engulf the long-doomed town stretch into dense forests of stone-pine, mingled with thick underbrush and thickets, through which roam buffalo and wild boar. And all this within twenty miles of the gates of Rome!

That an absolute wilderness should exist within a

few miles of a great city like this is something almost
incredible to an American mind. Yet so it is. There
being no public conveyance in this direction, we hired
a private wagon and driver, and set out under our own
leadership and guidance. The driver had never been
to Ostia, and did not know where it was, and we ex-
plored our way through guide-books and maps. The
road was sufficiently bad; at times, however, the surface of the old Roman "way" came to the ground, its
massive, irregular stone blocks giving us, at any rate,
a substantial foundation.

Leaving Rome, for about two miles we had a pleasant
entourage of farms and fields. This, I believe, is a
rather modern reclamation, the whole interval between
Rome and Ostia having been for centuries a desert.
These few farms, however, seemed to feel themselves
on the frontier of life and near the confines of the land
of death. There was a stillness and want of motion
that seemed lethargic, and almost oppressed you, even
passing through it. There were a few closed chapels
and some abandoned wayside altars falling to ruins.
Every haystack was surmounted with a cross, as if
appealing to heaven. At about the extreme limits of
cultivation there is a monastery, which, however, the
monks desert in the summer, fleeing for their lives.
In the winter they inhabit their possessions with comparative safety, tending some good vineyards, and, I
suppose, the chapels of the vicinage. Under the
stimulus of modern science they have recently undertaken the cultivation of the eucalyptus tree, which they
raise in groves, and from which they manufacture a
liquor which is claimed to be a useful preventive
against the malaria and fevers.

Very soon this meagre life died away, and we were
in a desert, with the domes and campaniles of Rome in
sight. From here to Ostia we rode through a dreary
waste—dismal, silent, and barren of cultivation. The
soil is good enough if reclaimed from the malarial

swamps, but man has given it up. The swamps, which, even in the time of Troy, were known as unhealthy, had been abandoned in modern times entirely, and had become a refuge for criminals and convicts. Here and there a straw hut, not any better than our Indian wigwam, attested the solitary presence of some outcast or waif-life, but even these were few and far apart. Within very recent years—since the government has undertaken the work of systematic exploration at Ostia —this kind of thing has been broken up, and travel is safe enough, although there has been one known case of brigandage this spring.

The sharp contrast comes when one remembers that centuries and centuries ago this desolated waste over which we rode was smiling with villas, the homes of opulence and cultivation. History tells us that there was once a time when Ostia, with its eighty thousand of inhabitants, was an actual suburb of Rome, the distance between the two being an unbroken line of country houses and residences, built on a scale of luxury and magnificence which has never been equalled anywhere or at any time else in the world. The classic writers speak of the "great mountains of white marble" seen far out on the sea which guarded this avenue of nations to the imperial city.

The Ostia which students go to see and savants to explore to-day is a town of twofold corporeal shape— old Ostia and new Ostia. Both are gone, and are to be seen only in their ruins. The one is a wreck of Roman greatness, pagan and imperial; the other, of Roman power, mediæval and Christian.

It is of old Ostia that I have been speaking so far, which to-day is simply a rough surface of field, broken by tumuli and ridges. Cropping out of this surface at odd intervals you see broken bits and masses of massive brick masonry, the surviving remnants of arches and temples and forums and tombs. In the sheltered niche of a storm-beaten and crumbling brick archway

32*

over the imposing gate of the city we fell suddenly
upon a half-wild bitch, of Campagna breed, with a
litter of pups—the only resident of the once-powerful
city. She looked as much startled as we were, but,
after a growl or two, settled down to friendship, and
was perhaps glad of an incident to break the unevent-
ful monotony of the wilderness.

Excavations at Ostia have been made during recent
years on a large scale and in an intelligent and judicious
manner. They are of peculiar historic value, as, the
story of the city being so well known, they cannot be
used to support theories or vague conjectures, but
become illustrative evidence of fixed history. Ostia
was also a purely Roman city. Its remains are the
remains of a purely Roman civilization, unembarrassed
by any Etruscan or Grecian admixture, and they reveal
in vivid form a perfect picture of the daily life of ancient
Roman society. Excavations have been made which
develop not only temples and baths and public buildings and detached walls, but long lines of streets entering into each other, and in one district running down
to the once-busy wharves. You can walk on the streets
in which these people walked, and enter the houses in
which they lived, see the frescos on the walls which
their eyes enjoyed, and go up the stairs by which they
ascended to the upper floors of their dwellings. You
see the ruts of their chariot wheels in the Roman pavement of the streets. Going down to the wharf, you
find their commission-houses and shipping-offices. All
around you, in vast quantities, lie fragments of pottery
—the remains of the vessels and utensils they used.
This pottery is generally coarser and embellished with
less ornamentation than that found in the ruined Aztec
cities of New Mexico and Arizona. You may tread
the forum where they met for business and exchange;
the temple where they gathered for worship—too bare,
however, of altar or image to know whom they worshipped; the baths, the great luxury of Roman life; the

theatre where they sat for pleasure and relaxation. You may go farther back up the hill, and meditate for half a mile among the tombs where they buried their dead.

Of course, but a small portion of the vast city is excavated, but enough is laid bare to give one a full idea of its daily walk and manner of life. The streets run in the same curving, irregular lines as those of Rome to-day, and are equally narrow. The ceilings are high, just as in the palaces of Rome to-day—the same climatic conditions producing the same results. The warmer and more delightful the climate the higher the ceiling everywhere, and the colder and moister the climate the lower the ceiling, as in Holland, England, and other northern countries.

The colors of the frescos here are as bright as at Pompeii; the rooms higher, and the stairways quite a marked feature, the Greek traditions which conditioned the architecture of Pompeii not conducing to high buildings.

Although a shipping-port and known only for its commercial traditions, Ostia was the home of great culture and taste, and her citizens must have been largely people of cultivation and refinement. Some of the finest treasures of antique statuary have been exhumed from these rooms,—exquisite works of art that the average well-to-do citizen of Liverpool or an American manufacturing town would hardly appreciate. In fact, the Vatican is full of them, a great portion of the excavations having been done under Pius V. And not only statuary, but tombs of masterly designs, sarcophagi, carvings, mosaics, etc. Noted among these rescued treasures are the familiar bust of the young Augustus, the Ganymede of Phædimus, and bas-reliefs of Endymion and Diana. In fact, the revelations of Ostia are conclusive evidence of the very great culture of the Roman people as a whole. This city was but an ordinary business-town, not pretending to any literature or art reputation, but its treasures are rare in quality and wonderful in number. The Ostian merchant of eighteen hundred years ago would have looked with curious contempt on the American millionaire of to-day furnishing his house with chromos or auction-room paintings, or engravings bought on the recommendation of a salesman. All this is the more wonderful when we remember that the cost of works of art was about equal to what it is now. A fairly good statue of full life-size cost $150, while a work of Phidias or Praxiteles brought $10,000 to $30,000. But to understand these values we must recollect that a slave could be kept for about ten cents a day, and that beef could be bought in the markets for four cents a pound.

It is a humiliating contrast between classic and modern civilization, that for hundreds of years the rude lime-kilns in the woods around Ostia have been supplied with sculptures from the ruins to make lime for Roman peasants, and Roman princes and cardinals, too, at times, I suspect.

The approach to Ostia to-day is a very pathetic reminiscence of past cultivation and grandeur. You cross the fatal Maremna, which here sinks into a watery marsh to-day, but in past times may have been flooded with the healthy waves of the sea, by a solid causeway of hard Roman pavement, built on piles and protected on each side by a low wall or railing of stone and marble. All along this causeway of over a mile in length, abandoned for centuries, half hidden by the reeds and thistles or half sunken in the poisonous marsh, stand on either side forgotten ranks of marble statues, —vanished gods, limbless heroes, headless queens and ladies, worn and time-stained senators. Some are fallen, some are leaning, all are forsaken. And this imperial approach, impressive even in its abandonment, leads up to a wretched Roman *trattoria*, the refuge of outcasts and petty brigands.

One of the marked features of the walls of Ostia, both interior and outside, is the variety of pleasing effects worked out by the simple use of brick, both in form and color—the very same effects within late years so largely introduced into the United States.

Ostia is lovingly remembered in Christian tradition as the home of St. Augustine, and the place where he parted with his mother, Monica, to bear the gospel to Saxon England.

Being the harbor and port of Rome, Ostia bore the brunt of all attacks made by sea, and her traditions are largely those of warfare and the repulse of pirates. At last, in the fifth century, she was utterly destroyed by the Saracens and razed to the ground. So utter was the ruin that no attempt was ever made to rebuild the town; but three hundred years later another town was laid out about a mile away from the river and became a place of importance and interest. This was mediæval Ostia, known to-day as "the new town." Here began again the fighting with the pirates, and the old Middle Age fortifications yet extant tell the story very graphically. That stalwart, fighting Pope, Julius II., when a cardinal, built here a castle so massive and secure that it yet stands in all its original strength, and is one of the best illustrations of mediæval military life which has come down to us. This compact little fortress is a capacious round-tower—a perfect circle—surrounded by bastions, which are linked with a curtain, and the whole encompassed by a wide and deep ditch. It is extremely picturesque, and, as it stands on level ground, was capable of indefinite defence in a time when it could only be taken by land. Nevertheless, the besieged were safe only by sleepless vigilance. Half an hour's carelessness would have let in the enemy.

For hundreds of years these castles and towers of Ostia—for there were others of them—maintained this fluctuating and eventful warfare with Cilician pirates and Saracenic armies; but at last, in the utter exhaustion which marked the fifteenth and sixteenth centuries, here, its life flamed away, and they, too, lay down in

ruin and weariness. We picked our way through a
marshy and treacherous plain that once was bright and
brilliant with the tents of the Saracen; under decadent
forests that not many hundred years ago had heard the
evening prayers of the Moslem. To-day an exhausted
Roman workman or two scraping gently on the edges
of an endless mass of ruin, a frightened wild animal, a
wretched peasant, the child, perhaps, of a convict, and
born in a land of death, were all there was to break the
melancholy solitude. Yet, after all, how much better
than that the Turk should have succeeded in fixing a
European camp here as well as on the Black Sea!

It is almost impossible for an American mind to conceive that here, within twenty miles of Rome, the altar
of the learning and culture of the world, there is a wilderness as silent, as savage, as desolate, as on the empty
plains or our untrodden frontier, where buffalo and wild
game range undisturbed; a sanctuary for criminals—if
there were anything to tempt crime or plunder; a solitude that seems abandoned of man and of God. And
it is a solitude, too, oppressive and stifling and appalling—for it is the silence of death and the grave, and
not like the fresh solitudes of our Western prairies, the
stillness of the morning.

Yet listen to Pliny as he pictures the scene of this
malarial desert nearly two thousand years ago: "Such
is its happy and beautiful amenity that it seems to be
the work of rejoicing Nature. For truly, so it appears
in the vital and perennial salubrity of its atmosphere,
in its fertile plains, sunny hills, healthy woods, thick
groves, rich varieties of trees, breezy mountains, fertil-
ity in fruits, vines, and olives; its noble flocks of sheep,
abundant herds of cattle, numerous lakes, and wealth
of rivers and streams pouring in upon it; many sea-
ports, in whose lap the commerce of the world lies,
and which run largely into the sea, as it were, to help
mortals."

Rome.

MODERN ITALY.

CHAPTER XLII.

NEW ROME.

The City of the New Quarter—The Union Army of Italy and its Civil Uses—Modernization of Rome—Convents as Government Buildings — Unmuzzled Bookstores—Politicians and Engineers—The American Church—The Protestant Graveyard.

Not the least among the astonishing sights of this famed and ancient city, and certainly the most unlooked for, is the New Rome that is arising every day strong and beautiful, clean and hygienic and lusty.

This is an entirely new-built section, where everything is modern, fresh, and recent. Whole streets of newly-erected houses meet one's view, the streets themselves wide and straight, well graded, and handsomely laid out, and the whole is of a few years' growth. It is such a quarter and development as one would expect to find in Cincinnati or Chicago, but the last thing looked for in Rome. The buildings in this new quarter are not architecturally handsome. The houses are very large, rectangular structures, affording only plain, straight lines to the eye. They are, however, palaces in their spaciousness, being very broad, the fronts measuring from fifty to one hundred feet, and as high in elevation as the best blocks in our cities. They are convenient to live in, but not picturesque structures, and although entirely different in construction from the American dwelling-house, the long succession of them, all of the same style and pattern, gives the effect of an American street. They are also as devoid of historical interest or association as the wooden-paved " avenues" of a ten-year-old Western metropolis. This new city lies from the Baths of Diocletian to the Esquiline Hill

and extending back to the walls, taking in all the
ground from the Porta Pia to the Porta Maggiore.
The backbone of the section is the broad *Via Nazionale,*
running from the new railway station to the Via
Quirinale. The races were transferred from the Corso
to this street at the Carnival of this year. There are here
large modern hotels, a fine new theatre, a handsome
American Protestant church up, ground broken for an
English one, and grand rows of palatial " flats." Along
with all this development there is the usual incident
of rising prices and speculation. Italian speculation,
however, is something very childlike and innocent to
American experience.

This whole quarter is a result of New Italy, and has
sprung into life entirely since Victor Emmanuel got the
reins and Cavour effected "The Union." It is the evidence that Italy has awakened at last to the modern
life, and is swinging into place in the column of the
nations. While we may regret the loss of the picturesque and the absence of scenic effect, it is an encouraging and hopeful sign, welcome to all who do not believe
in the saving grace of squalor and wretchedness, and in
the godliness of dirt.

There are many influences at work now to push forward the development of the Roman people. In many
respects the people strongly resemble us. They have
intelligence, versatility, adaptability to circumstances,
ready tact, and a very practical vein. There is the
same bright countenance, the same activity and lightness of motion seen in the best type of the American.
This is especially the case with the North Italians, who
will be the brain and power of the new kingdom.

The union of Italy, and the consequent birth of a
national instinct, has given a powerful impetus to
progress. Along with political freedom has come, too,
the removal of the frightful mental incubus of ecclesiastical tyranny. As long as an Inquisition could arrest
men in the night-time and try them in secret for their

beliefs and opinions, there was no hope for either moral, intellectual, or political advancement. The only relief lay through violence and bloodshed, and the odds were fearfully against the suffering victims. Now all that is changed, and the movement can go on, healthily and under the law.

As matters now stand, and as they must stand for some time, the bayonet is the saviour of Italy. It is a sad admission to make, but it is the truth, and measures the vast difference between the unhappy condition of this people and the fortunate circumstances of ours. The struggling people of Italy have secured their rights from the ecclesiastical aggression of ages only by the bayonet, and they hold them only by the bayonet. Disband the armies of free Italy, and the Church would reassume temporal power and rule in a month. The government of the people, for the people, would be replaced by the government of priests, with its hideous and appalling record of the last one thousand years. Education would give way to enforced ignorance, and civil rights be lost utterly as the light of the courts of justice went out in the hopeless night and outer darkness of the Inquisition. Americans, with their instinctive love of freedom, often resent the constant presence of the soldiery here, who throng the streets and stand on guard at every turn ; but they are in this case a necessary evil. It is unfortunate to have to rely on military power even for a season, but it would be still more unfortunate for Italy to abandon its protection at this moment. It would be a treason to humanity and to the trust of government, for it would be surrendering, without a struggle, all the work and cost and blood of the last thirty years.

Again, the army at present, in addition to its military uses, serves as a good school to the young men of new Italy. It educates them to the conception of nationality, and accustoms them to the use of civil force against ecclesiastical usurpation. Heretofore, to disobey a priest, who was in reality an unscrupulous politician, or to resist a corrupt bishop, has been looked on as a sacrilege and resistance to heaven, that might be followed by supernatural punishment. The people were in the unconscious bondage of superstition, which can be best broken up by the constant visible presence of the power of the civil law.

The soldiers of Italy are a fine-looking body of men, intelligent, cleanly, of resolute bearing, and in excellent condition and discipline. They are so far beyond their less fortunate brethren who are not in the ranks that I think the best thing, both for the State and the people, would be to draft the whole remaining population, and let every male in the kingdom have the benefit of a few years' service. In each regiment the recruit gets a good elementary schooling in the common elements of education; but beyond that he receives a moral training, inducing habits of self-reliance and self-respect, which are just what the peasant and poor artisan need after a thousand years of priest rule. The army is the common school of Italy, and it is the best she can have at present.

Again, it is the judicious usage of the war minister to shift the troops about, placing the northern battalions on duty in the south, the southern in the north, and so on, the very thing which is needed to break up the sectional and local feeling so disastrously strong in Italy. The young soldier, after his military service is over, feels that he is not any more a Genoese, a Pisan, a Neapolitan, a Roman, or a Florentine, but something better and greater,—an Italian.

One of the most conspicuous features of new Rome— the Rome that is open and free—is the new American church on the Via Nazionale. This handsome edifice, built by the present rector, Rev. Dr. Robert J. Nevin, of Pennsylvania, has been put up only since the opening of Rome by Victor Emmanuel. It is of large size, even for this city of basilicas, and is constructed in the

early Gothic of Northern Italy. The walls are of
travertine, the stone of the Colosseum and St. Peter's,
and it is floored inside with Venetian pavement,—a
kind of rough mosaic. The plan of the building is
that of the basilica, with apse, nave, and side-aisles.
The tower is of the campanile order, with ascending
stories of airy windows, openings which let out the
clear sound of the bells, a style almost unknown in our
land, but which harmonizes admirably with the skies
and landscape of Italy.

This beautiful church, with its twenty-three bells
ringing every Sunday over the seven hills, is a permanent monument to the free right of all men to worship
God according to their own faith. It stands in the
very camp of that great power which has always
denied this right, and we can justly be proud that it
has been placed there by American liberality, faith,
and courage. Already the example is bearing good
fruit. The Church of England is laying foundations
for a church on the *Quattro Fontane,* and some six or
eight congregations of various Protestant faiths are
organizing and building over a city where for long
suffocating centuries their worship went up to God
only from the torture-chambers of the Inquisition or
the sacrificial piazzas of the *auto-da-fe.*

Another feature of free Italy are the enfranchised
bookstores. In the old times, under the dead hand
of the *Index Expurgatorius,* bookselling, as may well
be imagined, was not a very flourishing calling, and
the shops had rather a meagre supply of still more
meagre matter. To-day an hour in any good Roman
bookstore will almost startle the stranger. The literature of every nation greets one from the shelves and
tables,—German, English, American, French, Spanish,
and the Italian is not mainly theological or religious,
as one unconsciously assumes, but largely devoted to
the physical sciences and practical treatises on mathe-
matics and engineering. For some reason politics and

engineering go together in Italy, as they do also in France, and this sympathy makes engineering a popular and prominent study. The average Italian candidate for political office is not a lawyer, as with us, but an engineer.

Modern Italian literature, however, is comparatively meagre and limited in its range. The popular want is, therefore, supplied by translating copiously from the literature of other nations, and it is surprising to see how thoroughly the better works of the world have been appropriated. All the standard English books and much of the current publications of the United States and England are reproduced in Italian. This is done promptly, and as that Canada thistle, the middleman, has not yet overrun Italy, books can be bought there comparatively cheap. They are much cheaper than with us, when our enormous markets are taken into account. These bookstores of which I am speaking are not confined to the new quarter, but have spread all over Rome, and now in the low precincts of the Pantheon or even under the spiked guns of San Angelo one may see modern scientific tracts exposed for sale among little tin hearts and cheap rosaries and the votive offerings of all kinds so well known and so flimsy, rude, and gaudy.

There is another movement which has operated largely to the modernization of Rome. The civil government in succeeding to the estate of the ecclesiastical government has taken many of the old conventual properties for public use. Thus, all the departments of State—the War Office, the Navy, the Post-Office, the Foreign Office—are now quartered in fine large monasteries, and brisk-walking, cleanly-clad officials have replaced the filthy-habited, flea-haunted monks who made the city picturesque and dirty only twenty-five years ago. This kind of appropriation has been on a very large scale, and quite changes the face of many localities.

Just beyond the Ostian gate through which the holy Apostle St. Paul was led to execution, and at the foot of the colossal pyramidal tomb of Caius Cestus, the only surviving monument of Rome which witnessed his martyrdom, nestles "The Protestant graveyard," also a field of the Italy of the nineteenth century. It is "outside of the walls," but a century or so ago Rome was not either civilized or Christian enough for even that.

This burial-ground is one of the loveliest places around Rome, and is full of tender and suggestive associations. It is the graveyard of those who die here out of the Roman communion, and is already, perhaps, the most Catholic spot in the city. Russians, Danes, Germans, French, English, Americans, Italians, and men I know not of what other tongues, lie here together awaiting the resurrection. Under its dark cypresses, and among its clustering roses, are some twelve hundred graves—a silent congregation from all the world. The title to the ground is vested in the German government, through whose courtesy and Christian charity and national courage the people of all the world find that consecrated rest which is denied them elsewhere in Rome by act of its Church.

This quiet and beautiful spot, covered with violets, swept softly by fragrant winds, sleeping, as it were, out of the world, is so restful and soothing that it has a singular charm for all who see it. Shelly sang it long ago—

"Where, like an infant's smile, over the dead
A light of laughing flowers along the grass is spread."

His heart rests in it to-day, right under the ruins of an ancient loop-holed tower in the old Aurelian wall. Keats is there, William Howitt, Gibson, the sculptor, and long lists of names familiar to our English tongue. Most of the graves are of the young—a touching memento of blighted promises and broken hopes. They

are those who, full of youth and hope, were cut down
on their travels—brides, perhaps, on their first journey, or those who sought life in foreign lands and
found death. By far the largest proportion of names
are from England. The English do not have that
semi-morbid desire for burial in their own land, under
any circumstances, which presses so heavily on the
American and Chinaman. On many of these tombs
are read the names of noble and wealthy families of
England; but although England is so near, and her
family burial-grounds are more beautiful and impressive
than those of any other people, when an Englishman
dies in Rome, no matter what his rank or position, he
generally sleeps there. Here they are in force among
the roses and lilies and oleanders of Italy, lords and
ladies and children, admirals and generals with their
slumbering effigies, poets and artists and travellers, at
peace forever. Indeed, so peaceful and beautiful is this
spot, so full is it of catholic association, so emblematic
is it of the fellowship and brotherhood of the whole
world, as it shall stand on the resurrection day, when
all the tribes and tongues and nations of the earth shall
meet together, that I do not wonder so many persons
of note and educated tastes have accepted it as their
final rest.

Rome.

CHAPTER XLIII.

UNITED ITALY.

ITALIAN POLITICS—THE GREAT WORK OF THE UNION OF ITALY—THE CHURCH IN POLITICS—SETTLING AN ESTATE OF KINGDOMS—SECTIONALISM—NORTH AND SOUTH ITALY—A LOOK INTO THE CHAMBER OF THE CONGRESS OF THE NEW KINGDOM OF ITALY—ENGLISH FEATURES OF THE HOUSE—MONTE CITORIO—THE MINISTRY—THE FLOOR OF THE HOUSE.

THE union of Italy is the keynote of modern Italian politics and political history, and it has been a grand achievement. The more one sees under the surface, and meets the leaders of the several interests and parties, the more he is impressed with the consummate abilities and energy of the men who achieved it. Our own Union in 1776–83 was but child's play compared with the work in Italy of the past twenty years, and our pending question of reconstruction is simple aside of the problems yet to be solved in this country before it becomes one nation, thoroughly united in heart and head, with common interests, common hopes, and a common future.

Let me for a moment briefly summarize some of the grand difficulties which have stood in the way. They fairly bristle as we call them up, starting back far through the centuries and enlisting all the human passions. They are historic—of blood, of climate, of religion, of civic pride, of finance, of ignorance, of topography.

And first of blood. The Roman race is at its best but a conglomerate one, but Italy is not even purely Roman. Naples and the country round about it was settled by Greek colonies, and the people to this day retain the peculiarities and show the traces of their Grecian ancestry. Sicily has even a marked proportion of Arab blood. Then, again, there is a North and a South Italy, far more marked in their differences and histories than the Northern and Southern States of our country. Their differences come from twenty centuries. Their special characteristics are rooted in the ages. But the dangers of sectionalism here are not limited to the clashing interests of two or three great natural sections.

In Italy sectionalism means city pride. As mentioned in a previous letter, the city has been the political unit of Italy for all its known and even legendary history. The walled city held no communication with its neighbors, save those of war, and they knew each other only by feuds and forays, or formal treaties with each other against others. Even to-day the people of one Italian town talk of each other as foreigners, and speak commonly of Genoese, Milanese, Neapolitans, Romans, Florentines, Pisans, just as they do of French, Germans, English, or Americans. It is in their blood and will not go out inside of this generation. They have to be educated, not from the conception of a province or a state up to the idea of nationality, but from the very primitive start of the municipal idea.

Again, there are the geographical troubles. Large portions of the new nation, such as Sardinia and Sicily, are islands " cut off," of course, from the instantaneous communication of rail—the new artery of the modern body politic. Even the mainland is not compact, but straggles through changing climates, inducing different modes of living, and therefore different habits and customs.

There is a North and a South Italy, with differences of temperament and tastes just as wide and deep-seated as any that exist between our Northern and Southern States. There is, indeed, a rather curious parallel between our two nations in this, North Italy holding much the same relation to South Italy as do our Northern States to our Southern ones. In the Northern Kingdom of Italy the people are industrious, active, and comparatively prosperous. Their children go to school. They themselves fall in as far as they can with the thought and movement of the age. The hold of the Roman Catholic Church loosens first in the North. Humbert, the Union king, comes from the Northern house of Savoy.

As you go southward these characteristics gradually weaken and disappear. Industry gives way to idleness, activity to laziness, school training to ignorance, religion survives in superstition, and the dirty mendicant monk becomes the true representative man of the country. The statistics of Italian illiteracy run exactly as do ours, from North to South. From the latest data in the *Annuario Statistico*, it appears that in every thousand of the population the number that could neither read nor write, in 1871, was, in Piedmont, five hundred; in Lombardy, five hundred and twenty-eight; in Tuscany, seven hundred and twenty-four; in the Roman provinces, seven hundred and seventeen; in the Neapolitan district, eight hundred and fifty-six; and in Sicily, eight hundred and seventy-two. It is the same descending scale as from Maine to Mississippi.

Worst burden of all for Italy is this appalling ignorance of the mass of the people, habituated for generations to a galling slavery of body and mind, ruled and owned from the cradle to the grave by priest or prince, and unused to self-management, self-providence, or self-control. These people, when brought face to face with the question of self-government, are pitifully ignorant. Ignorance is always suspicious, and they therefore mistrust experienced leaders, and are more apt to be controlled by unscrupulous cunning than intelligently convinced by argument. By a law of nature large masses of ignorance always gravitate against intelligence, and the party that raises and frees this people must expect to have them turn against it.　At this moment, Garibaldi, leading the radical element, and the Pope, representing the reactionary forces of the Vatican, alike agree in advocating universal suffrage.　Garibaldi asks it as a logical and necessary step in his plan, accepting the immediate risk in the faith of the good that is to come.　The Papal power is willing for this revolutionary step, knowing that it would bring to the polls legions of the *contadini*, the ignorant peasantry of the villages, who can neither read, write, nor think, and who are controlled absolutely by their priests.　At present suffrage is based on a property qualification, and is confined to a comparatively small proportion of the population.　The qualified voters of Italy are, by last statistics, just 2.26 to every one hundred of population, and, on an average, only sixty per cent. of the vote is ever polled.　Were the doors opened to manhood suffrage the mass of the Italian vote would be directed straight from the Vatican, and cast against the party of union and freedom.

The great disturbing element, however,—the ugliest trouble of all,—is the political claim of the Roman Catholic Church.　Its relation to Italy is not at all a religious one, as in our country, but a definitely political one.　It is not even the vexed question of Church and State—it is State or Church.　The Roman Catholic sovereignty here claims the temporal dominion of the old States of the Church as its right, and is fighting for it to-day by every means in its power.　It excommunicated Victor Emmanuel, and would excommunicate King Humbert and the two Chambers of Parliament, and all the personnel of government in an hour if it would do any good.　It is a political *imperium in imperio*, and a power of such strength and ramification that it cannot be struck down without endangering the very structure of society.　At this very day the kingdom of Italy is paying to the Pope, an active worker for its overthrow, an annual tribute of over six hundred thousand dollars. Imagine some vast, restless power in our land which controlled, nominally, at least, the religious belief of the entire population ; which owned every church-building in it, with one or two exceptions, and directed all the worship in them ; which had a vast machinery of paid, organized forces, men and women, always at work, and which, entering into every family, north, south, east, and west, and influencing all their members in their most sacred relations, reaching them in the cradle, at school, on the marriage-day, and at the hour of death, was restlessly and avowedly plotting for the overthrow of the government ; demanding it as a right, and adjuring all to aid in it as a religious duty ; imagine, further, that our people were so superstitiously devoted to this power that the government dare not strike at it, but must pay it a large pension—absolutely furnish it with means to carry on its claims—imagine all this, and you have some idea of the civil situation here, and begin to understand the appalling odds that confronted, and still confront, the leaders for union. They do not even hold their own camp.

But leaving the consideration of all these organic difficulties, inherent in the life of the people, when the hour of success at last came, and the act of union was consummated, the practical adjustment of the vested interests which were to be merged in the new nation was a matter of infinite tact, patience, and cost in money. It was, in fact, the settlement of an estate of seven king- doms.

New Italy has been formed out of seven distinct kingdoms or powers, each one of which had a ruling family whose rights and interests society, the social order of Europe, recognized. The house of Savoy got the crown of Italy, but all the rest had to be pensioned or provided for in some way.

Each of these kingdoms had its court, its army, its judiciary, its debt—all the machinery and burdens of sovereignty. The adjustment of these conflicting and

unequal interests involved endless trouble and infinite
concession and compromise. The debts of some of the
little countries were relatively heavier than those of
others ; had, perhaps, been extravagantly incurred, or
for ends distasteful and displeasing to some. The armies
of each little power, too, were different. Some were in
good order, others in poor. Some were relatively larger
than others. In some the rank of the officers was relatively higher than in others, in some the pay, in some
the proportion of officers to men.

The same difficulties presented themselves in the civil
list, and had to be adjusted—many of them by money.
Pensioning was the easiest way, retiring the older men
to make way for the younger, or the inefficient to make
room for better. This, although expedient and necessary, was expensive, and hence Italy enters the family
of nations with a respectable national debt.

Our own political troubles and perplexities look
small and petty when compared with these—but more,
the leaders in the march to Italian unity have had to
struggle against a moral opposition,—a traditional current of thought,—a stifling mental atmosphere, of which
we know nothing. I heard a deputy on the floor of
the chamber argue against the further extension of railways in the kingdom, because the facility of communication afforded the common people—the " working-
men" was the word used—was dangerous to the good
and peace of the country. " It produces," said he,
" discontent, socialism, nihilism. These have come with
the railways into Europe."

The longer and the deeper one studies Italy the
greater becomes the conception of the union of Italy—
the grander the proportions of the noble monument
which Cavour has reared to bear forever his name into
history.

The other day, through the kindness of a senator,
who showed me over the parliament building and in-

troduced me into the chamber of the representatives during the progress of an important debate, I had an opportunity of seeing the "plant" of the government and catching a glimpse of the legislative machinery in motion. The hall was arranged as an amphitheatre, the members' seats rising at a very steep ascent. The speaker and clerks sat in the arena, as did the cabinet of the king, who, as in England, have the privilege of the floor to defend or advocate their measures, and also that the representatives of the people may interrogate them at any time as to their conduct of affairs. They do not vote. The ministry shifts also with the parliamentary majority, as is the English usage. In this, in the presence of the ministers on the floor, and in paying them salaries and not paying the members, Italy has patterned closely after England, refusing our younger precedent.

The assembly seemed to be composed of men very much of the age and same relative station of life as the membership of our lower house at Washington. The house was quieter and more decorous than ours in the ordinary flow of business, but at one moment, when a little excitement did occur, it fluttered and quivered like a living thing in a way entirely impossible, perhaps, to a deliberative body of the Anglo-Saxon race. The little trouble flamed up instantaneously all around the circled walls of the chamber like powder in a pan, and while the feeling was intense and the whole floor—speaking at once—seemed to throb and pulse with excitement, you felt convinced all the time that it was not deep or dangerous, and would die out safely, as it did in a minute or two, without leaving a trace.

In this assembly the speaker calls the house to order by the ringing of a bell. It very effectually silences interruption and the discordant voices, but had to me something of a railway-depot effect, that being the signal here for the trains to draw out. As in the churches, however, they announce the presence of the Host by the ringing of a bell, it may have more dignified associations for Italian ears.

The senate is appointed by the king, the lower house chosen by the people, the electors, however, being but a limited portion of the population, suffrage resting on a property qualification. Congressmen—deputies they call them—receive no pay, but have high social and political rank by virtue of their office, a deputy taking precedence of a prince. This is a wise provision in a country where social rank is so great a force.

The congress of the new kingdom of United Italy does not sit in the old Capitol of historic tradition and legend, nor even on its site. That spot, so rich in association and suggestion, belongs to the city of Rome, and civic pride will not surrender it for the uses of the nation. It is a municipal treasure, and will not be given up. The chambers, therefore, sit in a massive old palace, which has been remodelled for their use. The palazzo Monte Citorio is plain, but very substantial, and seats commodiously the five hundred members. It contains library, reading-room, committee-rooms, and all the usual incidental accommodations. As the new kingdom is poor, all the fitting up has been done economically, and with a very praiseworthy avoidance of extravagance, or anything which could bear that interpretation. Economy, indeed, is the rule of the new kingdom, and is seen in everything that starts with the Union. The new cabinet ministers, for instance, receive salaries of but $4000. There are many expensive legacies of the past, however. This parliament-house is the only public building, civil or religious, I have seen in Rome which is not weighed down with statuary. There is not a single piece in it, nor did I see any paintings save one—a full-length portrait of Victor Emmanuel. All the embellishments of the halls, library, and reading-rooms were very modest engravings. Our country was recognized by an old but good likeness of

Washington, frame and all about one and a half by two feet in size. It would be a graceful act, and do good, if the Congress of the United States would send its card to young Italy in the shape of a large and full-size painting of the Father of that country whose Union has been the chart and sampler for the statesmen who conceived and are achieving the freedom of the Roman people.

The library is small, but started on a judicious plan, and will grow into a valuable collection. The leading papers of each country in the world, received daily and preserved bound, is one of its features. In the reading-room you sit and read the powerful journal of each nation. Everything here, as in the building at large, was severely plain and sensible, the best *materiel* of all kinds, but no show. The committee-rooms were entirely devoid of ornament, frescos, or sumptuous furniture, in sharp contrast with our gorgeous civic salons for this kind of use.

In the general service of the building there was something more of form than with us, but not as much as is common in a private palace here. When one of the speakers arose during my visit to make his argument, a servant in full livery bore to him some wine on a silver salver. All the employés of the house, —doorkeepers, pages, messengers—were liveried, and in addition wore a band or narrow sash of the national tricolor bound around the left arm, its breadth and varying degree of ampleness denoting their relative rank. Further, these servants of the legislative chambers differ very greatly from those at the Capitol in Washington, in not being under the impression that they are the most influential personages in the building.

ROME.

CHAPTER XLIV.

GARIBALDI.

THE RED-SHIRTED LEADER AT WORK ON A SICK-BED—PIC-
TURE OF A MIDDLE-CLASS ITALIAN HOME—A MILITARY
HEADQUARTERS WITH NO RED TAPE—A REVOLUTIONARY
COURT—CRYING THE DAILY PAPERS IN THE COLOSSEUM—
THE GARIBALDIAN CREED—EUROPEAN REPUBLICANISM—
THE EMERGENCE OF THE COMMON PEOPLE.

ITALY—Garibaldi. The two names reflect and
suggest each other to the American mind whenever it
thinks of the Roman people, or of Italian nationality.
And it is almost the same here. There are three pictures one meets everywhere in Italy,—in the streets
and shops, side by side, equal in the honor and affection of the people,—King Humbert, Queen Marguerite,
and Garibaldi. The soldier-king and the beautiful
young queen are the fortunate man and woman who
happen to represent in their persons at this hour the
power of all the organized forces of society, government, learning, culture, aristocracy, property, for two
thousand years. Twenty centuries are behind them,
and combine to make them. Garibaldi is the orator
of the common people. A man of themselves,—poor,
simple in manner and speech,—they have raised him
by acclamation to a seat beside princes in a land which,
from time immemorial, has been the heritage of princes.
His strength, too, represents a permanent force, and
not an emotion or transitory excitement, for his power
with the people is a sustained one, and has endured
through an eventful life, checkered by poverty, misfortune, and defeat.

Certainly, there is no man of Europe more worthy
of study than this one, who represents the people in an

age when their advent to political power threatens the whole structure of society as it has traditionally existed.

I had the good fortune of visiting Garibaldi the other day, in company with the proprietor of one of the leading New York dailies, and my brother, Rev. Dr. Nevin, of Rome, whose influence with a distinguished officer here, the chief of staff of the Italian army, had procured us a responsible introduction and an audience—the old revolutionary general being on a sick-bed, and too ill to see visitors except for good cause.

The surroundings of the old hero, although severely simple, were rather dramatic, and thoroughly in accord with the popular conception of his person and habits. We found him in an obscure street, at the house of his son,—the house a very plain one,—and, for this town, small. The family occupied the second floor, what in the United States would be known as the third story. The narrow hall and steps all the way up were stone, hard and cold, and the hall-windows looking into the street had no glass in them, were simply apertures in a thick stone wall; save in the sick man's bedroom, there were no carpets on any of the floors, but there were some brilliant and quite good frescos on the high ceilings. The first room along which we passed, and which was necessarily in full view of every visitor, was the kitchen, odorous and picturesquely dirty, as is the custom of the country. A young woman was at her work in it, careless of the fact that a historic character would eat of her food, and that a revolution might be brewing in the next room. The setting of the picture was, in fact, quite revolutionary. Two doors off, in the solid brick gateway of a large, cold building, stood, or rather lounged, three rough men, with the air of irregulars,—the very picture of a vigilance committee, —who eyed us closely and curiously as we entered the door. At the entrance of the Garibaldi apartments we were received by an old soldier, wounded, clad in coarse, civilian clothes, but wearing the red shirt. He viewed us rather suspiciously, as had several Garibaldians whom we passed, half-posted, half-lounging, in the porter's gate and entry, evidently looking on my brother's ecclesiastical dress with no friendly eyes, and as entirely out of place in that locality. The name of the Italian general, however, acted as a talisman. Distrust gave way to respect, and when we informed the old veteran that we were soldiers and Americans, come to see his chief, we had at once a warm friend at court. He had fought in America for freedom, he proudly told us, and welcomed his co-patriots with enthusiasm.

Here I should say, that in order to secure a more satisfactory and uninterrupted interview, we had left our letter of introduction and cards the day before with a secretary, and arranged with him for a fixed hour to call. In true Italian fashion, this had been the end of that forethought. Garibaldi had never seen the letter, or heard of it, and we had to introduce ourselves with no word of announcement save, I suppose, the kindly commendation of our red-shirted comrade.

Garibaldi lay on a narrow, iron-frame bed, of what we would call a hospital pattern, but which is of ordinary use here, his frame wasted, his face thin and worn, but his eye bright and sparkling, firing with enthusiasm, or softening into warm and genial sympathy as he spoke. He called in quick and nervous tones for the letter when he found it had not been delivered. A little granddaughter scudded around the bedroom, hunting on tables and chairs for the paper. The old soldier ran to a large heap of letters and documents piled on a side-table, without order or arrangement, and tumbled them over and over, but without effect. Some of them bore the official envelope of the Quirinal. Some women from an adjoining bedroom took part in the hunt, but without results, and at last, as the sound of many voices all talking at once cleared, and the clatter of hands and

feet stopped, the cry went up, "Menotti has it!"
Menotti was the son, and out of the house.

The old general spoke with some little effort, but to
the last with enthusiasm. He remembered America
with friendly kindness, and seemed unaffectedly pleased
when I told him that his name was a household word
with our people. His eye kindled as he spoke of the
united Italy, and seemed to thank the stranger that
took the friendly interest to ask about it and express
sympathy with it. In fact, the *raison d'être* of Garibaldi is the union of Italy. It is his instinctive sympathies with every impulse in this direction which give
him such a hold on the hearts, and make him the exponent of the will and aspirations, of the Italian people.
Union means the ultimate coming forward of the
masses. Coming out of the bedroom of the prostrate
soldier, I was curious to observe the manner of life of
the man and his following. It was intensely democratic.

In an ante-room there waited twenty-six people, six
of whom were women. Some of the waiting crowd
were foreigners, but the great bulk were Italians, and
apparently quite poor. Of all the native attendance
there was but one man whom we would call in our
country well dressed. There was a committee of seven
young men with an address,—a delegation from some
Italia irridenta club,—a rather combustible-looking
body. There was a poor woman, evidently come for
help; the correspondent of the London *Times;* a
bright, half-faded, dark-eyed woman of the adventuress
type; some more veterans, come likely to snuff up the
prospects for future work. It was emphatically a court
of the people, and in it you seemed to breathe the air
of uprisings and revolution. There was no formality
of any kind, but work went on of itself—with earnest-
ness if not with regulation. A secretary was writing
busily at a small table in the centre of the room, all his
papers and work exposed to the crowd. No cards were
sent in, but the red-shirted soldier acted as master of

ceremonies, communicating with Garibaldi from time
to time, and announcing results effectively by opening
the door and letting in such as were called for. There
was little furniture, and most of the visitors stood up
while awaiting their audience. On a wardrobe-top,
used for table purposes, lay some stray letters, newspapers, and a volume in the French language. I
picked it up. Its title was *La Papessa Jeanne.*

Garibaldi suffers great personal disadvantage in the
likeness of him which has gone over all lands, and
which is, perhaps, all that the photograph can do. He
needs a painter to give him to the world, and a painter
as great as himself. The accepted picture, which is
known the world over, may be a correct map of the
lines of his physical features, but it misses entirely the
real man. It is heavy and rather stolid. He is bright,
of fine intellectual cast, and with an exceptionally sympathetic smile that wins all hearts. It is this real,
earnest, world-wide sympathy which has made him the
leader of the common people of Europe. He is neither
a soldier nor a statesman, he is an impulse and an
enthusiasm. He has made military mistakes, and his
political moves are often erratic to a degree. They are,
in fact, not politic movements at all—simply straight-
forward demonstrations, in season and out, for the end.
His is the heart, not the head, power, and as the masses
of his forces have, at present, no higher sense of action
than the blind, personal following of some leadership,
his is the force that is needed. Being without governmental power, he has no responsibilities, and so far
does not need the strength of judgment and careful
policy. He represents the aspirations of a people that
long for the morning after the dreary night of the
Dark Ages.

And nothing but loving sympathy can do the work
for them. Nothing but that could sustain the leader
or hold the trust of this people, steeped in the dense
ignorance of centuries of slavery of mind and soul.

Ignorance is always its own hopeless foe by an inexorable law. The ignorant man is suspicious by reason of his ignorance. The suspicious man is a ready dupe to cunning and low suggestion by reason of his suspicions. When the battle of universal suffrage is fought by Garibaldi for the Roman people and won for them, they will turn against him and vote for the reactionary party, just as surely as did the negroes of the South with us. He has faith, however, and is willing to make the sacrifice, trusting in God for the ultimate result.

The struggle for the social advancement of the common people on this spot is a very discouraging one. Even the centuries work against it. The other day, in the shadows of the Colosseum, I heard a faint, thin cry. A newsboy, a youth of some nineteen years, had come in with half a dozen papers on his arm, which is a fair load here. He looked around, advanced reflectively, called out two or three times: " *Il Popolo Romano*" on a decrescendo scale, and then he too subsided into rest and meditation. The presence of the crowding years was too much, and this is largely the history of all action here. The great national force is inertia.

Garibaldi throws his great political influence with the king, who in this stage of affairs represents United Italy. When he came to Rome, some ten days since, weak and sick, carried almost like a dead man from the depot to his son's house, amid the cheers and wailing of the populace, the king paid him the first visit. Some days later Garibaldi repaid it, going in a carriage, which he was not able to leave. He was driven into the lovely gardens of the Quirinal, when the king came down, and, entering the carriage, sat with him during the interview. His relations with the established government are cordial and complete; in fact, he is drawing a large pension from the State.

While accepting the crown as the representative to-day of established government and Italian union, and throwing his influence with it in the interest of order, Garibaldi is in no way satisfied with the administration, and his political position is on the extreme left of the Lefts. It is doubtful, however, if he would be satisfied with any government. He is a poet, although a writer of bad verses, and lacks the practical grasp of statesmanship. It is his mission to arouse and destroy, not to protect and administer.

It would be a mistake to think of Garibaldi as an American Republican. He is a born revolutionist, with all those dangerous beliefs which European conservatism have made the creed of European Republicanism. Socialism, communism, nihilism, have his undoubted sympathies, and I think he would gladly break up the present order of society at any immediate cost. With the assassination of kings he has expressed more than sympathy. His deliberately written words are those of encouragement. It sharply defines the contrast between European and American Republicanism, between the fortunate condition of the people of America and the desperate state of the masses of Europe, to remember that assassination, which with us is never regarded save as an unmixed crime and a cowardly one, is, in Europe, dispassionately, and often intelligently considered as a political weapon, and that not as a remedy for evil, but merely to call attention to it. It is in many cases a deliberate act of self-immolation. Garibaldi has all his life been heading forlorn hopes against the entrenchments of privilege and vested power, and his feelings very naturally are very different from those of men who have never had to fight this battle.

For a whole lifetime Garibaldi has been the mover of the oppressed peoples of Europe, leading them in one desperate effort after another that has always ended in his defeat and disaster. To-day, as he nears death, his body worn away by the force of the still living and powerful soul within it, it is dramatic to think that he stands, like the leader of old on Pisgah's top, almost in reach of the promised land of his hopes and prophecies. In Germany an appalling military despotism, like a blind fate, is forcing the question of human rights to a violent issue on a grand scale. In England, to-day, the social and political power of the common people is steadily growing healthily and peacefully. In France they stand a guard in possession of the government. In Italy they wait in hope, under, perhaps, the freest constitutional government of the continent. In Russia they are blindly rising in crime and blood—illogically, illegally, but in a way that is striking terror into organized society all over Europe, and forcing the consideration of the situation on the fears and conscience of those now fortunate classes who, for a thousand years, have enjoyed the trust of government without ever being called on for an account of their stewardship, or, perhaps, ever thinking much of their responsibility.

ROME.

CHAPTER XLV.

MODERN ITALY.

KEEPING THE NATIONAL HOLIDAY OF THE UNION—THE PEOPLE OF NEW ITALY—TRANSITION CONTRASTS—THE AMERICAN AND ITALIAN PHYSIQUE—THE HEIRS OF IMPERIAL ROME—COMMON LIFE IN ITALY—MODERN ITALY—PUBLIC BUILDINGS—THE ROMAN SUNDAY—THE NEWSPAPERS.

TO-DAY, being the first Sunday in June, is the national holiday,—the Fourth of July of New Italy, —and it has been kept with a good deal of enthusiasm; the more so, perhaps, as it falls this year on Whit-Sunday, and both parties, the "blacks" (papal) and the "whites" (national), can join in gentle *vivas* and wearing flowers.

The streets were crowded all day long with well-dressed and intelligent-looking people. It has seemed to me that the throngs on the streets and piazzas were of a better class of persons—more prosperous, and brighter looking in face and manner—than those who turn out on the Church *fête* days. They are the people of New Italy. Among them were groups of peasants, men and women,—the men in their sheepskin clothing, and the women with their red shawls, outside corsets, and Ionic head-dress, giving local color to the scene, and relieving the otherwise dead level of the respectability of the multitude, which looked much like an American crowd.

The main feature of the day was a review of the troops and their parade before the king and the queen and their court. Some five thousand infantry were in line. The soldiery were in very good condition for field service, but they had not that finish of drill and accuracy of movement which our army had attained generally before its disbandment in 1865. Wherever I have seen the Italian troops this creditable feature comes out. They seem to be drilled and handled with constant reference to effective field use, and comparatively little attention paid to the parade side of the training. They always march with a long, swinging quickstep, and have achieved a wonderful celerity of movement.

After the review, the troops were formed in double lines, faced inward, along the broad and handsome Via Nazionale, leading to the Quirinal, and through these lines rode the queen in an open landau, with ladies and officers of state. Following her, about five minutes later, the king rode down the lines on horseback, accompanied by Prince Amadeo of Spain, a large and brilliant staff, and his body-guard, which is not a show troop of costumed dragoons, but an effective body of cavalry. I had the opportunity some weeks ago of inspecting this troop at their barracks, and was surprised to find how thoroughly they were equipped for field service, and how thoroughly the officers accepted this as their work, never for a moment seeming to think of themselves as being set apart for mere escort or ornamental duty.

As tne queen passed down the street there was a graciously hearty acclamation from the dense crowds which surged on both sides against the living walls of soldiery,—and it was repeated when the king appeared. The demonstration, however, while real and kindly, was not as vigorous as is our American fashion. I have seen a governor received in Philadelphia with far louder cheers and much more violent enthusiasm. The *vivas* and hand-clapping rather reminded me of the fashionable repressed and kid-glove encoring of our Academy of Music. Perhaps this may be explained by saying that the lower classes of the Italians have as gentle manners as the higher classes of Americans. I noticed this particularly in the behavior of the troops towards the people. They held their lines always intact and kept the street clear, but without a rough word or action,—officers and men had the manners and demeanor of gentlemen in a ball-room throughout all the movements.

The display of bunting was very moderate, and not at all equal to the ordinary American demonstration on the Fourth of July. The flags were few and small compared with our show on such an occasion. Indeed, the very largest in size was an American one, which floated from the campanile of the American Church, and directly under which the royal party passed.

In the evening there was an illumination of the city in honor of the event. Roman fireworks are noted the world over for their excellence and cheapness, and the display was creditably brilliant. The old Castle San Angelo, the centre of the illumination, stood out grandly, like a fortress of fire, and, as the successive explosions of the fireworks boomed through the city, one could almost imagine that some of the old warrior popes were at their work again. The Vatican was dark and silent. The national *fête* of to-day is a State anniversary, held in honor of the adoption of the modern constitution. As the pope is virtually a dethroned ruler here, and still keeps up his claims to the temporal sovereignty of his old kingdom, he would hardly be expected to join in the celebration of the adoption of the liberal constitution under which King Humbert administers the government.

The transition from the absolute autocracy of the Papal government to the very limited monarchy of the United Kingdom has not been a quiet or easy one, and the ecclesiastical and civil parties stand widely apart. Under the old *régime* the Church had gotten to be the main land-owner of the country. Two-fifths of all the real estate was said to be in its possession. The new government found it necessary to confiscate a large portion of this and return it to healthy uses. Laws were passed appropriating large properties for the immediate use of the government, and providing for the gradual extinction of the monastic establishments, which had grown plethoric with estate and meagre in membership. To-day nearly all the great department buildings are confiscated convents, and many others have been sold or rented for private purposes. These buildings often still retain their old legends and titles, and the effect is singularly confusing, and at times odd.

Over a restaurant, for instance, on this street you see *ave gratia plena.* The headquarters of the police department, which, however, is itself a somnolent institution compared with Scotland Yard or an American "Central Station," is full of ancient inscriptions from the catacombs in erudite abbreviated Latin. Along the front of a pension, not far off, I read every day that fine old sentence from one of the fathers : " *Per varias heic ætates et tempora vitæ omnes atque æternam tendimus patriam,*" and " *Dis Manibus,*" from half a dozen tombs, meets me every time I ascend the stairways to my own rooms.

In fact, the intrusion of classic association and tradition into the commonplace life of every day is incessant. Every morning our butter comes on the table stamped with an image of the she-wolf suckling Romulus and Remus, a favorite print here; and it is a sad come down to read S. P. Q. R.—those imperial initials, so fraught with transcendent power and meaning to our school-boy mind—on the municipal street-carts and the caps of the city lamp-lighters.

It seems like calling up the spirits from another and far-off world; and yet that world, perhaps, was much like our own. Any one going through the galleries of the Vatican and Capitol, where there are thousands and thousands of statues and busts, would be struck, I think, with the likeness of the old Roman politicians of the Republican period to the politicians of our own country, particularly those of the South and Southwest of the generation just previous to the war. There is the same gaunt, meagre, self-reliant face and figure, and often that half-careless and shabby swing or slouch of the body.

I have before mentioned that the Italian of to-day resembles strongly the best American type of this moment,—the man with fine-cut, intellectual face, symmetrical form of body, and light, elastic step,—that type which seems to prefigure the coming American man when the race shall have fully sloughed off the grossness and dross of its heterogeneous mixture and evolved its own distinctive form.

There is even now a strong parallel between the physical appearance of the two people which you can trace down into detail and to classes. The soldiery of New Italy strongly resemble the best regiments of our volunteers. They are both the armies of freedom. The upper middle classes of Italy, the hope of the new kingdom, have much the appearance of the middle classes of our own country,—the rank and file of the Republican party. Both classes are doing the same work for their respective countries,—leading them up and onward.

I may as well say here, for fear of misleading, that the Romans themselves acknowledge no kinship in any way with any Northern nation. From the high plane of their descent and traditions they look down on us all, English, Americans, Germans, and Russians, as barbarians. They are too polite to say this, and irreproachably courteous in their demeanor,—*noblesse oblige*, —but, nevertheless, they think it. They are polite and kind, not because it is our due, but because they owe it to their name and heritage. This feeling of infinite superiority extends to the lowest classes, who all look on themselves as old families compared with the outside world. Notwithstanding, they look on all foreigners as a fair subject of plunder,—poor wrecks sent by a kind Providence to be stripped and overcharged. I think the stranger in Italy pays just about double for everything. I have seen oranges sold out of the same basket at one price to the Roman and at more than double to *forestieri.* A curious illustration of this is found in physicians' bills. The regularly accepted tariff of the average physician is, for a visit to an Italian, ten lira (about two dollars); for a visit to a stranger, twenty lira. The populace thus, by a motion of their own, levy a high export duty on all goods sold out of their country, or to be taken out, and even on services rendered to an outsider.

Living is very cheap in Italy for many reasons. Labor is to be had in abundance at a few cents a day; lodging or house-rent comes to little, because the solid stone dwellings, built for a once greatly larger population, are still there, and are a free gift to the present generation; the cormorant middleman has not come yet, and the fish of the sea and generous fruits of the earth, olives, figs, grapes, cost almost nothing. But for the stranger on the trodden highways of travel, all

these things might as well not be. Among themselves,
the commoner classes of Italy, and indeed of all Europe,
live with an economy that is painful, and excites one's
involuntary pity, but the traveller cannot share in the
advantages of the cheap prices which this brings about.
Accounts in France are kept in francs, and here in lira,
pieces of about twenty cents, which tends to economy,
the mind making that the unit of expense, instead of
the dollar, as with us. The poorer people buy and sell
and keep their accounts in centesimi, the one-fifth part
of our cent. There is a small copper coin in circulation
here in value two centesimi,—two-fifths of a cent,—and
in Austria they have a coin of just half that value, or
two mills of our system. It is almost impossible for
us to feel that such a coin represents a distinct value,
or can purchase anything, or be worth having or saving,
but to the people of Europe it is a sharp fact. It is
these centesimi coins, I fear, that make communism.

The new central post-office on the piazza San Sil-
vestro is a fair illustration of the way in which the new
government is changing the face of old Rome. The
building is a spacious pile of confiscated convent property. A convent in Rome, I should say, means what
we commonly call a monastery. You enter it on either
side by a handsome hallway, possibly fifty feet high,
certainly forty, whose sides are adorned by immense
panels of oil-paintings,—emblematic pictures of the
genius of the railway and the telegraph. Once over
the tessellated pavements of these fine arches you enter
a grand interior court. So munificent is the provision
of room that this court or piazza is a beautiful square,
one hundred and fifty feet in length and breadth, lovely
with fountains, flowers, statuary, green plots of grass,
and with a covered corridor frescoed on ceiling and
wall and paved with bright marbles stretching all the
length of its exterior. Around this court the building
proper rises in three grand stories.

There are rooms and offices for every conceivable purpose, and those for the accommodation of the public nearly always in duplicate,—one for men and one for women. All these rooms are frescoed or painted, and equipped with furniture of massive style and artistic design. So lavish is the embellishment that the corridor affords a walk of six hundred feet of continuous pictorial design, much of it fantastic and quaint, and all on the theme either of the railroad or telegraph-wire, steam or fire. The building has just been opened to the public, and is daily thronged with groups of æsthetic Italians—which means the lower classes as well as what we call the educated—discussing with interest and animation the taste and execution of the work.

To present fairly the liberality and enlightened provision of the Roman government, it must be remembered that Rome is a city not one-third as large as Philadelphia, and that its people do not have the habit of writing and communication. There is, for instance, no newspaper mail at all as compared with ours. There are no large business establishments flooding a whole continent or the world with circulars. In fact, the circular is not known here in our sense. Finally, of the quarter of a million people here, there are vast numbers who never either send or receive a letter. I doubt if the amount of business of this office is one-tenth that of ours. As an illustration of the different habits of the people, among the wealth of rooms in the building (and there are so many that they seem at loss sometimes, I think, to know how to label them) there is one set apart for the public and common use of any one who wants to write his letters or address them, or do anything of the kind at the office. This room, all brilliant with painting, had in it four small tables, neatly fitted out with stationery, ink, pens, blotters, etc., two seats to each table, and was, in fact, a charming little retreat. Just one seat was occupied. In Philadelphia, or New York, or

Boston, one hundred chairs would be kept pretty well filled.

Even in so purely democratic a matter as post-office accommodation, both for the people at large and the men who serve them, we have something to learn from a monarchy.

Sunday is the central day of the week in Rome in social and civil as well as in religious life. Parliament, or congress, sits on this day as on any other. Most of the shops are open, although the attendance at church is good. It is, in fact, a mystery to me where the people in the churches come from, as the streets are full and the town busy. Political meetings are generally fixed for Sunday, although there are not many of them. The fresh cartoons appear on the walls and in the shops on Sunday. It is the visiting day, and the day for putting on cleanly-washed clothes among the poor people. It is a brilliant day on the Corso, that lively little avenue being crowded with equipages, and blue and scarlet with uniforms. In the evening there is always *the* opera of the week, and in the private houses balls and receptions. This social use of the day is not confined to the Italians or Roman Catholics, but holds among Protestants, and English and Americans as well, who readily fall in with the social usages of the country, and give their dinner-parties and receptions according to its customs. It is a national or Continental, not a religious, characteristic.

It is to be said for the Italians, if we would present the question fairly, that, while it is perfectly natural and a matter of course among them to use Sunday for their pleasures and recreation, it is also perfectly natural and a matter of course with them, as it is not with us, to go to church and worship devoutly on week-days. Service is going on all the time in the numerous churches here, and fairly well attended. You can hear a sermon every day in the week if you want to. Some

bb

people here perhaps do. A good number hear mass
every day, and a vast number enter their churches
daily for personal and private prayers. If the Italians
carry their pleasures into Sunday, as we do not, they
also carry their religion into the six week-days, as we
do not.

The whole Sunday question is at bottom like so
many others, one of climate and habit of life. The
differences grow out of different modes of life induced
by different clime and land. These people, having
warm sun and soft skies the year round, live out-of-
doors all the time, and have no family-life, in our
sense, where the family lives from morning to night
within walls to itself. They could not adopt our solitary observance of Sunday, simply because they have
no close houses to shut themselves up in. Our ordinary habits of life to them would be imprisonment.
They live on the street, under the trees, out by the
fountains, in open gardens, in their cool marble
churches, grand and lofty, and in the stone-flagged
plazas. If they stop working on Sunday they must
see each other.

Once upon a time, hundreds of years ago, there lived
here a tailor called Pasquino so witty that his sayings
were the talk of the town, and brought him custom from
all, both high and low, who loved to come to his little
shop and hear in clever phrase all the pungent scandal
of the day. This tailor-shop was a kind of liberal club
of those days. Right opposite it, on the angle of a wall
of a palace, stood a large statue of some person—as
is so often the case here—unknown. The friends of
Pasquino after his death, unwilling to give up their
diversion of witty criticism and satire, still kept on
forging their sharp comments on public men and
passing events, hanging them in written form on the
base of this statue for the amusement of the public.
The statue very easily took the name of Pasquino. To

help the thing along, the statue pretended to talk with a neighboring river-god in marble across the way, the comments taking the form of dialogue, or sometimes point-blank question and answer. From this incident we have our word *pasquinado.* The sayings were written and put up in the night, the authorities taking them down in the daytime, but they could not stop people circulating from mouth to mouth the clever sayings which had been found there in the morning, and which were the news of the day.

This thing kept up for generations and became a cherished usage. So exasperated were the popes, who were severely lampooned, that they removed therefrom the river-god to the museum of the Capitol, and one of them, Adrian V., wanted to remove Pasquino also, and throw him into the Tiber. His owner, a duke, objected to this and defended him, and here he is yet, badly mutilated, little more than a trunk, but talking still. His last great pasquinado was during the recent sitting of the Vatican Council, when there hung from the stumps of feet one morning the inscription, " Free as the Council," a bitter epigram to those who understand the inside working of that caucus-ridden instrument of the Vatican " machine."

For centuries this Pasquino image was the only organ of public opinion in Rome, and so strong is the force of habit that public opinion to-day finds expression in this " placard" form in preference to any other. The newspaper has come,—a great modern institution,—but the Italian mind hardly receives it. It prefers the placard, and uses it in every way. Political attacks are made on cheap colored cartoons sold in the shops and on the stands as we sell newspapers. Religious disputes are carried on in printed placards posted on the churches, and so many of them are they that they very thoroughly cover the town. Rome has been quite excited for some weeks over a discussion as to the adoration of the Virgin, and it is entirely carried on by printed posters. One morning you find a card of one side posted all over the place, and groups gathered reading it. In a day or two, or perhaps the third or fourth,—things move slowly,—appears a reply similarly posted. The people read it, and at their homes talk over it. Printing, of course, is cheap, and also posting. This usage extends even to advertisements, which will not go into the papers, although advertising is cheap enough, six to eight cents a line for one insertion. Does an Italian want to let an apartment he never thinks of advertising in a paper, but has a package of hand-bills struck off, and placards the town. The little advertising there is in the papers is done by English and Americans.

Under these circumstances the Italian papers, although there are plenty of them, are naturally thin and weak. They are all poor and able to spend but little money. The Italian does not ask for news with his morning maccaroni, and they, in consequence, do not give it to him. He knows nothing of the world outside of his city, and there is no correspondence. Only in one department do they compare with us, and in that they often surpass us. Their editorials are often strong, polished, timely, and scholarly. Here the paper, rejected by the mass of the people for their common uses, has a special function. It is the channel adopted by the leaders of New Italy to reach the thought and influence of the Nation. There is generally but one article, such as we call "editorial," a real leader, occupying the first column of the first page. It grasps the leading issue of the day and handles it with vigor and depth. There is a scope and breadth about many of these articles which reveal in their writers a large knowledge of the world, and that trained habit of thought which comes from the discipline of education. In this spirit and style the great questions of Church and State, of the right to the ballot, of the use of an army, of intervention or non-intervention in European politics, of home political construction, and the hourly arising problems and complications of the new Union are daily discussed, and this high plane of discussion is one of the most encouraging and hopeful signs for the Italy that is to come. This is not, of course, the character of all the editorials, nor of those of all papers, but it is of many of them,—enough to give tone and a character to the general press, or at least a liberal portion of it.

The reason for the strength and high character of this class of articles is clear,—they are not written for the mass of the people, who would perhaps be best moved by a very passionate and an *ad captandum* style of writing, but for the men who control and lead. They are the work of leaders reaching out to other leaders and men of influence and power. At present only these use the newspapers. The average Italian lets it alone. Hence the strong " Vatican" articles ; the strong " Parliamentary" articles ; the strong " Radical" articles, which one sees every week here in the several leading journals. The newspaper is a real channel here for the statesman.

The usual price for a daily paper in Rome is two cents. The circulation is small, but very many persons read the same sheet,—perhaps an average of ten. In time the newspaper will be a great popular institution in Italy, for the Italians are a people given to reading, and fond of talking about what they read, but at present it is foreign and strange to the ingrained habits of centuries and must work its way slowly.

CHAPTER XLVI.

THE ITALIAN LIFE.

KINSHIP OF THE MODERN ITALIAN AND THE AMERICAN—THE
VISIBLE BLOOD-TIE OF THOUSANDS OF YEARS AGO—THE
COMMON EDUCATION OF ITALY AND THAT OF THE UNITED
STATES—THE TWO CIVILIZATIONS—BRIGHT SIDE OF LOWER
CLASS LIFE IN ITALY—RULE OF THE ROMAN MIND—POLIT-
ICAL AND SOCIAL END OF TRAVEL.

WHEN one goes to Italy expecting to find there in
the people of to-day the full-blooded descendants of the
Roman senators and imperial pro-consuls who stalked
like demigods through our well-remembered school-
books, he suffers, of course, a foolish disappointment.
In race and blood the modern Italian is largely the
same manner of man as we are. His national fibre, in
good part, is like our own, Teutonic. Our race ancestry in one great branch—say in the male line—is
the same, and our common ancestor is not very far back.
Some few thousand years ago our Teuton forefathers
came swarming together out of those wondrous cavernous shades in Asia which neither Revelation nor history
have yet illuminated ; and only about twelve to fifteen
hundred years ago they separated, the Gothic branch
pouring over Southern Europe, Italy, lower France,
Spain, the Scandinavian branch streaming over Northern Europe. Certain Gothic tribes flooded over the
Alps into Italy, washed out the civilized people and
government of the soil and camped there in history.
Certain other tribes, their Scandinavian kin, pushed
for the northward and westward to barbarous Britain,
swept away the rude people and institutions, and made

their home there. Substitute the vanquished, savage Celt in place of the vanquished, polished Latin, and the modern Italian and Englishman, or American, are the same. When the Gothic Teutons that came into Italy submerged the people they found there and drove them out of history, they took from them a classic literature and art, and a social culture, that were the product of the two highest civilizations the world had yet seen. When the Scandinavian Teutons that came into Britain had disposed of its barbarian population, they found little there that was much better than themselves, and, consequently, took little by their conquest save the bare soil.

In all this our modern Italian relatives have this great advantage of us: their fathers married into a better old family than did ours. But even in these old families there was a distant, although forgotten, relationship, for the Celt and Latin were both of Aryan stock. The modern nationalities of Italy and the United States are not, therefore, quite brothers, but we are certainly cousins in the family of the world.

It is this far-off but strong blood-tie which accounts for the elusive traces of similarity, sometimes in physique, sometimes in mind, between the Italian and American which constantly challenges one's attention in Italy. The two people are so different and yet often so alike. The Italian is the American with his æsthetic and higher side fully and roundly developed, but to the neglect of his practical energies and lower activities. The American is the Italian with his lower or money-getting faculties acutely developed to the neglect of his æsthetic and higher culture. This is a rather blunt and not very complimentary way to ourselves of putting it, but it at least defines sharply the complementary relation which we seem to hold to each other as peoples. We are the same people differentiated by the special development for fifteen hundred years of different sides of our nature.

It is the advantage of comparative social studies that they enable us to see ourselves somewhat as other peoples see us, and as we cannot see ourselves. We Americans value certain things and prize them highly, and rank ourselves above all the world because we possess them, and despise those nations who do not possess them. The Italian values certain other things, achieves them, is proud of himself because he has achieved them, and contemns those who cannot understand his way of thinking and living. We despise the Italian as ignorant and lazy; he looks down on us as rude and uncultivated. He is just as honest and sincere in his contempt of us as we in ours of him. The decision must come from some higher and broader court than either nation.

The average Italian has leisure and cultivation, and he despises the American who has neither. The average American has food and clothing and work, and he despises the Italian who often has none of them.

Let us try to look at this question a moment with Italian eyes and not our own. In inviting a competitive international comparison the American would probably put forward as his first and strongest claim to superiority, "We are the better-educated people." "No," the Italian would surely say; "you are not. More, you are grossly uneducated. To be sure, you can all read and write and have an illusory proficiency in the lower branches of education, but in all higher education your national mind is a blank. Your average citizen can read type, but he cannot read a Titian or a Fra Angelico, as our humblest people can. He understands arithmetic, or book-keeping, or contracting, but he cannot understand a work of Michael Angelo or Phidias. He would not know a Praxiteles if he found it on the roadside, and could not enjoy it if it were given to him. Even your wealthy classes are too uneducated to purchase intelligently in our art mar-

ket. We send over to you our refuse—slop-shop paintings and ready-made statuary—because you prefer it,
and will not buy our best work. Engravings of the
masters will not sell in your great cities against modern, sentimental crudities that would not be exposed for
sale in an interior Italian town. Your millionaires are
incompetent to select the simplest picture for their
swollen houses filled with all gross luxuries. The
walls of their halls and drawing-rooms would often
offend the eye and shock the taste of many an Italian
peasant. You have a wonderful faculty for the practical application of the exact sciences to common uses,
which fits you pre-eminently to be laborers and traders
for all the world,—to supply their bodily wants,—but
you have not the higher flower of civilization, that
culture and perfection of those nobler faculties which
makes the whole man a desirable and gracious being.
You are fit to be manufacturers and mechanics for all
men, but not to sit with them. You have not that
mental and social grace which make companionship
with you desirable. You are excellent toilers and laborers, but you do not get higher,—you never reach the
intellectual and artistic side of work. Even your
professional mechanic is not the artisan of Europe."

Now this reply does raise the question, What is
education? And if there are varying educations, which
is the higher and better? Which makes the higher
and fuller and happier man? Which is the higher
accomplishment, the power to understand at once and
thoroughly enjoy a patent rat-trap or a piece of sculpture? Is it a greater national glory to produce a sew-
ing-machine or a steam-tug, or a school of art? Is it
a higher intellectual capacity to be able to read newspapers and science primers, or Correggios and Guidos
and cathedrals?

Leaving this question open, the advocate of the
American life would probably select his ultimate position in the general comfort and well-being of the body

of the nation, and from this intrenchment argue, "We are a prosperous people; every man among us is well fed, well clad, well housed." And so we are in comparison with Italy or any other European people. " But," says the Italian, "granting all that, is the body the man? Is its care and comfort the pursuit of happiness? The corpulent hog is well fed and warm and well housed, but what is he? You have attained physical well-being and material prosperity at the neglect of the culture of the higher man. Your prosperous, well-to-do, perhaps wealthy man—the man you call successful—is often of coarse instincts, of ignorant manners, of unpleasant and vulgar address. He is devoid of that personal cultivation—the culture of his mind and affections—which makes association with him agreeable, and which, if he possessed, would constitute for himself a far higher and truer source of enjoyment than anything that food and clothing and gross luxuries of any kind, or to any amount, can bring him. He has sacrificed everything that is high in him to the getting of material comfort, and the best one can say for him is, that he can never understand his utter mental and moral poverty, his meagreness and unloveliness as a man. The poor Italian, with leisure, gracious manners, fine perceptions, refined instincts, and, withal, content; with a capacity to enjoy the highest development of human thought and genius, is an infinitely higher type of man. What is even your power of money? You can make money, which is the lowest relation of man to wealth. You cannot spend it, which is the highest relation of man to wealth. Our poor, cultivated peasant is the superior of your vulgar rich man. Man does not live by bread alone; our civilization is a moral, not a material one, and must not be tried by material tests."

Here is another issue which must be left to the decision of some tribunal which is neither American nor Italian.

Whatever may have been our popular and conventional opinion of the Italian in times past, certain it is that the educated thought and thinking travel, both of England and America, are every day pronouncing a higher verdict on the modern Italian. And it is likely that this judgment will strengthen as we come to know more of him from personal knowledge, and as we gradually lift ourselves more and more above a provincial plane of mind.

The modern Italian has virtues which are not ours, an education which is not ours, a national wealth which is not ours, a national ambition which is not ours. He is badly handicapped by the centuries, but he has already achieved wonderful things both in political and social advancement. He has broken the fetters of a superstitious bondage, of whose appalling and merciless power we have no conception. He has set out towards self-government, with the achievement of a federal Union of states in the face of obstacles which make our work in 1776 to 1789 seem crude and infantile. He has established an order of society by classes, superimposed one above the other, but not so greatly at the cost of the lower orders as in England. One never meets in Italy the painful servility of the lower class Englishman. The Italian peasant has the self-respect of a prince. In this respect the social structure of Italy is a higher piece of work than that of England. The modern Italian bears a most burdensome national debt with a self-control and honesty which far surpasses that of the average American State or city. The repudiator has not yet appeared in Italian politics.

There is a positive wealth, too, throughout Italy of which we have no conception, for it is not our idea of wealth, and cannot be measured by statistics, like iron and pork and cotton. In every country town in Italy there are vast treasures of art of which the average American does not know enough even to go and see when he is over there. There are no circulating libraries in the Italian provincial towns, and perhaps no reading-circles or book-clubs, those excellent institutions of our country life, but there are museums stored with a wealth of art and æsthetic treasure such as no American city can have at all, however metropolitan its ambition, descended palaces filled with frescos and paintings and sculpture by the masters, and cathedrals whose architecture and statues are a liberal education in themselves. And cathedrals and palaces are alike open to the people. So overflowing is this wealth that it cannot be enumerated, and does not get even into the guide-books. The statuary in the lovely cathedral of Orvieto, for instance, almost unseen by the tourist, Cardinal Wiseman pronounces to be "the largest and most beautiful collection of the time of Michael Angelo." Orvieto is a town that over here might rank in our life with Carlisle in Pennsylvania, or the county towns of Massachusetts.

Still more, the commonest Italian is able to understand and enjoy all this wealth of art and education, and does have his enjoyment of it. All through Italy the galleries and private palaces, with all their statuary and paintings and tapestries and furniture and carvings and marbles and precious stones, are open to the public. On Sunday, at least, they are absolutely free to all without cost of any kind. The princely families living in them on that day retire to interior suites of apartments, and all day long their halls and elegant salons and magnificent corridors and stairways are swept by the populace. Imagine for a moment the palaces of the Fifth Avenue, New York, or the costlier dwellings of Boston and Philadelphia being opened in this way. Yet this very week the costliest art treasures of all the world in the grand palaces of Florence and Rome are being exposed in just this way.

It is the most pleasing sight in all Italy, as it is one of the most suggestive, to wander into one of these lordly palaces on a Sunday. Sauntering quietly and composedly through hall and chamber and gallery and state-room, you see little groups of the humblest Italians, private soldiers, laborers, peasants, with their wives and sweethearts. They stroll at will over the palace, at perfect ease, discussing pleasantly and intelligently among themselves the works of art. You always find them clustered before the best statues and the rarest paintings, arguing on their merits or pointing out to each other their hidden perfections. And this they do without the aid of guide-books or catalogues, which, if they had, they most probably would not read. They are far beyond the northern barbarian's stage of culture.

Again and again this mortifying conclusion is forced on one in such scenes. Of the people in this drawing-room or gallery the Italians are of the lower classes of their country. What do they show? They have a perfect ease of manner, grace of movement and conversation, an intelligent appreciation of the master-work around them. The English and American people present are of the better classes of their countries or they would not be able to be here. And what do they show? One-half of them at least only ignorance and vulgarity. Heavy-faced millionaires, looking bored and hopelessly lost among the finest treasures of the world; overdressed daughters, giggling and awkward, uncertain how to move in a palace; wives with dull, expressionless faces, who you know are going to mispronounce English if they open their mouths.

In personal refinement and cultivation and æsthetic education the lower classes of Italy have reached a point of civilization beyond that of our poorer classes, and our classes of uneducated wealth, and it is needless to add, far beyond the similar classes of England. Here, indeed, is the presentable side of the Italian nation, for the higher classes do not seem to improve on the lower in proportion to their advantages. Their education is not advanced proportionably, and they seem to lack in virility and nerve. The fire of conquest, the lust of achievement, seem to have died out both from the Gothic and Roman lines of blood.

Perhaps even here, however, the Italian would take issue and come in with a new claim. "We conquer not any longer by physical conquest, as did our forefathers in ruder days, and as you Northern nations essay to do now. We rule the world in these latter ages, not by force of arms, but by force of mind. The Roman Law to-day administers the justice of the world. You see it in the flesh in your own code of Louisiana, and on the statute books of Colorado and Utah, and it is the soul of the Equity Courts of England and the United States."

"And the Papacy,—the Second Roman Empire,—is it not a magnificent demonstration of the genius of the Roman mind for rule? Is not this grand ecclesiastical empire the lineal successor of the First Roman Empire? Rome under the Cæsars ruled the world for half a dozen centuries by force of arms,—under the Popes she has ruled it, or the greater part of it, for twice six centuries by force of intellect. She changed the form of empire, not the fact. And is it not a greater achievement to hold the mind of the world in subjection than its territory? This is just what Rome did when the Papal Pontiffs took the chair of the Imperial Pontiffs."

Certain it is there is a subtlety in the Italian mind which is beyond our power to follow, and with which we cannot successfully compete. We may condemn it in morals, but there it stands in fact, an intellectual development beyond our own, a refinement or intensity of mental action which has not been given us. On this plane we cannot grapple with the Italian on even terms. On this field, which is one of mental force, he leads us.

There is no greater good of foreign travel than this, that it gives us the opportunity for comparative contrast and study of our own country, our government, our social institutions, our whole civilization, with those of other countries. It is only against the background of other countries and civilizations that we can see our own, and detect their failings or defects, or dangerous tendencies. And these are the points we should look for and study. Where we are better than other nations —and that is, happily, in very many things—there is no danger ahead, and nothing to be won, and, consequently, nothing to be learned. Where we are behind other peoples there may be national danger in store for us, and there is certainly something to be achieved and secured. It is on this principle that in this volume I have considered chiefly those features of foreign life which are superior to ours.

The conditions of life for all in this country are much higher and more fortunate than they are now, or ever have been before, for any other people. If there is power in the people to govern themselves, as we all believe, and on which belief we have staked our national existence, there is no good reason why all the people of this country should not in time reach the privileges and culture and advancement which, in times past and in other countries, have only been reached and enjoyed by the very few at the cost of the many. This is our goal, and for this reason the liberal study of the institutions and civilizations of older countries is a practical political and social duty of the American citizen. It is part of the education which he owes to himself and to his country, that he may discharge fitly and safely the high functions of his citizenship.

To be of avail under our structure of society and government this education must come directly to the whole body of the people, and not to or through one higher class; and this, perhaps, under Providence, is the meaning of the surges of American travel which yearly flood the face of Europe, the countless hosts of a new race moving over an old world, with gentler manners and aims, but impelled just as blindly and unconsciously as the fateful hordes of their Gothic forerunners.

Rome.

APPENDIX.

APPENDIX.

HINTS OF TRAVEL.

Customs of Travel Abroad and at Home—The Red Books —Some Unwritten Laws of European Life—Hand-book Equipment — The "Impedimenta" — Routes —Railway Usages—Hotels—Luggage— Guides — Special Centres of Shopping—Food—Languages.

In closing this series of papers let me hastily throw together some notes, the sum of repeated experiences, which may save, perhaps, to future travellers some time, labor, and the annoying quest of unwritten information. The usages of strange countries are more foreign than their languages, and it is these which the unfamiliar traveller needs to have translated.

Routes.—Distances are so short in Europe that in travelling in any one country, or even between countries, it is hardly worth while to try to take everything in in one consecutive line or trip. It is better, if you wish to see any prominent person, or to be at any certain place at any fixed time, or to accept an invitation to visit, to do so, and double on your route for the rest of your journey. In other words, there is no economy in controlling your movements by distances, as there generally is in our vast territory. It is better to pay no attention to this, as railway fares will not be found to be the proportionately larger item of travelling expenses they are with us. It is the hotels that eat up one's funds.

From the great centres of London and Paris, Rome and Berlin, you can work out everywhere with more economy than by trying to take in all you want to see on a consecutive schedule of time and route. Again, as a rule, there is no economy in Europe in buying through tickets, as there always is with us. One thousand miles of travel in England and on the Continent, made over the same route, cost exactly the same whether you purchase one ticket for the entire route or divide it into fifty,

435

—except in the case of a few "circular" tickets purchased through agencies and sadly limited as to time of use. Further, when you are going to stop off frequently, a long ticket may become a positive nuisance, so hampering and embarrassing are the conditions and limitations of its use. As a rule, it must be *viséd* or endorsed by somebody wherever you intend to use it after having once stopped, and this form takes quite as much time and trouble as buying a new ticket. By a ridiculous inversion of thought and business tact, the railway regulations abroad are all made for the convenience of the railway and police officials instead of for that of the passenger.

Luggage.—Contrary to the common impression at home, the arrangements for handling baggage abroad are better and cheaper than ours. The registering is just as safe as our checking system. The only difference is between a paper check and a metal one, while the train and station employees are infinitely more careful in moving and storing baggage than with us. Only the traveller must not attempt to take care of himself after the American fashion. Let him trust himself at once to a porter, who for a few pennies will arrange everything, gather his luggage together, remove it from the station, call a good cab, and give the proper directions to the driver. The traveller's only care should be to secure the most experienced and reliable-looking porter on the ground. He will place you in your carriage in a very few moments, and you will get from the station to your hotel much quicker, cheaper, and more pleasantly than you can make the same trip in any American city I know of. In Italy a cab for two persons, with a trunk and hand-baggage, will cost only from a franc to a franc and a half; in great London, for the usual course, not over fifty cents.

Hotels.—Always select a small hotel abroad in preference to a large one of the same grade. You have better service and are more comfortable. Europe is beginning to build huge hotels after the American fashion, but they are not a success, and generally combine the vices and defects of both systems. On the Continent hotels are advertised as first- and second-class. The first is the more elaborate and expensive house, and generally very comfortable; the second is cheaper, everything is plainer and more limited, but of its kind it is solid and good. The second-class European hotel is not a shabby or nasty imitation of a first-class one. The proprietor is not ashamed of the grade of his house, but advertises it openly, and is as proud of keeping an excellent second-rate hotel as of doing anything else well and honestly, in which he differs largely from his American brother, who is always assuming to offer first-class accommodations for a second-class price. In England, the railway hotels, as a rule, are excellent, and travellers need not avoid them on principle, as one does here. They are owned and managed by the railway companies, and as the road is so they are.

Food.—Our country is, of all the world, the land of good food, cheap, plenty, and in rich variety. There is no European country that can begin to compare with us in this blessing, and the American stranger abroad must expect for a time to really suffer for the want of his accustomed luxuriance of table. The poverty of an English hotel breakfast-table is something inexplicable,—sole bacon and chops is the same dreary fare all the kingdom over and every day in the year. Although true to her traditional reputation for grand roasts of beef and generous legs of mutton, England does not have at all the sirloin steak, the highest American conception of beef. Nor has she game in our sense and use of it. Coffee is never good at a British public table; the tea, however, is generally excellent and superior to ours. Coffee in France is always good and tea poor. In Italy, at a provincial inn, both are looked on as curiosities, and served as such if one is erratic enough to call for them.

The severe meagreness of an English or Continental table is, however, in its fruit and vegetables. They simply do not have them at all as we know them. At the private tables of those classes whose tastes are cultivated and somewhat cosmopolitan there is some provision of vegetables; the fruit, however, will be only a miniature dessert course. At an English public table one gets a rigid and unvarying allowance of just two vegetables, —always the same,—potatoes and Brussels sprouts. These are invariably set before one at every inn without the least change, even when the green-grocers' stand in the same street may have onions, beans, cabbage, and others of our coarser and plainer vegetables in reasonable plenty for sale. I have had them sometimes, but it was only on a special order and after serious consultation with the inn authorities. Fruit is rarely in the house, and if a peach, or bunch of grapes, or cherries are at last produced, it is at the price of a peck or bushel of them here.

It is this lack of fruits and vegetables, and the consequent want of their acidulous contribution to the blood, which, I think, makes Europe a wine-drinking land. The body demands this acid for the proper working of the system, and gets it in the wine. We get it in the fruit and vegetables we consume so largely and continuously. This same reasoning goes to show that we will never be a wine-drinking country,—at least while our present affluence in this kind of food exists. Our luxuriance of tropical fruit—bananas, oranges, citrons—is absolutely unknown to the common table of England.

Hotel Expenses.—As a whole, the hotel expenses in England and in the larger cities of the Continent are much heavier than with us. The attendance is better, and more personal and individual to each guest, but the provision and accommodations are more limited in their range. Even at plain country inns in such places as Reading, Chester, York, Carlisle, one must spend sixteen to twenty shillings per day, and then take rather plain meals. The best hotels in the same kind of towns in this country would not cost over $2.50 to $3. The whole hotel life and management is so different here and abroad that it is difficult to institute any direct comparison of expenses, but it is safe to say that there is not in any large city of all Europe any hotel where one can get the accommodations of the St. George, in Philadelphia, the Windsor, in New York, or the Grand Pacific, in Chicago, for their moderate prices, or for anything like them. In the provincial towns of France and Italy, however, the hotels are good and very moderate,—two or three dollars covering all expenses, including a wine something better than the *ordinaire.*

Guides, valets de place, etc.—If you have any knowledge at all of the language of the country you are in, or a slight amount of self-reliance, avoid guides altogether, and especially those ghastly, flaccid, half-alive creatures who start out from behind columns and dark recesses in old churches or dog your steps in gateways and porches. It is better to miss some things than to have everything spoiled by the disagreeable presence and incessant, unintelligent, parrot-like recitation of a mendicant guide. If you are rushing through any town in a few hours, it may be necessary to employ a guide to find your way and economize your minutes; but if you have reasonable time, any intelligent man can readily see everything for himself with the aid of his hand-book. Wherever you take a professional guide you lose absolutely the impression and associations of the place.

The red books.—There is no greater saving in travelling— saving of time, money, fatigue, temper, and opportunity—than that which is made in the procuring of good guide- or hand-books. It is economy to be extravagant in the way of buying them.

In the English and French provincial towns which one may want to see thoroughly one always finds two or three local guides, —shilling or two-franc pamphlets. It is best to buy them all. Each will be likely to have some feature worth its cost.

The very best of foreign-edited guide-books as a series are *Baedeker's.* They are wonderfully minute and explicit, giving a street-plan of nearly all towns of any size or interest, and going into the detail of expenses of cabs, tramways, hotels, rooms, lights, fires, restaurants, etc., in each town, and also of railway fares. The series now covers pretty much the travelled world, excepting our own country. They are very honest and upright in their editorship. I have always found their information reliable, and never detected any evidences of blackmailing or advertising in the text, which is more than can be said of a good many hand-books. They are also portable,—a very essential requisite,—and reasonable in price.

Baedeker's series have also the advantage of being published in French and German as well as English, and by getting the edition in one of these tongues one can perfect himself in a foreign language in using them.

Black's guides are good in their excellent pictures of places, rivers, and scenery, fine wood-engravings of good design and finish. I have never used their text.

Murray's series are elaborate and crowded with matter, but rather undigested and heavy. They seem to suit the English traveller better than the American or Continental.

The Satchel Guide, issued from Boston, is an admirable little work for Americans who want to make a hurried two or three months' run over Europe. It is scholarly and practical, and also thoroughly honorable and trustworthy in its information.

Whitaker's Almanac, large edition, is an almost indispensable companion for any one travelling in England who wishes to make an intelligent study of the country as he goes along, and to acquaint himself with its higher interests, machinery of government, form of society, diplomatic relations, etc. It can be had anywhere in London.

The Sportsman's Guide, an established British publication, is invaluable as a directory of private estates, and of hunting and fishing leases over England and Scotland.

John Bellows' English-French and French-English pocket-dictionary is, in some mechanical respects, the most wonderful book ever published, and the very best thing to be had in the way of a travelling dictionary of the languages. The genders in French, for instance, are all distinguished by types, a feminine word, wherever used, being printed in Italic. Many other things are thus presented at once to the eye by the use of typographical signs. The condensation of incidental information is also something admirable. It is a volume of only a few—two or three—inches in size, bound in fine flexible morocco for pocket use, rich in excellent miniature maps and carefully worked-out tables ; costs fifteen shillings, but is amply worth it.

In visiting in Italy there are numerous French and German works of travel which it is desirable to get and read. One not only reads up the country thus, but enjoys the advantage at the same time of seeing it through French or German spectacles as well as his own, and of studying the French or German mind in the same act with the Italian character. You make thus a comparative study of three or four nationalities instead of one. This process can be reversed, of course, according to what country one is in, as all the European countries with literatures have written of one another. The newspapers of each land and city are also very useful in the way of letting one rapidly into the current life of the country.

Learning Languages.—It is a common impression that foreign languages can be "picked up" *en route* as an incident of travel. Adult travellers, I think, will find this a mistake, and their inability to do this will be in proportion to their intelligence and mental vigor. The education of travel is a higher one than that of the grammar book, and the mind has too much on hand to grasp with interest the small detail of words and idiomatic rules; and unless it does grasp them with vigor there is no retention of them. One can study history, politics, social science, on a flying tour, but hardly languages.

Travelling-parties.—All over Europe the cab, hansom, or voiture is hired by the course or the hour, as you please, but you pay for the use of the whole cab, and not for the number of persons carried, as often with us. The ordinary vehicles have seats for either two or four. It costs, therefore, as much for one person as for two, for three as for four. The fee, also, at a gallery, palace, or museum on the Continent for one will do for two, and a party of four would pay the same as three. In dining, also, a whole bottle of wine costs a trifle less than two half-bottles, and is better; and in the restaurants, as in our clubs at home, two can make a better and cheaper dinner by ordering a number of courses of one portion than either could by ordering separately.

A single gentleman *en route* pays also about as much to the servants at the hotels—garçons, chambermaids, concierge, etc. —as he would if accompanied by a wife.

Two or four is, therefore, an economical party of travel.

Shopping.—As to shopping, which holds such a prominent place in the minds of intending travellers, all idea of it had better be abandoned at once. With the exception of certain local specialties, some of which are noted farther on, the American will get everything cheaper and better in his own country than abroad. I do not mean to say that there is nothing in Europe which we do not have in our home stores at the same rates. In London and Paris there are unquestionably many articles sold cheaper than our best stores can afford to offer them, but the stranger will not get them. There is one price for home customers and another for "foreigners" all over Europe.

As a rule, the American can do better by purchasing at home, where he is known and where it is the merchant's interest to retain his custom, than by venturing among the sharpers of strange towns.

There are certain special centres worth mentioning, however, which are the homes of certain manufactures, where really good articles may be had very cheap, and where the articles themselves have some additional value as mementos. For instance, Oxford is the best place in the world to buy Bibles,— the King James's version; Dieppe for ivory-carving, crosses, bracelets, card-cases, hair-brushes, etc., etc., in wonderful variety of designs and wonderfully cheap, as the carving is a small home industry, whole families working all the year round in their own dwellings at this labor and selling their work in their little village homes; Genoa for silver filigree-work and velvets; Venice for its wonderful colored glassware and beautiful toys; the Swiss towns for wood-carving, but the wood is apt to warp in our dry climate; Naples for raw-silk clothing; Pisa for small marbles and casts; Inverness for Scotch tweeds; Dublin for ulsters and Irish linens; Berlin for amber ornaments; Italy for coral; Scotland for pebble and cairngorm jewelry; Brussels for laces; silks and velvets from the "Lyons looms;" London for India shawls and goods, if you cannot get to India; Paris and Naples for kid gloves.

Gratuities, fees, vails.—A petty but endless trouble of the traveller in Europe for the first time is the matter of gratuities. You give a trifle all the time to every one who does you the least service. Even for an apparently friendly word of information on the street you are expected to pay in this way. In England it is " a tip ;" in France, the *pour-boire ;* in Italy, *buono manu,*—" the good hand ;" in Germany it is *trinkgeld,*—" drink money ;" in the East *backshish.* It is not much money in any one instance, but foots up pretty well after an active day's work. The practical trouble, however, is to know *what* to give. The inhabitants and the servants themselves know exactly what they are *entitled* to, for it is a matter of right just as much as any other charge, although the amount is never fixed or published in any written form for the information of strangers. They must learn it by experience.

We, as a rule, to whom the European measures are new, give too much. Englishmen of rank and wealth complain that Americans raise the costs of travel wherever they go.

For the gratuity to cab-drivers, waiters at restaurants, etc., the recognized European usage is in England one penny for every shilling spent in fare or at the table, and in France and Italy two sous for every franc spent. This rule disposes of a large portion of the cases.

For porters, twopence in England and two sous on the Continent for every piece of luggage handled, if it is only to carry it across a pavement. An umbrella or a shawl is a piece as well as a trunk. The driver of an omnibus cab, or fiacre, as a point of etiquette and out of professional consideration for the porters, will refuse to touch a piece of luggage himself,—even to lift it from three feet away into his vehicle.

Visiting at private houses of the upper classes in England the servants expect their tips in gold coin if your stay is over a day or two. The smallest English gold coin is a ten-shilling piece, —$2.50. You fee the footman who attends your bedroom ; the maid, if you have ladies, who serves their chambers ; the butler who has charge of the dining-room and force of waiters ; the keeper, if you hunt: the groom you use if you ride, or the head of the stables if there are several ; and generally any servant that you specially use. One soon learns by intuition how to grade these fees according to the rank of the servant and the length of his visit. The guard on a gentleman's stage-coach running on a line of travel expects a half-crown ; the guard on a public coach something less,—about a shilling.

On first-class ocean-steamers the gratuities are much analogous to those in a gentleman's house. The steward who waits on you at the table and the one who attends your state-room will each expect a fee in gold—ten shillings, $2.50, at least— from a single passenger, a pound if you have baths brought into your room every morning, are particular about having your wines warmed or iced, or, in short, use the servants up to their full capacity. When the passage is $60 to $75 or less, these fees are less,—about one-half of the figures above. The "Boots" also looks to be remembered,—about one-half the amount given the steward.

There is an aristocratic affectation in the use of coin in England. The fashionable world always gives its charities and subscriptions in guineas and not pounds, and in return its pet tradesmen and swell shops always charge in guineas for their wares or work. The difference is just one shilling on the pound, the pound being twenty shillings, the guinea twenty-one. There is no guinea coin. In its smaller tips, too, fashion uses the half-crown, and not the two-shilling florin. I confess that to myself, a stranger, the florin was always a particularly objectionable and low-bred looking coin, although I could never understand the reason of the prejudice.

The expense of this gratuity business in ordinary travel is, in general, rather exaggerated. The sums given are very small, and you get a great deal for them, a willing, perfect, and kindly service which you do not get in our country at all. To the traveller the custom is an annoyance rather than a burden. It must be borne in mind that for the most part in foreign lands these fees are not largess or bounty, but a right,—the regular wages for specific labor performed. The porter or garçon or driver has a right to them and from you. And in the matter of imposition these persons are fully as much sinned against as sinning. No one who has travelled much but has noticed again and again outwardly respectable enough looking people attempting to steal away from servants or evade the proper tariff of drivers and porters.

The worst feature of the whole business is the demoralization and want of self-respect which it engenders on the part of the classes who receive their compensation in this way as a gratuity, and not as wages. Persons in the habit of accepting gratuities and doing their service for these are certainly not in fit training for the independent responsibilities of citizenship, and in this view the custom, which, without its European foundation of right, is creeping into this country, has a special social interest for us.

The habit of accepting bounties degrades, demoralizes, and unmans the recipient, and that fairly-earned compensation should be systematically paid in this way—that whole classes should be forced to receive their return for their labor in this humiliating form—is but another proof of that fatal despising of humanity and the common manhood of all men which so thoroughly pervades the European life. It is sad to think that a very great portion of the people of Great Britain and Europe do now receive their wages in this way, look for it, and feel no humiliation in the transaction. You can hardly insult anybody across the water by an offer of anything, no matter what appears to be his or their official position. I have given a shilling in London to uniformed policemen and a franc in Paris to magnificent-looking hotel managers. A Philadelphia acquaintance in London had several hundred dollars brought to him from his banking-house—one of the largest there—by a clerk of the establishment, and the nattily-dressed young gentleman asked for a shilling for his services. Imagine the consequences of offering ten cents to a conductor on the Pennsylvania Railway who had shown you to your seat in the car and given you information as to when to get out; yet this is done all over England every day, and the middle-aged uniformed and respectable-looking guard hangs around stickily till he gets his sixpence.

There is nothing, on the whole, for which one may feel prouder of our country, in contrast with others, than the moral stamina and self-respect of the American employee, who would resent as an indignity the gratuity for which the European begs. That legendary fellow-countryman of ours spoke out of a full heart and with a just national pride, who, homeward bound, from the bridge of his Liverpool steamer, addressed the crowded wharf: " If there is any man, woman, or child on this island to whom I have not yet given a shilling, now is the time to speak."

ANCIENT CLASSICS FOR ENGLISH READERS

EDITED BY

REV. W. LUCAS COLLINS.

20 Volumes. Small 12mo. Fine Cloth, $1.00 each. The
20 Volumes, in neat Cloth Box, $20.00. Complete
in 10 Volumes, in neat Cloth Box, $15.00.

NOW COMPLETE, EMBRACING

1. HOMER'S ILIAD.	*11. PLINY.*
2. HOMER'S ODYSSEY.	*12. EURIPIDES.*
3. HERODOTUS.	*13. JUVENAL.*
4. CÆSAR.	*14. ARISTOPHANES.*
5. VIRGIL.	*15. HESIOD & THEOGNIS.*
6. HORACE.	*16. PLAUTUS & TERENCE.*
7. ÆSCHYLUS.	*17. TACITUS.*
8. XENOPHON.	*18. LUCIAN.*
9. CICERO.	*19. PLATO.*
10. SOPHOCLES.	*20. GREEK ANTHOLOGY.*

The aim of this delightful series of books is to explain, suffi·
ciently for general readers, who these great writers were, and what
they wrote; to give, wherever possible, some connected outline
of the story which they tell, or the facts which they record, checked
by the results of modern investigations; to present some of their
most striking passages in approved English translations, and to
illustrate them generally from modern writers; to serve, in short,
as a popular retrospect of the chief literature of Greece and Rome.

" Each successive issue only adds to
our appreciation of the learning and
skill with which this admirable enterprise of bringing the best classics within
easy reach of English readers is conducted."—*New York Independent.*

" There is not a volume of this most
admirable and useful series that is not
done in a very masterly manner, and
worthy of the highest praise."—*British
Quarterly Review.*

⁎ A Supplemental Series in the same size and type is being
issued. It will not be extended beyond eight or ten volumes

VALUABLE WORKS OF REFERENCE.

Lippincott's Pronouncing Biographical Dictionary.

Containing complete and concise Biographical Sketches of the Eminent Persons of all Ages and Countries. By J. THOMAS, A.M., M.D. Imperial 8vo. Sheep. $15.00. 2 vols. Cloth. $22.00.

Allibone's Critical Dictionary of Authors.

A Dictionary of English Literature and British and American Authors, Living and Deceased. By S. AUSTIN ALLIBONE, LL.D. 3 vols. Imperial 8vo. Extra cloth. $22.50.

Lippincott's Pronouncing Gazetteer of the World.

A Complete Geographical Dictionary. New Edition of 1880. Thoroughly Revised. Royal 8vo. Sheep. $10.00.

Allibone's Dictionary of Prose Quotations.

By S. AUSTIN ALLIBONE, LL.D. With Indexes. 8vo. Extra cloth. $5.00.

Allibone's Dictionary of Poetical Quotations.

By S. AUSTIN ALLIBONE, LL.D. With Indexes. 8vo. Extra cloth. $5.00.

Chambers's Encyclopædia.
American Revised Edition.

A Dictionary of Useful Knowledge. Profusely Illustrated with Maps, Plates, and Woodcuts. 10 vols. Royal 8vo.

Chambers's Book of Days.

A Miscellany of Popular Antiquities connected with the Calendar. Profusely Illustrated. 2 vols. 8vo. Extra cloth. $8.00.

Dictionary of Quotations,

From the Greek, Latin, and Modern Languages. With an Index. Crown 8vo. Extra cloth. $2.00.

Furness's Concordance to Shakespeare's Poems.

An Index to Every Word therein contained, with the Complete Poems of Shakespeare. 8vo. Extra cloth. $4.00.

Lempriere's Classical Dictionary.

Containing all the Principal Names and Terms relating to Antiquity and the Ancients, with a Chronological Table. 8vo. Sheep. $3.75. 16mo. Cloth. $1.50.

☞ The above Works are also bound In a variety of handsome extra styles

MRS. FORRESTER'S NOVELS.

12mo. Extra cloth. $1.25 each. 16mo. Paper cover. 50 cts. each.

RHONA.

"The author is one of the most popular writers of the period, and this is esteemed among her best."—*Baltimore Gazette.*

DOLORES.

"This is a delightful book. One of the best romances of the day."—*Philadelphia Chronicle.*

DIANA CAREW;
Or, For a Woman's Sake.

"A story of great beauty and complete interest to its close."—*Boston Traveller.*

MIGNON.

"Will be counted her best, as it is full of a keen interest both in its plot and character, and is written in a refined and exceedingly pleasing style." —*Publishers' Weekly.*

VIVA.

"A work of unusual power and interest. The plot is deeply attractive, the characters are striking, and the management of the story throughout is very skilful."—*Boston Saturday Evening Gazette.*

THE "DUCHESS" SERIES.

PHYLLIS.

12mo. Extra cloth. $1.25. 16mo. Paper cover. 50 cts.

"It is fascinating to a high degree. . . . We lay aside the book with a sigh of regret that the pleasure is over, after mingling our laughter and tears with the varying fortunes of the charming heroine."—*New York Ev. Mail.*

"Certainly 'Phyllis' is one of the most fascinating little novels that has appeared this year."—*N. O. Times.*

MOLLY BAWN.

12mo. Extra cloth. $1.25. 16mo. Paper cover. 60 cts.

"Is really an attractive novel. Full of wit, spirit, and gayety, the book contains, nevertheless, touches of the most exquisite pathos. There is plenty of fun and humor, which never degenerate into vulgarity. All women will envy, and all men fall in love with, her. Higher praise we surely cannot give."—*London Athenæum.*

AIRY FAIRY LILIAN.

12mo. Extra cloth. $1.25. 16mo. Paper cover. 60 cts.

"The airiest and most sparkling contribution of the month is a brilliant romance by the author of 'Phyllis.' It is as full of variety and refreshment as a bright and changeful June morning. Its narrative is animated, its dialogue crisp and spirited, its tone pure and wholesome, and its characters are gracefully contrasted."—*Harper's Magazine.*

GEORGE MACDONALD'S WORKS

MALCOLM.

8vo. Paper cover. $1.00. Fine cloth. $1.50.

"It is the most mature, elaborate, and highly-finished work of its distinguished author, whose other novels have had an extraordinary success. —*Philadelphia Evening Bulletin.*

THE MARQUIS OF LOSSIE.

8vo. Paper cover. 75 cents. Fine cloth. $1.25.

"One of the best of George Macdonald's novels, stronger in incident than his stories are wont to be, and not less strong in the delineation of character."—*New York Ev. Post.*

SIR GIBBIE.

8vo. Paper cover. 75 cents. Fine cloth. $1.25.

"The story is one of strong interest from opening to conclusion. It is, in fact, one of Macdonald's best, and there are thousands of readers who know how high a recommendation as to the interest of the story that means." —*Detroit Tribune.*

PAUL FABER.

8vo. Paper cover. 75 cents. Fine cloth. $1.25.

"An absorbing novel—in some, if not in all, respects Macdonald's best; and his novels are among the best of our time."—*San Francisco Alta-California.*

RANALD BANNERMAN'S BOYHOOD.

12mo. Profusely Illustrated. Extra cloth. $1.25.

"Mr. Macdonald writes of youthful experiences in a way unequalled by any other author of the day, and this volume is in his best style."—*Boston Post.*

THE PRINCESS AND THE GOBLIN.

12mo. Profusely Illustrated. Extra cloth. $1.25.

"This is one of the most attractive books for the young published this season, in respect both to contents and appearance. It is fascinating in its interest."—*Pittsburgh Gazette.*

THE

"ODD TRUMP" SERIES.

8vo. Fine cloth. $1.25. Paper cover. 75 cts.

THE ODD TRUMP.

" Deserving the highest praise. . . . Its incidents are all pure; it is the apotheosis of chivalric bravery and courtesy; and is written in elegant English, with a purity of style that is in itself refreshing."—*Louisville Courier-Journal.*

HARWOOD.

"A good novel in the best sense of the word."—*Indianapolis Journal.*

THE LACY DIAMONDS.

"Will more than ever stamp its author as one of the foremost popular novelists of America, or it may be of the world."—*New York Commercial.*

FLESH AND SPIRIT.

"We do not at all wonder that these novels are popular. They deserve popularity for being precisely what they are meant to be and what they profess to be."—*New York Evening Post.*

THE CLIFTON PICTURE.

"A novel that the most exciting taste will revel in. It is brimful of situations, bright and entertaining." —*Boston Post.*

THE GHOST OF REDBROOK.

"It is a thoroughly readable novel, pure and vigorous in tone, with plenty of love, romance, and humor, and not much ghost. The plot is worked out most skilfully, and will puzzle even the inveterate novel readers."—*Louisville Courier-Journal.*

"A LIBRARY IN ITSELF."

CHAMBERS'S ENCYCLOPÆDIA,

A Dictionary of Universal Knowledge for the People.

AMERICAN REVISED EDITION.

Illustrated with numerous Wood Engravings and Maps. In Ten Volumes, royal octavo. Bound in various styles, at prices ranging from $22.50 upwards.

The Publishers have the pleasure of announcing that they have concluded the revision of CHAMBERS'S ENCYCLOPÆDIA, and that the work is now complete in TEN ROYAL OCTAVO VOLUMES, of over 800 pages each, illustrated with about 4000 engravings, and in some of the editions embracing FORTY MAPS; the whole, it is believed, forming the most complete work of reference extant.

The design of this work, as explained in the Notice prefixed to the first volume, is that of a *Dictionary of Universal Knowledge for the People*—not a mere collection of elaborate treatises in alphabetical order, but a work to be readily consulted as a *Dictionary* on every subject on which people generally require some distinct information. The editors confidently point to the Ten volumes of which it is composed as forming the most *Comprehensive*—as it certainly is the *Cheapest—Encyclopædia* ever issued in the English language.

AN INTERESTING WORK.

CHAMBERS'S BOOK OF DAYS

A Miscellany of Popular Antiquities in connection with the Calendar,

INCLUDING

ANECDOTE, BIOGRAPHY, AND HISTORY, CURIOSITIES OF LITERATURE, AND ODDITIES OF HUMAN LIFE AND CHARACTER.

Revised under the Supervision of Robert Chambers. Profusely Illustrated. Two volumes, royal 8vo. Price per Set: Cloth, $8.00; Sheep, $9.50; Half calf, gilt extra, $12.00.

THIS WORK CONSISTS OF

I. Matters Connected with the Church Calendar.
II. Phenomena Connected with the Seasonal Changes.
III. Folk-Lore of the United Kingdom: namely, Popular Notions and Observances Connected with Times and Seasons.
IV. Notable Events, Biographies, and Anecdotes Connected with the Days of the Year.
V. Articles of Popular Archæology, of an entertaining character, tending to illustrate the Progress of Civilization, Manners, Literature, and Ideas.
VI. Curious Fugitive Pieces and Inedited Pieces.

A Work of Great Value to every Reader and Student of the Bible.

The Englishman's Critical and Expository

BIBLE CYCLOPÆDIA.

By the Rev. A. R. FAUSSET, A.M.,

Joint author of the "Critical and Experimental Commentary," etc.

With more than 600 Illustrative Woodcuts from Photographs, Coins, Sculptures, etc. Quarto. 750 pages. Price, cloth, $5.00; library sheep, $6.00; half Turkey, $7.00.

The aim of this work is to put within the reach of all Bible students, learned and unlearned alike, the fruits of the latest modern criticism and research, and at the same time set forth briefly and suggestively those doctrinal and experimental truths which the written word itself contains.

"We recommend it with confidence as a volume for the library and as an aid in the study of the Bible."—*Independent.*

"A vast storehouse of Scriptural information in a most compact and accessible form."—*Messenger.*

"A storehouse for those who teach and those who would themselves be taught in all Biblical matters."—*Episcopal Register.*

"More nearly realizes our ideal of a Bible Dictionary for all classes than anything that has ever come under our observation."—*Lutheran and Missionary.*

A MAGNIFICENT AND UNRIVALLED WORK.

A NEW VARIORUM EDITION

OF

SHAKESPEARE.

Edited by HORACE HOWARD FURNESS.

In large 8vo volumes. Superfine toned paper. Fine cloth. Uncut edges. Gilt top. $4.00 per volume.

In this *New Variorum* edition of SHAKESPEARE will be found:

First.—On the same page with the text, a collation of the ancient copies, folio and quarto, and of the majority of modern critical editions.

Secondly.—The notes (also on the same page with the text) of all the editors whose texts are collated, together with other notes, emendations, conjectures, and comments.

Thirdly.—In an appendix will be found reprints of the early quartos; also, criticisms and illustrations.

Now Ready.—ROMEO AND JULIET, MACBETH, HAMLET, KING LEAR.

J. B. LIPPINCOTT & CO.'S DICTIONARIES
OF THE
French, German, and Spanish Languages.

CONTANSEAU'S PRACTICAL DICTIONARY OF THE FRENCH and English Languages. Composed from the French dictionaries of the Academy, Boiste, Bescherelle, etc., and from the best English dictionaries, followed by abridged vocabularies of geographical and mythological names. By LEON CONTANSEAU. Crown 8vo. Extra cloth. $2.50.

CONTANSEAU'S POCKET DICTIONARY OF THE FRENCH and English Languages. By LEON CONTANSEAU. 18mo. Extra cloth. $1.50. *Tourist's Edition.* 2 volumes. 32mo. Cloth flexible. In case. $1.75

LONGMAN'S POCKET DICTIONARY OF THE GERMAN AND English Languages. By F. W. LONGMAN, Balliol College, Oxford. 18mo. Extra cloth. $1.50. *Tourist's Edition.* 2 volumes. 32mo. Cloth flexible. In case. $1.75.

"We have not seen any pocket dictionary (German and English) that can bear comparison with this. It is remarkably compendious, and the arrangement is clear."—*London Athenæum.*

NEUMAN AND BARETTI'S POCKET DICTIONARY OF THE Spanish and English Languages. Compiled from the last improved edition. 18mo. Extra cloth. $1.50.

ANNOTATED POEMS OF ENGLISH AUTHORS.
EDITED BY THE
Rev. EDWARD T. STEVENS, M.A. Oxford,
and Rev. DAVID MORRIS, B.A. London.

16mo. With Illustrations. Bound in cloth, limp.

THIS SERIES INCLUDES:

GRAY'S ELEGY IN A COUNTRY CHURCH-YARD. Price, 20 cents.

COWPER'S TASK. Book I. THE SOFA. Price, 25 cents.

GOLDSMITH'S DESERTED VILLAGE. Price, 20 cents.

SCOTT'S LADY OF THE LAKE. Canto I. Price, 35 cents.

GOLDSMITH'S TRAVELLER. Price, 25 cents.

The above Series bound in ONE VOLUME. *Illustrated. 16mo. Extra cloth. $1.00.*

"It is a good work well done, and we cannot commend the little volume too earnestly to the attention of teachers who are wise enough to appreciate the need there is for giving a larger and better place to English classic literature than it now has in our schemes of education."—*New York Evening Post.*

"The growing interest manifested in all our American schools in the study of the English classics will make these little volumes eminently useful."—*New England Journ. of Education.*

STANDARD
Architectural Works.

SLOAN'S HOMESTEAD ARCHITECTURE.

Containing Forty Designs for Villas, Cottages, and Farm Houses, with Essays on Style, Construction, Landscape Gardening, Furniture, etc.

Illustrated with over 100 Engravings. By SAMUEL SLOAN, Architect. Second Edition. 8vo. Extra cloth. $3.50.

HOBBS'S RURAL ARCHITECTURE.

Containing Designs and Ground Plans for Villas and other Edifices, both Suburban and Rural, Adapted to the United States.

With Rules for Criticism, and an Introduction. By ISAAC H. HOBBS & SON, Architects. Illustrated with over 100 Engravings. 8vo. Extra cloth. $3.00.

SLOAN'S CONSTRUCTIVE ARCHITECTURE.

A Guide to the Practical Builder and Mechanic.

In which is contained a Series of Designs for Domes, Roofs, Spires, the Interior Construction and Finish of Bays, Window Shutters, Sliding Doors, etc. Illustrated by 66 Plates. With Explanatory Text. By SAMUEL SLOAN, Architect. Quarto. Cloth. $7.50.

CITY AND SUBURBAN ARCHITECTURE.

Containing Numerous Designs and Details for Public Edifices, Private Residences, and Mercantile Buildings.

Illustrated with 131 Plates. With Explanatory Text. By SAMUEL SLOAN, Architect. Folio. Extra cloth. $10.00.

THE MODEL ARCHITECT.

A Series of Original Designs for Cottages, Villas, Suburban Residences, etc.

Accompanied by Explanations, Specifications, Estimates, and Elaborate Details. With 210 Plates, the majority of which are handsomely colored. By SAMUEL SLOAN, Architect. Two volumes. Imperial quarto. Half Turkey. $18.00.

BULWER'S NOVELS.

Each Complete in One Volume.

The Caxtons.
Pelham.
Eugene Aram.
The Last of the Barons.
Lucretia.
Devereux.
The Last Days of Pompeii.
Rienzi.
Godolphin.
A Strange Story.
Kenelm Chillingly.

Night and Morning.
Ernest Maltravers.
Alice.
Zanoni.
Harold.
Leila, Pilgrims of the Rhine, and Calderon.
Paul Clifford.
The Disowned.
The Parisians.
Pausanias, the Spartan.

Each Complete in Two Volumes.

My Novel.   What Will He Do With It?

THE LORD LYTTON EDITION.

Complete in 25 Volumes. Large 12mo. With Frontispiece. Extra Cloth, Black and Gilt, $1.25. Price per Set, $31.25.

"We know of no series so desirable in every respect as this."—*Philadelphia Evening Bulletin.*

"It makes one of the most attractive and valuable series to be found in any library for reading in distinction from reference. It is at once handsome and cheap."—*Chicago Evening Journal.*

THE GLOBE EDITION.

Complete in 25 Volumes. Printed on Tinted Paper. 16mo. With Frontispiece. Fine Cloth, $1.00. Price per Set, $25.00.

"We have more than once commended the Globe as the best edition of Bulwer accessible to American readers."—*Cincinnati Gazette.*

. . . "The convenient size, beautiful style, and cheapness of this edition is worthy the attention of book-buyers."—*Pittsburgh Gazette.*

LIBRARY EDITION.

Complete in 47 Volumes. Large Type. Fine Tinted Paper. 12mo. Extra Cloth, $1.00. Price per Set, $47.00.

EACH NOVEL SOLD SEPARATELY.

COMPLETE IN FIFTEEN VOLUMES.

THE

NEW STANDARD EDITION

OF

PRESCOTT'S WORKS

WITH THE

Author's Latest Corrections and Additions.

EDITED BY

JOHN FOSTER KIRK.

AS FOLLOWS:

HISTORY OF FERDINAND AND ISABELLA.
Three Volumes.

HISTORY OF THE CONQUEST OF MEXICO.
Three Volumes.

HISTORY OF THE CONQUEST OF PERU.
Two Volumes.

HISTORY OF THE REIGN OF PHILIP II.
Three Volumes.

HISTORY OF THE REIGN OF CHARLES V.
Three Volumes.

PRESCOTT'S MISCELLANEOUS ESSAYS.
One Volume.

This Edition is Illustrated with Maps, Plates, and Engravings,

Price per volume, 12mo, in fine English cloth, with black and gold ornamentation, $2.00; library sheep, $2.50; half calf, gilt back, $3.50.

www.ingramcontent.com/pod-product-compliance
Lightning Source LLC
Chambersburg PA
CBHW031826270326
41932CB00008B/557